PHOTOSHOP DOWN & DIRTY TRICKS FOR DESIGNERS

Corey Barker

Education and Curriculum Developer for the
National Association of Photoshop Professionals

The *Photoshop Down & Dirty Tricks for Designers* Book Team

CREATIVE DIRECTOR
Felix Nelson

ASSOCIATE ART DIRECTOR
Jessica Maldonado

TECHNICAL EDITORS
Kim Doty
Cindy Snyder

TRAFFIC DIRECTOR
Kim Gabriel

PRODUCTION MANAGER
Dave Damstra

STOCK IMAGES COURTESY OF
iStockphoto.com
fotolia.com

Published By
New Riders

Composed in Frutiger, Museo, and ITC Script by Kelby Media Group, Inc.

Trademarks
All terms mentioned in this book that are known to be trademarks or service marks have been appropriately capitalized. New Riders cannot attest to the accuracy of this information. Use of a term in the book should not be regarded as affecting the validity of any trademark or service mark.

Photoshop is a registered trademark of Adobe Systems Incorporated.

Warning and Disclaimer
This book is designed to provide information about designing in Adobe Photoshop. Every effort has been made to make this book as complete and as accurate as possible, but no warranty of fitness is implied.

The information is provided on an as-is basis. The author and New Riders shall have neither the liability nor responsibility to any person or entity with respect to any loss or damages arising from the information contained in this book or from the use of the discs or programs that may accompany it.

THIS PRODUCT IS NOT ENDORSED OR SPONSORED BY ADOBE SYSTEMS INCORPORATED, PUBLISHER OF ADOBE PHOTOSHOP.

ISBN 10: 0-321-82049-5
ISBN 13: 978-0-321-82049-5

9 8 7 6 5 4 3 2

Printed and bound in the United States of America

www.newriders.com
http://kelbytraining.com

For Blue

Acknowledgments

Scott Kelby—There just aren't enough good things I can say about Scott Kelby. It was his first *Photoshop Down & Dirty Tricks* book that lit up my creativity way back when, and now I am honored that he has the confidence in me to carry on the name to a new generation of Photoshop creatives. It is unfair that so few of us can experience the joy of working for such an awesome guy, who has the passion to share the knowledge that has made him an inspiration to so many! Thank you Scott!

Mom and Mark—You guys have always supported everything I ever did with great enthusiasm, and I've always enjoyed our movie banter. We've all certainly seen life's ups and downs, but we've always known how to make the best of it and look ahead. Thank you for all you've done!

Dad and Sue—You two were there when this all started nearly 20 years ago, when you dropped me off at art school in Sarasota, Florida. It has since been one awesome journey, and I want to thank you for all your help and encouragement along the way.

Shelley Giard—You inspire me with your determination. You, Zane, Baleigh, and Brie were my cheering section during this whole process and I can't thank you enough.

Dave Moser—I can always count on you to have a good military metaphor to fit any situation, and yet as silly as they sound sometimes, you always get the point. Thanks for being a strong leader and great mentor. I, like many others in the company, am quite comfortable knowing you are at the helm.

Felix Nelson—This man is definitely one of the best digital artists on the planet, and I have always been a fan of his work. Now, we talk movies and Photoshop, and that alone inspires ideas. Thanks for just being awesome!

The Photoshop Guys—I most definitely have to give a shout out to my fellow Photoshop Guys: Matt Kloskowski, Rafael "RC" Concepcion, Dave Cross, and Pete Collins. You guys are the reason it is fun to come to work every day. Thank you Matt for being a great leader and being the glue of the team. RC, remember the old *Layers TV* days? Ah, good times! Glad we are able to work together. You are wealth of knowledge. I can always count on Dave Cross to be the rational one of the bunch. Thanks to you for being a good friend and great mentor. Pete, since you just started recently, you get mentioned merely by association, but I'm glad you're here!

Bert Monroy—Having been a huge fan of Bert's work, I never thought I would meet him, and we have since become good friends. You are truly an inspiration and I would not be where I am today without your teachings. Oh, and I am actually in Bert's *Times Square* painting, as well. How cool is that?

Cindy Snyder & Kim Doty—You guys are the real deal. This being my first book, I have only heard about what it is like doing a book with you guys. Now I can see that I cannot think of anyone else I would want to do a book with. You guys are solid pros!

Jessica Maldonado—Your talents and expertise have made this book look as cool as it could possibly be, from cover to cover. Thanks for all your hard work and design genius!

Adobe Systems, Inc.—To my good friends at Adobe: Zorana Gee, Russell Brown, and Pete Falco, to name a few. So glad that I have gotten to know all of you, and glad for all the work we have done together over the years.

iStockphoto—A big thanks to all the folks over at iStockphoto for all their help, especially Brenda Bazylewski for providing me with everything I needed to create the dazzling images you see throughout the book.

New Riders & Peachpit Press—A big thanks to the entire gang over at Peachpit Press: Ted Waitt, Sara Jane Todd, Gary-Paul Prince, and Scott Cowlin. You guys are the ones that make learning accessible and fun! Keep up all the good work and thank you for this opportunity.

Alicen Rehnert—You have become a treasured friend, and I knew I could always count on you when I needed a favor. You were always helpful when I was on the seminar tour, and always had a solution for any problem, even when 1,000 miles away.

Tomasz Opasinski—I have always admired your body of work, both commercial and personal. I thank you for letting me share some of your magic within the pages of this book.

Lastly, a big thanks to the late Steve Jobs. The impact he has made on my career is profound, and I feel fortunate that I was able to experience the impact he had on our world. You were truly a renaissance man.

About the Author

COREY BARKER

Corey is an Education and Curriculum Developer at the National Association of Photoshop Professionals (NAPP). An award-winning designer and illustrator, Corey is the Executive Producer of the Planet Photoshop website (www.planetphotoshop.com), and has regular columns in *Photoshop User* magazine. He is also a featured instructor at the Photoshop World Conference & Expo, and is an Adobe MAX Master Instructor. He has taught thousands on the *Photoshop Down & Dirty Tricks* seminar tour, traveling to cities across the country. Corey has produced numerous online training courses and DVDs on Photoshop and design for Kelby Training, and was a contributing author of *Photoshop CS4 Down & Dirty Tricks* with Scott Kelby. He was also a contributing author of *3D in Photoshop: The Ultimate Guide for Creative Professionals*. Corey holds a BFA in Illustration from the Ringling College of Art & Design in Sarasota, Florida.

iMAGiNE

TGIF

ELEGANCE IN THE MOST
EXTREME CONDITIONS

SWAT

GFX

12 Important Things About This Book

I'm excited to present to you the *Photoshop Down & Dirty Tricks for Designers* book. The Photoshop Down & Dirty Tricks series has been immensely popular over the years, since it was started (with Photoshop 6) by best-selling author Scott Kelby. I'm incredibly honored that Scott has passed the torch on to me with this newest volume, and I couldn't be happier to have had this opportunity to put some of my most popular techniques, and a lot of new ones, into this book. But, first, here are some important things you'll want to know about the book:

1. You'll learn exactly how to create the final image.
The problem I've always had with other Photoshop books on designing is that they tend to show a really cool image, and I always think that's what I am going to learn, only to find out the author wants me to open a file that's 60% done, and the tutorial only shows how to create that last 40%. But, what about that first 60%? Well, in this book, nearly every project either starts with a basic photo, a simple graphic, or a blank document. So, when you flip through these pages, the end product you see is exactly what you are going to learn how to do... from the beginning!

Before

After

2. The order of things.
This book is designed so that you can open it up to any project and get started. You do not need to follow the chapters in sequence. You will notice I tend to use some images or effects created earlier in the book on some of the other projects throughout the book. This is to show you the various uses of certain textures and brush effects. You'll see these referenced throughout the book, directing you to where you can learn how to create them. But, while some projects make reference to other projects in the book, each project is self-contained.

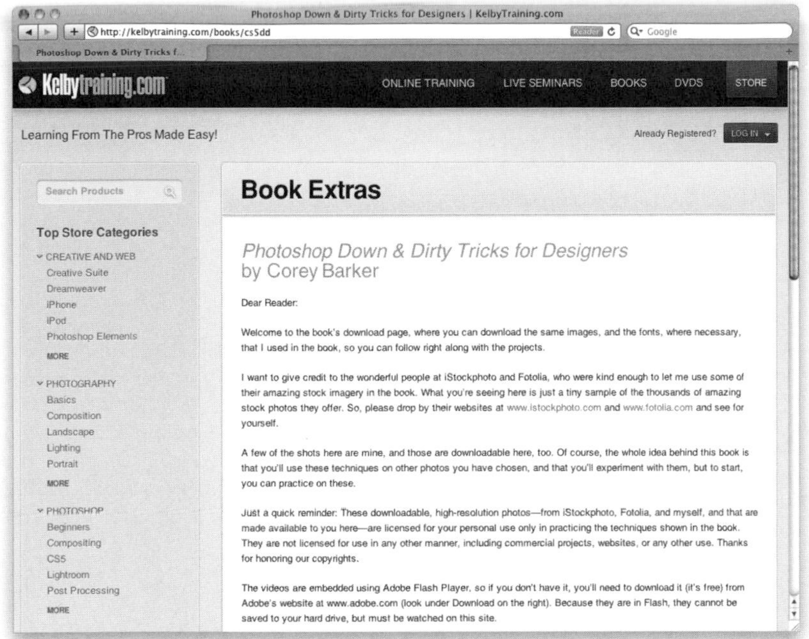

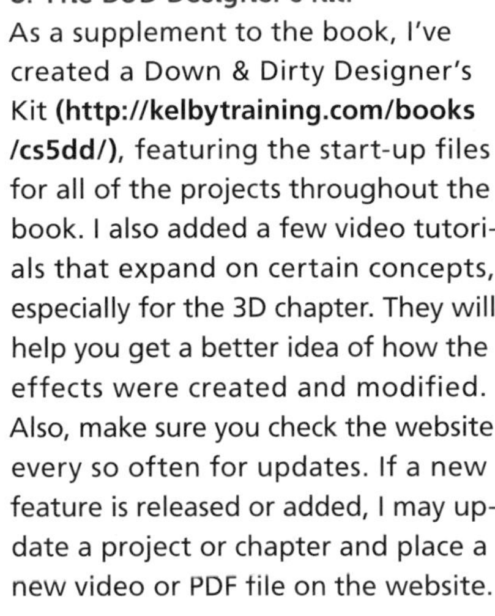

3. The D&D Designer's Kit.
As a supplement to the book, I've created a Down & Dirty Designer's Kit **(http://kelbytraining.com/books/cs5dd/)**, featuring the start-up files for all of the projects throughout the book. I also added a few video tutorials that expand on certain concepts, especially for the 3D chapter. They will help you get a better idea of how the effects were created and modified. Also, make sure you check the website every so often for updates. If a new feature is released or added, I may update a project or chapter and place a new video or PDF file on the website.

4. What about the fonts?
Like in previous editions of this book series, I tried to use common fonts available on most systems. But, in some designs, I used specialized fonts just to finish the effect. I have provided some fonts as part of the D&D Designer's Kit downloads, but would also encourage you to go beyond what's used in the projects and try other typefaces. One great resource for free fonts to experiment with is www.dafont.com.

5. What user level is this book?
While this book is classified as Beginner to Intermediate, it's really for all user levels. Most projects do assume you have some working knowledge of Photoshop, although being an expert is not required. All you need is the desire to learn and a little patience. Also, most projects can be completed using almost any version of Photoshop, but some techniques make use of the newer features in CS5 (like in the 3D chapter).

6. What file size should I use?
I always feel this needs to be addressed, because it can confuse some people. Throughout this book, you'll notice I create the files at small dimensions and low resolutions for several reasons. The most obvious is speed. And, since I was creating these images for the book, they did not need to be super-sized. Just remember: if you are re-creating these effects (with your own images) for actual print, then be sure to build them high-res.

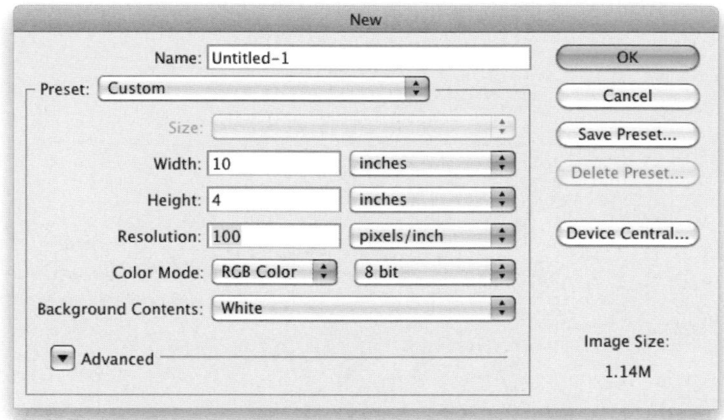

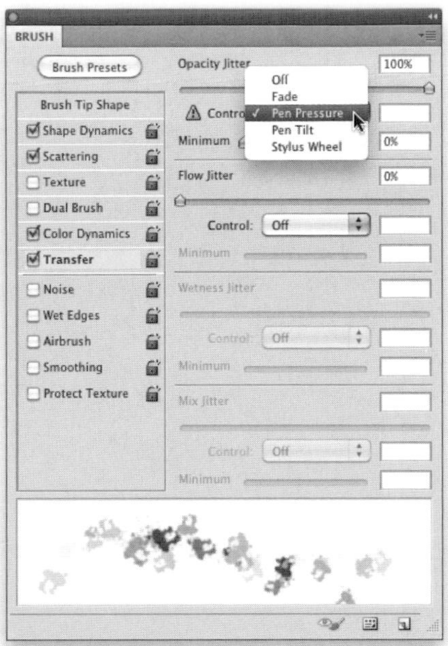

7. Get a pressure-sensitive tablet.
If you are a working designer, or an up-and-coming designer, then you should seriously consider a Wacom pressure-sensitive tablet. Photoshop has a number of features built specifically to take advantage of pressure sensitivity, which gives you unmatched control over your work, not to mention a pen has a much more natural feel than a mouse.

8. This is an effects book for all creatives.
This book is not a course in graphic design, but was written for designers, artists, and even creative photographers that want to be able to create eye-popping effects, either from scratch or using photos. True, the title says this book is "for Designers," but this book is really for anyone who wants to learn how to make cool stuff in Photoshop.

9. Use stock images.
One of the best secret weapons in any designer's arsenal is the availability of stock photography, especially with as much as is available today. Most of the projects in this book utilize assets I found over at iStockphoto's website (www.istockphoto.com). They have a vast collection of not just photos, but illustrated graphics, logos, and video clips—just about anything you need—for very reasonable costs. A big thanks to the folks over at iStockphoto for helping me out with the images for this book.

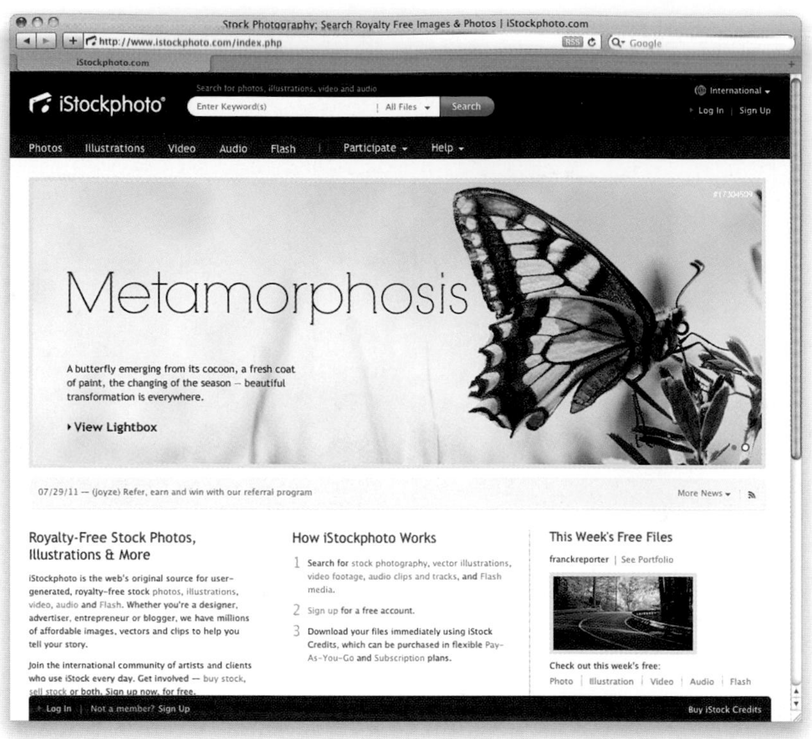

10. The 3D Chapter.
As I mentioned before, most of the techniques in this book are relevant to most recent versions of Photoshop, although some features are specific to Photoshop CS5. However, the 3D chapter at the end of the book is only specific to Photoshop CS5 Extended (it has changed from CS4). Now, if you do not yet have CS5 Extended, then I would still suggest reading through the 3D chapter so you can get an idea of what is possible with 3D in Photoshop. If you want to set yourself apart as a designer, you can only help yourself by getting a little 3D experience!

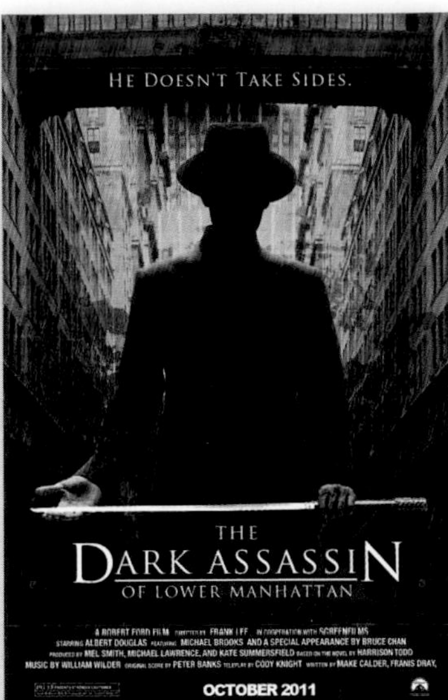

The splat brush, created in Chapter 1, was used in both of these designs

11. Experiment, experiment, experiment!
While I do encourage you to follow the projects in the book step by step, be sure to experiment with your newfound knowledge. Think of these projects as a vehicle for a real project you're working on. Chances are most of you won't actually be creating a movie poster or title effect, but that doesn't mean that the concepts can't be applied to your own projects. Master the technique, and then add your own flavor to it. Most of the effects in this book were created through my own experimentation, both from things I've seen or things I just thought would look cool.

12. Be creative and have fun!
Finally, I just want to thank you for taking the leap forward and making this small investment in your creativity. Sometimes, just seeing what is possible is enough to light up your creative brain to new ideas. That is one of the reasons I had the final images in this book made as large as possible, so you can really take in what the final result is and get inspired. I hope you enjoy the fun times to be had within these pages and remember to be creative and have fun!

Strokes of Creativity

brush effects

"Give a man a fish and you feed him for a day.
Teach a man to fish and you feed him for a lifetime."

—Old Chinese Proverb

I like the quote above, because it sums up nicely what I think about the brush engine in Photoshop. You can indeed follow a tutorial step by step and end up with what someone intended, and that would be it. You can also follow a tutorial and then take what you learned and go further by experimenting with other features and settings. Thus, you will feed your creativity for a lifetime. As you go through this chapter, and through the rest of this book, for that matter, try to keep in mind to go out of your mind. What I mean is that you should think beyond the obvious use for the things you see here, and contemplate other directions by experimenting. Have fun fishing!

Bokeh Brush Effects

Here, we're going to create a brush that recreates the out-of-focus lights you see in photos, known as bokeh—the optical effect adds an interesting look in photos and movies. Now, what if you could have that bokeh effect on tap right here in Photoshop, and have it be customizable to a number of different images and scenarios? Well, here's how:

STEP ONE:

Select the Brush tool **(B)** from the Toolbox. Then, click on the Brush Panel icon in the Options Bar (between the brush thumbnail and the Mode pop-up menu) to open the Brush panel and see the brush options. Click on Brush Tip Shape at the top left to access the basic brush features. Then, select a basic round brush from the Brush Picker at the top right. Here, I've selected a 60-pixel brush. Set the Hardness to 75% and increase the Spacing to 250%. You can see these changes take effect in the preview area at the bottom of the panel.

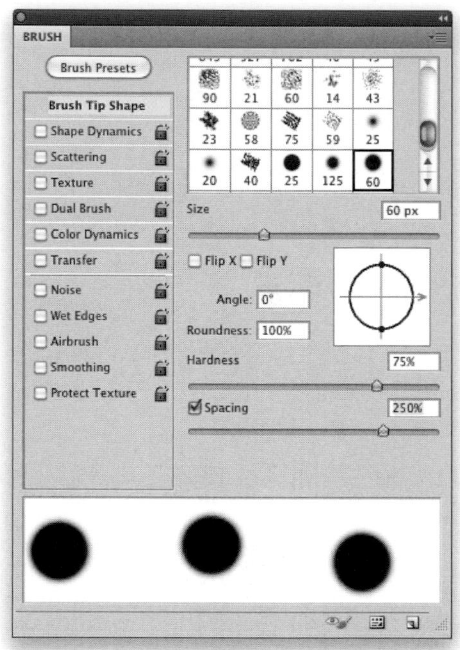

STEP TWO:

Next, click on Shape Dynamics on the left to turn it on. All we are going to do in this section is increase the Size Jitter to around 15%. This will give you a slight variation in size as you paint. You can increase this if you want to space them out more. As an option, if you are using a pressure-sensitive tablet, you can set the Control pop-up menu to Pen Pressure, and the size will vary based on how hard or soft you press down on the tablet.

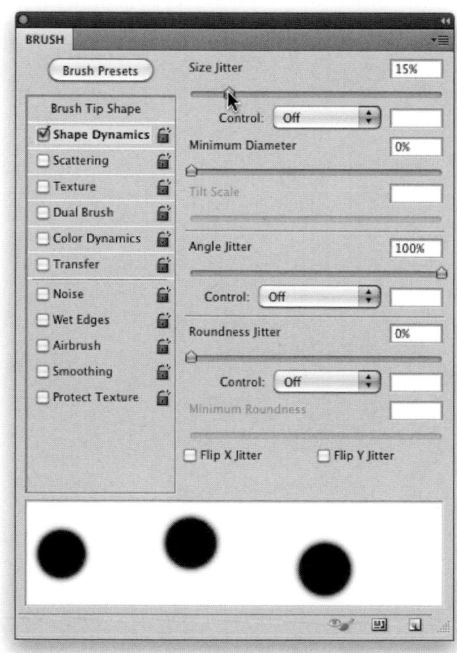

STEP THREE:

Next, click on Scattering on the left to turn it on. Turn on the Both Axes checkbox at the top, then raise the Scatter setting to the maximum of 1000%, and change the Count to 2.

STEP FOUR:

Now, click on Texture on the left to turn it on and click on the texture thumbnail to open the Texture Picker. Click on the right-facing arrow in the upper-right corner and, from the flyout menu, choose **Texture Fill 2** from the presets at the bottom. Locate the texture called Weave 3 and click on it to select it. Turn on the Invert checkbox, and leave the Scale set to 100%. Set the Mode to **Subtract** and drop the Depth to around 20%. This will make the texture a little subtler—if you were to look at real bokeh, when there is a visible texture, it is often very subtle.

Continued

STEP FIVE:

Click on Transfer on the left now to turn it on. To help with the subtlety of the texture and the overall bokeh effect, for that matter, set the Opacity Jitter to 100%. This will vary the density of each bokeh instance. Set the Flow Jitter at 50%. Again, you could also take advantage of pressure sensitivity here by simply choosing Pen Pressure in the Control pop-up menu.

STEP SIX:

Now, you can see that once you choose a new Foreground color, you can add a very interesting and realistic bokeh effect to your images by simply creating a new blank layer and painting on it with this brush. Also, if you change your brush size, and paint each size on a separate layer, you can vary their looks by changing the blend modes or opacities separately in the Layers panel. Of course, feel free to experiment with the brush settings to achieve variations of the same effect. You can change the colors, randomness, size, and even the texture to get a vast array of bokeh looks. In fact, what if you wanted to have bokeh lights of varying colors? Just click on Color Dynamics on the left and then adjust the Hue Jitter. This lets you vary the color of each bokeh instance as you paint. Set this around 50% to start, but then try higher or lower settings—lower settings vary fewer colors, whereas higher settings increase the number of colors quite dramatically.

Note: It is important to paint with a color. If your Foreground color is set to black or white, it won't vary the color. If you choose warmer colors, then you will consistently get warmer hues. Conversely, if you choose cooler colors, you will get consistently cooler hues.

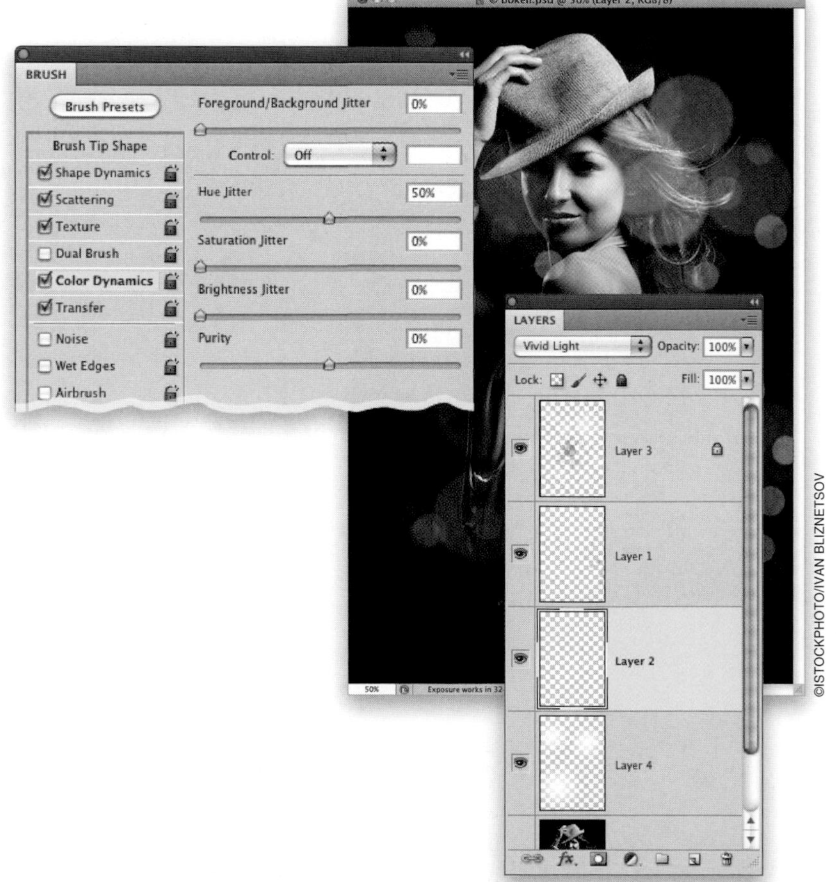

©ISTOCKPHOTO/IVAN BLIZNETSOV

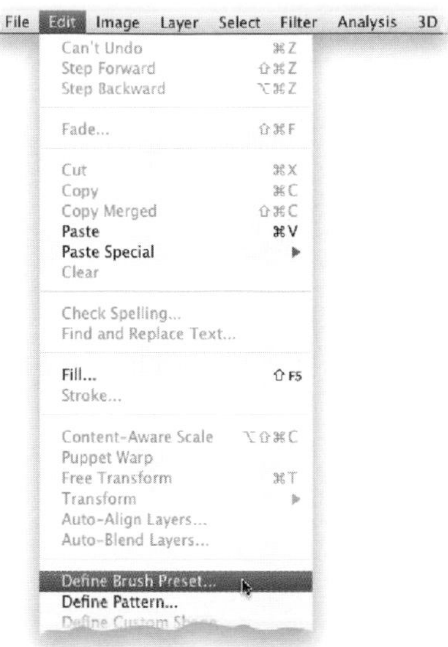

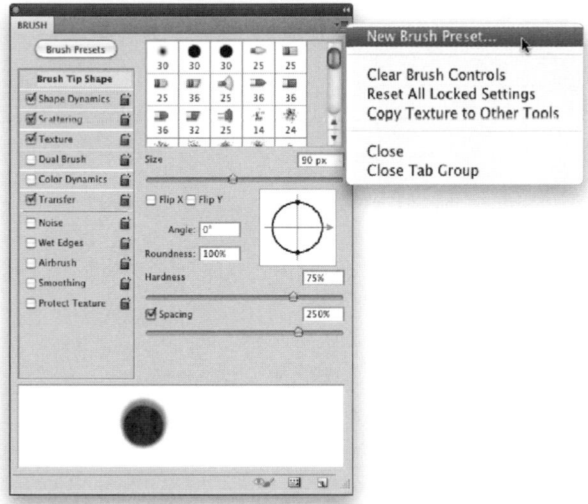

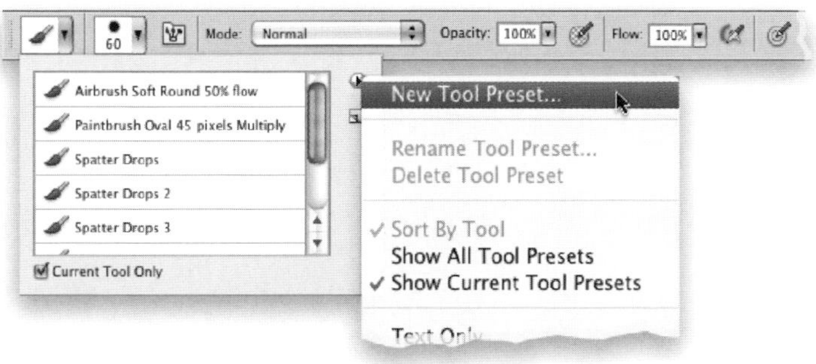

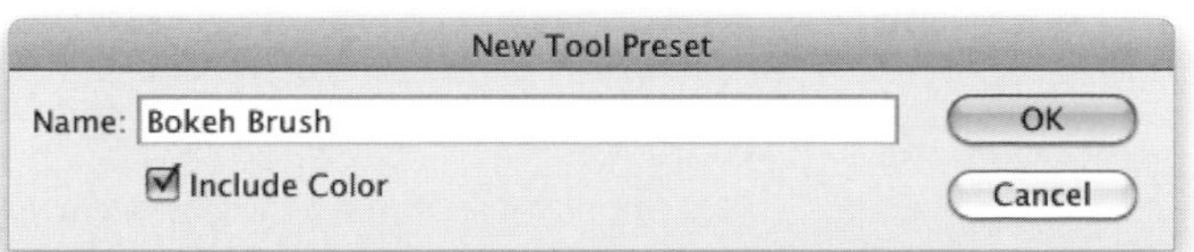

STEP SEVEN:

Now that you've created the brush, you may want to save it for future use, so you don't have to go through this process every time. I tend to use this brush a lot, and not always for a bokeh effect. I'll vary the settings and use it on a layer mask to create a stylish masking effect, or paint with straight, solid colors for a more graphic effect. It was experimenting with these settings that helped me develop this bokeh effect in the first place!

There are three ways to save the brush, and it's important to know the difference: First, you can go under the Edit menu and choose Define Brush Preset (we'll do this later). This saves only the brush tip—all the settings in the Brush Tip Shape section in the Brush panel, but no others. You can also use this to create a brush from an image or part of an image. To save all of the settings in the Brush panel, but not the color or any settings from the Options Bar, you can go to the Brush panel's flyout menu and choose New Brush Preset. Finally, you can save it as a Tool preset (as we'll do with the bokeh brush), which saves all the brush settings, the color, if you want, and the Options Bar settings.

So, with the Brush tool selected, in the Options Bar, click on the Tool Preset thumbnail (the first one on the left) to get the Tool Preset Picker. Then, from the Picker's flyout menu, choose **New Tool Preset**. Name it, and turn on the Include Color checkbox to save the current color of the brush (I made mine a light yellow), then click OK. Now you can go to the Tool Preset Picker anytime and choose your custom brush.

Continued

Final Image

Just so you can see that this has multiple uses, here's another design that uses the same bokeh brush, only this time, I changed the color and changed the size of the brush. You can even go back into the Brush panel's options and change the behavior to work with whatever effect you want.

Hollywood-Style Flare Brush

I actually like to call this effect the "J.J. flare," because no one in Hollywood goes crazier with optical flare than J.J. Abrams. Anyone who has seen his films knows exactly what I mean, although the reason he uses it is because it looks cool. Well, here I'm going to show you how to create a flare from scratch, and then define it as a brush to be used anytime you want. In fact, you'll see me use this several times throughout this book.

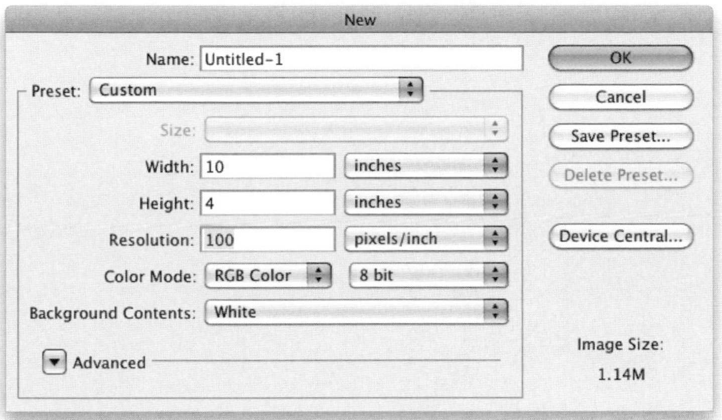

STEP ONE:

Start by going under the File menu, choosing **New**, and creating a new blank document to create the brush on. It's going to be a wide brush, so create a document that is 10 inches wide by 4 inches tall at 100 ppi.

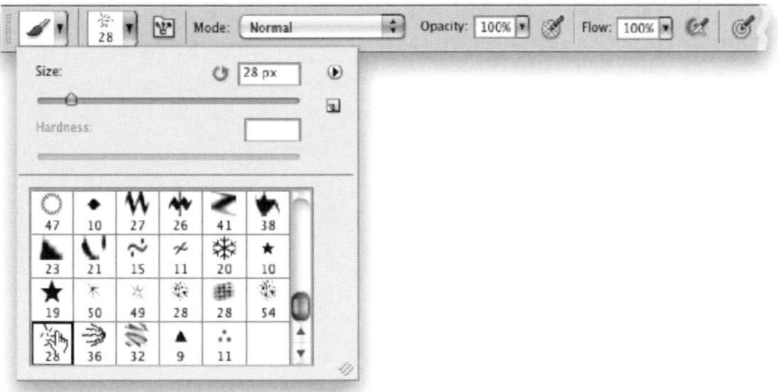

STEP TWO:

Next, select the Brush tool **(B)** from the Toolbox and then click on the brush thumbnail in the Options Bar to open the Brush Picker. Then, click on the right-facing arrow in the upper-right corner and, from the flyout menu, choose the **Assorted Brushes** preset. You can choose to append it to the existing list or replace the existing list altogether. I chose to append it. Locate the brush called Texture 4, which looks like a cluster of little lines. Select it, then open the Brush panel by clicking on the small folder icon to the right of the brush thumbnail in the Options Bar.

Continued

STEP THREE:
Click on Brush Tip Shape on the left side of the panel, and set the Size to around 45 px. Then, for Roundness, type in 75%. This will squash the brush down a little bit.

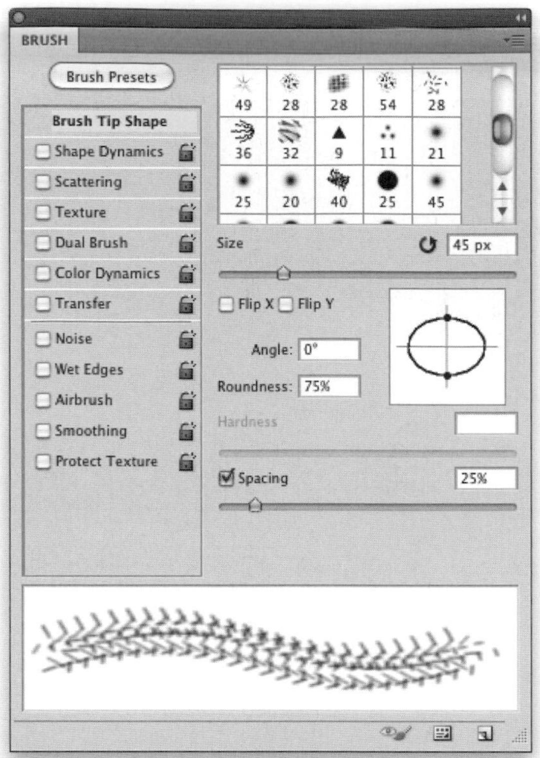

STEP FOUR:
Press **D** to set your Foreground and Background colors to their defaults of black and white, then press **Option-Delete (PC: Alt-Backspace)** to fill the Background layer with black. Now, press **X** to switch your Foreground color to white. Click on the Create a New Layer icon at the bottom of the Layers panel to create a new blank layer. Then, press-and-hold the Shift key and click-and-drag to paint a short horizontal stroke in the middle of the canvas, as seen here.

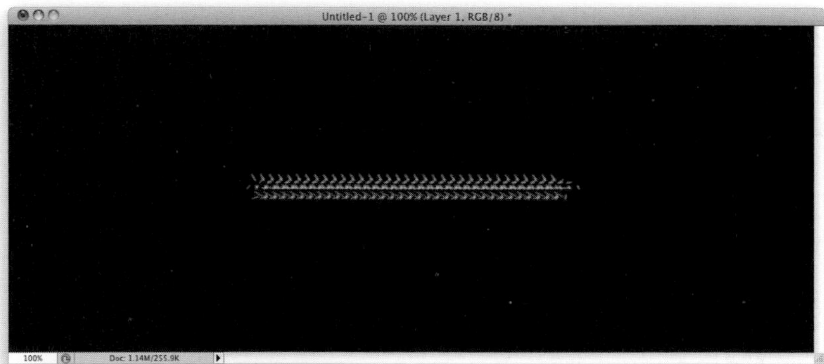

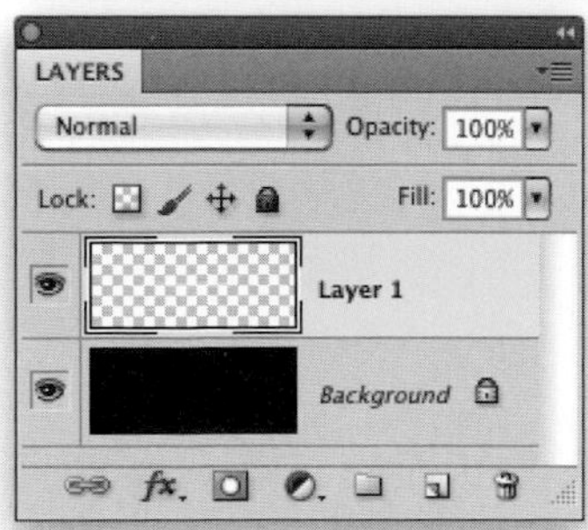

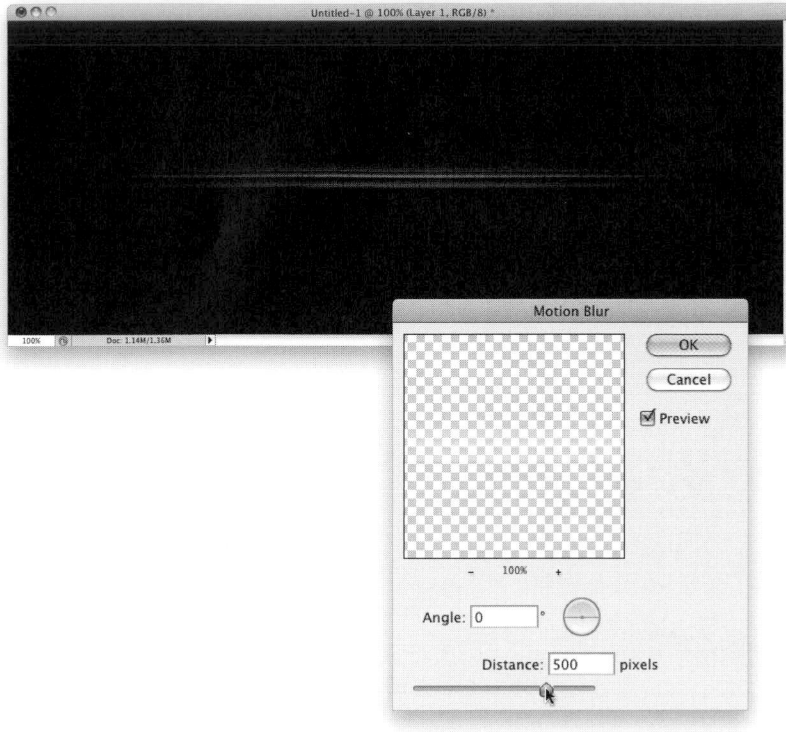

STEP FIVE:

Now, go under the Filter menu, under Blur, and choose **Motion Blur**. Set the Angle to 0° and the Distance to 500 pixels. This will give you a nice horizontal streak effect. Click OK.

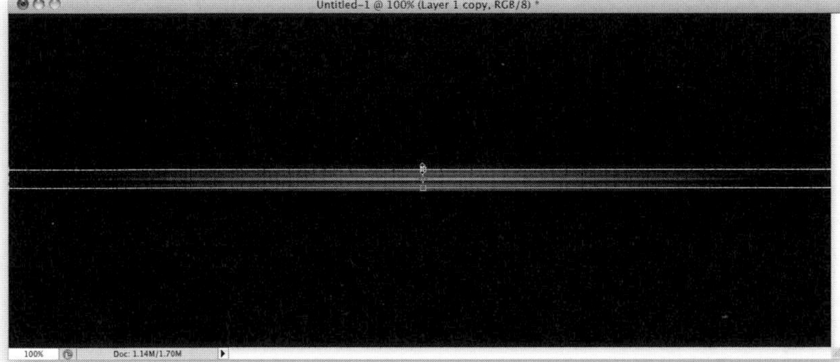

STEP SIX:

Make a duplicate of this layer by pressing **Command-J (PC: Ctrl-J)**. Now to stretch it a bit further, put the shape in Free Transform mode by pressing **Command-T (PC: Ctrl-T)**, then press-and-hold the Option (PC: Alt) key to anchor the transformation to the center, grab any of the corner handles, and squash the flare down and stretch it to near the edges of the canvas. Press **Return (PC: Enter)** when you're done to commit the change.

Continued

STEP SEVEN:

To enhance the glare on this part of the flare, we are going to add a Bevel and Emboss layer style. That's right: Bevel and Emboss. I have discovered over the years that by playing around with the various layer styles, you can achieve some interesting effects in ways that these features weren't necessarily designed for. For instance, here I want to generate a more stylized glow on the streak. So, with the duplicate layer selected, click on the Add a Layer Style icon at the bottom of the Layers panel and choose **Bevel and Emboss** from the pop-up menu.

In the Layer Style dialog's Bevel and Emboss options, in the Structure section, set the Style to **Emboss** and increase the Depth to around 490%. Keep the Direction set to Up and increase the Size to around 54 px. At the top of the Shading section, set the Angle to 176° and the Altitude to 21° (you can also just grab the small target inside the circle and move it around to change the angle of the effect). Then, go to Highlight Mode, set it to **Hard Light**, and leave the color set to white. Increase the Opacity to 100%. Then, for Shadow Mode, also choose **Hard Light**, but then click on the color swatch, and choose a really light gray color (but not white). Leave the Opacity at 75% and click OK when you're done.

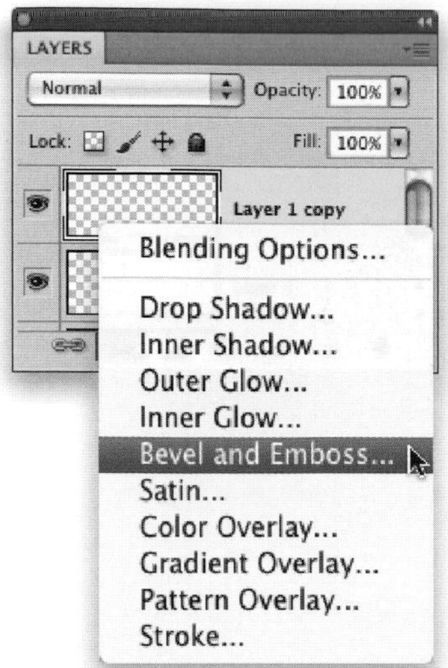

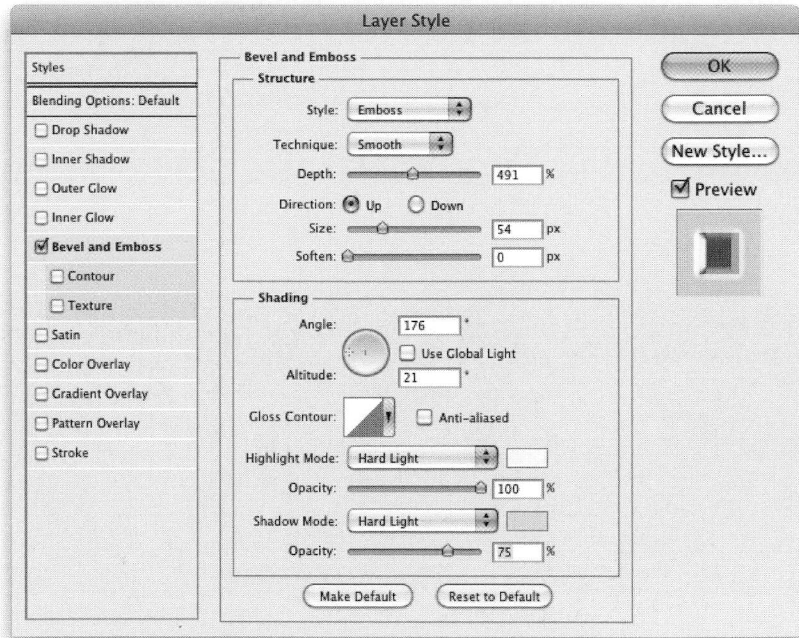

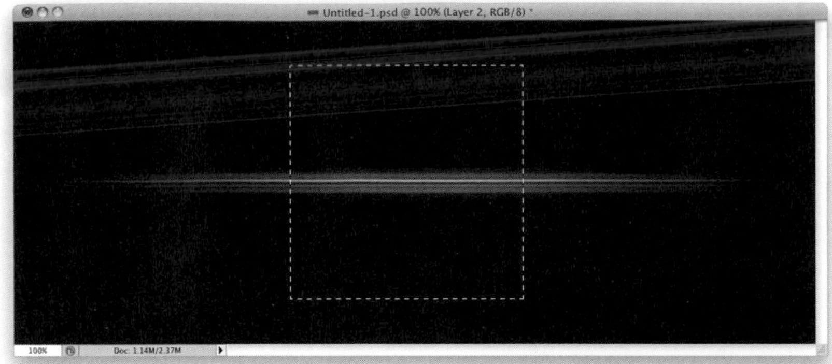

STEP EIGHT:

Now, let's move on to the next part of the flare. We need to create a point of origin for the light itself, with intense light beams. So, start by creating a new blank layer, then get the Rectangular Marquee tool **(M)**. We need to create a perfect square in the middle of the streak, so press-and-hold Option-Shift (PC: Alt-Shift), click in the center area of the streak, and drag a square selection out from the center, stopping just short of the edges of the canvas.

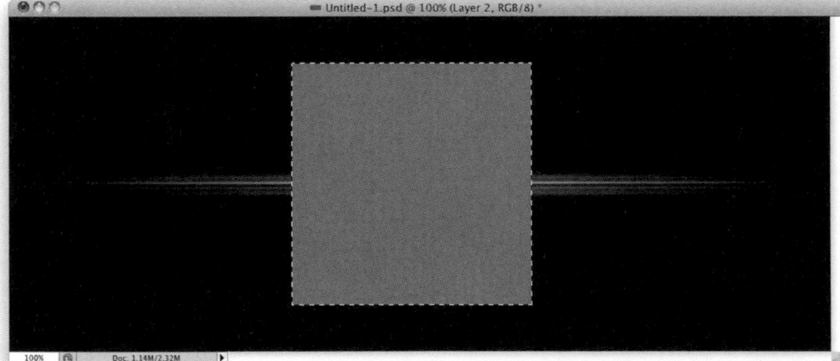

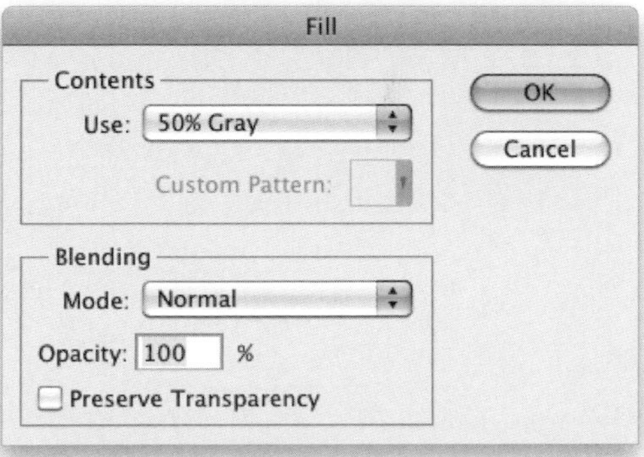

STEP NINE:

Press **Shift-Delete (PC: Shift-Backspace)** to open the Fill dialog. Then, choose **50% Gray** from the Use pop-up menu and click OK.

Continued

STEP 10:

Press **D** to set your Foreground and Background colors to their defaults of black and white. Then, go under the Filter menu, under Render, and choose **Fibers**. Set the Variance to 16 and the Strength to 10. Click OK.

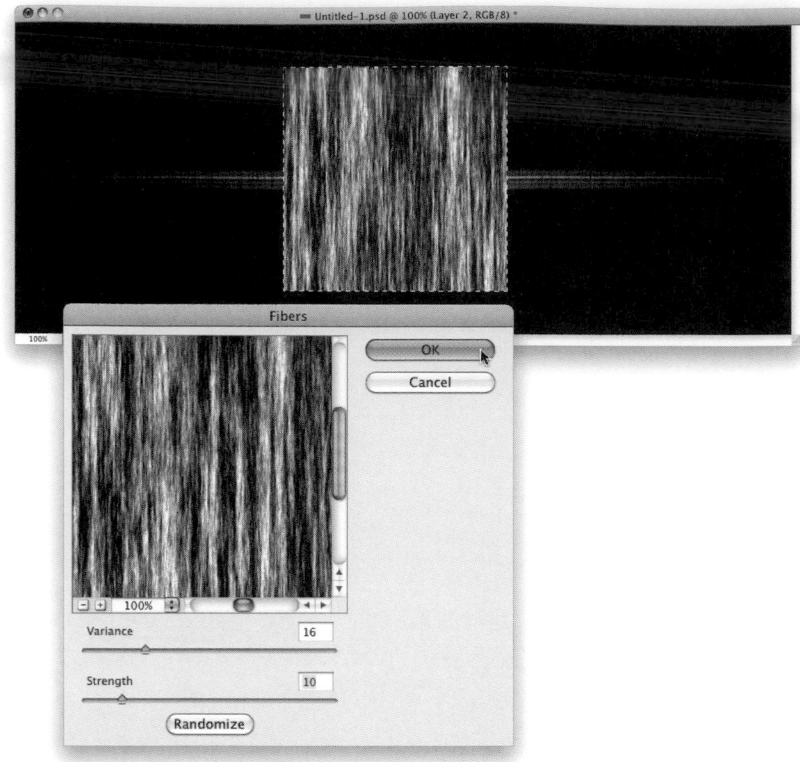

STEP 11:

We need to run a motion blur on this, but I've noticed that the blur is applied more smoothly and evenly by locking the transparency of the layer, rather than using a selection. So, deselect by pressing **Command-D (PC: Ctrl-D)**, then click on the Lock Transparent Pixels icon near the top of the Layers panel. Now, go to the Filter menu, once again, under Blur, and choose **Motion Blur**. Set the Angle to 90° and the Distance to 400 pixels to give the flare a streakier look.

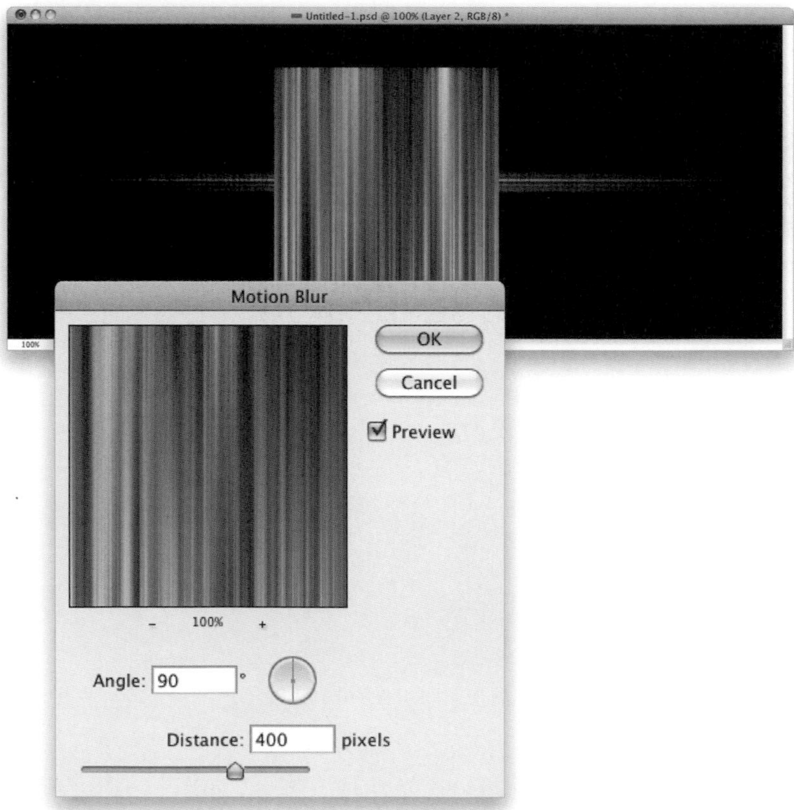

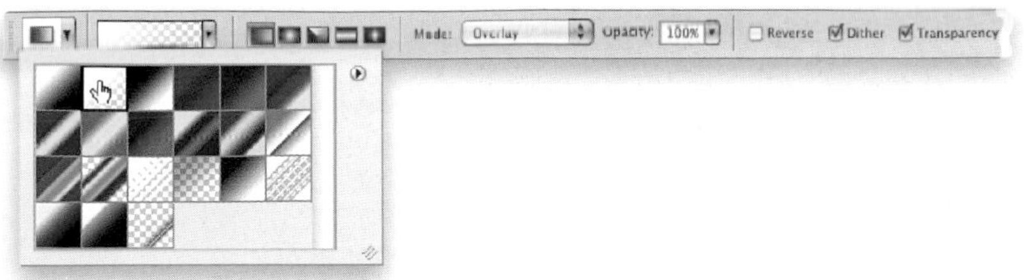

STEP 12:

Now we need the streaks to fade to black at the bottom. We'll do this using a gradient, but in a slightly different way than you might be used to. Get the Gradient tool **(G)** from the Toolbox, then click on the down-facing arrow next to the gradient thumbnail in the Options Bar to open the Gradient Picker, and choose the Foreground to Transparent gradient (the second one in the top row). Also, make sure the Linear Gradient icon to the right of the gradient thumbnail is selected. Lastly, change the Gradient tool's blend Mode to **Overlay**.

STEP 13:

Make sure your Foreground color is set to black and, starting at the bottom of the square shape, press-and-hold the Shift key, and click-and-drag up almost to the top edge of the square. Notice that some streaks remained more prominent than others. This randomness is due to the Overlay blend mode, which affects the varying gray tones differently, resulting in streaks of more random lengths, as opposed to what you would get just using a plain black gradient. Simply apply the gradient one or two more times (dragging a shorter distance) to take care of any other streaks that might be still going to the edge (as shown here).

Continued

STEP 14:
Reload the shape as an active selection by pressing-and-holding the Command (PC: Ctrl) key and clicking on the layer's thumbnail in the Layers panel. Then, go under the Filter menu, under Distort, and choose **Polar Coordinates**. Choose Rectangular to Polar. This will wrap the streaks around a center point, giving the effect of a light burst. Click OK, then deselect.

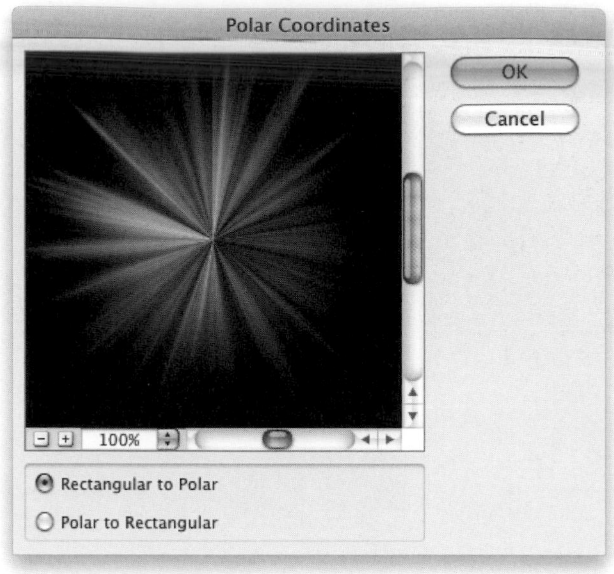

STEP 15:
Now, to blend the burst with the streaks we already created, change the burst layer's blend mode to **Screen**. Then you can adjust the positioning, if necessary.

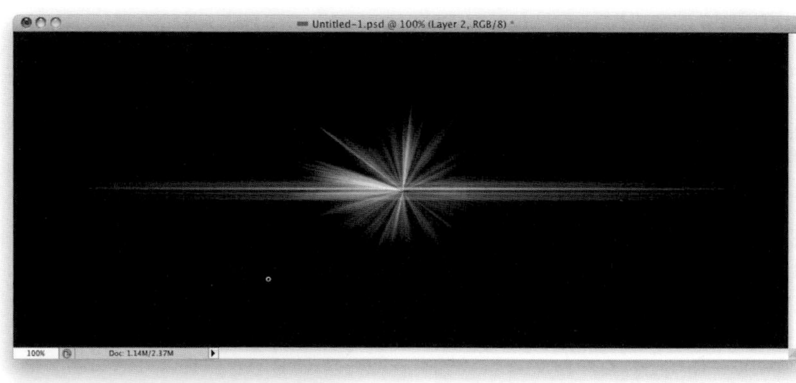

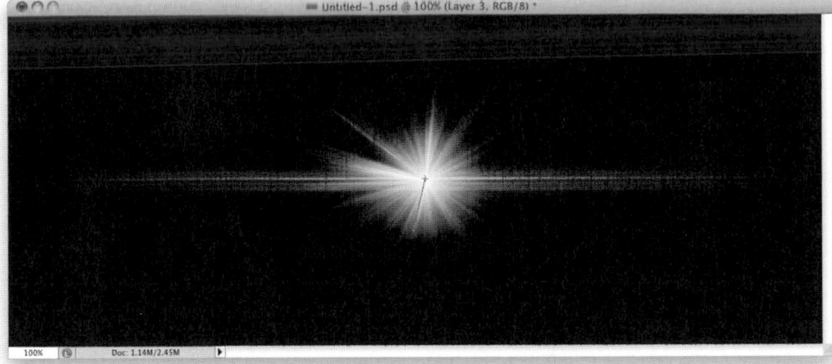

STEP 16:

The flare is really taking shape, but it needs to be a bit brighter in the center area. Go ahead and create a new blank layer and, with the Gradient tool still selected, keep the Foreground to Transparent gradient, but change the gradient type to Radial (the second icon from the left) and change the blend Mode back to **Normal**. Press **X** to swap your Foreground and Background colors, making white your Foreground color. Start at the center of the burst and draw a small white radial gradient.

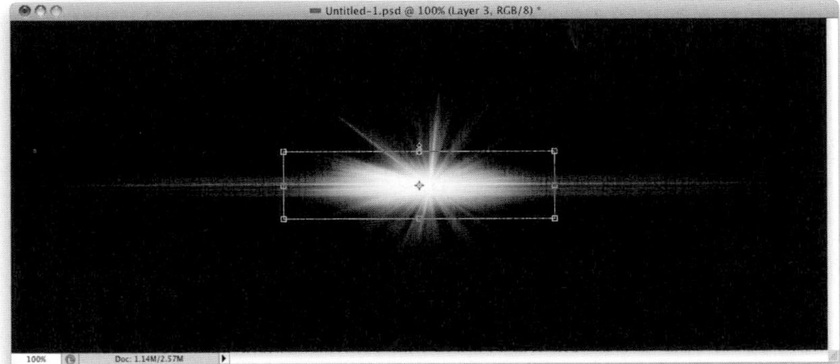

STEP 17:

Then, press **Command-T (PC: Ctrl-T)** to go into Free Transform, grab any control handle, and scale the gradient so that it is less circular and more oval by scaling more horizontally than vertically. When you're done, press **Return (PC: Enter)**.

Continued

STEP 18:

Next, click on the Add a Layer Style icon and choose **Outer Glow**. In the Structure section near the top of the Layer Style dialog, click on the color swatch and change the color to white. Then, in the Elements section, increase the Size to around 150 px. This will add an enhanced ambient glow to this element. Click OK.

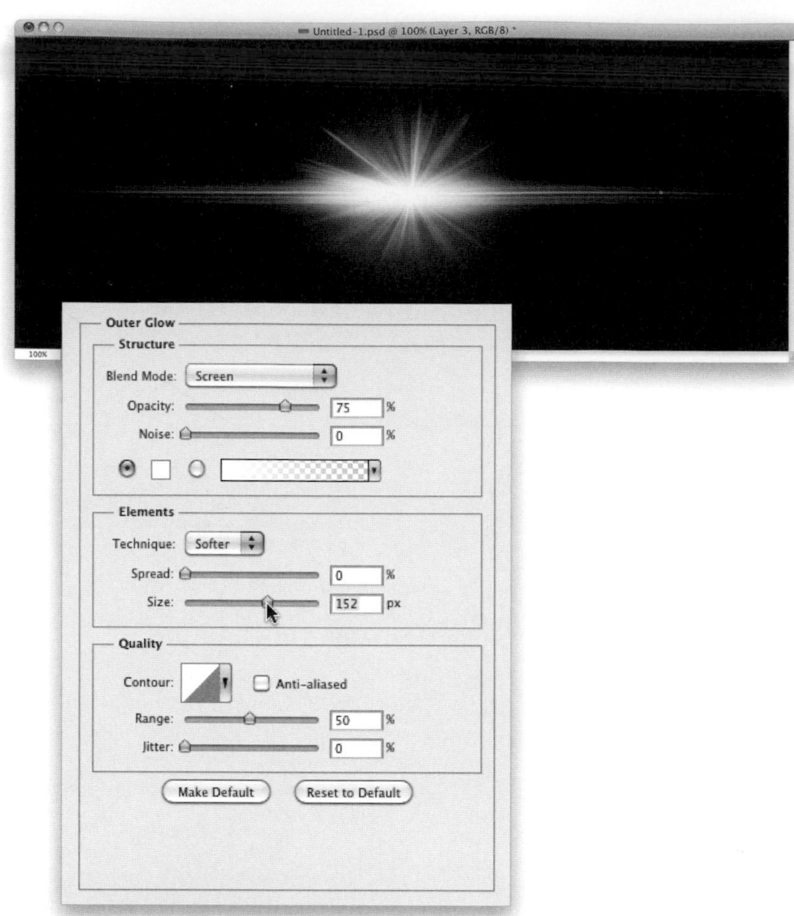

STEP 19:

Now we are ready to make the brush. When defining a brush in Photoshop, the darkest areas of the image will be the most opaque areas of the brush. Up until now, we have been building this graphic on a black background for the sake of visibility and it's how a flare would look, but now we need to invert these values to create the brush. So, start by selecting the topmost layer in the Layers panel, then press **Command-Option-Shift-E (PC: Ctrl-Alt-Shift-E)**. This will create a merged version of all your layers (the overall flare) on a new layer at the top of the layer stack.

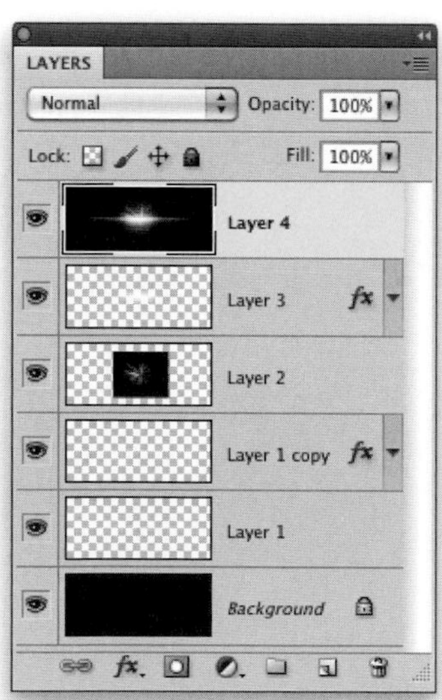

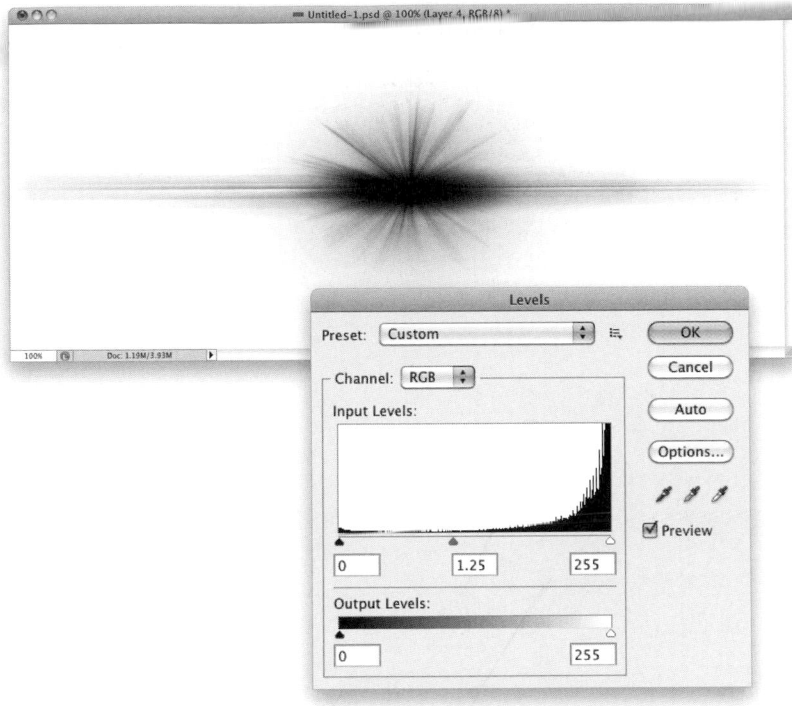

STEP 20:
Go under the Image menu, under Adjustments, and choose **Invert** (or press **Command-I [PC: Ctrl-I]**). This will make the flare black and the background white. Once the image is inverted, you may notice some areas that are a little gray and need adjusting. Simply apply a Levels adjustment (press **Command-L [PC: Ctrl-L]**) to increase the contrast a little bit. Now we are ready to define the brush.

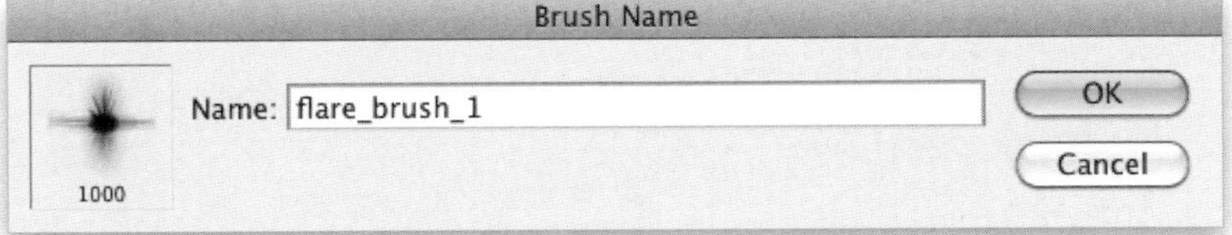

STEP 21:
Go under the Edit menu and choose **Define Brush Preset**. You don't need to select the flare first, as Photoshop will automatically ignore all the white areas, leaving only the black area in the shape of the flare. Just give the brush a name and there you have it. You can access the brush from the Brush Picker and use the Brush panel to modify its appearance. As you will see, this brush can have many uses. Have fun!

Continued

Final Image

Before

After

©FOTOLIA/YUGANOV KONSTANTIN

©ISTOCKPHOTO/ICONOGENIC

Here, and throughout the book, you can see some different uses for the flare brush. Remember, you can add to and modify the layer style to get a different color. Once the flare is on a layer, you can scale and rotate it with Free Transform, like any other graphic element.

Custom Brush Effects

Here's a great way to use various design elements defined as brushes to create cool image effects. Whether it's a stock image or a picture taken with your phone, there are numerous ways to create brushes with them, and even more possibilities with the options in the Brush panel. Here's a cool effect I saw on a video game cover recently:

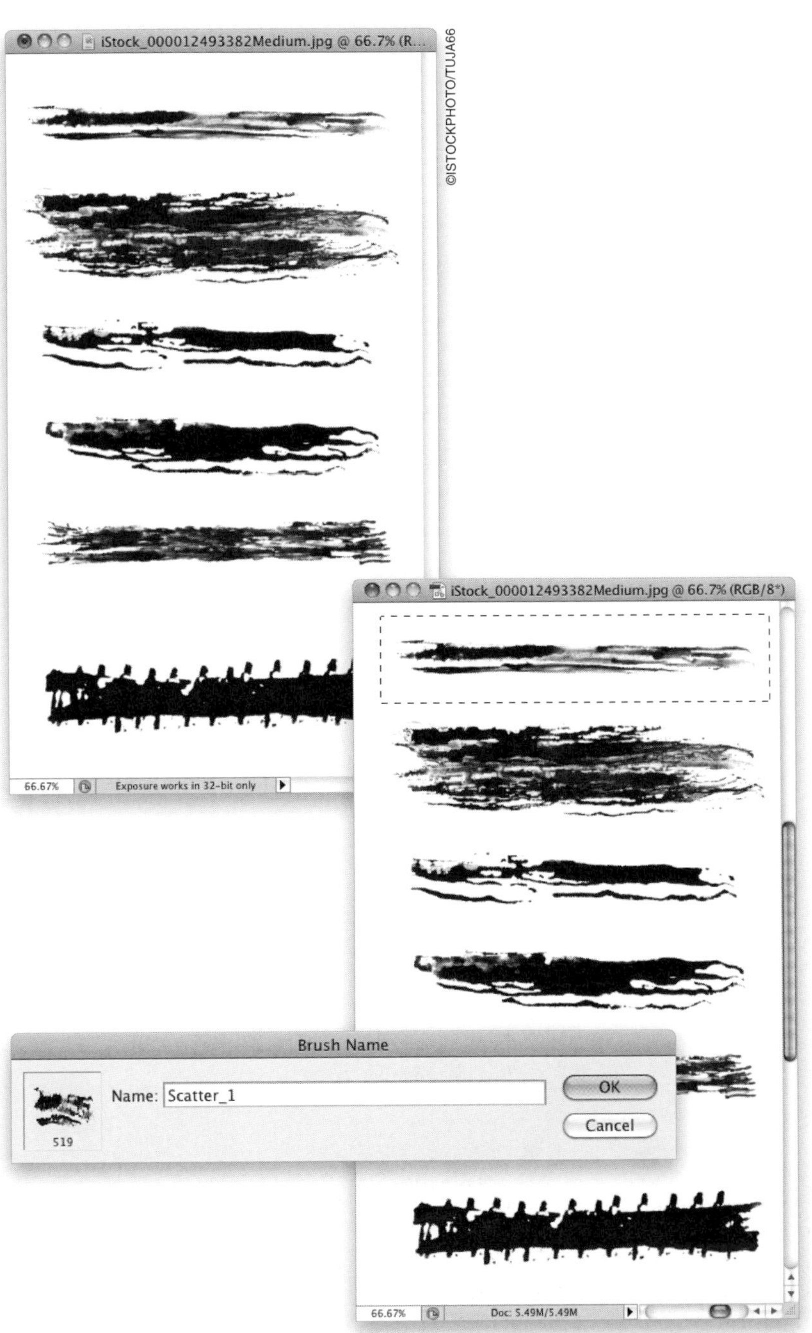

STEP ONE:

To begin, we'll start with a stock image of some abstract shapes that I got from iStockphoto (www.istockphoto.com). The cool part is that this one file contains several different shapes, so we have a choice as to which one we want to make a brush.

STEP TWO:

Grab the Rectangular Marquee tool **(M)** from the Toolbox and draw a selection around the top shape. Then, go under the Edit menu and choose **Define Brush Preset**. Give the brush a name and click OK.

Note: Notice that I didn't make any adjustments to the graphic, as I felt that it had a nice balance of dark and light areas to make a good brush. However, if you have a graphic that could use a contrast fix, then go ahead and run a quick Levels adjustment. Just press Command-L (PC: Ctrl-L).

Continued

STEP THREE:

Next, open the image of the football player we'll be applying the effect to. We need to separate the player from the background, so grab the Quick Selection tool **(W)** from the Toolbox, and then click-and-drag over the player to select him. If you miss a spot, just paint over it and it will be added to your selection. If you select something you didn't mean to, press-and-hold the **Option (PC: Alt)** key and paint over it to remove it from your selection. Once he's all selected, press **Command-C (PC: Ctrl-C)** to Copy the selected area to the clipboard.

©ISTOCKPHOTO/JASON LUGO

STEP FOUR:

Press **Command-N (PC: Ctrl-N)** and create a new document that's 7 inches wide by 12 inches tall at 125 ppi. Then, press **Command-V (PC: Ctrl-V)** to Paste the image into your new document. Press **Command-T (PC: Ctrl-T)** to go into Free Transform, press-and-hold the Shift key, and click-and-drag a corner handle inward to scale the image to fit in the canvas area (if you can't see the corner handles, press **Command-0** [zero, **PC: Ctrl-0**]). Press **Return (PC: Enter)** when you're done.

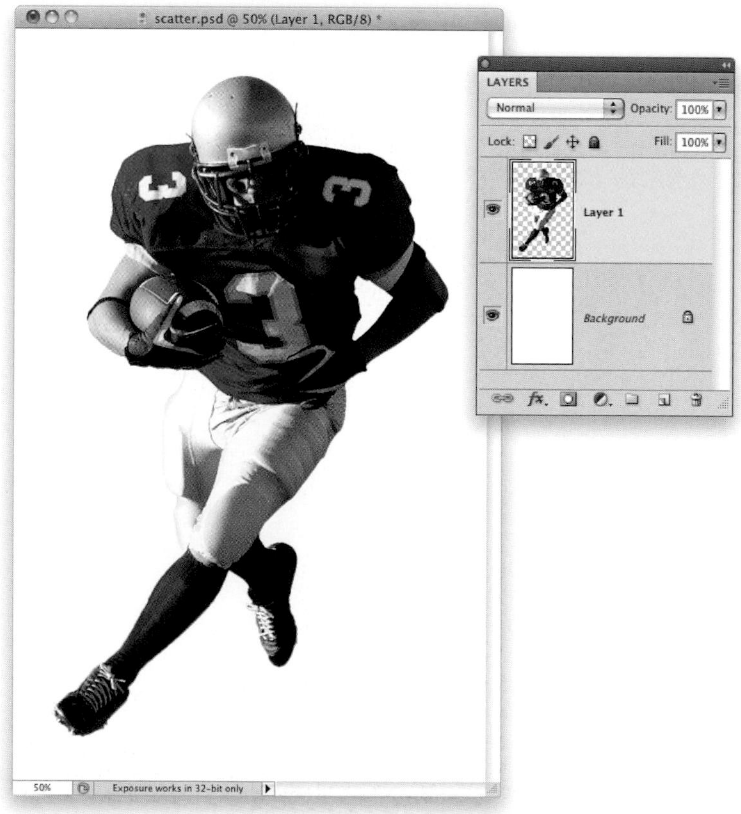

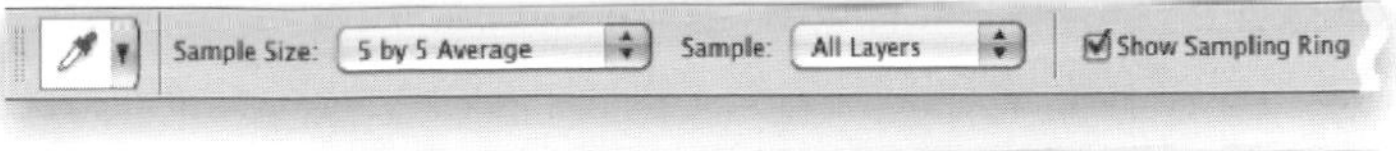

STEP FIVE:

Get the Eyedropper tool **(I)** from the Toolbox, and make sure the Sample Size setting in the Options Bar is set to **5 by 5 Average** at the minimum. Click in the rich red area of the jersey, just above the football. This will make that color your Foreground color.

STEP SIX:

Press-and-hold the Command (PC: Ctrl) key and click on the Create a New Layer icon at the bottom of the Layers panel to add a new layer below the currently active layer. Then, press **Option-Delete (PC: Alt-Backspace)** to fill this layer with the sampled red color.

Continued

STEP SEVEN:
Click back on the layer containing the player and convert it to a smart object by Right-clicking in the blank area of the layer and choosing **Convert to Smart Object** from the pop-up menu. This will allow us to stylize the photo with some filters without actually altering the original pixels.

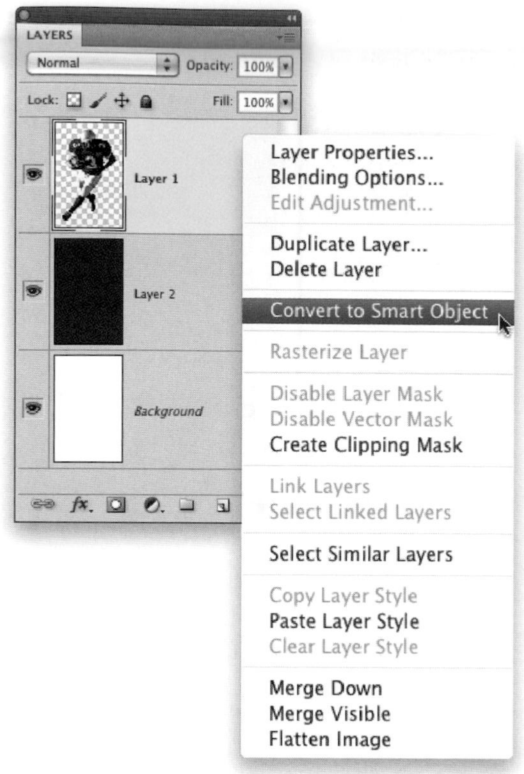

STEP EIGHT:
To make the photo look less like a photo, go under the Filter menu, under Texture, and choose **Grain**. In the filter dialog, change the Grain Type to **Speckle**. Then, set the Intensity to 60 and the Contrast to 0. Click OK.

STEP NINE:
Next, go under the Filter menu again, and under Artistic, choose **Poster Edges**. Set the Edge Thickness to 0, the Edge Intensity to 1, and the Posterization to 6. This will greatly enhance the overall effect, probably even a little more than you want.

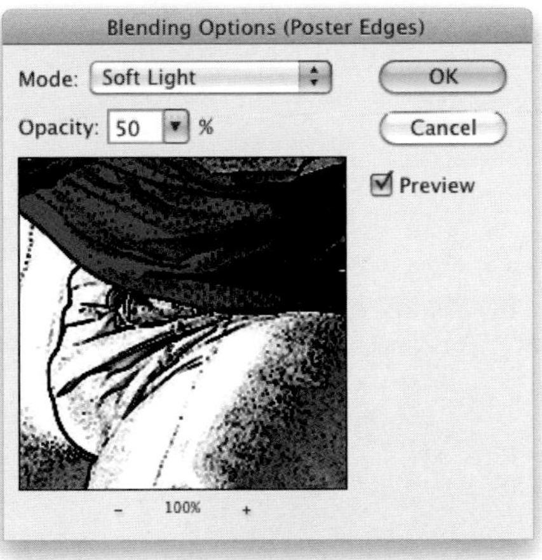

STEP 10:
If that last effect looks good, but looks too intense, then you can go into the Layers panel and double-click on the small icon to the right of Poster Edges. This will open the Blending Options dialog, which allows you to modify the appearance of the filter by changing the blend mode or the opacity. In this case, change the blend Mode to **Soft Light** and set the Opacity to 50%. This will lessen the effect quite a bit. (*Note:* Normally this feature is only available right after you have applied a filter, but when that layer is a smart object, as it is here, you can access this feature any time.)

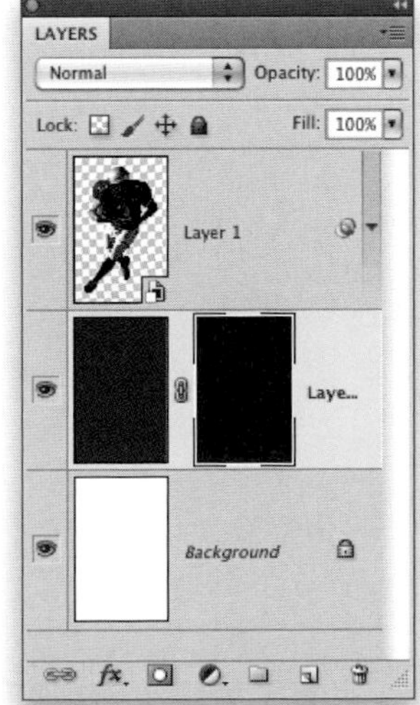

STEP 11:
Click on the layer with the red color fill again. Add a black layer mask (to hide everything on that layer) by pressing-and-holding the Option (PC: Alt) key while clicking on the Add Layer Mask icon at the bottom of the Layers panel. We'll paint that red color back in using the brush we made back in Step Two.

Continued

STEP 12:
Choose the Brush tool **(B)** from the Toolbox and click on the brush thumbnail in the Options Bar to open the Brush Picker. The new brush should be the very last brush in the list. Just scroll to the bottom and select it.

Click on the icon to the right of the brush thumbnail to open the Brush panel, and click on Brush Tip Shape near the top left first. Set the Angle of the brush to 30°, set the Roundness to 75%, and increase the Spacing to about 50%.

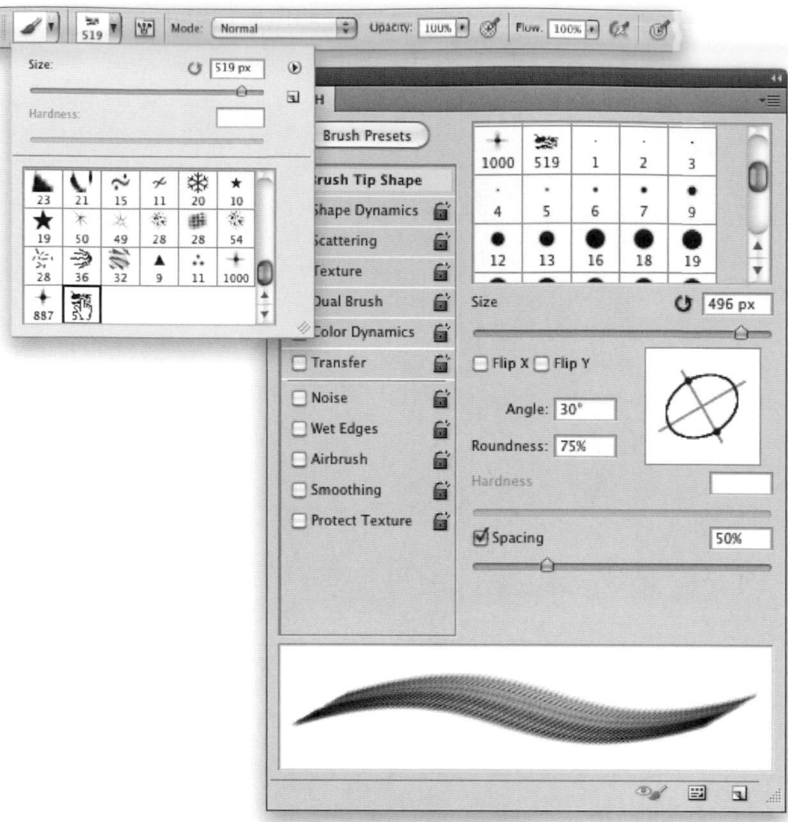

STEP 13:
Next, click on Shape Dynamics on the left to turn it on. Set the Size Jitter all the way to 100%. Of course, if you are using a pressure-sensitive tablet, you can also set the Control to Pen Pressure. Then, turn on the Flip X Jitter and Flip Y Jitter checkboxes at the bottom to add some more variation to the brush tip.

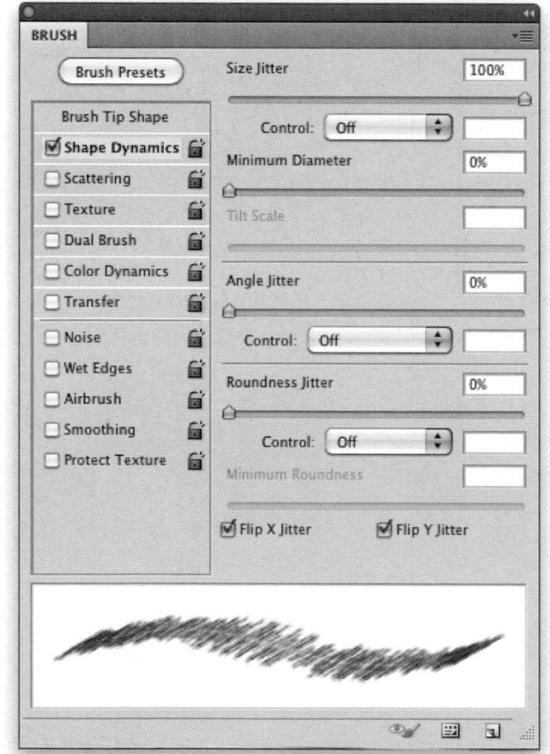

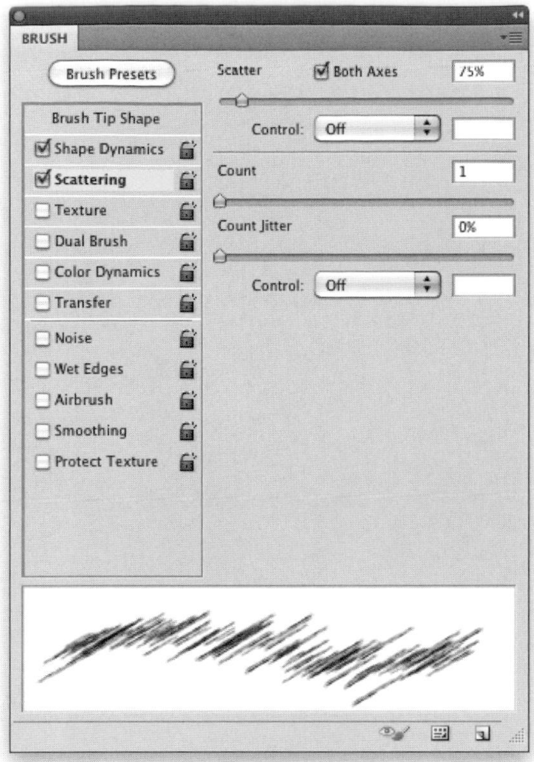

STEP 14:

Now, click on Scattering on the left to turn it on. Make sure that the Both Axes checkbox is turned on and set the Scatter amount to 75% to start. If you don't like the way this works, simply increase or decrease this setting.

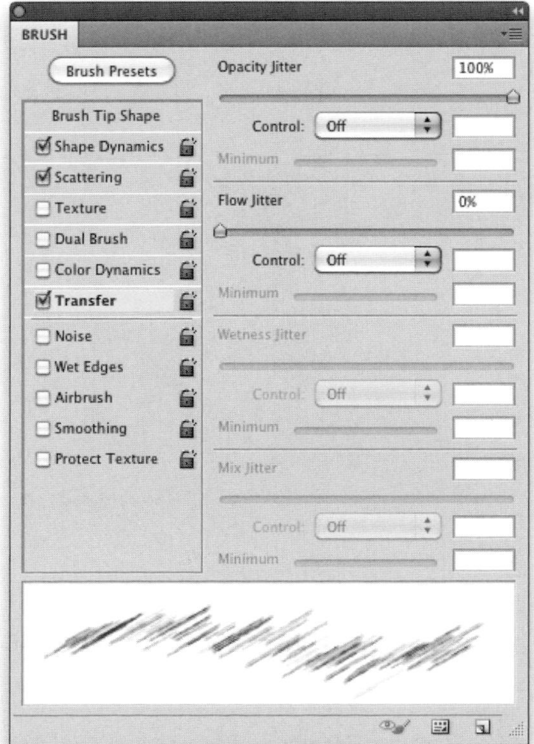

STEP 15:

Finally, click on Transfer on the left to turn it on. All you need to do here is set the Opacity Jitter to 100% to vary the density of the brush tip as you paint.

Continued

STEP 16:
Make sure the layer mask is selected on the red-color-filled layer and your Foreground color is set to white, and then just randomly paint the area around the player to reveal the red in a very stylish way with the new brush. Notice the varying sizes of the brush strokes, as well as the varying opacity. All with a simple brush and its options.

STEP 17:
You can definitely take it a step further and add a white (reveal all) layer mask to the Smart Object layer, by clicking on the Add Layer Mask icon. Then, press **X** to switch your Foreground color to black and, using the same brush, randomly paint areas around the player to mask them, giving the appearance that the effect is wrapping all around the player. So, you're using the same brush and brush properties to hide and reveal different parts of the image, creating a very interesting result.

To finish off the image (as shown on the next page), I clicked back on the red-color-filled layer, then clicked on the Add a Layer Style icon at the bottom of the Layers panel and added Inner Glow, Gradient Overlay, and Pattern Overlay layer styles. I used a Black, White reversed radial gradient, and the Herringbone 2 pattern from the Patterns presets. Then, on a new blank layer, I drew a rectangle with the Rectangle tool set to Fill Pixels and my Foreground color set to white, used Free Transform's Warp set to Bulge, lowered the layer's opacity, and added a black Outer Glow layer style to it. Finally, I added some text over the shape.

Final Image

Similarities in Nature

Here's something that I actually stumbled upon by accident: I was attempting to take a photo of lightning and create a brush from it, so I could have lightning when I needed it. However, in my pursuit of this, I had a "Eureka!" moment. When you look at the lightning image below, what does the shape of the lightning resemble? Read on to find out.

STEP ONE:
Here, we'll start with this simple stock image of a lightning strike. It's always good to have a folder of images that contain generic elements like this. You just never know what you might be able to use them for.

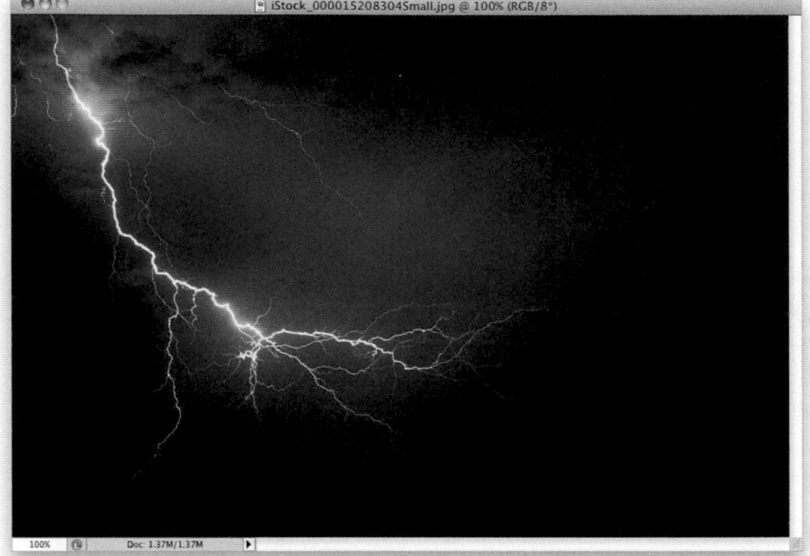

©ISTOCKPHOTO/CHEE MING WONG

STEP TWO:
To create the brush, we are going to start with the image's channels. Open the Channels panel by going to Window>**Channels**. Toggle through the individual channels and locate the channel that defines the lightning pretty well, while the background is as dark as possible. In this case, it looks like it will be the Red channel. So, make a duplicate of the Red channel by dragging it down onto the Create New Channel icon.

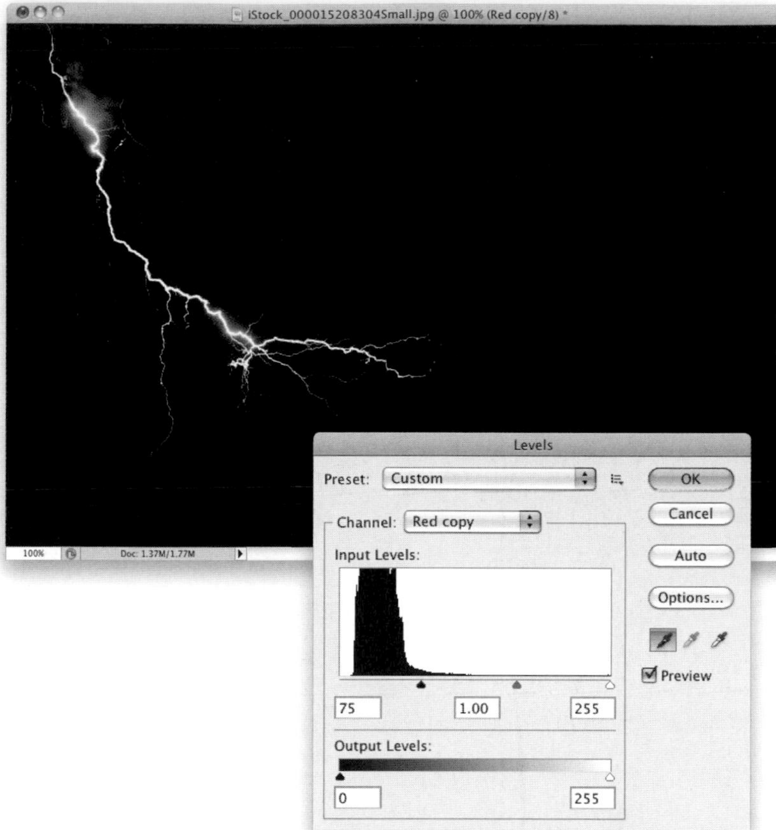

STEP THREE:

With the Red copy channel active, press **Command-L (PC: Ctrl-L)** to open the Levels dialog. Grab the black (shadows) eyedropper below the Options button, and click on the light gray area next to the lightning bolt. This will force everything that is that shade of gray or darker to go black. Then, if necessary, move the sliders to tighten up the contrast a bit more (I ended up dragging the center gray Input Levels midtones slider to the right a little to 0.75), and click OK.

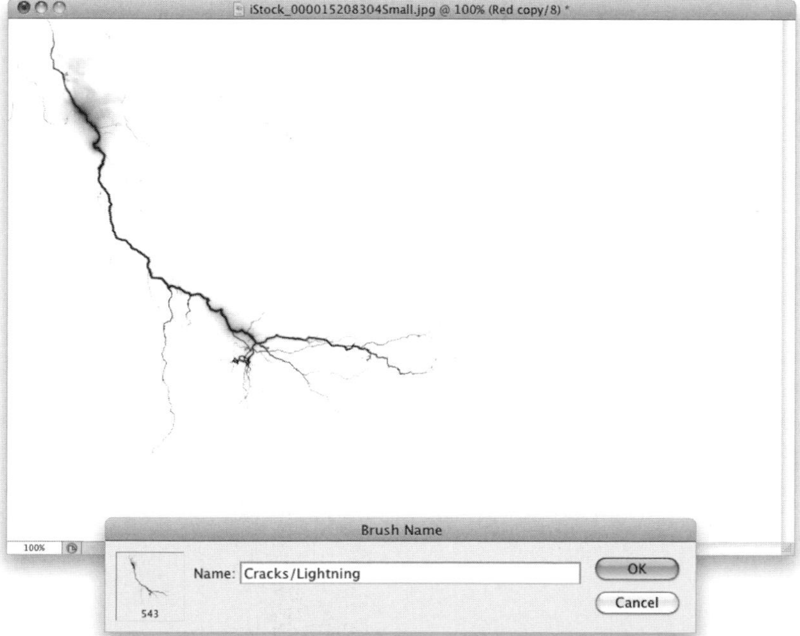

STEP FOUR:

As we saw before when defining a brush, Photoshop will disregard the white area, only defining the black areas and any little hints of gray there might be. So, press **Command-I (PC: Ctrl-I)** to Invert the image, so the sky is white and the lightning is black. Now, go under the Edit menu and choose **Define Brush Preset**. Then just give the brush a name and there you have a lightning brush.

Continued

STEP FIVE:

At this point, we have achieved what we first set out to do, which was to create a lightning brush. But, if we think a little outside the box, we can use it for more than just lightning. Click on the brush thumbnail in the Options Bar to open the Brush Picker, and select your new lightning brush. Then, click on the icon to the right of the brush thumbnail to open up the Brush panel. Click on Brush Tip Shape on the left and set the Spacing to 60%. Notice, also, that the brush size is set to what it was defined as. But, we'll use a handy keyboard shortcut to change the size later while painting.

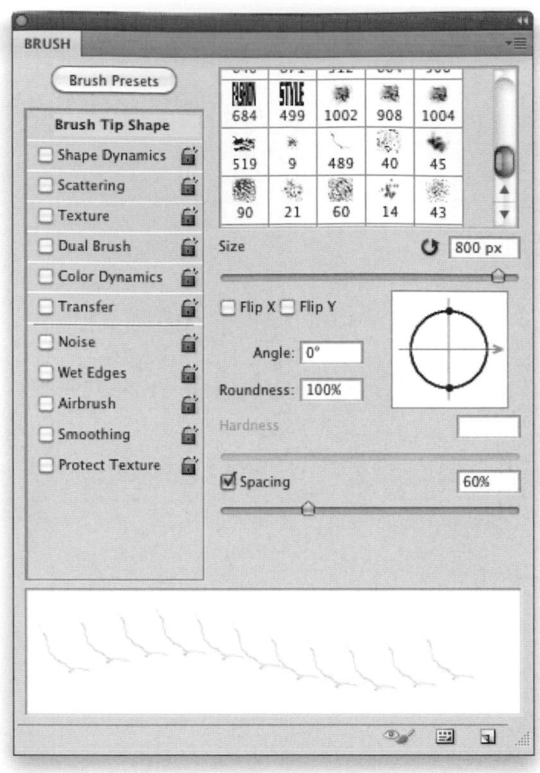

STEP SIX:

Next, click on Shape Dynamics on the left to turn it on. Set the Size Jitter to 100% and make sure the Control pop-up menu is set to **Off**. Then set the Angle Jitter to 100%, as well, and again leave the Control menu set to **Off**. Finally turn on the Flip X Jitter and Flip Y Jitter check-boxes at the bottom to add variation to the brush effect.

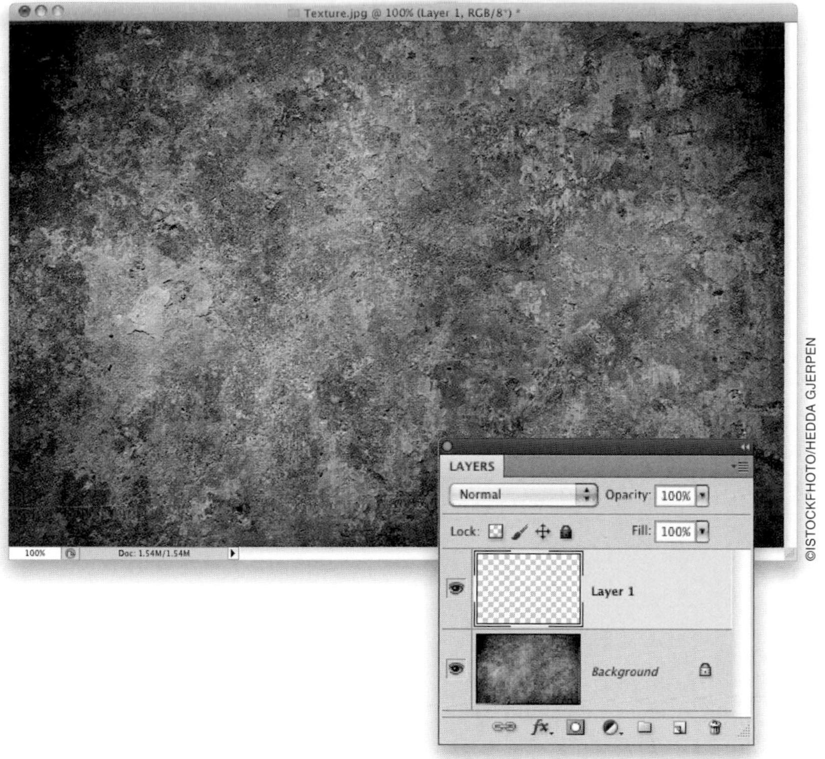

©ISTOCKPHOTO/HEDDA GJERPEN

STEP SEVEN:

Now, open the stone texture file I supplied on the book's download site (mentioned in the book's introduction), or open any texture file you want to try this effect on. Remember when I said that if you look closely at the shape of the lightning, you can see more than the obvious? I look at it and see a cracked effect. So, click on the Create a New Layer icon at the bottom of the Layers panel to create a new blank layer to paint on.

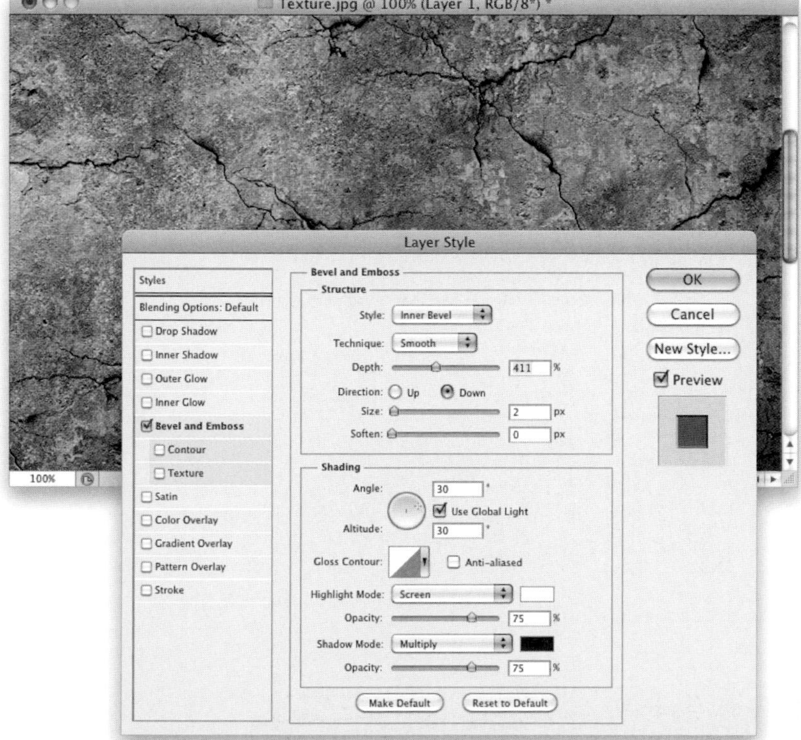

STEP EIGHT:

Before we paint, click on the Add a Layer Style icon at the bottom of the Layers panel and choose **Bevel and Emboss** from the pop-up menu. Using the settings you see here will give the cracks a little edge depth, making them a little more realistic. Now, press **D** to set your Foreground color to black and paint on the blank layer with the new brush. You can see how it gives you the effect of cracks in the stone just by painting a few strokes.

Continued

STEP NINE:

To finish off the image here, add some text, using a heavy font (here, I used Swiss721BT), and change the text layer's blend mode to **Overlay**, so you can see some of the cracks through it. Then, Command-click (PC: Ctrl-click) on the text layer's thumbnail to select the text, and press **Command-Shift-I (PC: Ctrl-Shift-I)** to Inverse your selection. Now, click on your cracks layer and switch back to the Brush tool. Use the **Left Bracket Key ([)** to make your brush size smaller, and paint back and forth around and over the text to make it look like it's so heavy it crumbled the stone when it dropped onto it. Press **Command-D (PC: Ctrl-D)** to Deselect.

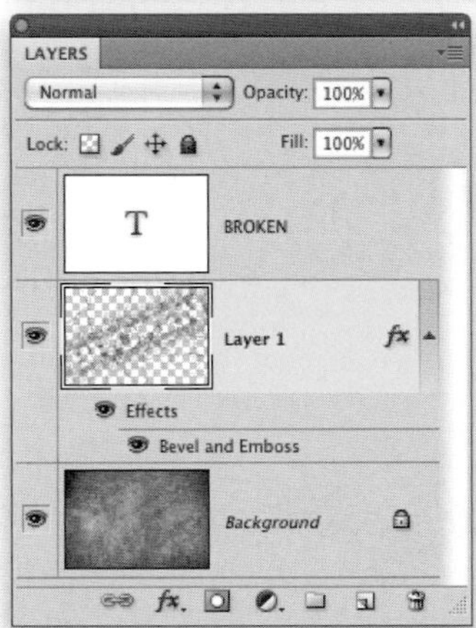

Final Image

By changing your Foreground color to white and adding a light blue Outer Glow layer style with the Blend Mode set to Hard Light, you can actually get a really cool lightning effect, essentially on a brush. This can give you some electrifying results.

Virtual Paintball!

Okay, not only does this brush have a cool effect, but it's also a lot of fun to just goof around with. By defining a brush from a graphic of a paint splat, you can set the brush up to paint as if your cursor were a paintball gun, allowing you to get pretty creative with paint splat effects. The best part? It's nowhere near as messy!

STEP ONE:
Here, we're starting with a stock image of some different ink splats. As with our previous custom brush, the great thing here is that we have quite a few different splats in this one file, so we can create several different types of brushes.

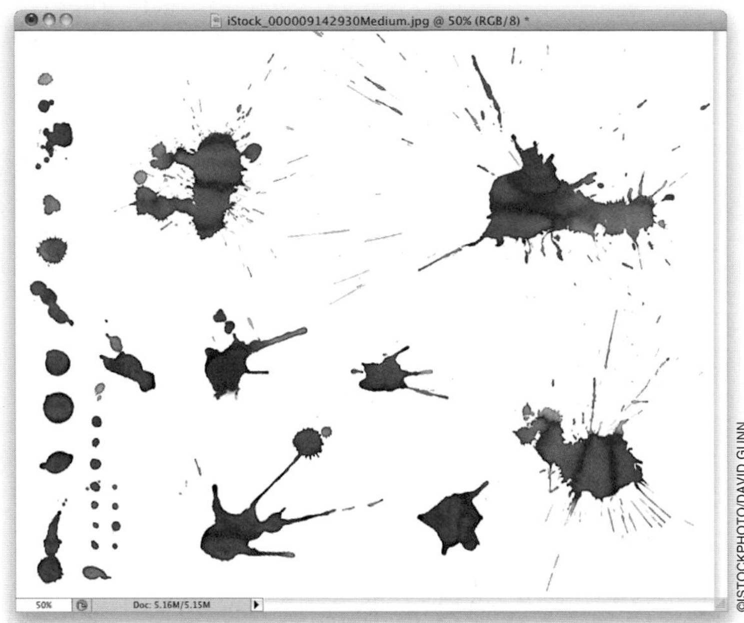

©ISTOCKPHOTO/DAVID GUNN

STEP TWO:
Go to the Toolbox and choose the Lasso tool **(L)**. Choose a splat in the image and draw a lasso selection around it. The splats are in color, but we don't need them to be, so press **Command-Shift-U (PC: Ctrl-Shift-U)** to remove the color from your selected splat.

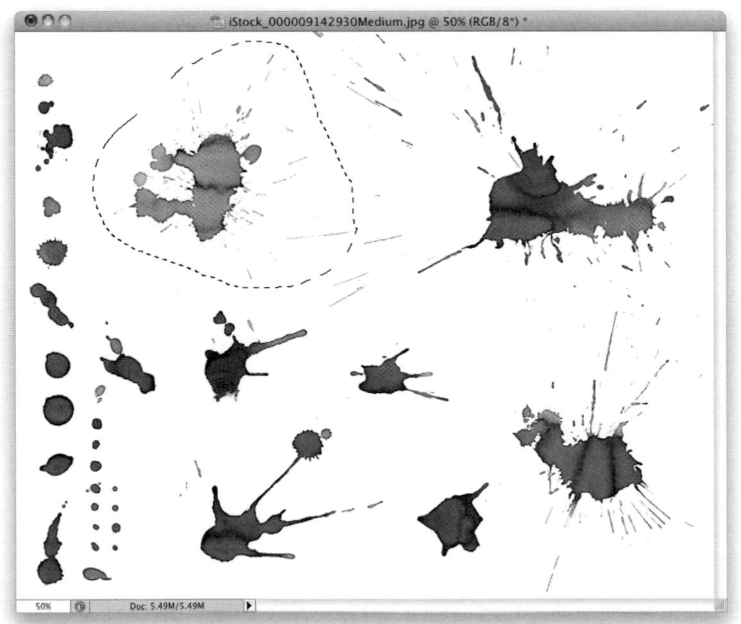

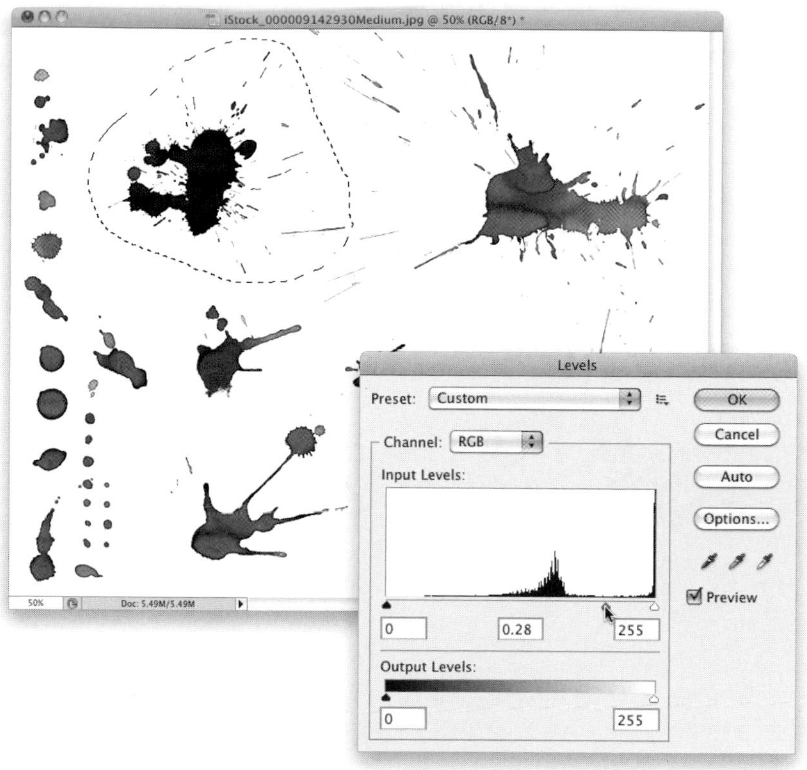

STEP THREE:

The graphic is a somewhat light gray now, and if it was defined as a brush, it would be fairly transparent. So, I think a quick Levels adjustment is in order to darken the overall splat. Press **Command-L (PC: Ctrl-L)** to bring up the Levels dialog. Then, just drag the Input Levels midtones (gray) slider to the right to about the 0.28 mark, and click OK. This will leave some gray, so that there is a little bit of transparency in the brush, but not too much.

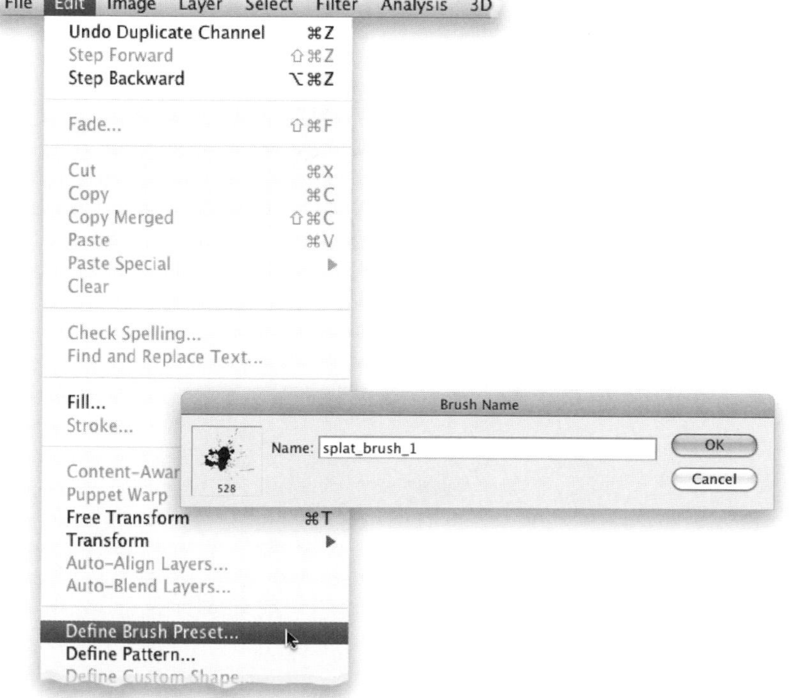

STEP FOUR:

Of course, by now you should know the drill (if you've read any of the other projects in this chapter). With your splat still selected, go under the Edit menu, choose **Define Brush Preset**, and give the brush a name. Click OK.

Continued

STEP FIVE:

With the brush defined, let's set up the image to paint on. Open the image of the jumping girl, or another silhouette or shape you want to use. To get a better selection of the girl or shape, click on the Create New Adjustment Layer icon at the bottom of the Layers panel, and choose **Levels** from the pop-up menu. In the Levels options in the Adjustments panel, move the black shadows slider beneath the histogram all the way over to the right. This will greatly darken the image, making it easier to get the selection.

©ISTOCKPHOTO/NICOLAS HANSEN

STEP SIX:

Get the Magic Wand tool from the Toolbox (or press **Shift-W** until you have it), and click on the white background. Make sure the Tolerance is set to the default of 32 in the Options Bar, and that the Contiguous checkbox is turned on, as well.

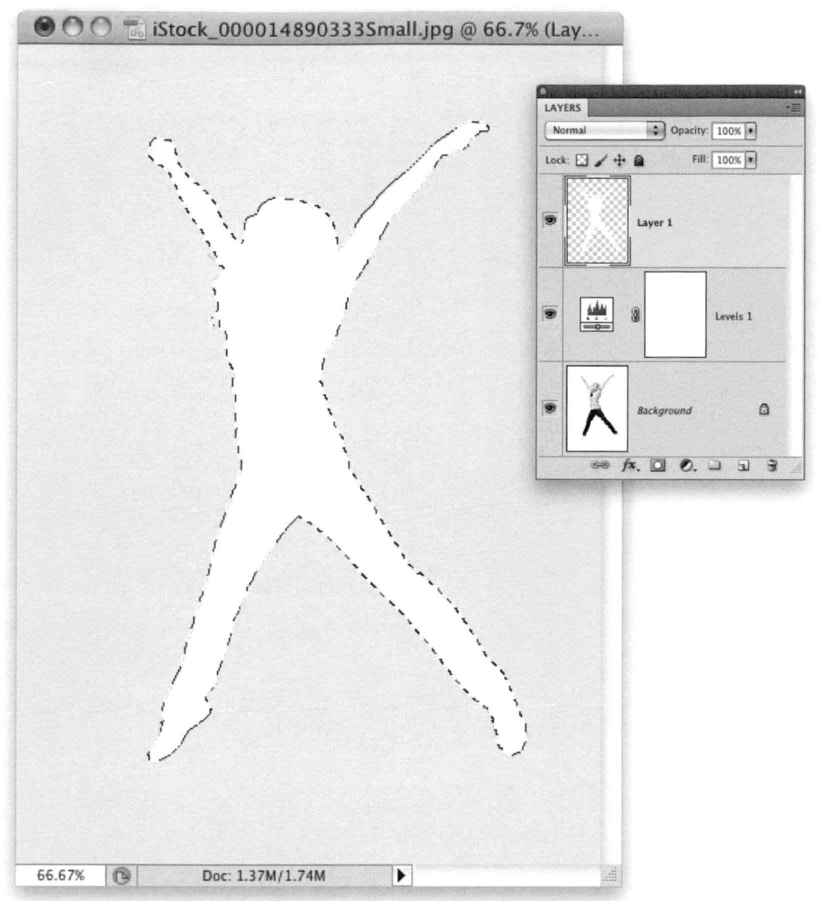

STEP SEVEN:

Then, press **Command-Shift-I (PC: Ctrl-Shift-I)** to Inverse the selection of the background and select the shape of the girl. Click on the Create a New Layer icon at the bottom of the Layers panel to create a new blank layer, press **D** to set your Foreground and Background colors to their defaults of black and white, then press **Command-Delete (PC: Ctrl-Backspace)** to fill this active selection with white.

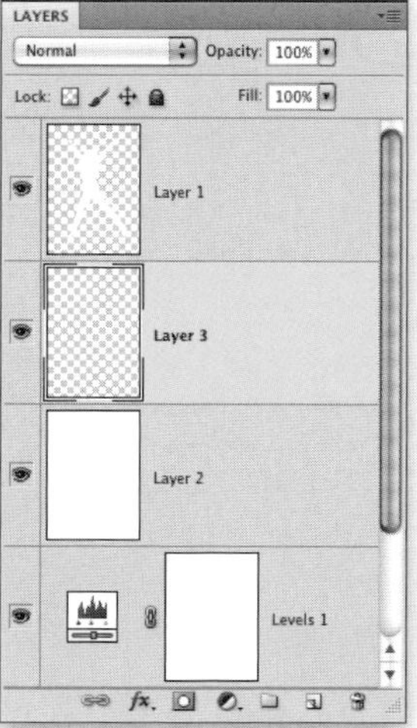

STEP EIGHT:

Press **Command-D (PC: Ctrl-D)** to Deselect. Create another new blank layer below this layer by pressing-and-holding the Command (PC: Ctrl) key while clicking on the Create a New Layer icon. Fill this entire layer with white, as well. This will leave you with a white silhouette layer over a white background layer. Add one more new blank layer in between these two layers and leave it blank.

Continued

STEP NINE:
Select the Brush tool **(B)** from the Toolbox, then click on the brush thumbnail in the Option Bar, and locate the splat brush we defined in Step Four in the Brush Picker. Then, click on the icon to the right of the brush thumbnail to open the Brush panel, and click on Shape Dynamics on the left. Set the Size Jitter and Angle Jitter to 100%. Also turn on the Flip X Jitter and Flip Y Jitter checkboxes to vary the orientation more.

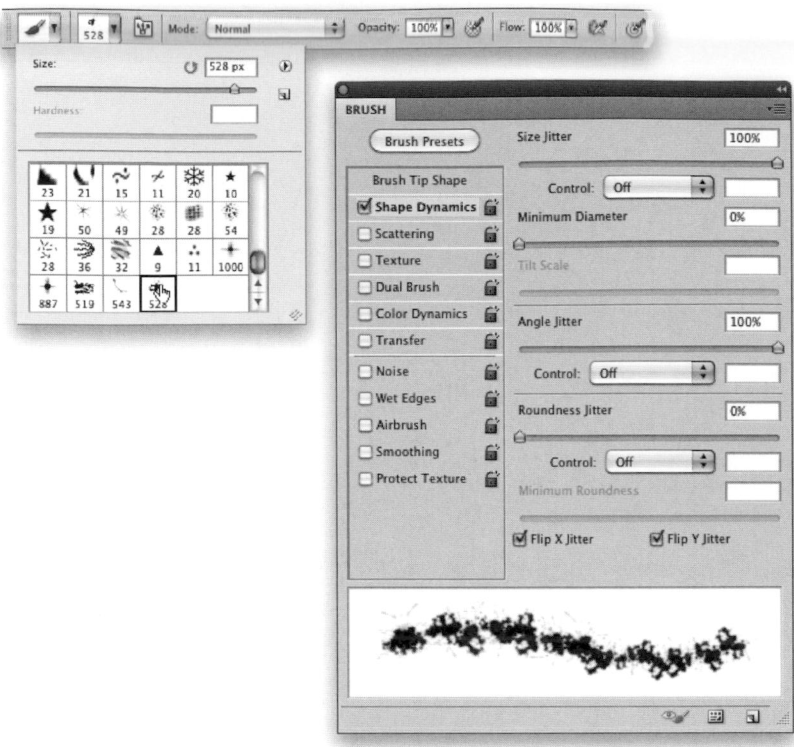

STEP 10:
Next, click on Scattering on the left to turn it on. Make sure the Both Axes checkbox is turned on, and set the Scatter amount to 140.

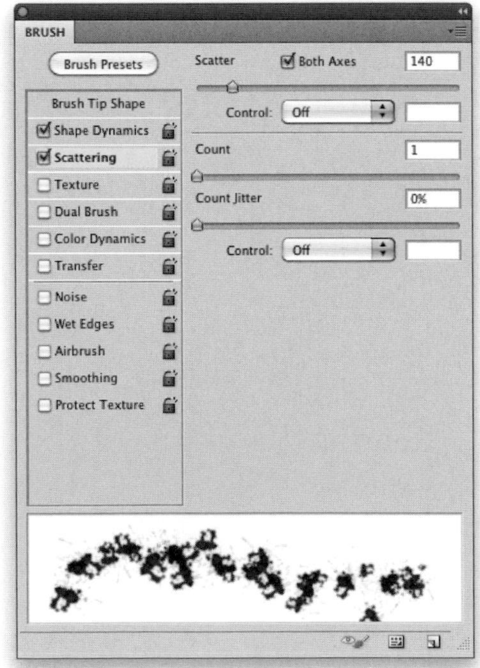

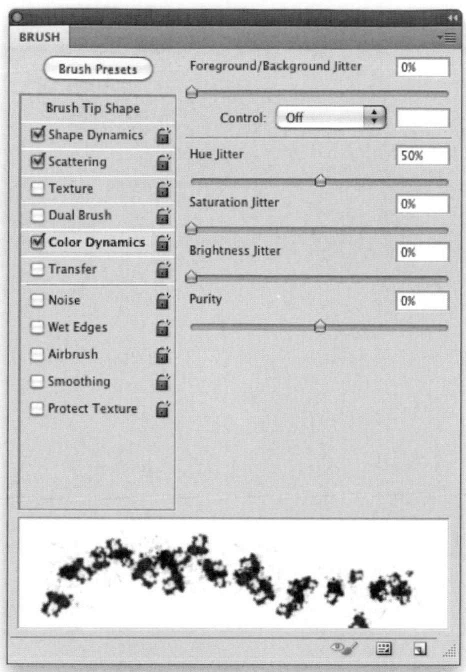

STEP 11:
Click on Color Dynamics on the left to turn it on and set the Hue Jitter to 50% to start. Feel free to try other settings to get a different effect altogether.

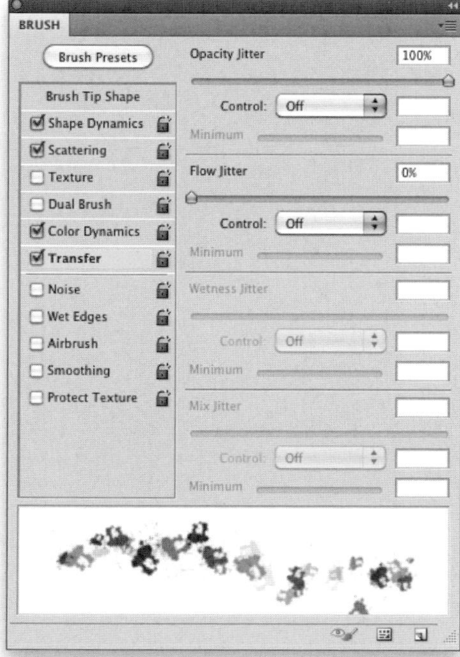

STEP 12:
Lastly, as an option, you can click on Transfer on the left to turn it on, and set the Opacity Jitter to 100%. I like this because it varies the opacity with better control than if the brush had been defined at that light gray color (without the Levels adjustment).

Continued

STEP 13:
Now, click on your Foreground color swatch and choose a color to start with. Then, paint on that blank layer (Layer 3). Remember (we talked about this when we made the bokeh brush), the Hue Jitter only works with colors, so black or white is no good. Also remember, the color you start with makes a difference, as well. Start with a cool color and you'll get more variations of cooler hues; start with a warm color and it'll produce warmer hues.

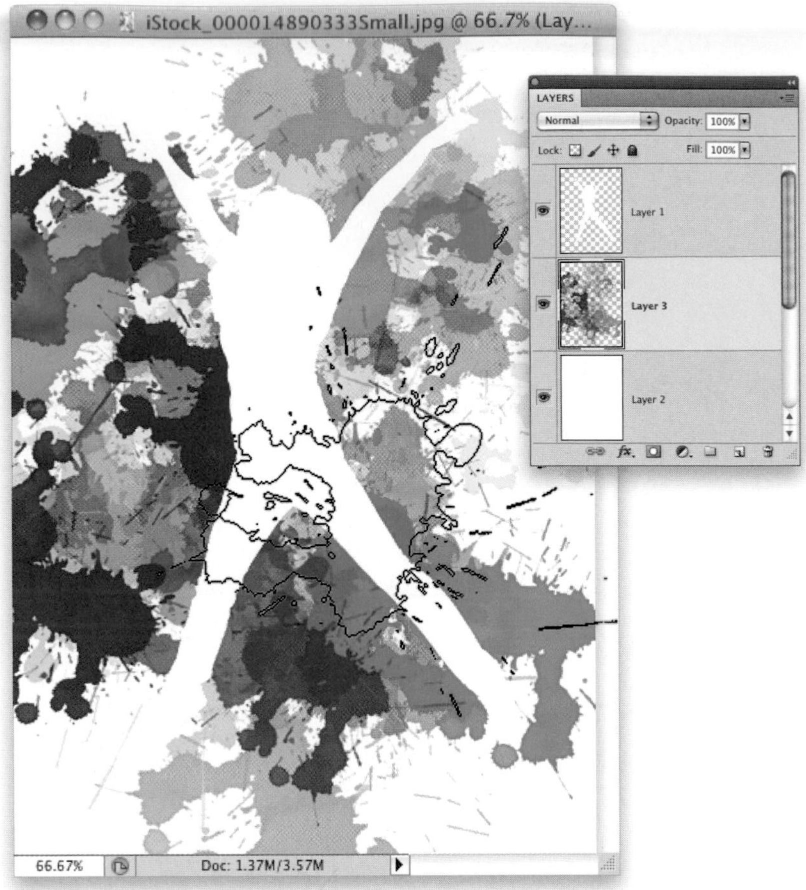

Final Image

With the splat defined as a brush, you can select it at any time and just change the initial color to get different results. Here, I started with a warm color to get an overall warmer feel. Be sure to experiment with the brush settings for different effects.

26-Piece Tool Set

type effects

Of all the tool sets available to the modern designer today, one of them remains the most important: those 26 characters we call the alphabet. Every designer will use text at some level in their design work, whether it is a simple paragraph of formatted text or a full logo effect with graphics and images. Using text effectively is, in and of itself, an art form. In this chapter, we will explore ways to use the strengths of Photoshop to create effects that will help you see text more as a design element. Pay close attention to more than what the text represents, to each letter's physical appearance and shape. Even observe the negative space inside and around the text, and see what emerges. With 26 letters and the numbers 0 through 9, you have an infinite number of possibilities. So, what do you say?

Hollywood Title Effect

Nowhere can you find cooler text effects than in the movies! Well...almost nowhere. And there's no reason why you can't incorporate a little Hollywood flair into your designs. Here, we're going to create a text effect that I was inspired by a while back, and that now seems to be everywhere. By getting creative with layer styles and using a brush effect we created in Chapter 1, you'll see these types of effects are easier to create than they seem!

STEP ONE:

Start by going under the File menu, choosing **New**, and creating a new document that's about 11 inches wide by 4.5 inches tall at 100 ppi. With your Foreground color set to black, press **Option-Delete (PC: Alt-Backspace)** to fill the Background layer with black, then select the Horizontal Type tool **(T)** from the Toolbox, and click on the canvas to create a text layer. Here, I have typed the word "INSPIRED" in a font called Eurostile, because it has a sort of cinematic feel to it. Regardless of what font you choose for this effect, I do recommend you use a sans-serif font, as bolder typefaces work best. Once done, select the text, then click on your Foreground color swatch, and choose a light gray color.

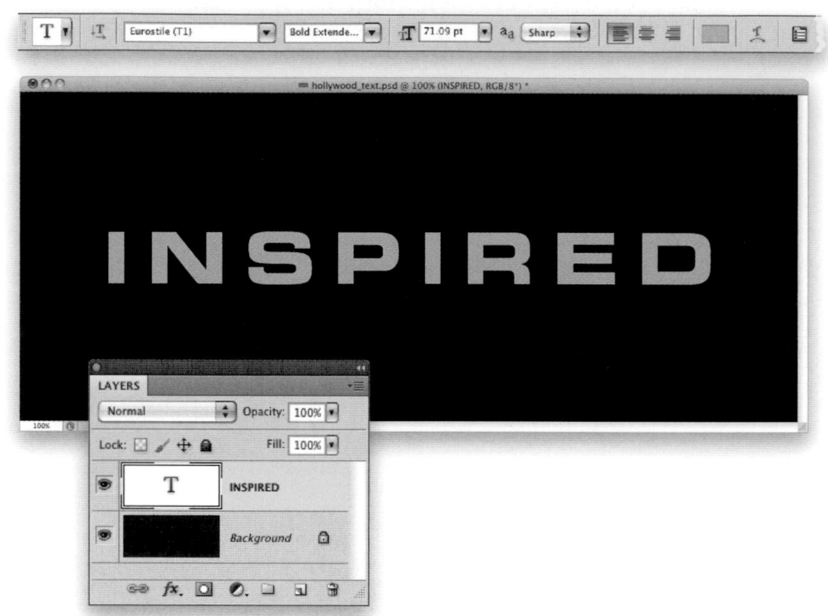

STEP TWO:

At the bottom of the Layers panel, click on the Add a Layer Style icon, and choose **Gradient Overlay**. In the Layer Style dialog, click on the down-facing arrow next to the gradient thumbnail and choose the Black, White gradient (the third one from the left in the top row), then change the Blend Mode to **Overlay**, set the Opacity to 90%, and increase the Scale amount just a bit. Also, turn on the Reverse checkbox to flip the colors.

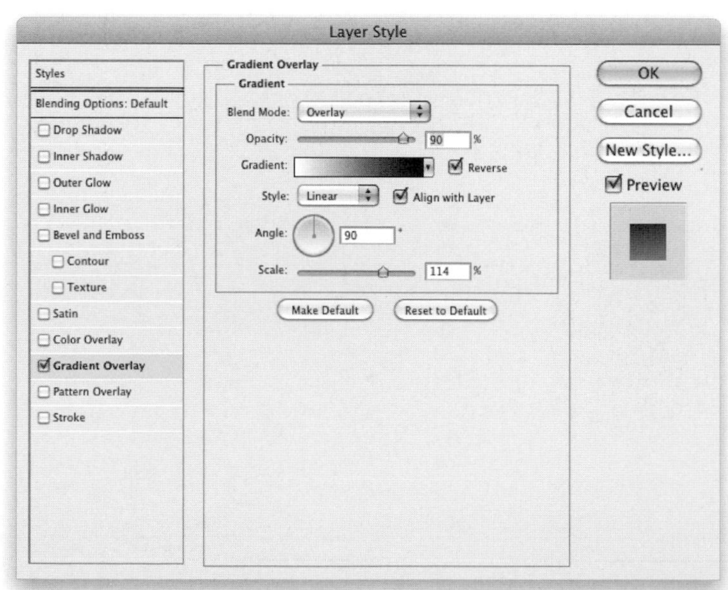

STEP THREE:

Now, load the shape of this text as an active selection by pressing-and-holding the Command (PC: Ctrl) key and clicking on the text layer's thumbnail (as shown here).

STEP FOUR:

Click on the Create a New Layer icon at the bottom of the Layers panel to create a new blank layer and fill the active selection with your Foreground color (the same gray color used to fill the original text layer) by pressing Option-Delete again. With the selection still active, from the Select menu, choose **Transform Selection**. This will put the selection into Transform mode. In the Options Bar, click on the Maintain Aspect Ratio icon (the chain link) between the width and height settings to lock the aspect ratio. Change the H (height) setting to 102% and the width will automatically change proportionately. Once done, press **Return (PC: Enter)** to commit the change and then press **Delete (PC: Backspace)** to remove the area inside the selection. What's left outside the selection now gives us the illusion the text is 3D.

Continued

STEP FIVE:

To help give this a bit more dimension, just add a Gradient Overlay layer style to this layer the same way we did to the original text layer. This time, though, leave the Blend Mode set to **Normal**, reduce the Opacity to 75%, leave the Scale amount set to 100%, and do not reverse the gradient (so it will be opposite the other gradient). Click OK and then press **Command-D (PC: Ctrl-D)** to Deselect.

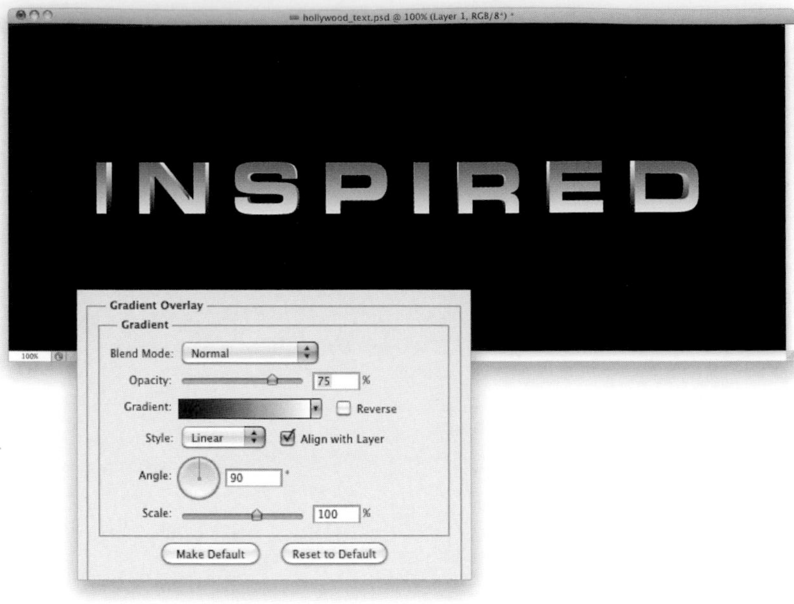

STEP SIX:

Now, the only problem I see here is in the letter "N." Notice how the inner corners don't look right? Zoom in on the letter, then grab the Rectangular Marquee tool **(M)** from the Toolbox, and draw small selections over the areas where the gradient is missing (as shown here). Press-and-hold the Shift key to create multiple selections and press-and-hold the Option (PC: Alt) key to remove areas from the selections. Then, just fill these areas with the same gray we used before, and deselect. The layer style will automatically redraw over the new area, completing the shape.

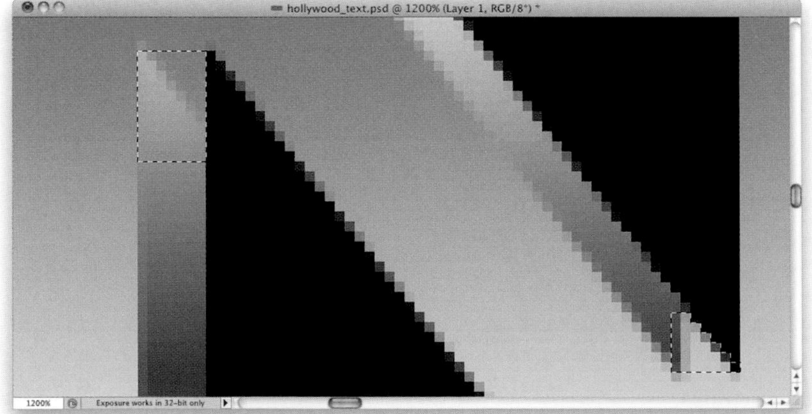

STEP SEVEN:

Now to give the text some color. Sure we could have given the text a color when we started, but I like using an adjustment layer over gray-tone elements, because it makes it much easier to change the color when needed. So, go to the bottom of the Layers panel again, click on the Create New Adjustment Layer icon, and choose **Hue/ Saturation**. In the Adjustments panel, turn on the Colorize checkbox, then set the Hue to 215, the Saturation to around 40, and the Lightness to –18. This will give you a nice blue cast over the text. Of course, feel free to play around with other color variations to get a different look.

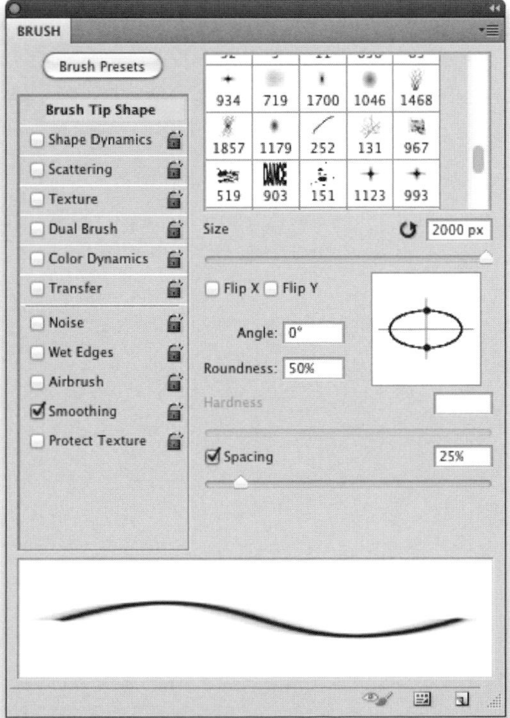

STEP EIGHT:

To add a final touch, we're going to add some cinematic flares to enhance the effect. Add a new blank layer, get the Brush tool **(B)**, and then choose the flare brush we created in Chapter 1 from the Brush Picker. Go to the Brush panel and, in the Brush Tip Shape options, set the Roundness of the brush to 50%. This will squash the brush down, making the flare a bit thinner. Also, increase the Size of the brush to 2000 px.

Continued

STEP NINE:

Press **D**, then **X** to set white as your Foreground color, then zoom out of the document and click-and-drag out the bottom-right corner of the image window, so you can see the pasteboard area outside the canvas. Position your cursor to the side of the text, just outside the edge of the document, and click once to paint one instance of the flare. You can see here this adds the outer parts of the flare to the visible canvas area, giving the effect that the light is just out of view.

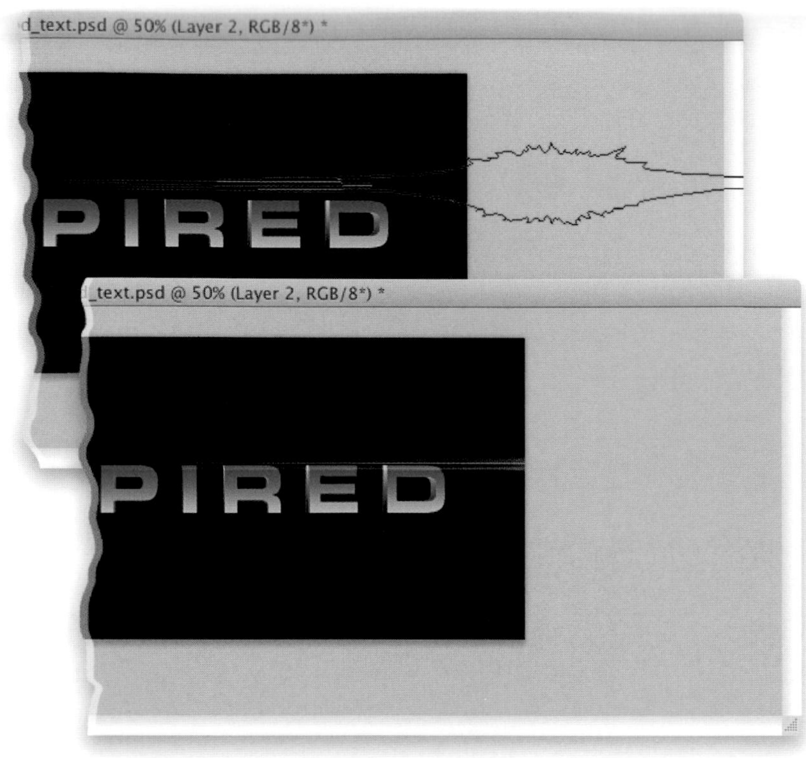

STEP 10:

To enhance this flare even more, click on the Add a Layer Style icon and, from the pop-up menu, choose **Outer Glow**. Click on the color swatch and choose a light blue color, or sample a blue color from the text. Set the Blend Mode to **Hard Light** and increase the Opacity to 100%. Set the glow Size to around 2 px and click OK when you're done. As an option, you can put the flare into Free Transform mode and scale it vertically to basically "stretch" the pixels to cover more area. As a result, this will add a blur effect to the flare as you scale.

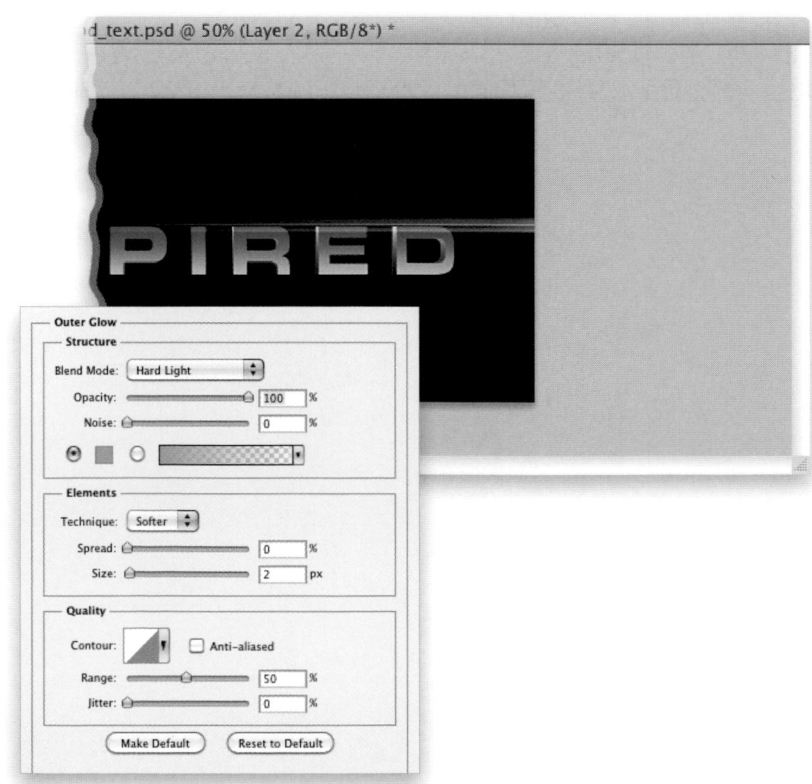

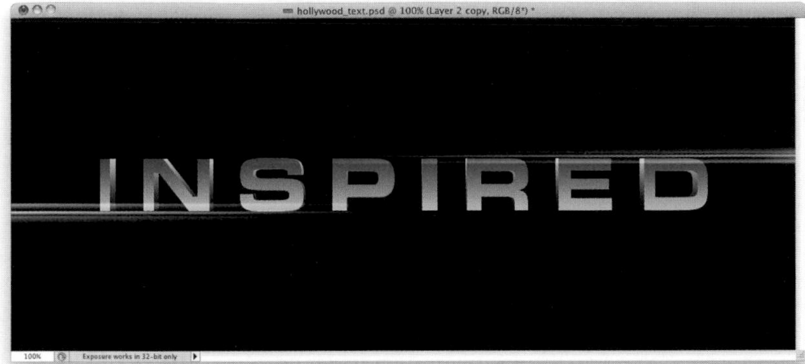

STEP 11:

Now use this same technique to add a flare from the other side of the canvas (or just copy the first flare layer, go into Free Transform, Right-click on it, and choose **Flip Horizontal**, then drag it to the left and beneath the text). Be sure to vary the position and scale of the flare to make it more interesting. Then, add the same Outer Glow layer style (by Option-clicking [PC: Alt-clicking] on the layer style in the Layers panel and dragging it onto the second flare layer).

STEP 12:

You can size the brush down using the **Left Bracket key ([)** and add a small flare at the bottom of the letters. Make sure you add the same Outer Glow layer style to this one, too, to complete the effect. You can see how the text has the illusion of being in 3D with very dramatic lighting effects utilizing the flare brush in another interesting way.

Continued

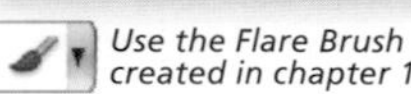
Use the Flare Brush created in chapter 1.

Final Image

Ah, Those Darn Swirls!

As a designer, there's just no escaping the ubiquity of swirls as a design element. They're just one of those things that never seems to go out of style. Some designers like to create their own swirls, and some like to just find them elsewhere and use those. I like doing both, but in this project, we'll take a look at using a stock image of a swirl graphic and the different ways we can implement it into our designs.

STEP ONE:

Go under the File menu, choose **New**, and create a new document measuring 12 inches wide by 7 inches tall at 100 ppi. Then, select the Horizontal Type tool **(T)** from the Toolbox and click on the canvas to create a text layer. For this effect, it's better to use a thick bold font—thinner fonts won't reveal the effect as much. Here, I've typed the word "iMAGiNE" in Helvetica Black and centered it in the canvas area.

©ISTOCKPHOTO/CAJOER

STEP TWO:

Open the file of the swirly graphic. This one I found over on iStockphoto's website (www.istockphoto.com). To get this shape into our layout, we need to first extract it from its background. So, go to the Channels panel (Window>**Channels**), press-and-hold the Command (PC: Ctrl) key, and click on the RGB channel. This will load the luminosity of the image as a selection. Since the image is straight black and white, it will select all of the white area, but we need the graphic selected, so go under the Select menu and choose **Inverse**.

Continued

STEP THREE:

Go to the bottom of the Layers panel and click on the Create a New Layer icon to create a new blank layer. Press **Shift-Delete (PC: Shift-Backspace)** to open the Fill dialog, choose **White** from the Use pop-up menu, and click OK. Now we have a white version of the original swirly shape. Press **Command-D (PC: Ctrl-D)** to Deselect.

STEP FOUR:

Use the Move tool **(V)** to drag-and-drop this shape onto the document with the text. Press **Command-T (PC: Ctrl-T)** to enter Free Transform, press-and-hold the Shift key to keep it proportional, and scale the shape to fit on the canvas area. Also, make sure this layer is above the text layer in the Layers panel. Change the layer's blend mode to **Difference** and this will invert the colors over the background elements—keeping the swirly shape white in the areas over the text, and black over the background area, even though the shape is still white. Press **Return (PC: Enter)** to lock in your transformation.

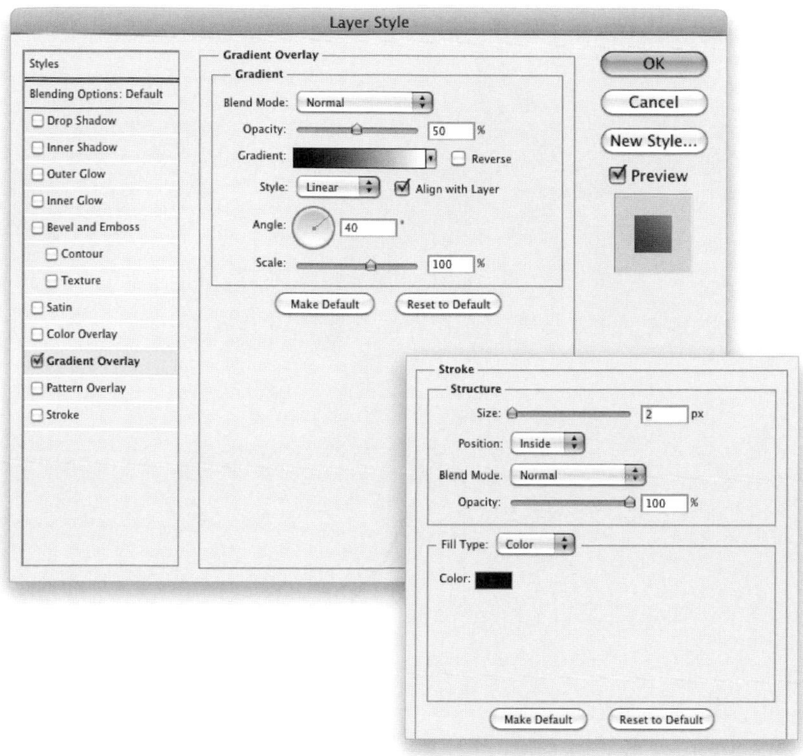

STEP FIVE:

Now let's add the swirly shape inside the text, but it won't look all that great on straight black text. Some layer style effects could work here, so click back on the text layer in the Layers panel to make it active, then click on the Add a Layer Style icon at the bottom of the panel and choose **Gradient Overlay**. Use the default **Linear** style with the Black, White gradient (choose it in the Gradient thumbnail's Gradient Picker), but drop the Opacity down to 50% and change the angle to 40°. Next, click on Stroke on the left to turn it on, and set the Size to 2 px and the position to **Inside**. Then, click on the Color swatch, set the color to black, and then click OK in the Color Picker, and again in the Layer Style dialog.

Continued

STEP SIX:

Click back on the swirly shape layer (the top layer) and press **Command-J (PC: Ctrl-J)** to make a duplicate of it. Change the blend mode back to **Normal** and then move this layer down just above the text layer in the Layers panel. Press-and-hold the **Option (PC: Alt) key** and click in between this layer and the text layer below to create a clipping mask. This will make the duplicate shape visible only inside the text area. Go into Free Transform mode, then press-and-hold the Shift key, and scale the shape down, so more of it can be seen in the text. Click inside the bounding box and drag it to reposition it wherever it looks best, and then press Return to lock in your transformation.

STEP SEVEN:

If you'd like, you can make another duplicate of the original Difference layer, then scale it down and reposition it to add more swirls.

STEP EIGHT:

Now, you may be wondering what you can do with it at this point. You certainly have many options, but here's one to consider: With the top-most layer selected in the Layers panel, click on the Create New Adjustment Layer icon at the bottom of the panel and choose **Invert**. This will make the text and swirls white and gray, while making the background area black. This allows us to make a selection of the entire graphic from within the Channels panel without having to flatten the file.

STEP NINE:

Just like we did back in Step Two, in the Channels panel, click on the RGB channel to make it active (along with the others below it), then press-and-hold the Command (PC: Ctrl) key, and click on the RGB channel to load the selection.

Continued

STEP 10:

Create a new layer in the Layers panel, then click on the Foreground color swatch, pick a dark purple color, and press **Option-Delete (PC: Alt-Backspace)** to fill the selection with the new color. Now you can take this top layer and drop it into any layout in any color you want. Be sure to save this file as a layered document, so you can modify and create new versions of the graphic in no time!

TIP: Turn It into a Brush

You can also turn this graphic into a brush. Just skip the Invert adjustment layer step (Step Eight) and, instead, create a merged copy of all the visible layers by pressing **Command-Option-Shift-E (PC: Ctrl-Alt-Shift-E)**. Then, go under the Edit menu and choose **Define Brush Preset**. Now you can play around with some of the brush effects we saw in Chapter 1 to get some really interesting effects.

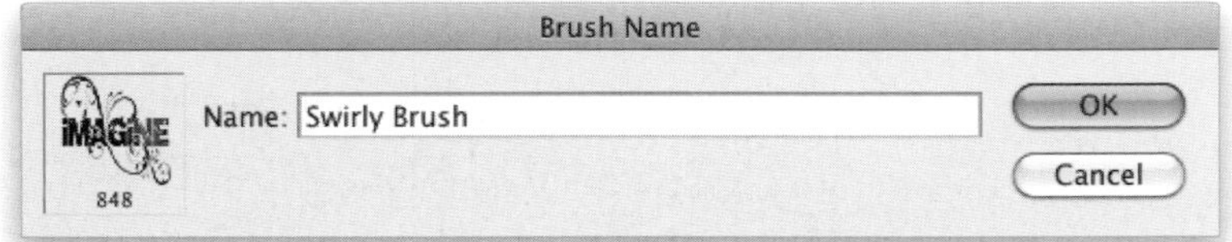

Final Image

In this alternate version, I changed the Stroke layer style's color and changed the Gradient Overlay layer style to Radial. I also added a texture over the background and masked part of it out, then positioned a swirl in the background, below the text, but above the main swirl. Finally, I added a blue Hue/Saturation adjustment layer on top.

Paint with Words

No, this is not a tutorial on writing poetry. I mean we're going to literally paint with words. With so many possibilities using Brush tool options, why not define brushes made of letters or words as a way of adding interesting text elements to a design?

STEP ONE:

Start by going under the File menu, choosing **New**, and creating a new document that is 10 inches wide by 4 inches tall at 100 ppi, and then select the Horizontal Type tool **(T)** from the Toolbox. Here, we're going with a fashion theme, so we'll start with the word "FASHION" set in a stylish bold typeface—I am using a font called Serpentine Bold. Keep the text at a larger size of around 100 points and make the color black.

STEP TWO:

Press the **Esc key** then go under the Edit menu and choose **Define Brush Preset**. Give the brush a name and click OK.

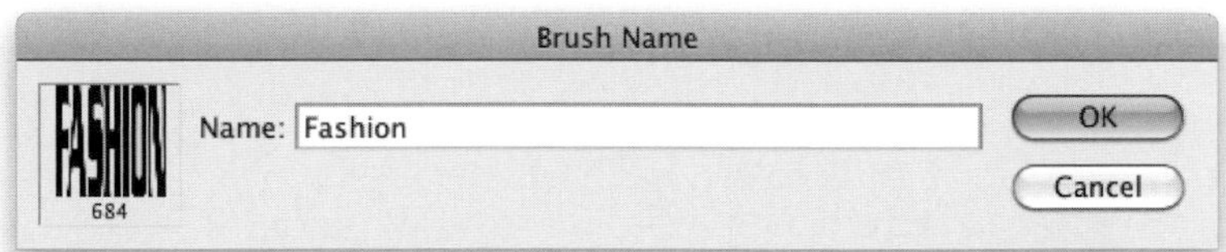

STEP THREE:

Now, double-click on the text layer's thumbnail in the Layers panel to highlight the text, and type a new word to go along with the theme, like "STYLE." Then, define this as a brush preset, as well. You can continue to create new word brushes on this theme, but I think you get the idea.

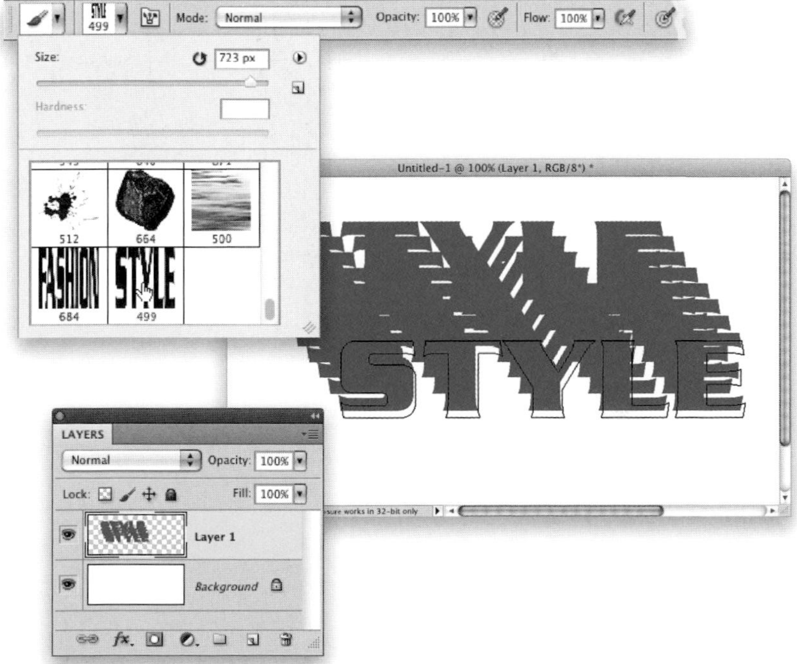

STEP FOUR:

With the brushes defined, choose the Brush tool **(B)** from the Toolbox, then click on the brush thumbnail in the Options Bar and locate your new word brushes at the bottom of the Brush Picker. Select one of the word brushes and then click on your Foreground color swatch and choose a color for your brush (here, I chose a medium blue). Click on the Create a New Layer icon at the bottom of the Layers panel to create a new blank layer (you can delete the text layer now) and then just paint on the canvas. You can see the default brush behavior is very basic and boring. This is where we need to get creative with the brush options.

Continued

STEP FIVE:

Click on the Brush Panel icon (to the right of the brush thumbnail) in the Options Bar to open the Brush panel. Now, first, in the Brush Tip Shape section, set the Size to around 250 px and increase the Spacing to 250%.

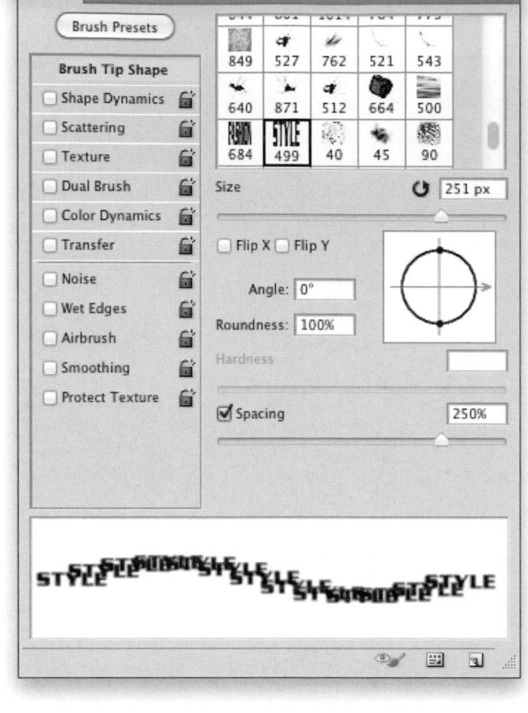

STEP SIX:

Next, click on Shape Dynamics near the top left of the Brush panel to turn it on, and set the Size Jitter to 100%. If you're using a Wacom pressure-sensitive tablet, then go ahead and choose Pen Pressure from the Size Jitter Control pop-up menu.

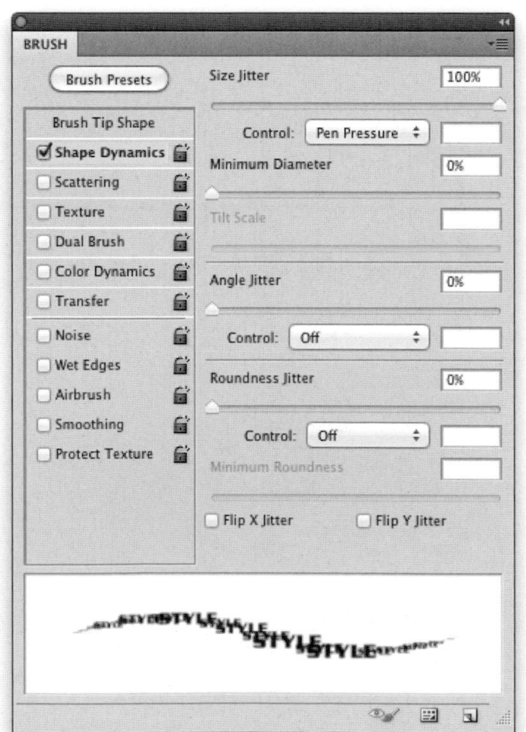

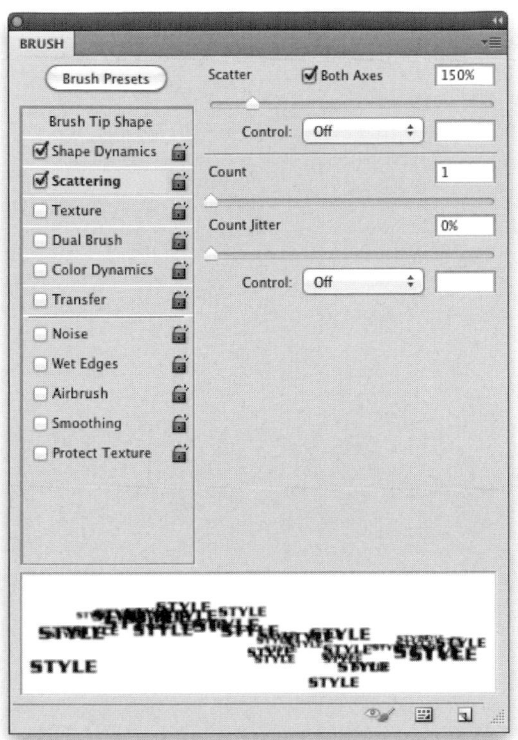

STEP SEVEN:

Next, click on Scattering on the left to turn it on. Make sure the Both Axes checkbox at the top is turned on, and then set the Scatter to 150%.

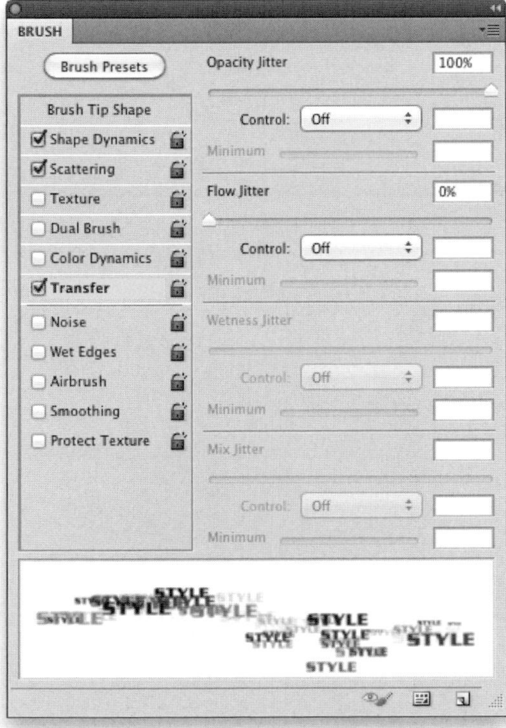

STEP EIGHT:

Lastly, click on Transfer on the left to turn it on, and set the Opacity Jitter to 100%. As these changes are made, you can get a good idea of how the brush will behave by looking at the brush stroke preview at the bottom of the panel. But, you'll also want to try the brush out on the canvas area to see how it will really look (as shown in the next step).

Continued

STEP NINE:

Once these settings are in place, it's always a good idea to save this brush with these settings, so you won't have to do this every time. So, save it as a tool preset by clicking on the Tool Preset thumbnail at the left end of the Options Bar, and then from the Tool Preset Picker's flyout menu, choosing **New Tool Preset**. In the New Tool Preset dialog, give it a name, click OK, and now you can find this brush with these settings in the Tool Preset Picker.

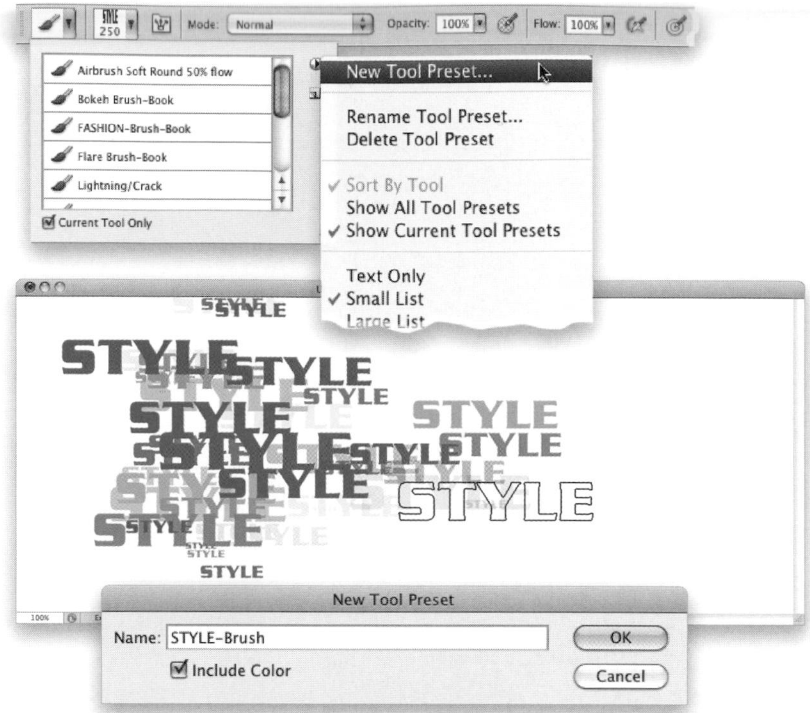

STEP 10:

Now, open up the image of the model to start building the design (you can go ahead and close the document you used to create your brushes). This image is perfect to create a multi-layered word scatter effect. But, first, we'll need to extract our subject from the background.

SCOTT KELBY

STEP 11:

Using the selection tool of your choice (here, I used the Lasso tool **[L]**), make a selection around the subject and then click the Refine Edge button in the Options Bar. In the Refine Edge dialog's Edge Detection section, move the Radius slider to around 14 px and turn on the Smart Radius checkbox. This will refine the selection quite a bit. However, here, the area around her hair needs some adjusting.

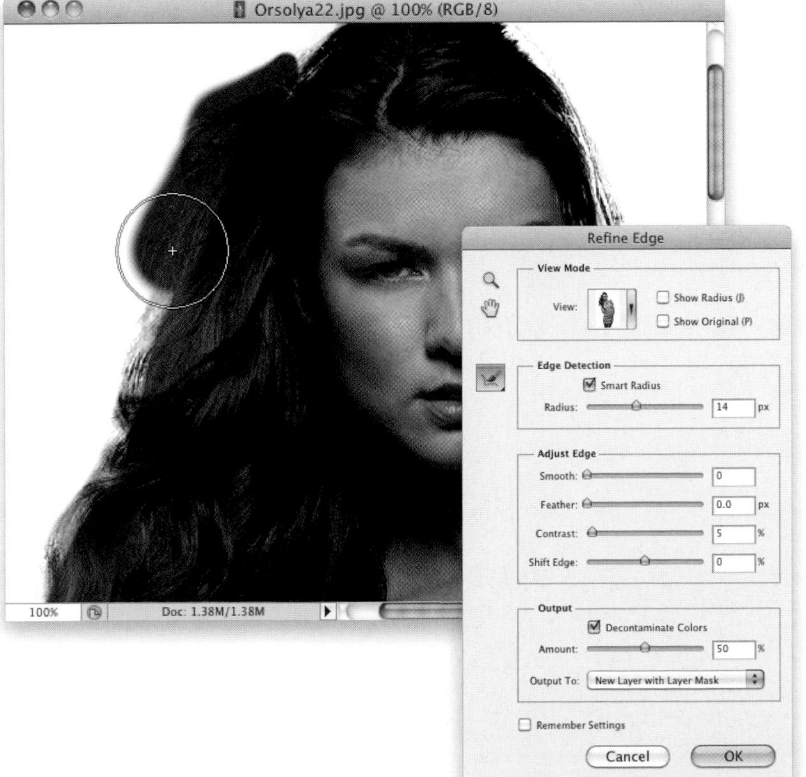

STEP 12:

Click on the Refine Radius tool **(E)** to the left of the Edge Detection section, and then choose **On White** from the View pop-up menu near the top. Use this tool to paint around the edge of the hair to let Photoshop know where to refine the selection. After that, you can tighten the selection up a bit by increasing the Contrast to around 5%. Lastly, turn on the Decontaminate Colors checkbox to remove any color that might be spilling onto the subject from the background, then choose **New Layer with Layer Mask** from the Output To pop-up menu and click OK.

Continued

STEP 13:

Next, let's make her fit a little better in the image. Click on the Eye icon to the left of the Background layer's thumbnail to turn it off. Press **Command-T (PC: Ctrl-T)** to go into Free Transform, then press-and-hold Option-Shift (PC: Alt-Shift) to keep it proportional and resize from the center, and click-and-drag a corner point outward (if you can't see the corner points, press **Command-0** [zero; **PC: Ctrl-0**]). Center her in the image and then press **Return (PC: Enter)** to lock in the transformation.

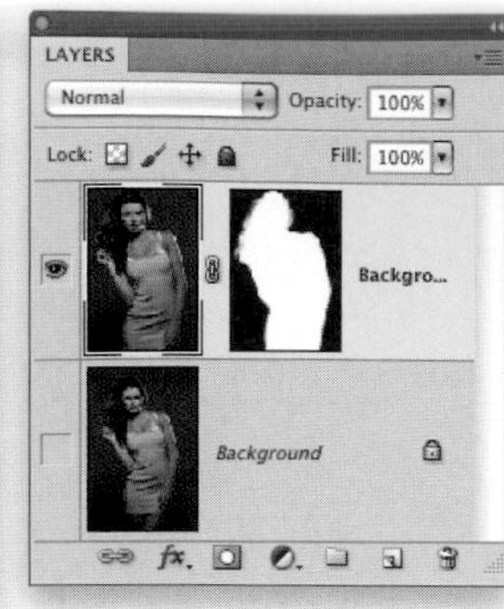

STEP 14:

Now, in the Layers panel, click on the Background layer, and then click where the Eye icon used to be to make it visible again. Go under the Filter menu, under Blur, and choose **Average**. There's no dialog for this filter. It will just look at the dominating tone of the image and fill the Background layer with that color. In this case, it's a warm gray.

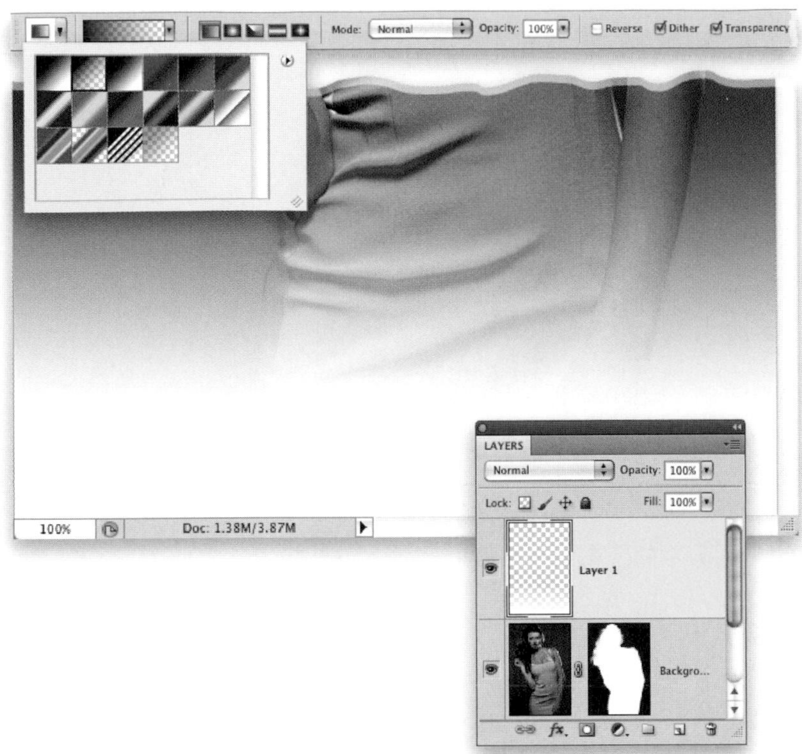

STEP 15:
Click on the Create a New Layer icon at the bottom of the Layers panel to create a new blank layer and move it to the top of the layer stack. Select the Gradient tool **(G)** from the Toolbox and then click on the down-facing arrow to the right of the gradient thumbnail in the Options Bar. Choose the Foreground to Transparent gradient (the second one from the left in the top row), and then press **X** to set your Foreground color to white. Click-and-drag the gradient from the bottom edge of the document up to around the elbow of the subject.

STEP 16:
Switch to the Brush tool **(B)**, and from the Tool Preset Picker in the Options Bar, choose the Style brush that we created earlier. Then, starting in the white area of the gradient, paint with the word brush, varying the direction and pressure (if using a tablet) as you build the effect upward. Remember, if you don't like what you get as you paint, then simply press **Command-Z (PC: Ctrl-Z)** to Undo and try again. Because of the randomness of the brush settings, you will sometimes need two or three tries to get what you want.

Continued

STEP 17:

When you're done with that brush, create a new blank layer and move it between the Background layer and the subject layer. Choose the other word brush from the brush thumbnail's Brush Picker, apply the same settings to it in the Brush panel that we applied to the Style brush (don't forget to save it as a tool preset), and then go nuts painting on this layer (you'll see what you do here will appear behind your subject). The point here is to maintain some sense of balance in the design as you paint—which can be a challenge when the tool is so random.

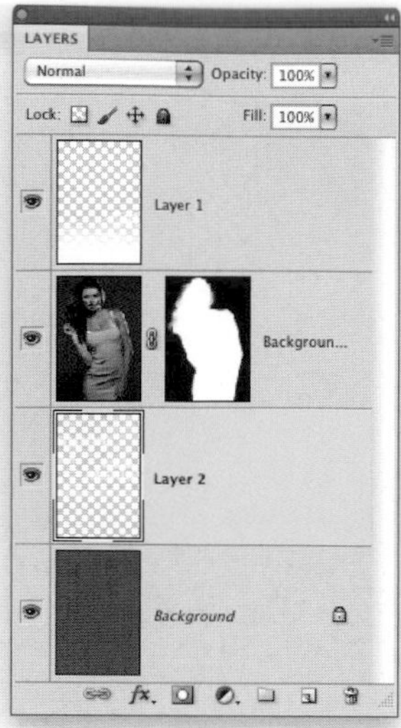

STEP 18:

Now, let's add some final touches to the background. First, click on the Create New Adjustment Layer icon at the bottom of the Layers panel, and choose **Hue/Saturation**. To get a blue color for the background (and the words that were added back there), turn on the Colorize checkbox, set the Hue to 220, and the Saturation to 25. Also, drop the Lightness to –20 to darken the overall effect a little bit.

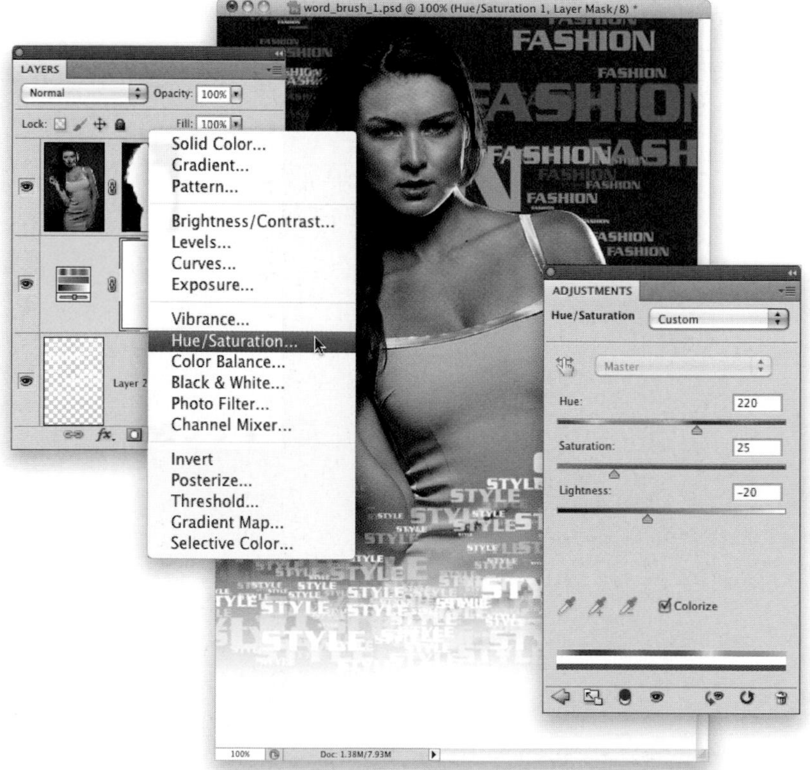

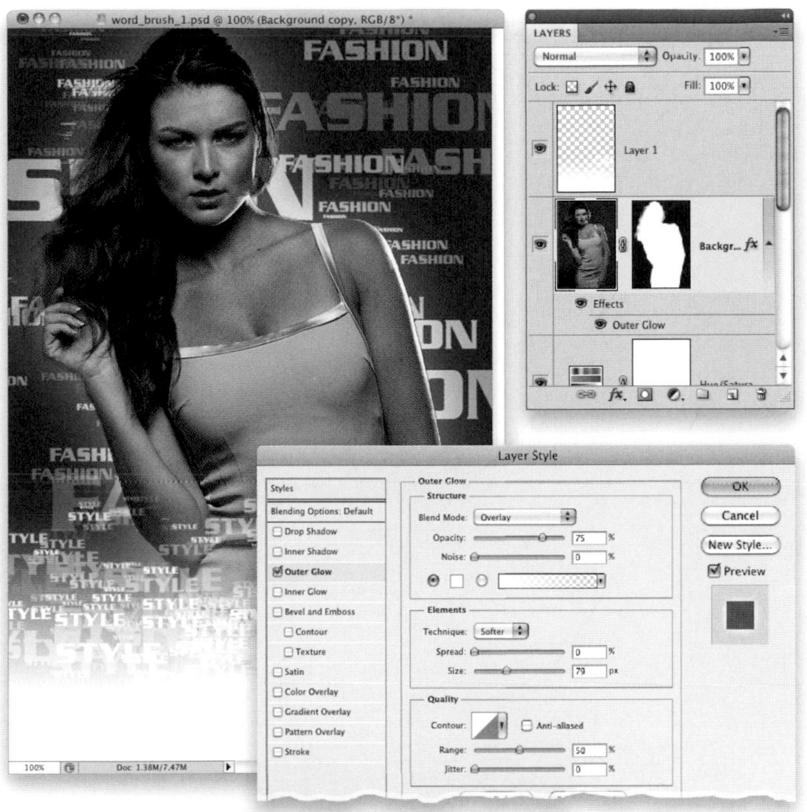

STEP 19:

Next, let's add a glow behind the subject. Click on the subject layer in the Layers panel to make it active, then click on the Add a Layer Style icon at the bottom of the Layers panel and choose **Outer Glow**. Change the Blend Mode to **Overlay** and leave the Opacity set to 75%, then click on the color swatch and choose white. In the Elements section, increase the Size to around 75 px, and then click OK when you're done.

STEP 20:

Finally, let's add some contrast to the subject. With the subject layer still active, press **Command-J (PC: Ctrl-J)** to duplicate it. Then, press **Command-Shift-U (PC: Ctrl-Shift-U)** to Desaturate the duplicate layer, change its layer blend mode to **Soft Light**, and lower its Opacity to 50%. Also, you can delete the layer style that was duplicated when you copied the subject layer by clicking on the *fx* icon and dragging it onto the Trash icon at the bottom of the panel.

Continued

Final Image

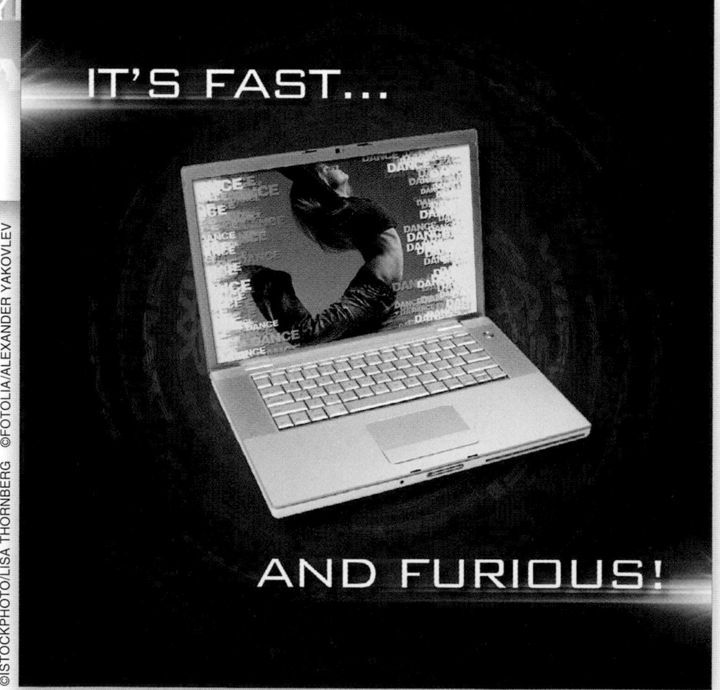

As cool as this effect is, we must continue to think outside the box. Whatever word you use for your brush, you can also paint along the bottom of the canvas with it, rotate the document 180°, then go under the Filter menu, under Distort, and choose Polar Coordinates. Choose Rectangular to Polar, which makes the text wrap around a center point, then just position it where you want.

 *Use the Flare Brush created in chapter 1.*

Words & Graphics

Often, a complex text effect will involve building a graphic around it as part of the whole theme. This is an effect I saw for the new *The Three Musketeers* movie, and it demonstrates how to build elements from photos and graphics that cater to the text, which creates the overall theme for the title effect.

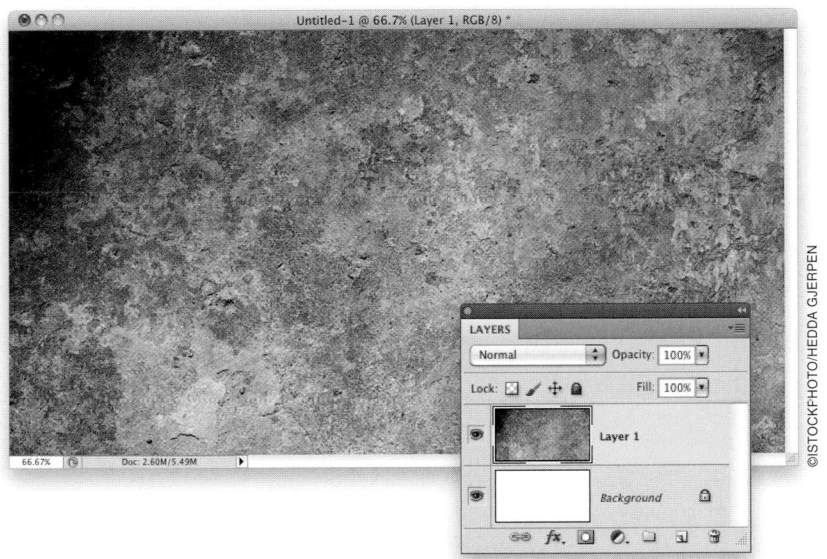

STEP ONE:

We'll start by creating the background to build the effect on top of. So, open the texture file shown here, which will be the base texture for the design. Press **Command-A (PC: Ctrl-A)** to select the entire image, and then press **Command-C (PC: Ctrl-C)** to Copy it. Go under the File menu, choose **New**, and create a new document that is 13 inches wide by 7 inches tall at 100 ppi. Now, press **Command-V (PC: Ctrl-V)** to Paste the texture into the new document.

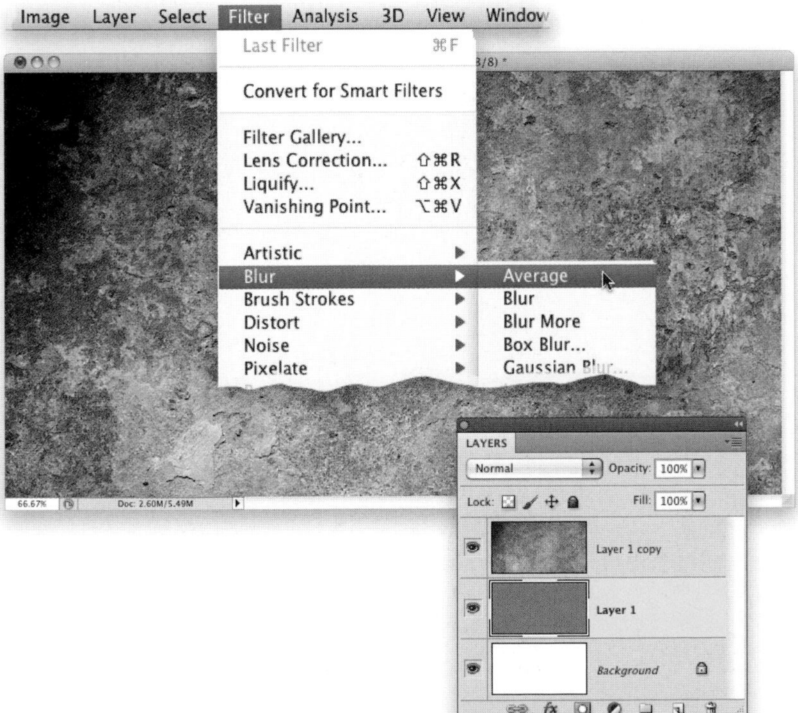

STEP TWO:

Now, while the texture is nice, it's a little too rough. So, here's a cool trick to lessen the effect: Make a duplicate of this texture layer by pressing **Command-J (PC: Ctrl-J)**, then click back on the original texture layer just below it. Go under the Filter menu, under Blur, and choose **Average**. There's no dialog for this filter. It will just fill the layer with the dominating color of the overall texture (but you won't see any change in your image, yet).

Continued

STEP THREE:
Click back on the duplicate texture layer and drop the layer Opacity to 50%. This will smooth down the texture quite a bit, while maintaining the overall color tone.

STEP FOUR:
Let's add a dramatic light effect to this texture. Press **D**, then **X** to set your Foreground color to white. Grab the Gradient tool **(G)** from the Toolbox. In the Options Bar, click on the down-facing arrow to the right of the gradient thumbnail, and choose the Foreground to Background gradient (the first one in the top row), then click on the Radial Gradient icon (the second icon to the right of the gradient thumbnail). Click on the Create a New Layer icon at the bottom of the Layers panel to create a new blank layer at the top of the layer stack, and then click-and-drag the gradient out from the center of the canvas, going just outside the edge of the document.

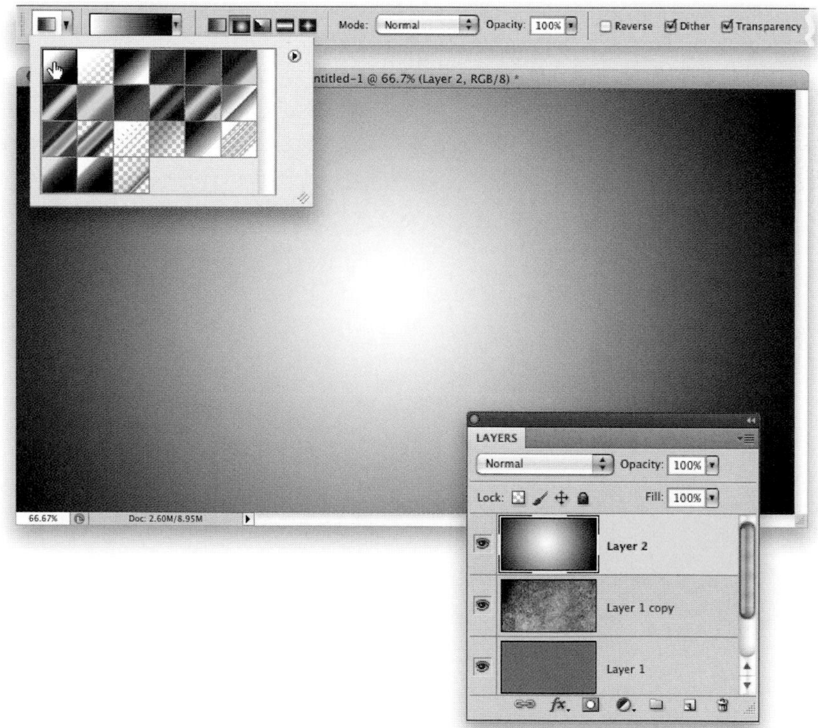

STEP FIVE:

Once the gradient is drawn, change the layer's blend mode to **Linear Burn** and lower the Opacity to 75%. Now we have a smooth texture backdrop with a dramatic light effect to build the rest of the design on.

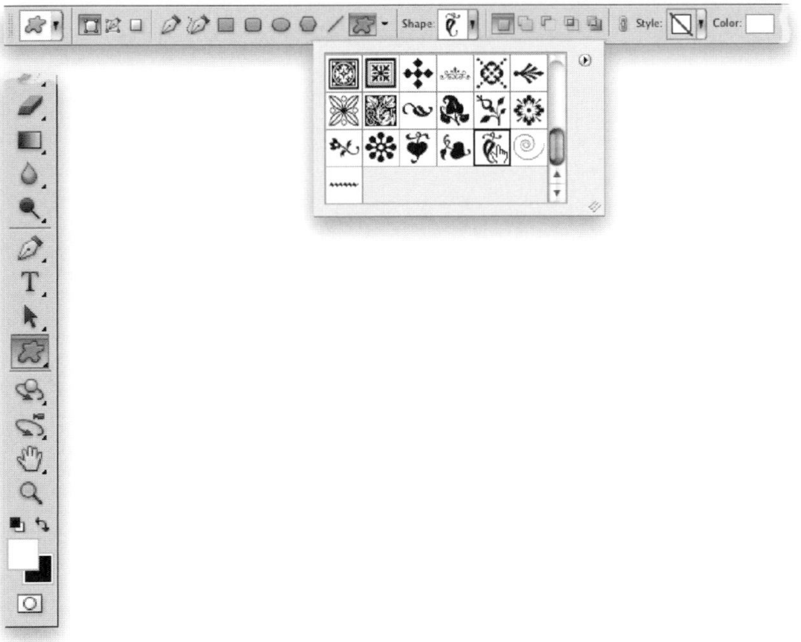

STEP SIX:

Let's begin creating our Musketeer text graphic. We'll start by creating a background design element that has a metallic surface and everything we need to do this is here in Photoshop. Start by selecting the Custom Shape tool from the Toolbox (or press **Shift-U** until you have it). Then, in the Options Bar, click on the Shape thumbnail to open the Shape Picker. Click on the right-facing arrow in the top right and choose **Ornaments** from the flyout menu (they are built into Photoshop). Then, click Append in the warning dialog to add this set of shapes to the Shape Picker, and choose the shape called "Hedera 3."

Continued

STEP SEVEN:
On the left side of the Options Bar, click on the Shape Layers icon (the first one on the left) to create a vector shape layer, which will make the graphic scalable without affecting image quality. Finally, on the right side of the Options Bar, click on the Color swatch and choose a color for the shape. Here, I am using R: 141, G: 121, B: 84.

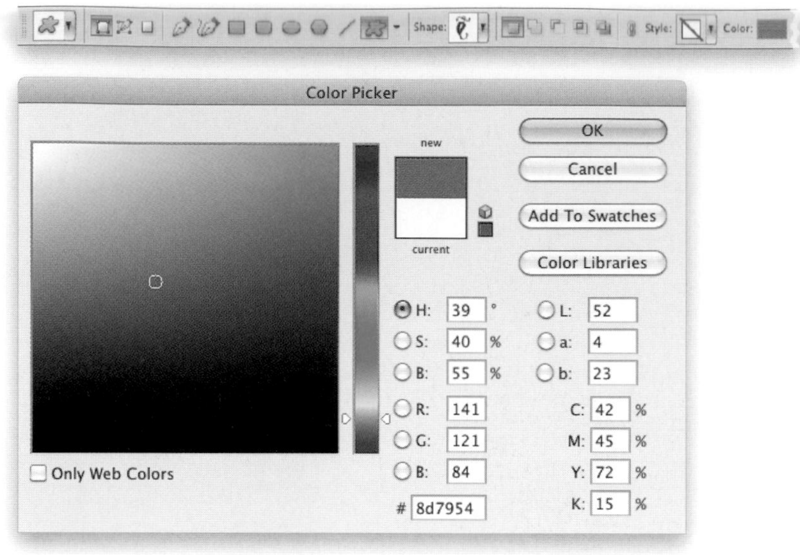

STEP EIGHT:
Now, press-and-hold the Shift key and click-and-drag the shape onto the canvas. A new Shape layer will be created and automatically filled with your selected color. Press **Command-T (PC: Ctrl-T)** to enter Free Transform, Right-click inside the bounding box, and choose **Rotate 90° CCW** to flip the shape so it's horizontal. Press **Return (PC: Enter)** to lock in the transformation.

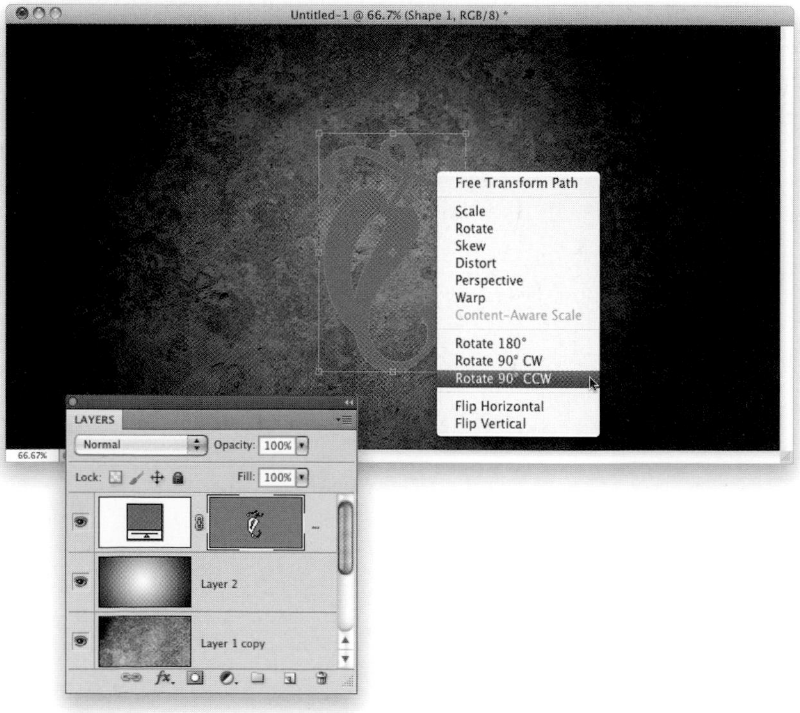

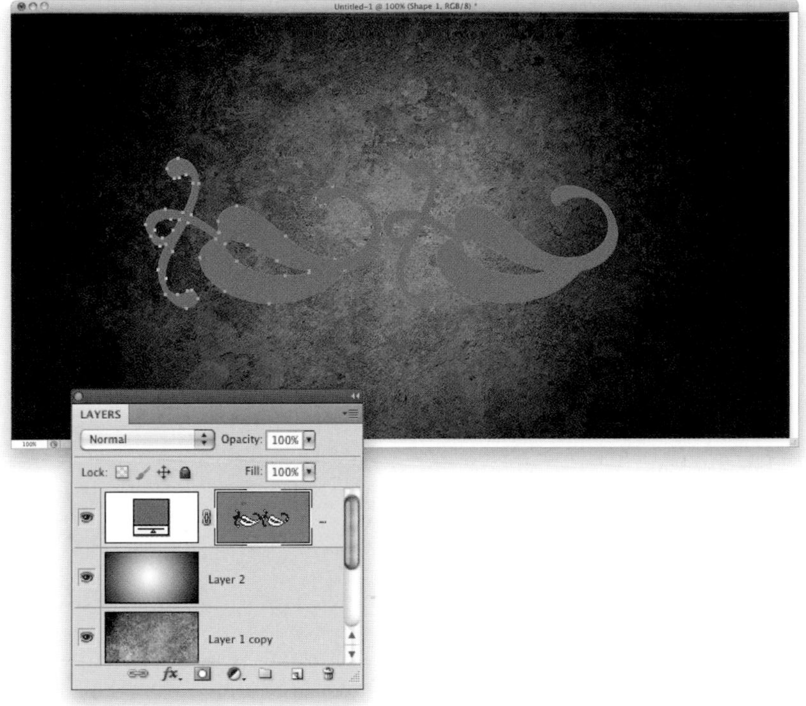

STEP NINE:

Now, choose the Path Selection tool **(A)** from the Toolbox, make sure the Show Bounding Box checkbox in the Options Bar is turned off, and click on the shape to select it. Then, press-and-hold Option-Shift (PC: Alt-Shift) and click-and-drag the shape to the left. This will drag a duplicate of the shape, but will still keep both shapes in the same Shape layer (adding the Shift key will constrain the left/right axis).

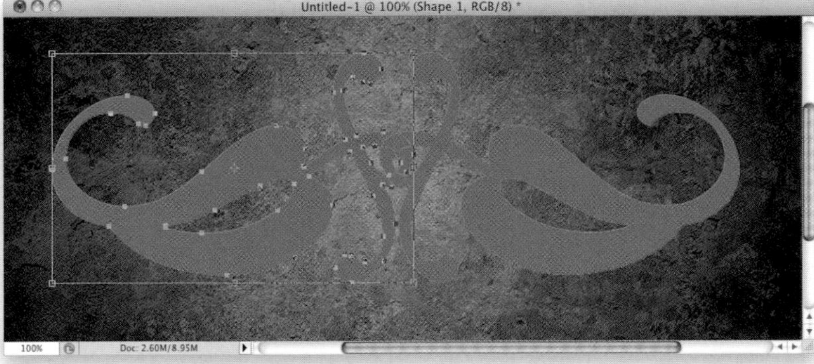

STEP 10:

With the duplicate still selected, press Command-T again, then Right-click inside the bounding box, and choose **Flip Horizontal**. Use the **Left and Right Arrow keys** to nudge the shapes to create a symmetrical design element, like you see here, then press Return to lock in the transformation, and click outside the shape to deselect it.

Continued

STEP 11:

Now, to give this shape some surface and dimension, we'll use some layer styles. Start by clicking on the Add a Layer Style icon at the bottom of the Layers panel and choosing **Bevel and Emboss**. In the Structure section, increase the Depth to around 320% and increase the Size to 10 px. In the Shading section, set the Angle to around 150°, then click on the down-facing arrow to the right of the Gloss Contour thumbnail and choose Ring (the second contour in the second row). This will greatly affect the appearance of the bevel. Next, choose **Overlay** from the Highlight Mode pop-up menu. Then, choose **Color Dodge** from the Shadow Mode pop-up menu, click on the color swatch to its right, and choose a light gray color. You can see the metallic effect starting to take shape. Don't click OK, because we're not done yet.

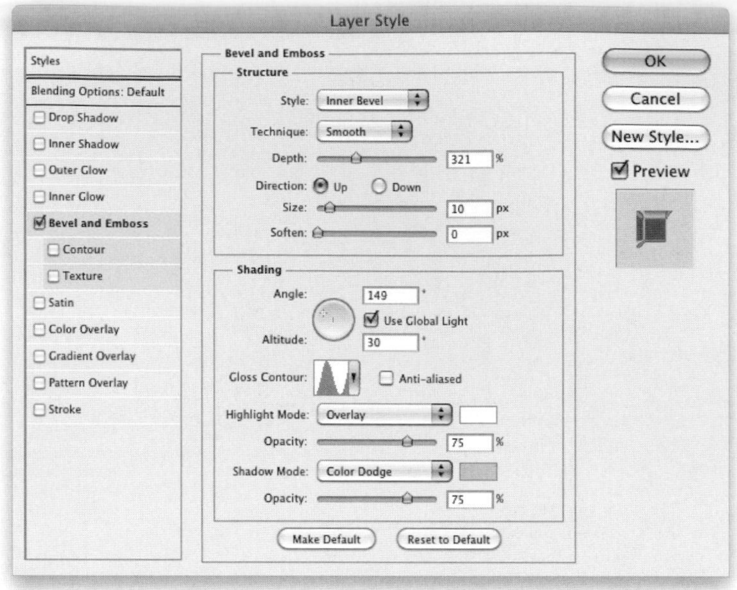

STEP 12:

Next, click on Satin on the left to turn it on, and set the Angle to 26° and the Distance to 31 px. This enhances the metallic look more by giving the illusion of reflected elements.

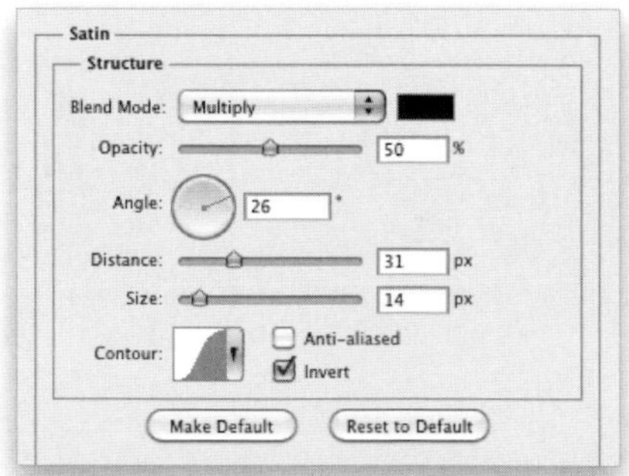

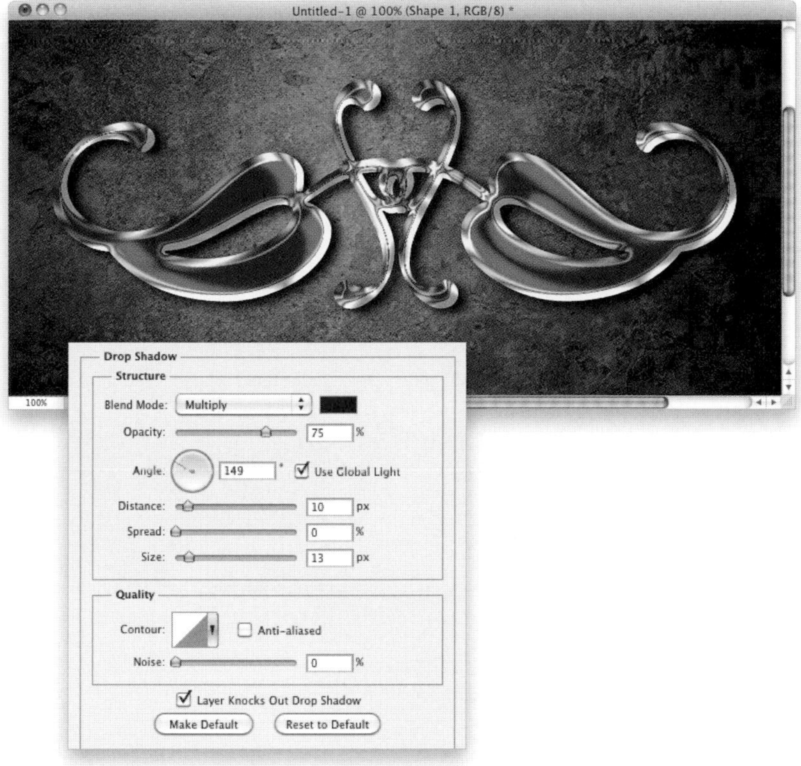

STEP 13:

Finally, click on Drop Shadow on the left to turn it on, and increase the Size to around 13 px to soften the shadow. For the Distance, you can input the setting I have here (10 px) or you can click-and-drag the shadow around in the image window to exactly where you want it. When you're done, click OK.

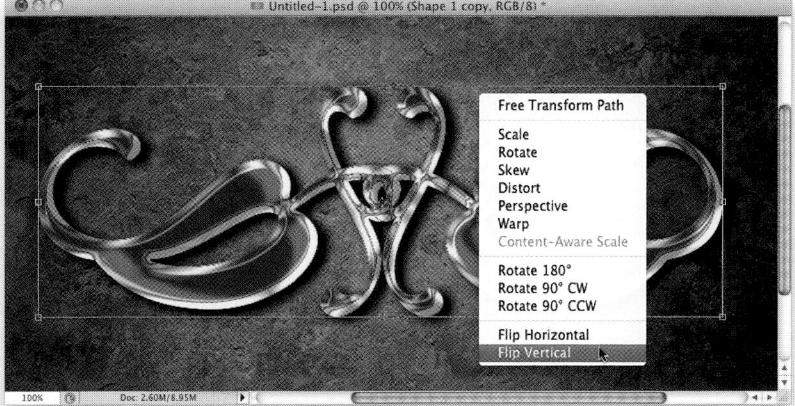

STEP 14:

Now, press **Command-J (PC: Ctrl-J)** to make a duplicate of this shape, then press Command-T (PC: Ctrl-T) once again to go into Free Transform. Right-click inside the bounding box, and this time choose **Flip Vertical** from the pop-up menu.

Continued

STEP 15:

With Free Transform still active, press-and-hold Option-Shift (PC: Alt-Shift) and then click-and-drag any one of the corner handles inward to scale the shape down proportionately to the center. Then, nudge the shape upward and press Return (PC: Enter) to add an extra element to the symmetrical design, completing the shape.

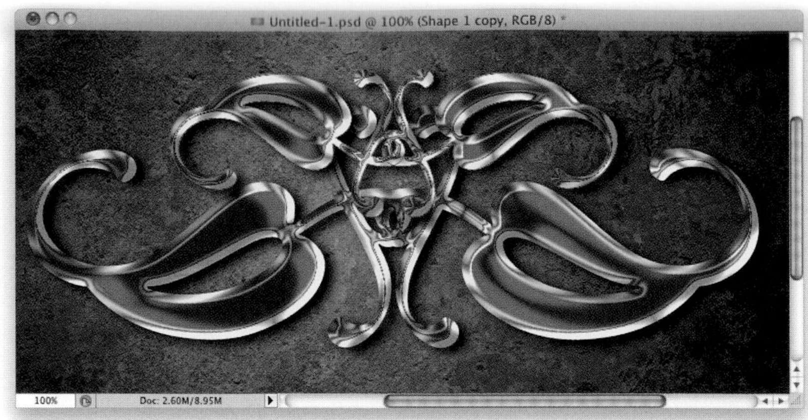

STEP 16:

The next design element we're going to add is a vintage sword image. I found this nice sword over on iStockphoto's website, and it has a white background, which makes it easier to extract to its own layer. Just get the Magic Wand tool (press **Shift-W** until you have it) and click on the white background to select it. Inverse the selection by pressing **Command-Shift-I (PC: Ctrl-Shift-I)**, and then press Command-J (PC: Ctrl-J) to copy the sword to a new layer (I turned off the Background layer here, so you can see the selected sword on its own layer).

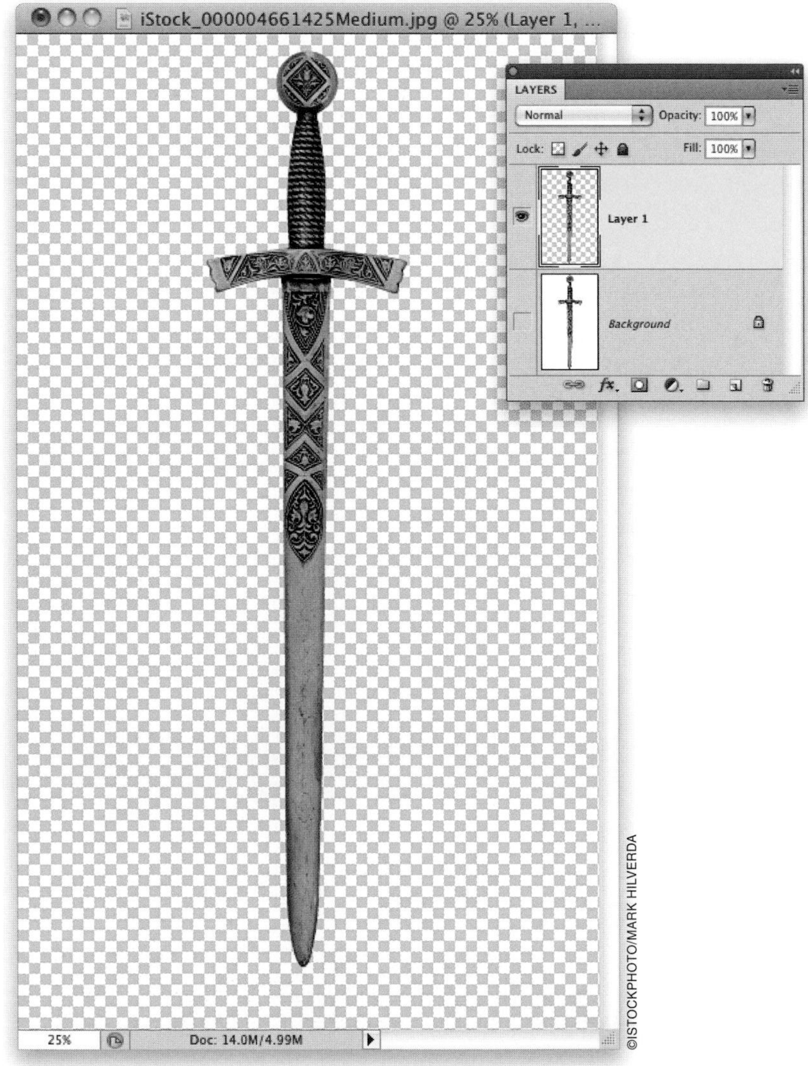

STEP 17:

Now, use the Move tool **(V)** to drag and drop the sword layer into the working design document. Move the sword into the middle of the design and use Free Transform to scale it to fit in the area, like you see here. Also, when I moved the sword into my document, I thought the shape graphic looked too big. So, I Command-clicked (PC: Ctrl-clicked) on both Shape layers in the Layers panel and used Free Transform to decrease their size a bit.

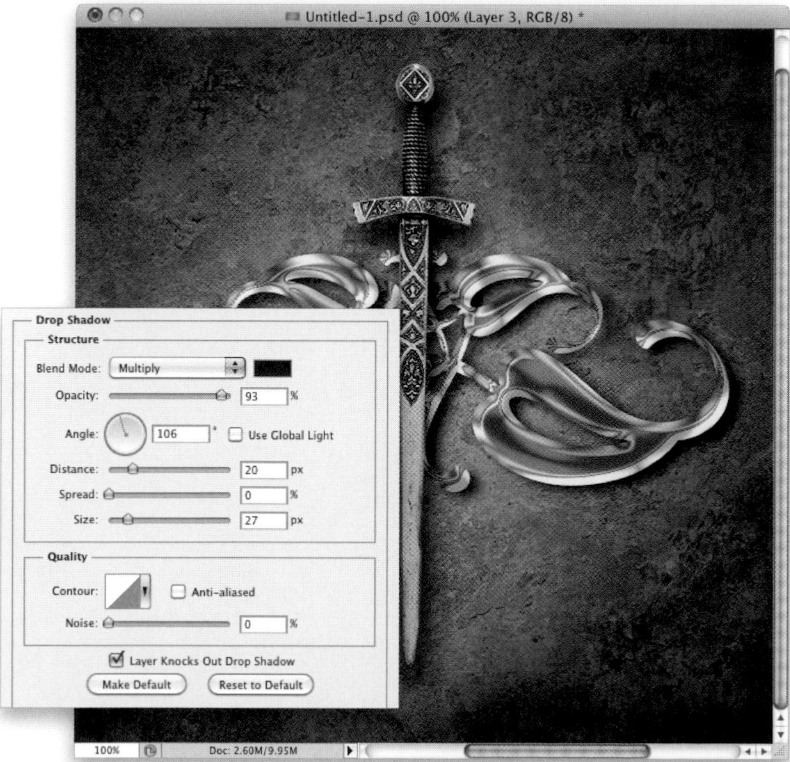

STEP 18:

To finish off the sword, add a Drop Shadow layer style to it, using the settings shown here.

Continued

STEP 19:

We have one more graphic element to add and that's a vintage pistol. This will add more interest to the overall look, while reinforcing the theme of the design. Open the pistol image, extract it the same way we did the sword, and place it on its own layer. Don't forget to select inside the trigger guard, as well. Once extracted and placed on a new layer, press Command-J (PC: Ctrl-J) to make a duplicate of this layer, then change the blend mode of the top layer to **Hard Light**. This will greatly enhance the contrast of the pistol.

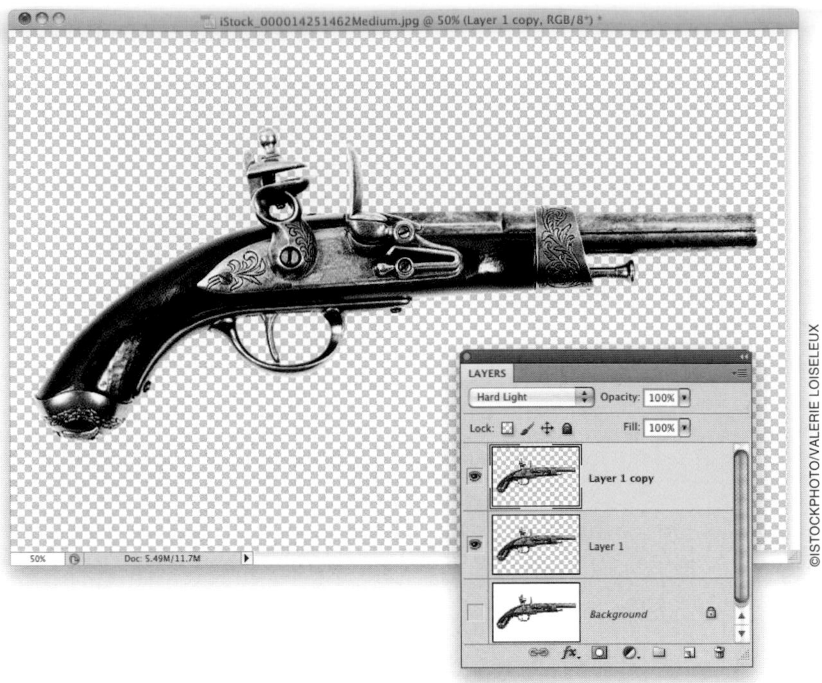

©ISTOCKPHOTO/VALERIE LOISELEUX

STEP 20:

Next, click on the Create New Adjustment Layer icon at the bottom of the Layers panel and choose **Hue/Saturation**. In the Adjustments panel, turn on the Colorize checkbox, set the Hue to 30, and then set the Saturation to 40. Change the layer's blend mode to **Multiply**. This will add a yellowish cast over the pistol to keep it consistent with the rest of the design colors.

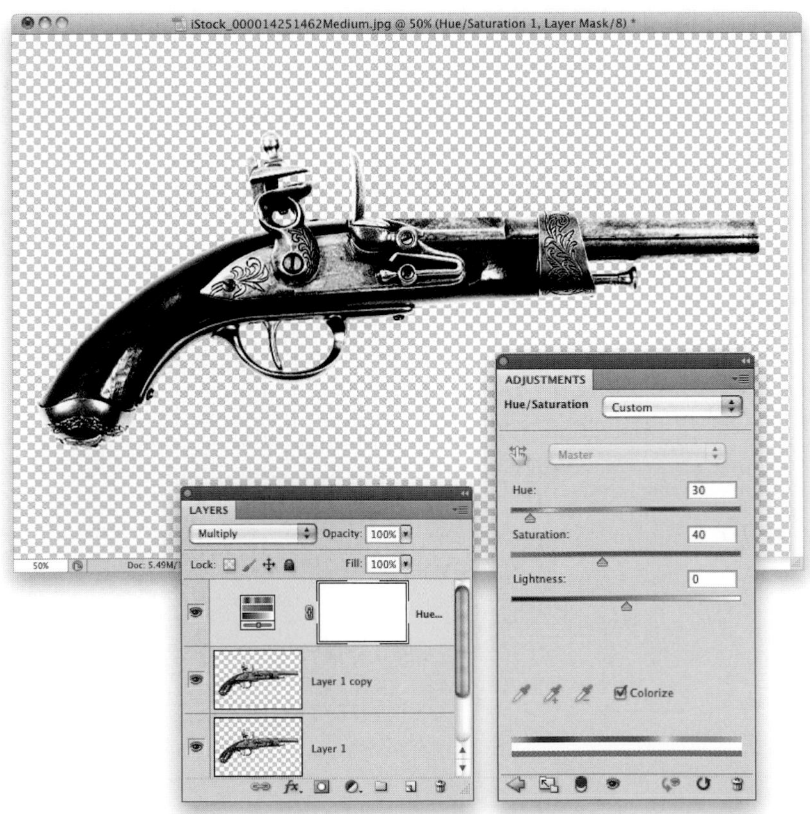

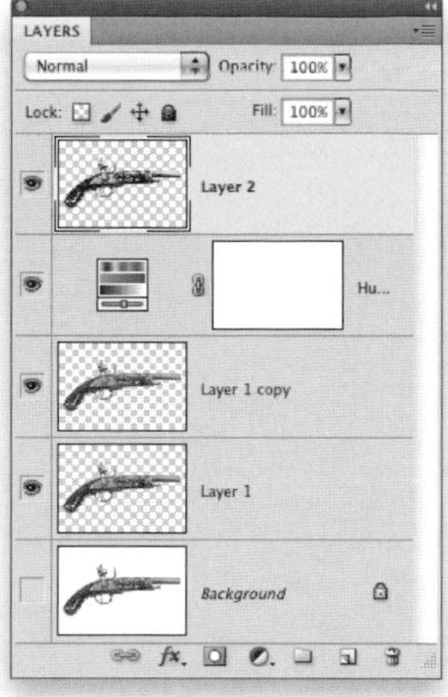

STEP 21:

Now, we need to get this element into the design layout, however we want to bring it over as one layer, but keep this document's layers intact. So, if you hadn't already, click on the Eye icon next to the Background layer to turn it off, so you only see the transparent background around the pistol. Then, press **Command-Option-Shift-E (PC: Ctrl-Alt-Shift-E)** to create a merged layer of the visible layers—basically, flattening the image without actually flattening the layers. Now, drag this merged layer into the working document and then save the pistol file as a PSD file, in case you want to make any changes to it later.

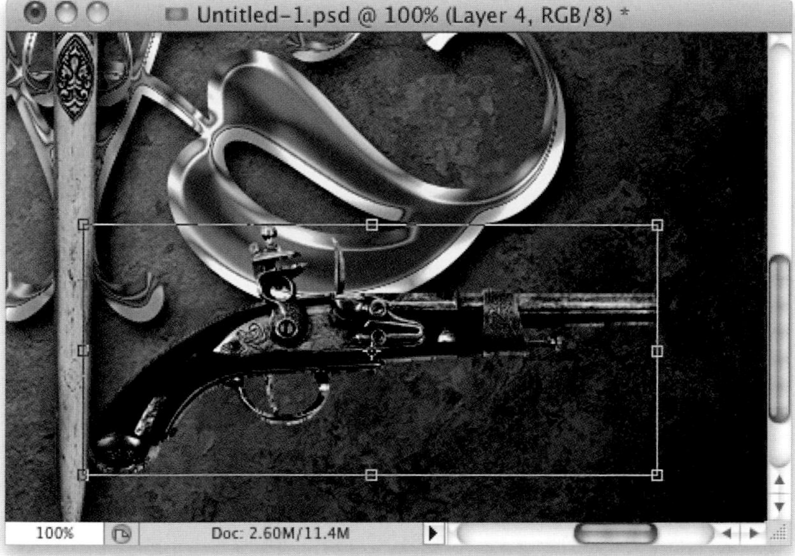

STEP 22:

Once the pistol is in the main design file, use Free Transform to scale and position it so that it touches the bottom-right edge of the sword and covers the bottom edge of the background graphic on the right. Notice the barrel of the gun, here, extends just a little way beyond the right edge of the Shape layer. I also ended up selecting the background Shape layers again, going into Free Transform, and pressing-and-holding the Option (PC: Alt) key while dragging a side handle inward to resize the shape again.

Continued

STEP 23:

Next, duplicate this pistol layer, then go into Free Transform, flip it horizontally, and place it directly opposite the one on the right, just like I have it here. Press **Command-E (PC: Ctrl-E)** to merge the two pistol layers into one layer and then add a Drop Shadow layer style to the pistol layer using the settings shown here.

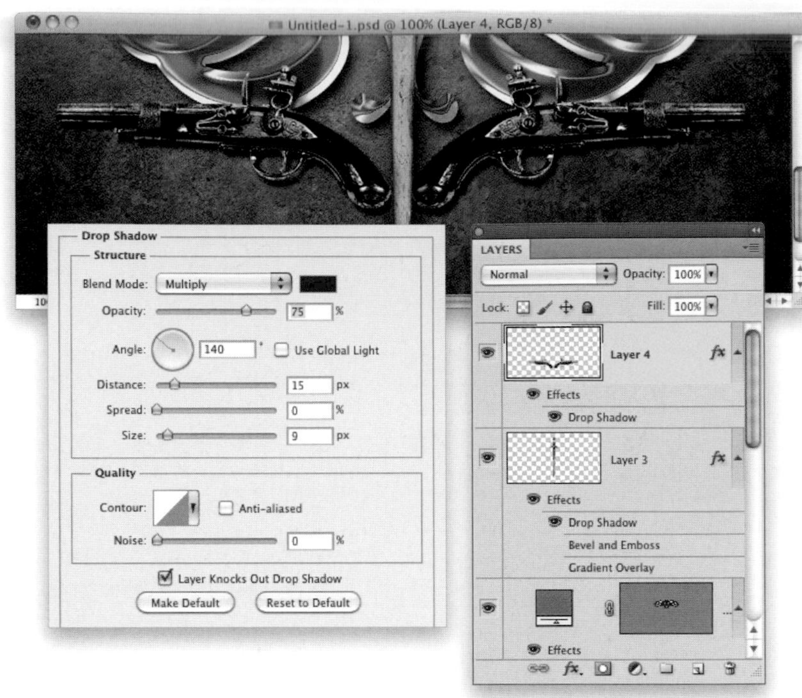

STEP 24:

Now, we're ready for the text. So, select the Horizontal Type tool **(T)** from the Toolbox and, in the Options Bar, set the font to Trajan Pro Bold, set the point size to around 68 pt, and then click on the color swatch and choose white. Click on the canvas and type "MUSKETEERS." Center align the text to the document by clicking on the Move tool in the Toolbox, pressing **Command-A (PC: Ctrl-A)** to Select All, then clicking on the Align Horizontal Centers icon in the Options Bar (as shown here). Press Command-D (PC: Ctrl-D) to Deselect. Now, go under the Window menu and open the Character panel. Then, switch back to the Horizontal Type tool, select your text, and in the Character panel, increase the Font Size to 110.75 pt and set the Vertical Scale to 65%. Highlight the first letter of the word, then press-and-hold **Command-Option-Shift (PC: Ctrl-Alt-Shift)** while pressing the **> (Greater Than) key** two times. This will increase the size of this letter by 10 pts each time you press the > key. Also do this to the last letter to create a balanced type effect.

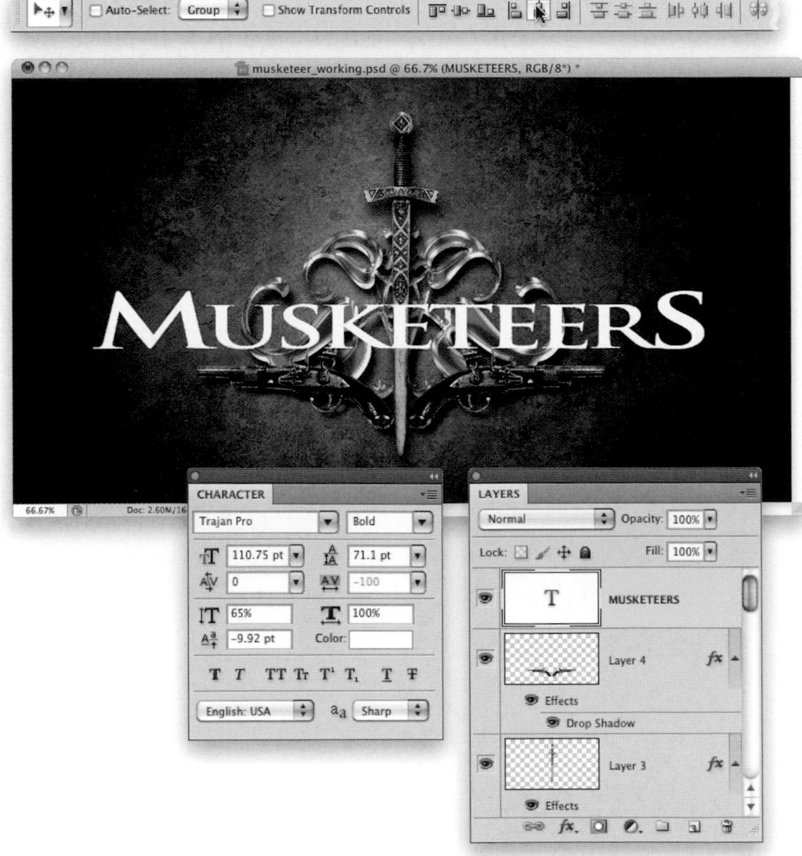

STEP 25:

Next, we'll add layer style effects to this text. When we create the other text objects, we'll be able to just duplicate this layer and change the copy, while maintaining the layer styles. So, click on the Add a Layer Style icon, choose **Bevel and Emboss**, and apply the settings you see here. This will give the text a little edge dimension.

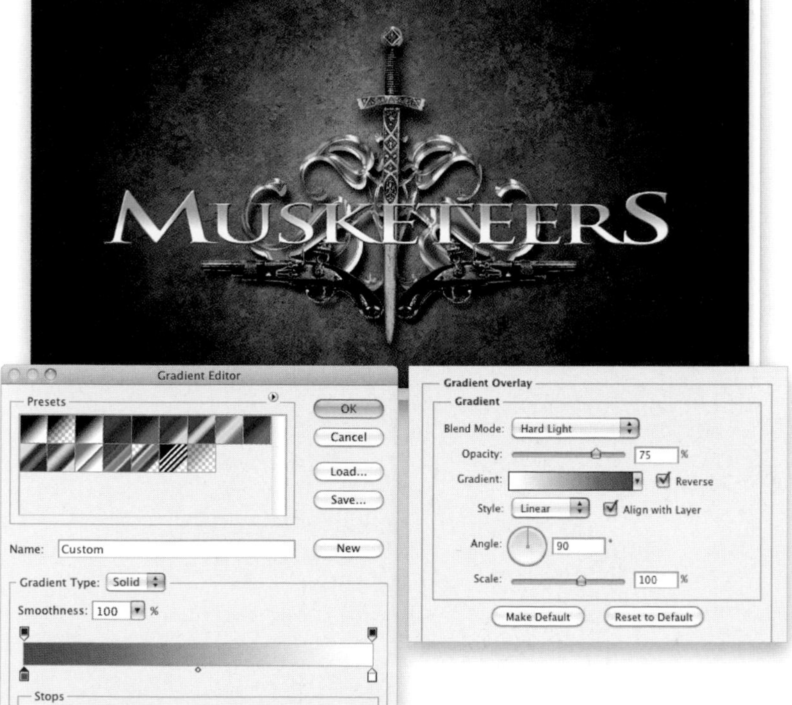

STEP 26:

Click on Gradient Overlay on the left to turn it on, and then click on the Gradient thumbnail to open the Gradient Editor. Keep the default Black, White gradient preset, but then double-click on the black color stop beneath the left side of the color ramp and set this color to a grayish blue, making the gradient blue-gray to white. Click OK. Now, change the Blend Mode to **Hard Light**, set the Opacity to 75%, and turn on the Reverse checkbox. Here, I also ended up clicking on the gradient in the image window and dragging it down just a bit.

Continued

STEP 27:
Next, click on Pattern Overlay on the left to turn it on. Click on the Pattern thumbnail, then click on the right-facing arrow in the top right of the Pattern Picker and choose **Artistic Surfaces** from the flyout menu (you can append the existing list of patterns or replace it altogether). Choose the Granite (128 by 128 pixels, RGB mode) pattern, then leave the Blend Mode set to **Normal** and the Opacity at 100%.

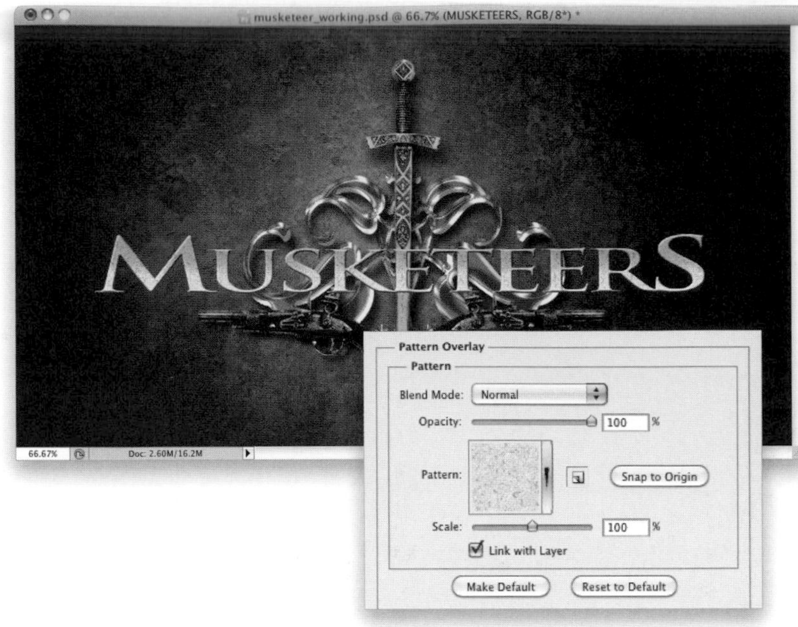

STEP 28:
Almost there. Click on Stroke on the left to turn it on, and then click on the Color swatch and set the color to a light gray. Set the size to 2 px and make sure the Position is set to **Outside**.

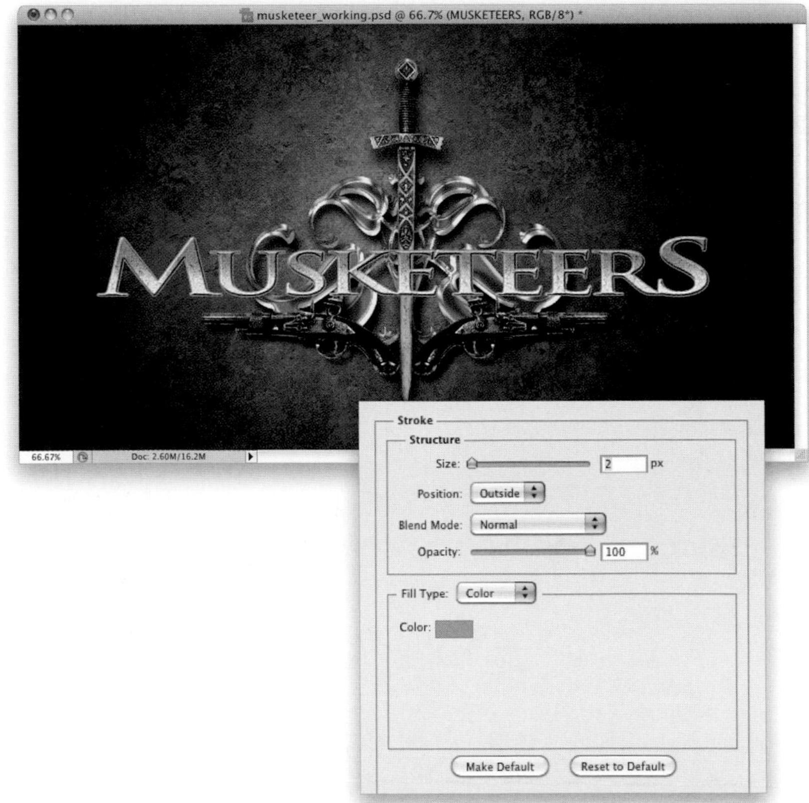

STEP 29:

Lastly, click on Outer Glow on the left to turn it on. Click on the color swatch and change the color to black, then change the blend mode to **Multiply**, and set the Opacity to 75%. Down in the Elements section, set the Spread to 10% and the Size to 40 px. This will give us a nice dark glow to separate the text from the background. You can now click OK in the Layer Style dialog.

STEP 30:

Now, with all that work out of the way, adding the remaining text is easy. Just press-and-hold the **Option (PC: Alt) key** and click-and-drag a duplicate of the text upward, directly above the original text. This will automatically create a duplicate layer, along with the layer styles, in the Layers panel. Now, just highlight the text and type the word "FIRST." The layer styles will update with the new text. Go into the Character panel and scale the text, if you want, and then align it again when you're done (here, I scaled it down some). Finally, drag a duplicate above this text layer, highlight the text, and type the word "the." This will complete the overall title effect. Feel free to fine-tune any positioning or aligning before the final step.

Continued

STEP 31:

Okay, so here's a cool trick to complete the overall look: With the top-most layer active in the Layers panel, press **Command-Option-Shift-E (PC: Ctrl-Alt-Shift-E)** to create a new merged layer. Then, change the layer's blend mode to **Soft Light**. This will enhance the contrast and add a color and light effect that seems to unify the whole design. If it seems too intense, then just drop the layer's opacity. Here, I ended up dropping it to 60%. As a final touch, I created a new blank layer, and then used a scaled-down version of my flare brush from Chapter 1 to create tiny glares on the graphic.

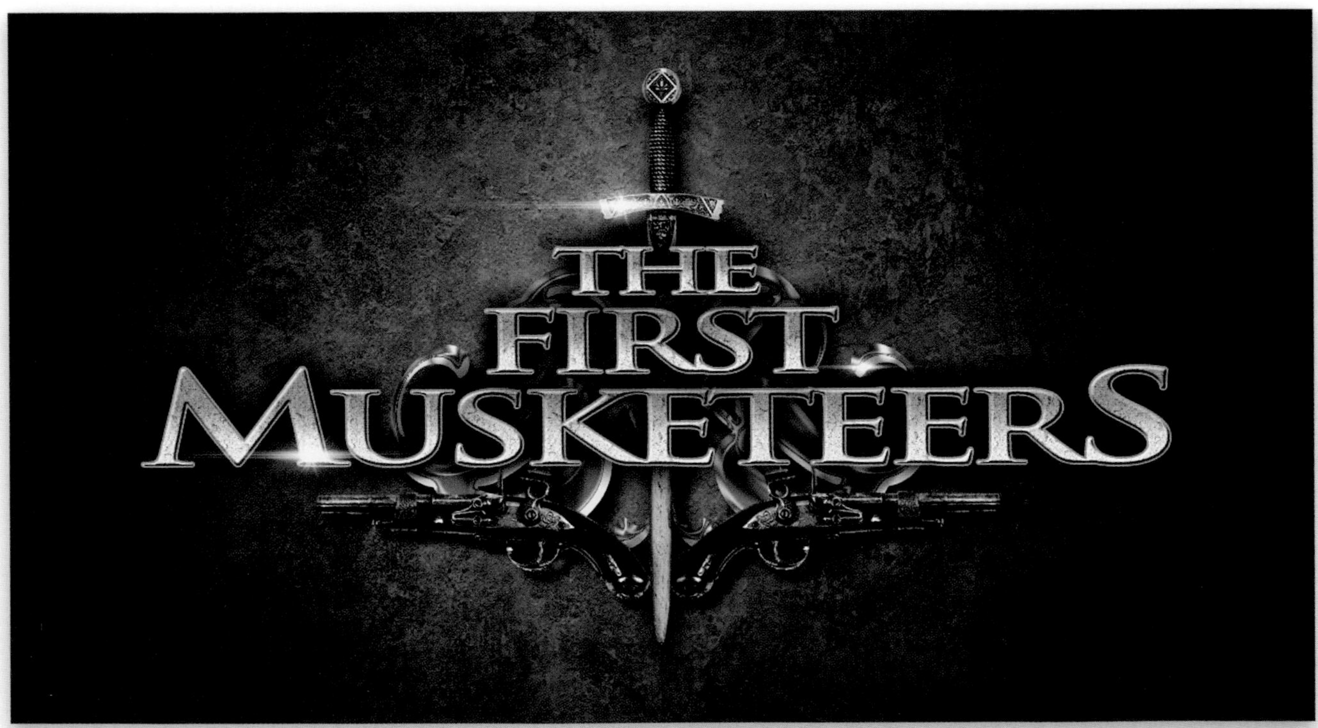

Use the Flare Brush created in chapter 1.

Final Image

The Elusive WOW! Factor

design effects

As a designer, you're always seeking that "Eureka!" moment that grabs you in an instant and shoots a feeling through your spine that lets you know that: a) you need to see a chiropractor soon, or b) you've discovered that elusive WOW! factor. It's that moment when you see a spark of an idea that tells you you're on the right track. Unfortunately, there's no formula for getting that WOW! factor every time. It really depends on the designer and how much you choose to see. The best I can do here is present you with some strategies that will kick-start your creative mind in the hopes that, along the way, you'll see that spark that sets you off on your own creative journey into the unknown. Lately, it seems to be the road less traveled by many designers. Be bold and see where your mind takes you.

Layer Style Effects

This technique demonstrates really well how effective layer styles can be for more than just a drop shadow or a simple bevel effect. They can be used to create so many different variations that, after using Photoshop for more than 15 years, I am still discovering new stuff. Well, at least for as long as Photoshop has had layer styles.

STEP ONE:
Here, we'll start with a seamless texture pattern I found on iStockphoto's website. It helps that the pattern is seamless, so if you choose to create your own texture, be sure to make it seamless.

©ISTOCKPHOTO/JAMIE FARRANT

STEP TWO:
Once the pattern image is open or created, go under the Edit menu and choose **Define Pattern**. Name your pattern and click OK.

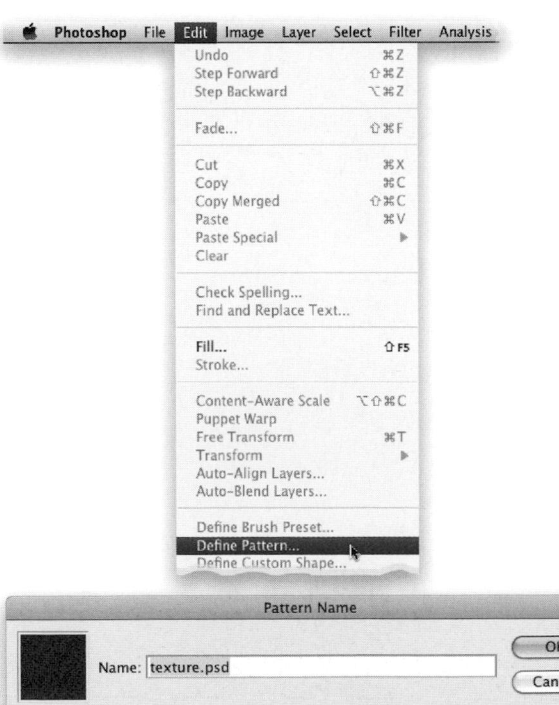

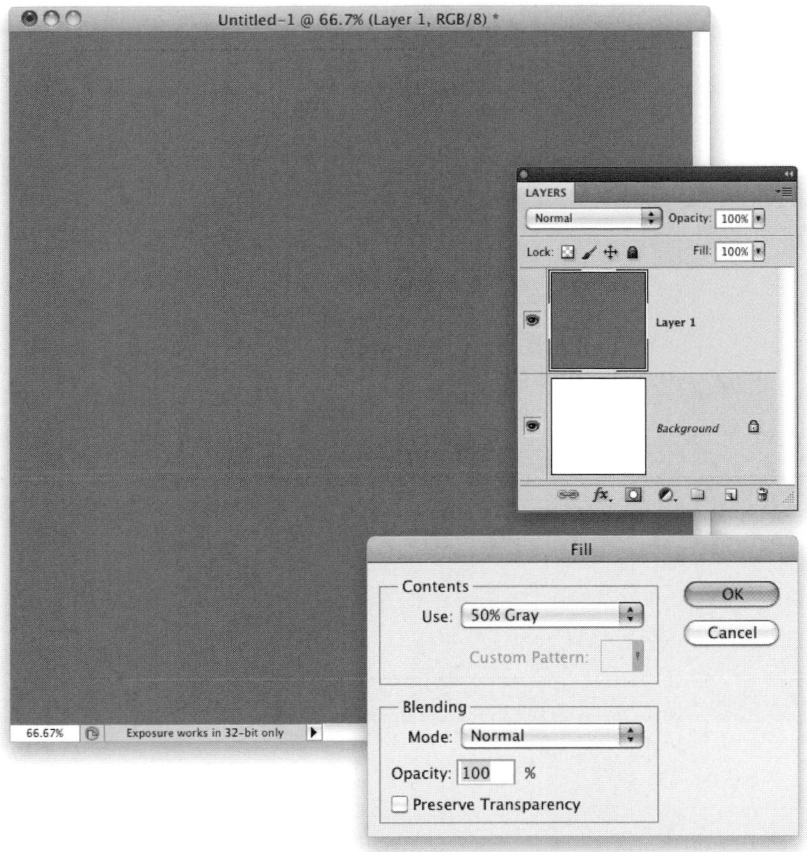

STEP THREE:

Now, go under the File menu, choose **New**, and create a new document that is 7 inches by 7 inches at 125 ppi. Then, click on the Create a New Layer icon at the bottom of the Layers panel to create a new blank layer. Fill it with 50% gray by pressing **Shift-Delete (PC: Shift-Backspace)** and choosing **50% Gray** from the Fill dialog's Use pop-up menu, then clicking OK.

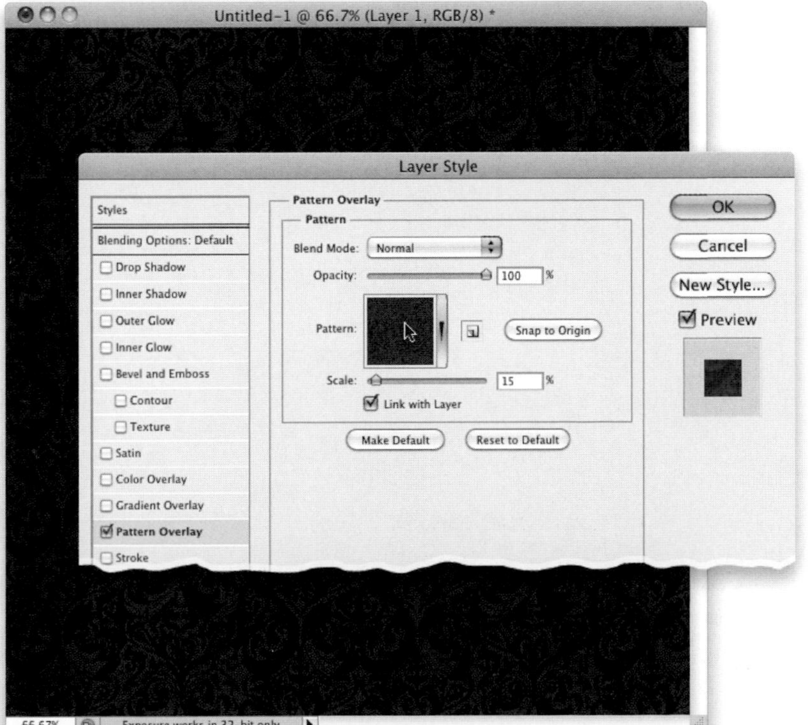

STEP FOUR:

Click on the Add a Layer Style icon at the bottom of the Layers panel and choose **Pattern Overlay** from the pop-up menu. Click on the Pattern thumbnail to open the Pattern Picker, locate the pattern we just defined, and click on it (it should be the very last one). Then, set the Scale to 15%. Now, depending on the pattern, you can move the pattern around manually by moving the Layer Style dialog off to the side, then clicking-and-dragging the texture around in your image window. Don't click OK yet.

Continued

STEP FIVE:

Click on Gradient Overlay on the left to turn it on. Keep the default Black, White gradient (if you don't have it, click on the down-facing arrow next to the Gradient thumbnail to open the Gradient Picker, and click on the third icon from the left in the top row). Change the Blend Mode to **Overlay**, and make sure the Opacity is set to 100%. Turn on the Reverse checkbox next to the Gradient thumbnail, and change the Style to **Radial**. Go down to the Scale setting and increase it to 150%. If it still seems too small, then move the Angle over to around 110° (as I did here) to widen the scope of the gradient just a little bit. Just like with the Pattern Overlay layer style, you can manually move the gradient around to change the overall light effect it is creating (I moved it to the right a bit here).

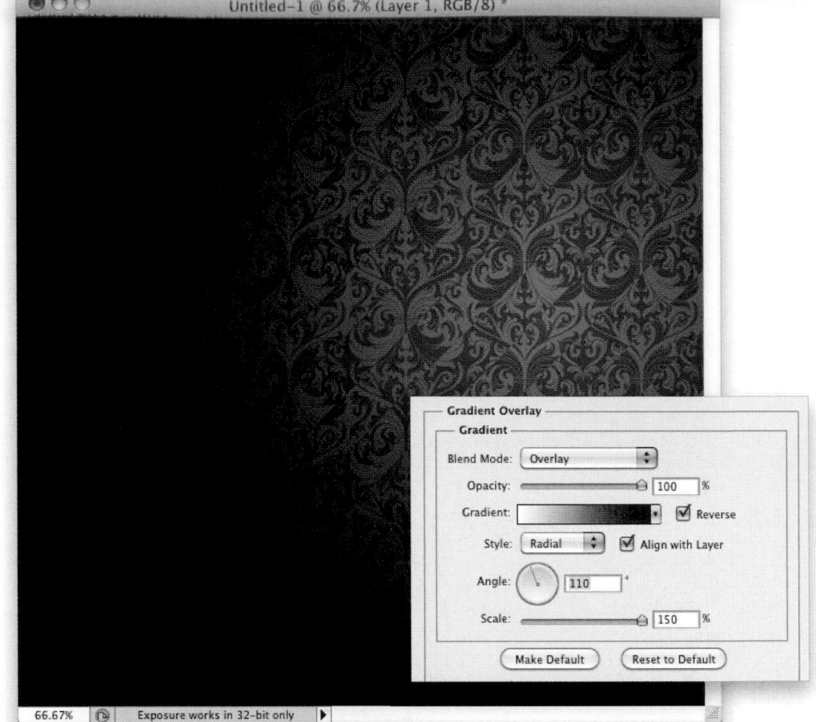

STEP SIX:

Next, click on Color Overlay on the left to turn it on, then click on the color swatch to the right of the Blend Mode pop-up menu and choose a color. Here, I'm using R: 58, G: 81, B: 148. Change the Blend Mode to **Overlay** and make sure the Opacity is set to 100%. Click OK when you're done.

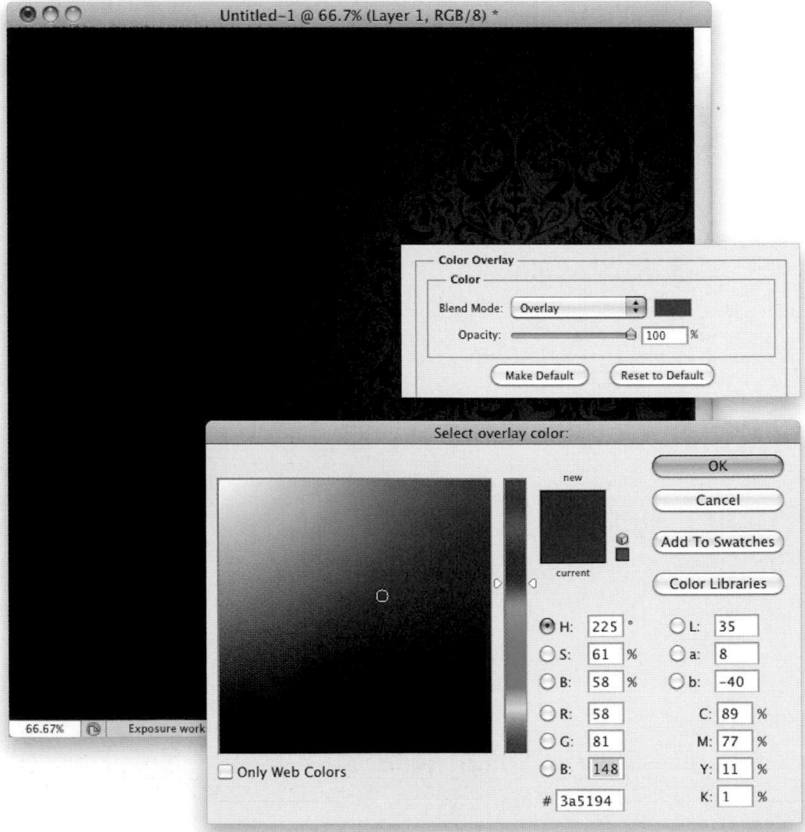

©ISTOCKPHOTO/ERIC HOOD

STEP SEVEN:

Okay, now that we have the background set, let's bring in the subject, which, in this case, is this image of a violin. The first thing we need to do is to extract it from the background by grabbing the Magic Wand tool from the Toolbox (or pressing **Shift-W** until you have it) and then clicking on the white background area to select it. Make sure the Contiguous checkbox is turned on in the Options Bar. With the background selected, press **Command-Shift-I (PC: Ctrl-Shift-I)** to Inverse the selection from the background to the subject. Then press **Command-C (PC: Ctrl-C)** to Copy the violin image.

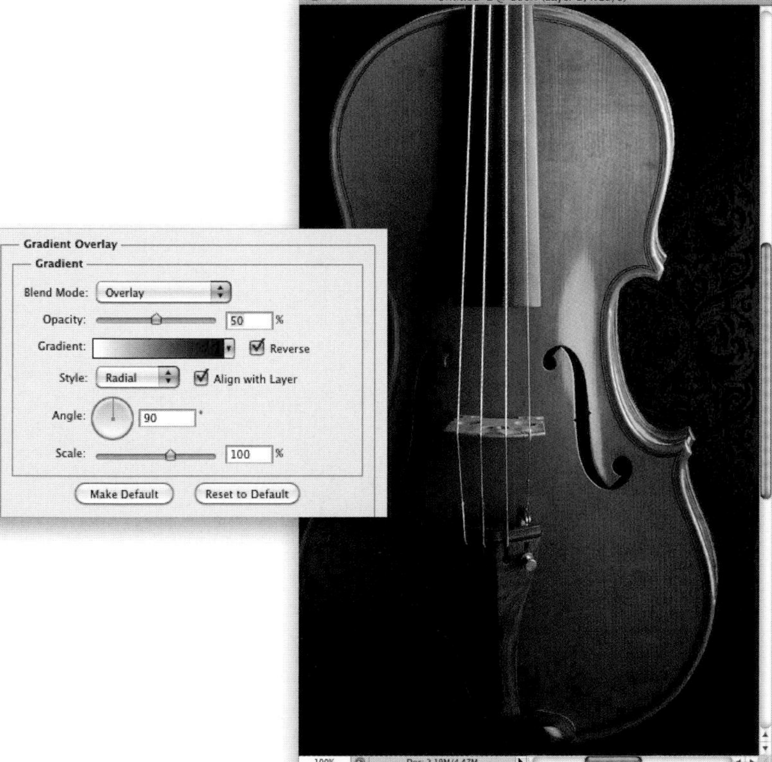

STEP EIGHT:

Switch back to the pattern working layout you created and press **Command-V (PC: Ctrl-V)** to Paste the violin into it. Use the Move tool **(V)** to position it toward the left side of the image. Here, we're going to apply a similar layer style to the one we used on the background, but we don't need the color effect or the pattern—we're just going to use the Gradient Overlay layer style to add a light effect. So, add a Gradient Overlay layer style, change the Blend Mode to Overlay, turn on the Reverse checkbox, set the Style to Radial, and reduce the Opacity to 50%. Now, you can, of course, click on the image and drag the gradient around to change the effect of the light to create different moods.

Continued

STEP NINE:
To give the image some depth, click on Drop Shadow on the left to turn it on, drop the Opacity to around 50%, increase the Distance to around 45 px, and increase the Size to around 15 px to make the shadow much softer. Turn off the Use Global Light checkbox and set the Angle to 90°. Then, just like with the gradient and the pattern, click on the image and manually reposition the drop shadow around to where it looks best.

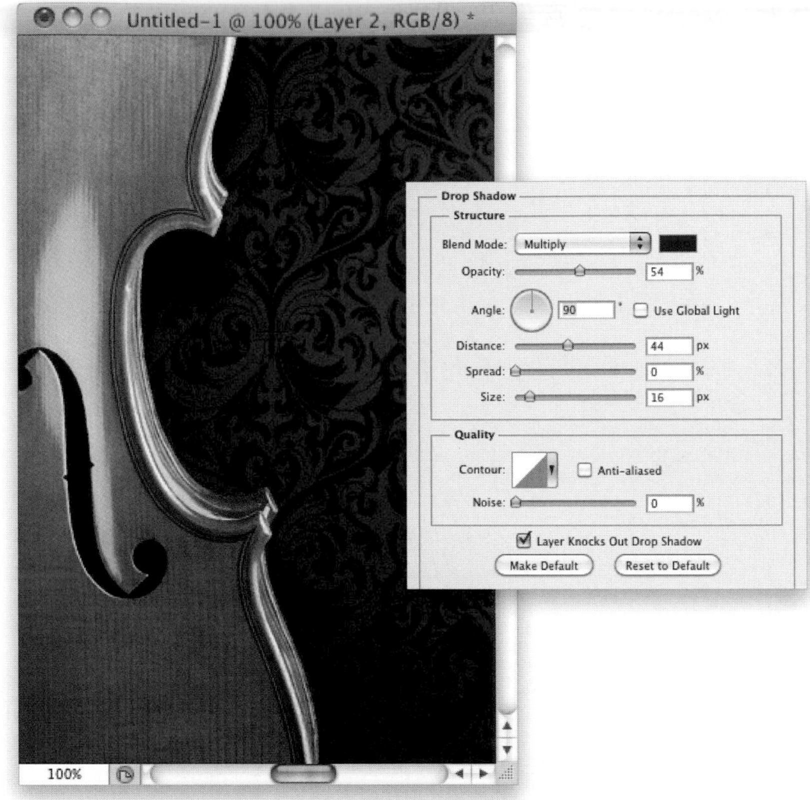

STEP 10:
I added a text element as a final touch. I set "Classical Masters" in Trajan Pro and filled it with white, and then added a Drop Shadow layer style, with the Opacity set to 75%, the Angle set to 120°, and the Distance and Size both set to 5 px.

Now, the great part about this is that these lighting effects are live, non-destructive layer styles that can be modified on the fly and even copied to other layers for different lighting effects.

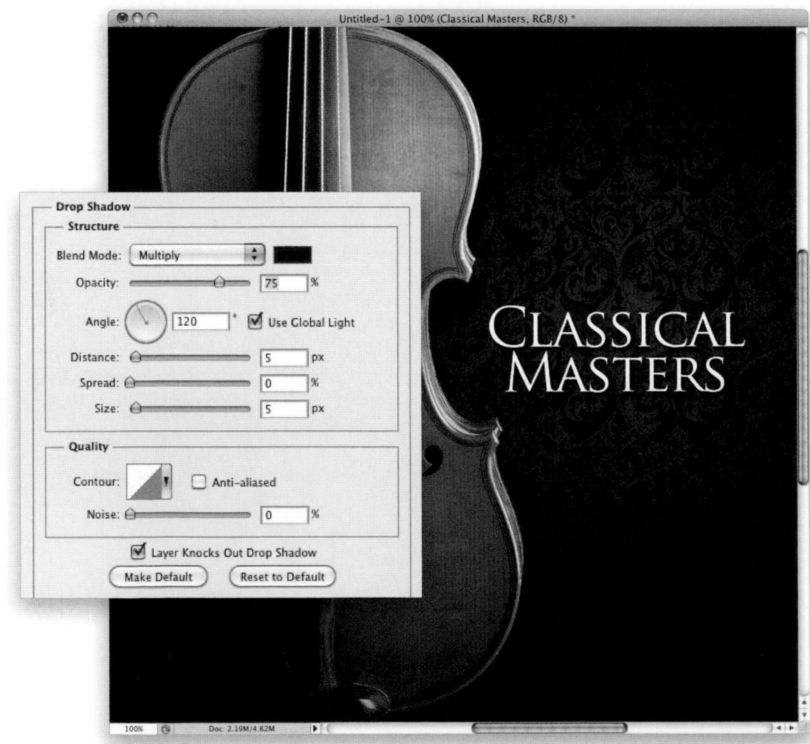

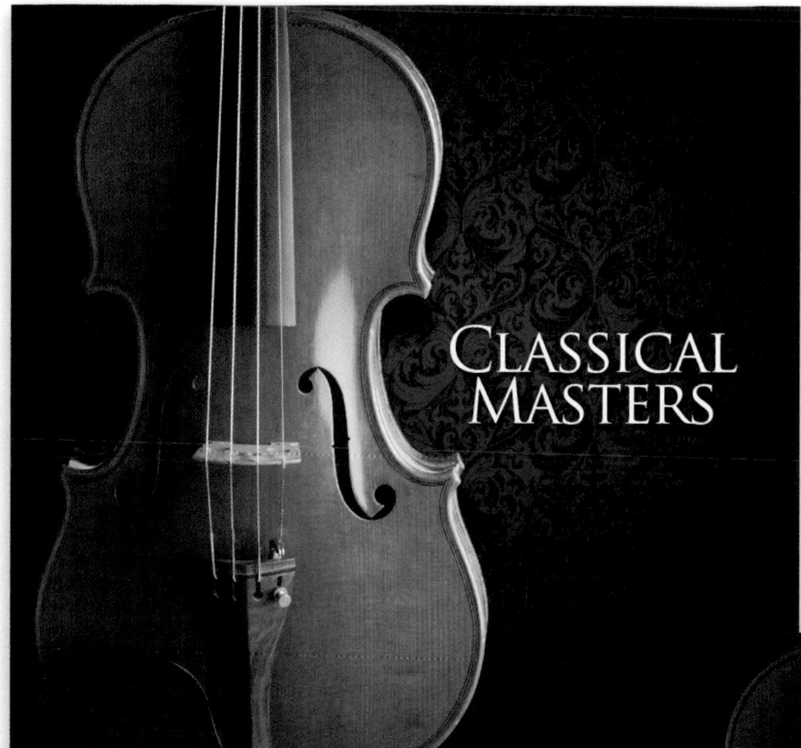

Final Image

Here, in this second example, I increased the size of the pattern and changed its color overlay. I also moved around the gradient overlays on both the background and subject layers to create a different look altogether.

Water Splash Elements

Oftentimes, there are images that you just can't get in the camera. Especially when it comes to the unpredictable nature of water. Here, we're going to combine a photo of a dancer jumping in the air with some water elements in a way that would be next to impossible or just plain impractical to try to shoot.

STEP ONE:
Start by going under the File menu, choosing **New**, and creating a new blank document that is almost 6 inches wide by 8.5 inches tall at 100 ppi.

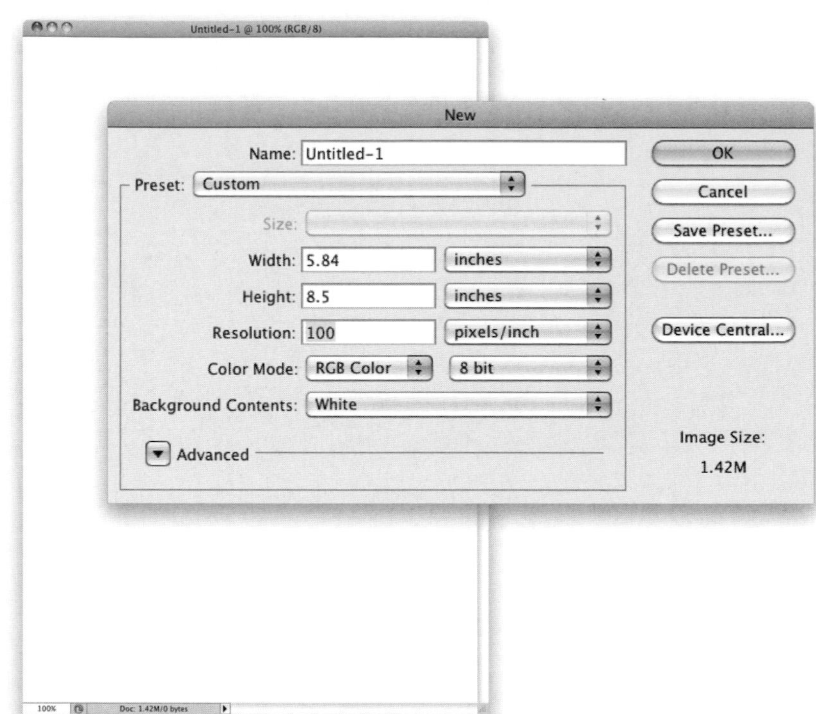

STEP TWO:
Select the Gradient tool from the Toolbox (or press **G**). Press **D** to set your Foreground and Background colors to their defaults of black and white, and then press **X** to invert them, so that black is the Background color. Click on the white Foreground color swatch at the bottom of the Toolbox, and set the RGB colors to R: 30, G: 109, B: 178. Click OK.

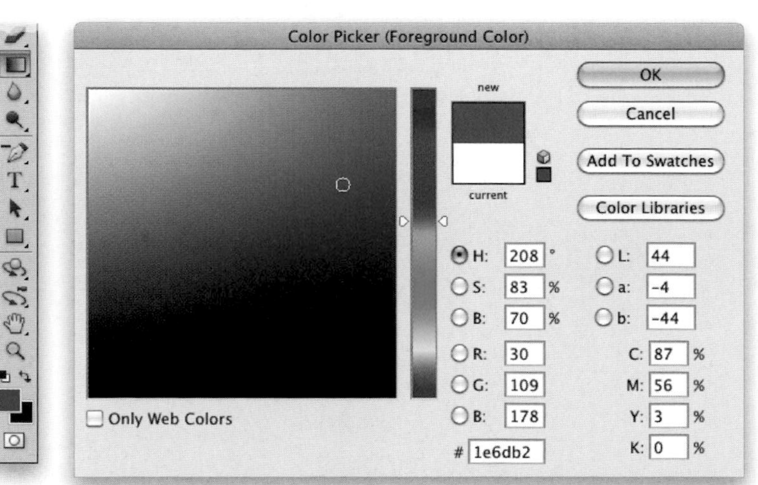

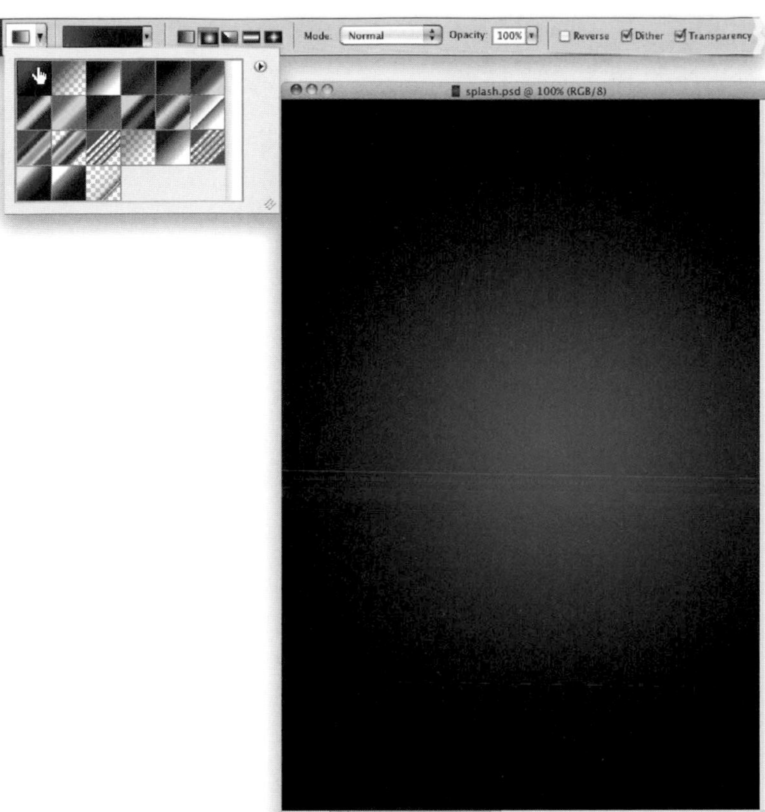

STEP THREE:

With the Gradient tool selected, go to the Options Bar and click on the down-facing arrow to the right of the gradient thumbnail to open the Gradient Picker. Choose the Foreground to Background gradient (the first one in the top row), then click on the Radial Gradient icon (the second icon to the right of the gradient thumbnail) to choose it. Now, click-and-drag the gradient out from the center of the canvas area. It doesn't need to be perfectly centered, but close.

©ISTOCKPHOTO/ALEXANDER YAKOVLEV

STEP FOUR:

Next, open the image of the dancer. The position of the subject in this image lends itself well to the effect we're going for here. However, I would like to grunge it up a bit to give the subject some texture. The HDR Toning feature (new to CS5) will work great for this.

Continued

STEP FIVE:

The HDR Toning feature, though, will only work on a flattened image, meaning you cannot have any layers except the base Background layer. But, we're going to need him selected off that background later, so make a duplicate of the entire file by going under the Image menu and choosing **Duplicate**.

STEP SIX:

With this duplicate file active, go under the Image menu, under Adjustments, and choose **HDR Toning**. I would honestly rather call this the grunge feature, because while it does give you a decent fake-HDR look, I like to use it to get a really high-contrast grunge look.

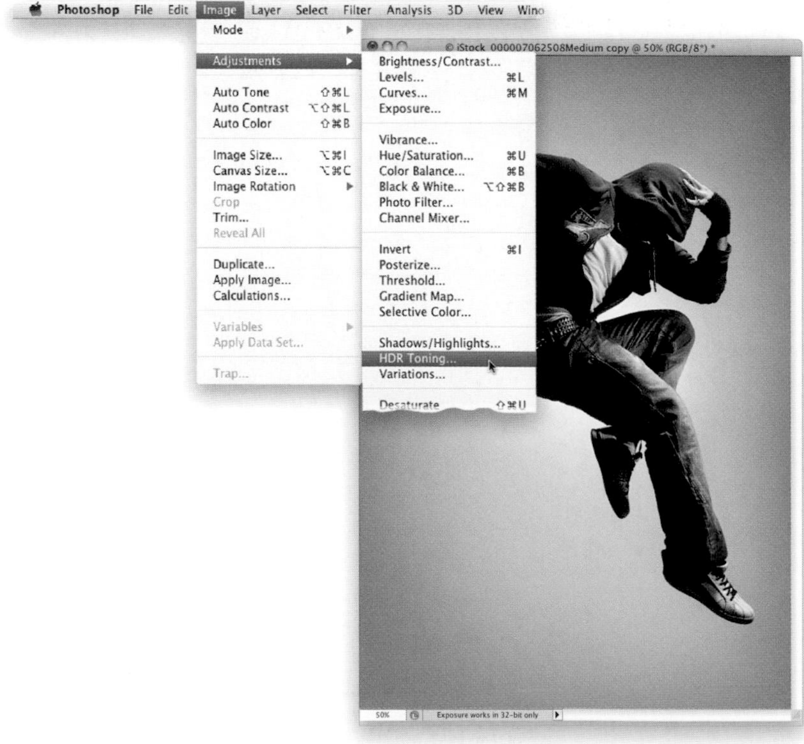

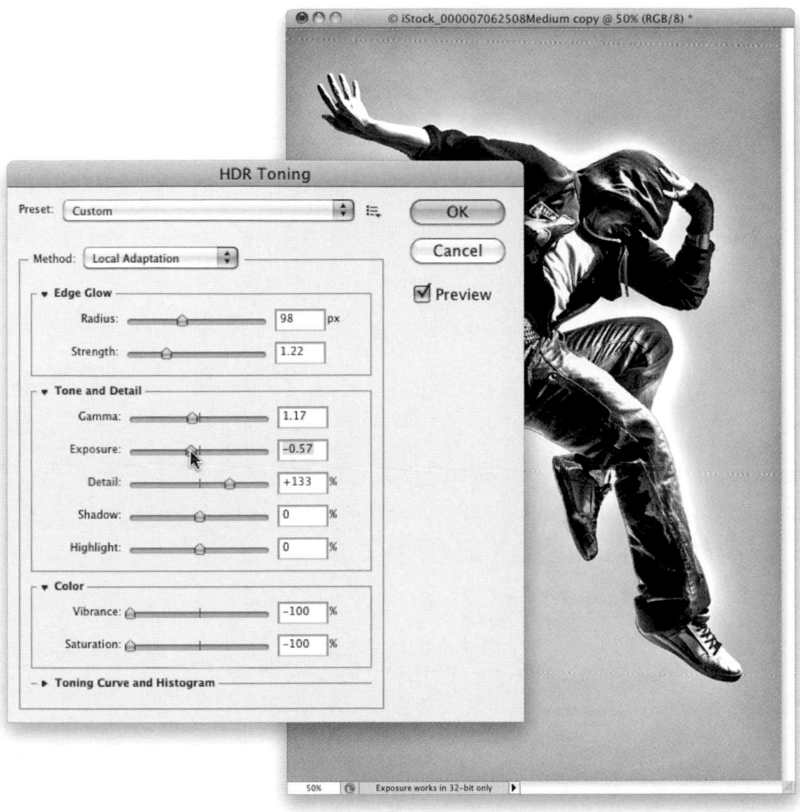

STEP SEVEN:

As I've learned using this feature, there is no real formula for what works. Each image is different. The best thing to do is to experiment and see what works and what does not. For this image, I started by first increasing the Detail setting to +133% in the Tone and Detail section. Since I planned to blend this adjusted image with the original, I went ahead and dropped the Saturation to –100%, removing all color. Then, I moved up to the Radius and Strength sliders and dragged them to the right to modify the effect and fine-tune the detail areas. I also nudged the Gamma up a little and dropped the Vibrance to –100%. If the image gets too bright in some areas, you can lower the Exposure to recover some lost detail. Again, feel free to play around with this dialog, as there are numerous possibilities to create interesting image effects. Sometimes, color saturation can make things worse, so remember to perhaps lower the Saturation to recover detail lost by color saturation.

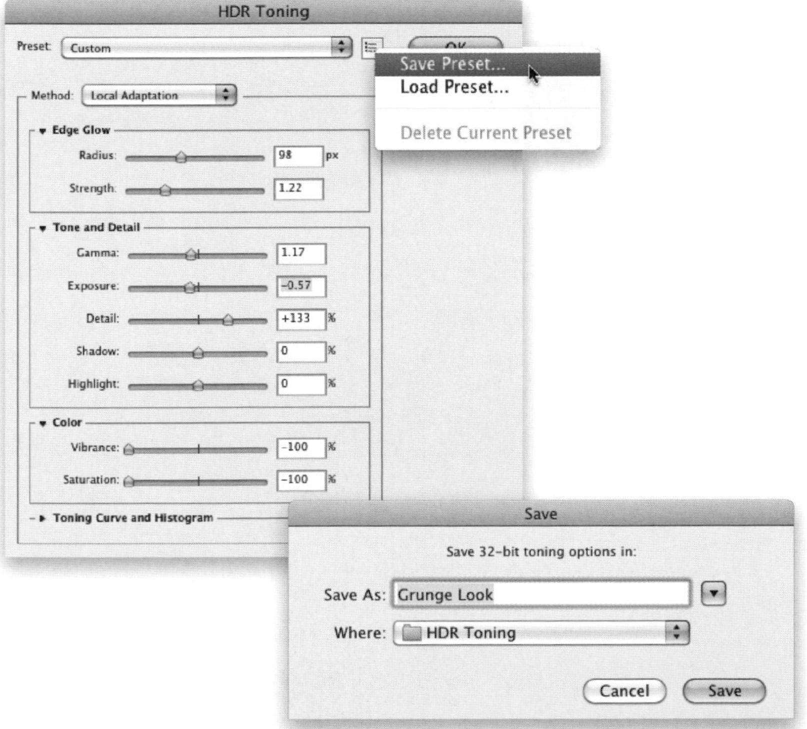

STEP EIGHT:

If you like the final effect, you can save it as a preset by clicking on the Preset Options icon to the right of the Preset pop-up menu, and choosing **Save Preset**. Name your preset and click Save. Now your preset will appear in the Preset pop-up menu.

Continued

STEP NINE:

Click OK in the HDR Toning dialog when you're done. Now, the result looks pretty good, but I want to increase the contrast just a tad more by running a quick Levels adjustment (press **Command-L [PC: Ctrl-L]**). You can see here, I made the light areas considerably brighter and only made the dark areas just a little darker.

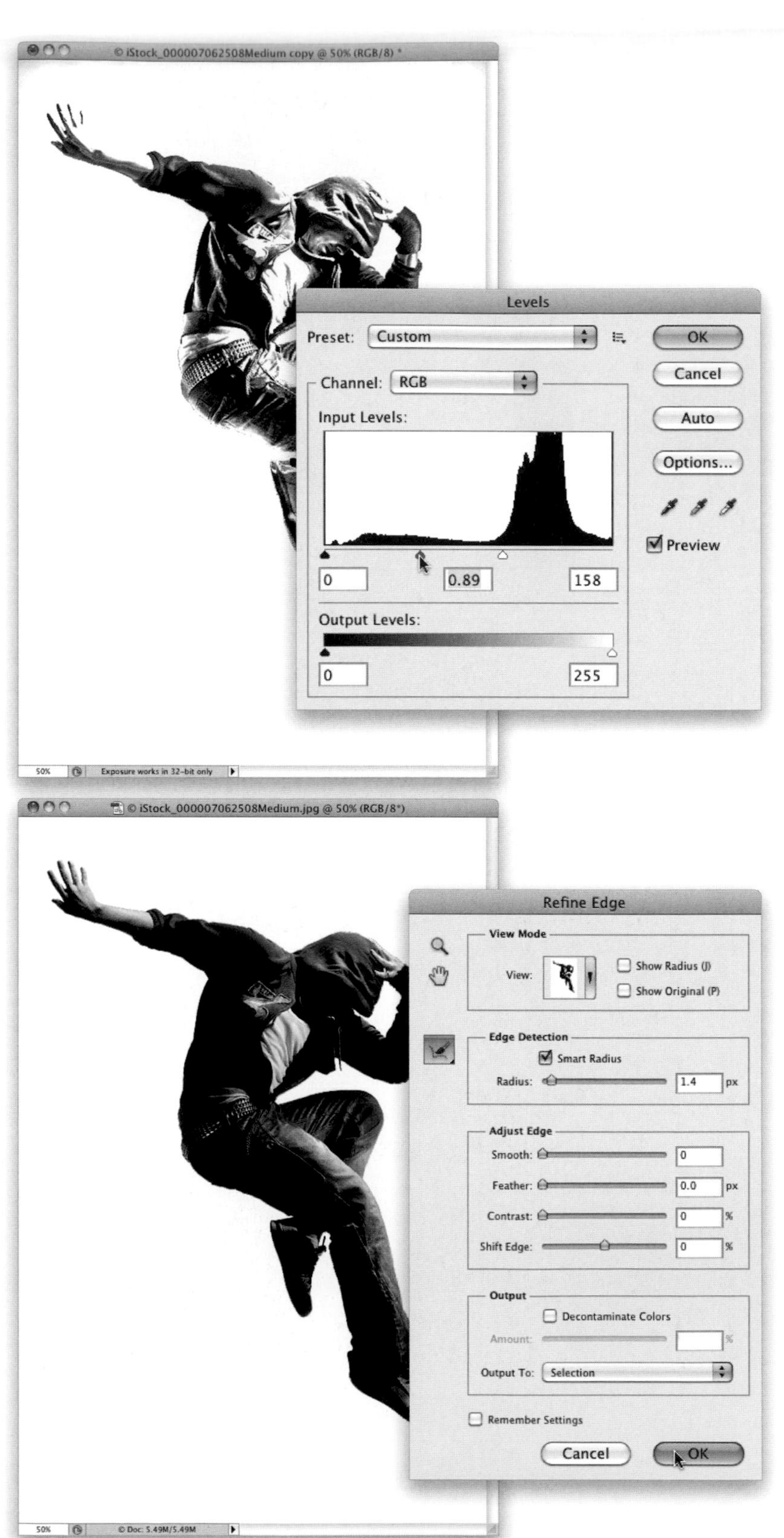

STEP 10:

Now, go back to the original dancer image and then choose the Quick Selection tool **(W)** from the Toolbox (it's grouped with the Magic Wand tool). Click-and-drag over the subject to select him and then click on the Refine Edge button in the Options Bar to fine-tune the selection. Here, I went ahead and turned on the Smart Radius checkbox, and increased the Radius only slightly to 1.4. In the Output section, set the Output To pop-up menu to **Selection**, then click OK.

STEP 11:

Press **Command-J (PC: Ctrl-J)** to copy the selection up onto a new layer. Then, go back to the duplicate image we applied the HDR Toning to, get the Move tool **(V)**, and click-and-drag it over to the file with the selection on a new layer. Make sure to press-and-hold the Shift key as you drag to line the two images up. Once it's in place, press **Command-Option-G (PC: Ctrl-Alt-G)** to clip this layer inside the extracted layer just below. Then, change the clipped layer's blend mode to **Soft Light**.

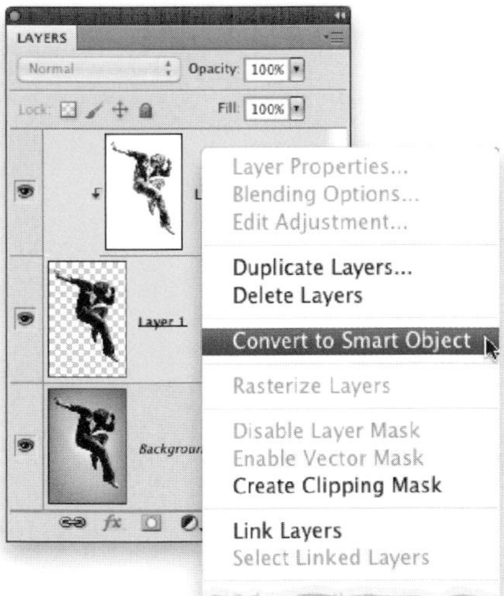

STEP 12:

Command-click on the original extracted layer to select both it and the top layer, and then nest them into a smart object by Right-clicking on one and choosing **Convert to Smart Object**. Then, click-and-drag this Smart Object layer into the working layout (with the blue-to black gradient). Press **Command-T (PC: Ctrl-T)** to go into Free Transform, then press **Command-0** (zero; **PC: Ctrl-0**) to see the Free Transform handles, and scale your subject down to fit in the frame (press-and-hold the Shift key while you drag to keep it proportional). Press **Return (PC: Enter)** when you're done.

Continued

STEP 13:

Go ahead and open up the first water splash image that we're going to composite with the dancer image. To extract the splash, open the Channels panel (under the Window menu), then press-and-hold the Command (PC: Ctrl) key while clicking on the RGB composite channel. This will load the brightness, or luminosity, of the image as a selection.

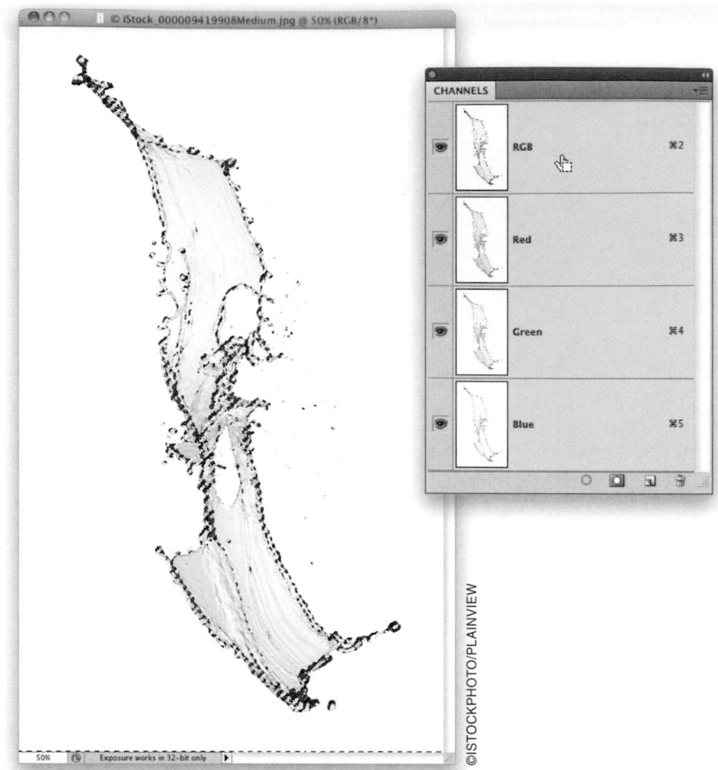

©ISTOCKPHOTO/PLAINVIEW

STEP 14:

Press **Command-Shift-I (PC: Ctrl-Shift-I)** to Inverse the selection. Then, go to the Layers panel and click on the Create a New Layer icon to create a new blank layer. Press **Shift-Delete (PC: Shift-Backspace)** and choose **White** from the Fill dialog's Use pop-up menu to fill the active selection with white. Press **Command-D (PC: Ctrl-D)** to Deselect. Click back on the Background layer, press Shift-Delete again, but this time choose **Black** from the Use pop-up menu to fill the Background layer with black. Now you can see a nicely extracted white water splash.

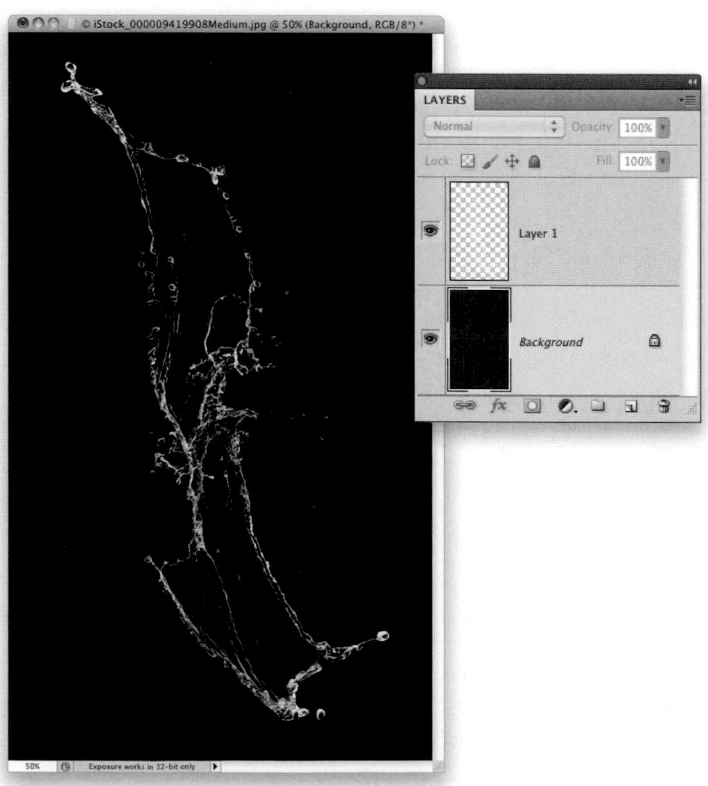

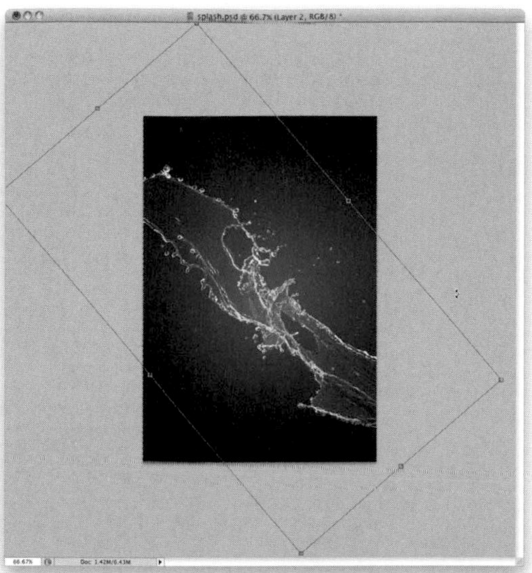

STEP 15:

Now, with the Move tool, click-and-drag the water splash layer over to your working layout. (Here, I turned off the dancer layer, so you could see the water splash better.) Go into Free Transform mode, then scale and rotate the water splash to fit in the composition just as you see it here. Press Return when you're done.

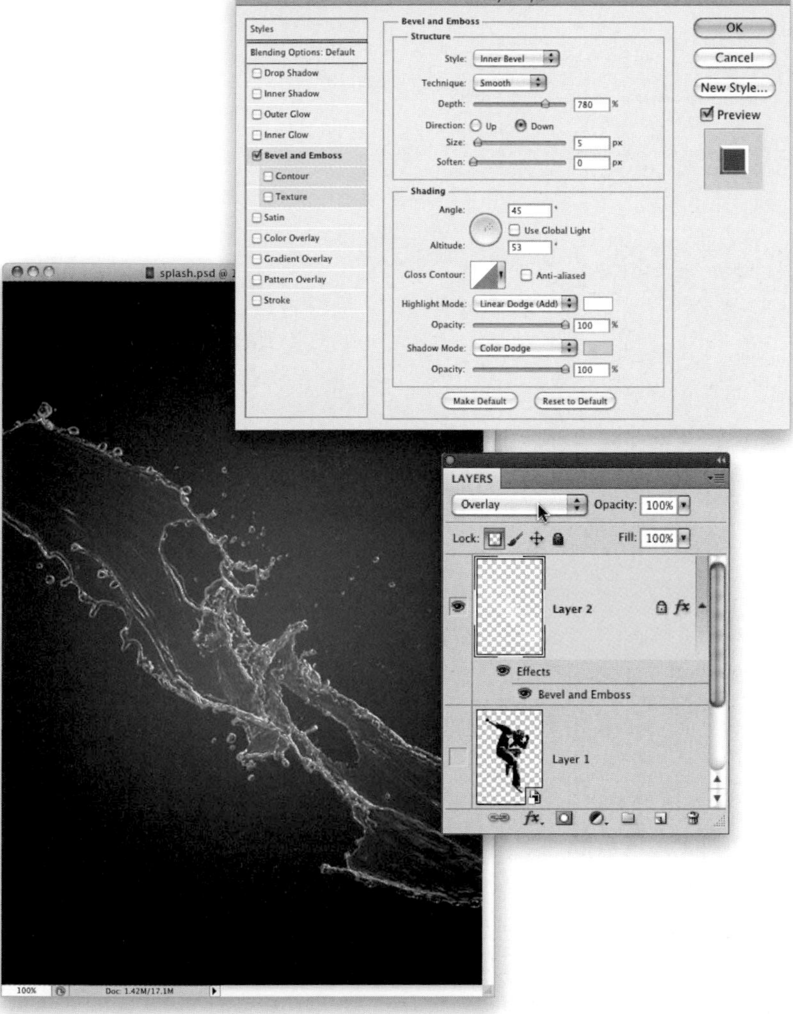

STEP 16:

Let's add a layer style to it to enhance the highlights a bit more. Click on the Add a Layer Style icon at the bottom of the Layers panel and, from the pop-up menu, choose **Bevel and Emboss**. Set the Style to **Inner Bevel**, the Technique to **Smooth**, the Depth to 780%, the Direction to Down, the Size to 5 px, and leave Soften at 0 px. Next, turn off the Use Global Light checkbox, and set the Angle to 45° and the Altitude to 53°. Then, set the Highlight Mode to **Linear Dodge (Add)**, its Opacity to 100%, the Shadow Mode to **Color Dodge**, its Opacity to 100%, and the shadow color to a lighter gray (I used R: 213, G: 213, B: 213). Try to vary these settings as you apply them to see the different looks that are possible. You may even stumble on something that works better for you. How do you think I got to these settings? Click OK and then change the layer's blend mode to **Overlay**.

Continued

STEP 17:
Press **Command-J (PC: Ctrl-J)** to make a duplicate of this splash layer to intensify the water effect on the background even more. If it seems too intense, just lower the layer's Opacity setting. If you turned if off, turn the dancer's layer back on again, and click-and-drag it to the top of the layer stack in the Layers panel, so he appears in front of the water.

STEP 18:
Now, open the second water splash image and extract this splash the same way we did the first one. When you're done, bring it over to the working layout and use Free Transform to scale it down, so it looks like what you see here.

©ISTOCKPHOTO/OKEA

STEP 19:

Next, apply the same layer style we applied to the first splash by **Option-dragging (PC: Alt-dragging)** the layer style (*fx*) icon on the first splash layer to the second splash layer. Also, remember to change the layer's blend mode to Overlay.

STEP 20:

Now, just duplicate this splash layer, like we did with the first one, to make it brighter. This will add to the effect of the dancer colliding with the water. We'll make that happen next.

Continued

STEP 21:

Click back on the first splash layer we added to make it active and then make another duplicate of it. Press **Command-T (PC: Ctrl-T)** to go into Free Transform mode, then Right-click inside the bounding box and choose **Flip Horizontal**. Press **Return (PC: Enter)** to lock in your change.

STEP 22:

For better visibility, turn off all the other splash layers by clicking on the Eye icons next to their image thumbnails, leaving just this one splash and the dancer. Click-and-drag the layer to the top of the layer stack, so it looks like it's in front of the dancer. Now, put the splash into Free Transform mode once again, scale it down, and rotate it around, so that its positioning is similar to what you see here. This is the splash we're going to make a displacement map from to distort the dancer.

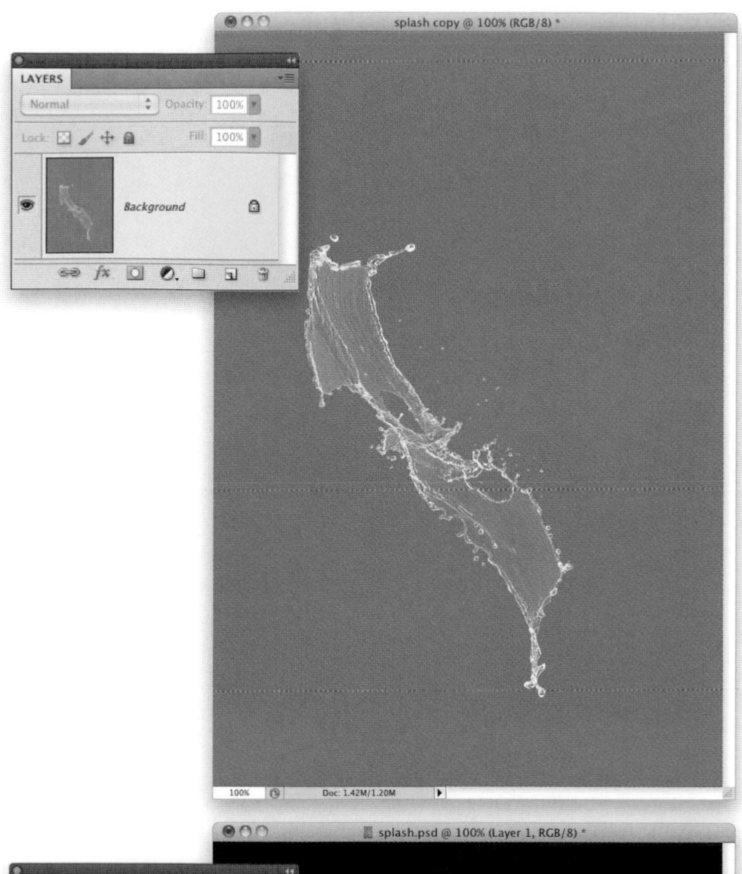

STEP 23:

Make a duplicate of this file by going under the Image menu and choosing **Duplicate**. Turn off all the layers, except this splash layer we just rotated and the Background layer. Click on the Background layer, press **Shift-Delete (PC: Shift-Backspace)**, choose **50% Gray** from the Fill dialog's Use pop-up menu, and click OK. What you should have is that newly repositioned water splash against a gray background. This is our displacement map. The Displace feature affects an image based on the light and dark areas of another image. Gray areas are ignored, so, in this case, the image will only be affected by the white areas of the splash. Go under the Layer menu and choose **Flatten Image** (you can discard the hidden layers), then save this file to your desktop and close it.

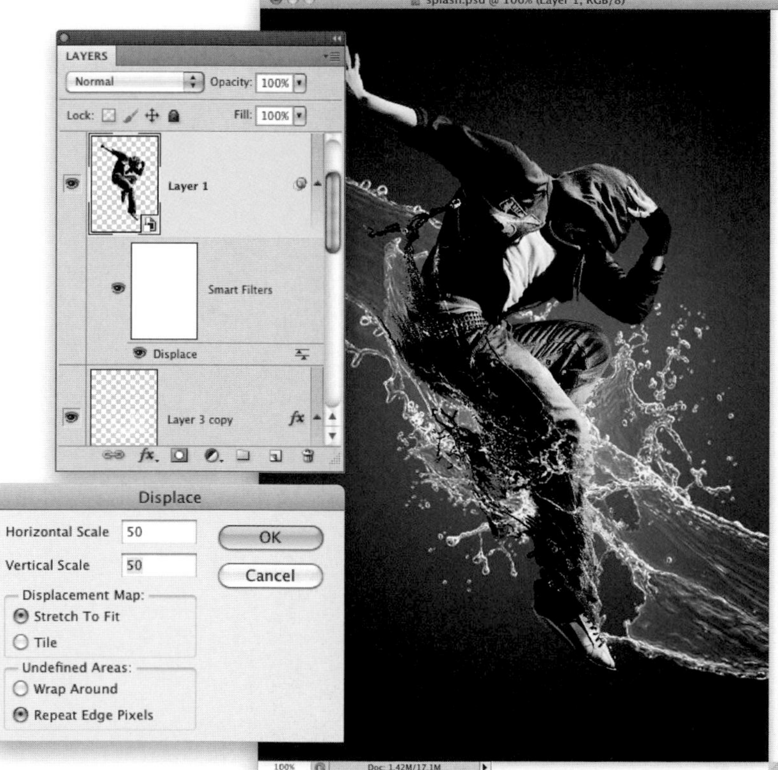

STEP 24:

Go back to your original working layout file and click on the Smart Object layer of the dancer to make it active. Go under the Filter menu, under Distort, and choose **Displace**. Set the Horizontal and Vertical Scale each to 50. Leave the other settings as they are, and click OK. When the Choose a Displacement Map dialog appears, locate the displacement file you just created, select it, then click Open. Notice how the dancer now appears to be distorted through the splashing water, making it seem more believable that he's colliding with the water. Turn all the other splash layers back on by clicking where their Eye icons used to be.

Continued

STEP 25:

Press-and-hold the Command (PC: Ctrl) key and click on the image thumbnail for the splash layer that we used to create the displacement map (Layer 2 copy 2) to load it as a selection. Then, click on the dancer layer and Option-click (PC: Alt-click) on the Add Layer Mask icon at the bottom of the Layers panel. This will hide the subject in the area where the distortion is, adding to the effect.

STEP 26:

To make it look more like his foot is plunging through the water, duplicate the first water splash layer we used one more time, drag it to the top of the layer stack, then use Free Transform to scale and rotate it to cover his foot, so it looks like what you see here.

STEP 27:

Now, on the dancer layer's layer mask, we're going to make the foot look like it is disintegrating as it passes through the water. Get the Gradient tool again and, in the Options Bar, make sure you are using the Foreground to Transparent gradient (the second icon from the left in the top row of the Gradient Picker). Change the tool's blend Mode to **Dissolve** and lower the Opacity to 75%. Also, make sure you have the Radial Gradient icon selected and your Foreground color is black. Now, with the layer mask (on the dancer layer) active, start at the tip of the shoe and draw the gradient just a little way up. Combined with the water effect, the foot will look like it is just disintegrating away. As you move up the foot and leg, though, it looks a little too speckled, so take the Blur tool (right below the Gradient tool in the Toolbox), reduce the Strength to 25%, and paint over the back of the foot and up the leg. This blends it better and makes it look more like solid water.

STEP 28:

To make him stand out more, click on the image thumbnail of the dancer, then click on the Add a Layer Style icon at the bottom of the Layers panel and choose **Outer Glow**. Change the Blend Mode to **Overlay**, set the Opacity to 100%, click on the color swatch and change it to white, then set the Size to 104 px, and click OK.

Continued

STEP 29:

After adding the glow, I think the colors in the dancer's clothing need to be more saturated. So, click on the Create New Adjustment Layer icon at the bottom of the Layers panel, and choose **Hue/ Saturation**. In the Adjustments panel, drag the Saturation slider to +25. To make the adjustment only apply to him, press **Command-Option-G (PC: Ctrl-Alt-G)** to clip the adjustment layer to the dancer layer.

STEP 30:

As a final element, I added a distorted white shape in the background (just above the Background layer) to help bring the elements together (I turned off all the other layers, so you could see it better). To do this, I drew a rectangle with the Rectangle tool set to Fill Pixels, and my Foreground color set to white. Then, I went into Free Transform, Right-clicked and chose **Warp**, chose **Bulge** from the Warp pop-up menu in the Options Bar, grabbed the top-center control handle, and dragged down a bit. Then, I Right-clicked again and chose **Skew**, and angled it so it was higher on the left. I added a Drop Shadow layer style to it (using the settings shown here), and hid part of it behind the dancer by adding a layer mask and drawing a black radial gradient on it. Was it really needed? Not necessarily, but I like it.

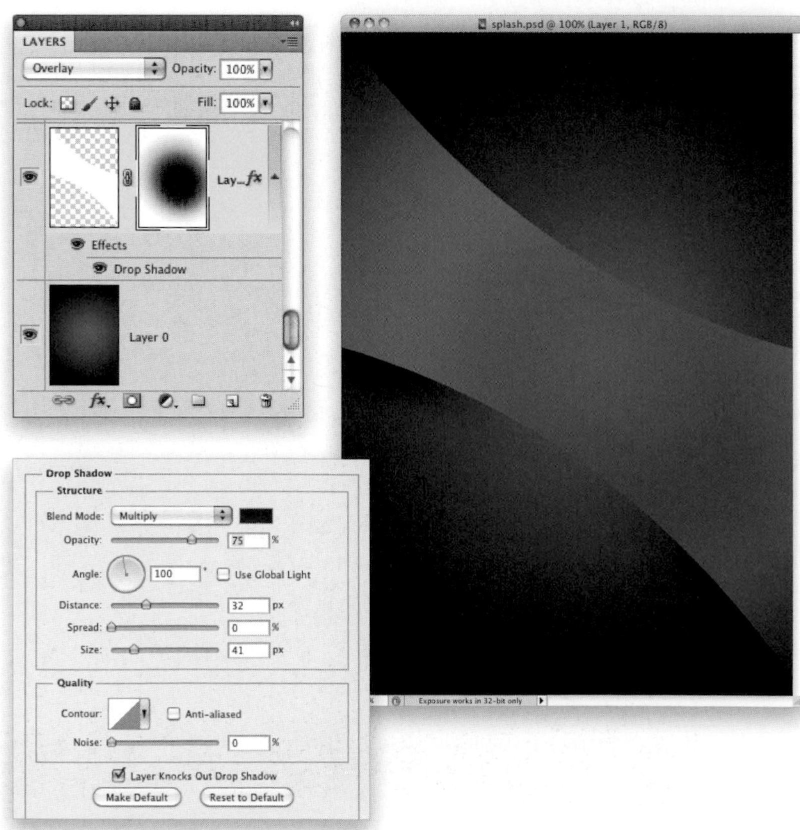

Final Image

Step & Repeat Effects

One of the coolest hidden features in Photoshop is the step-and-repeat command. It's a very clever way to get some really interesting repeating effects and patterns. While we'll be concentrating on one use here, you'll definitely want to play with this feature with different graphics and images to get some crazy graphic effects.

STEP ONE:

Go under the File menu, choose **New**, and create a new document measuring 7 inches by 7 inches at 200 ppi. Then, press **D** to set your Foreground color to black, and press **Option-Delete (PC: Alt-Backspace)** to fill the Background layer with black.

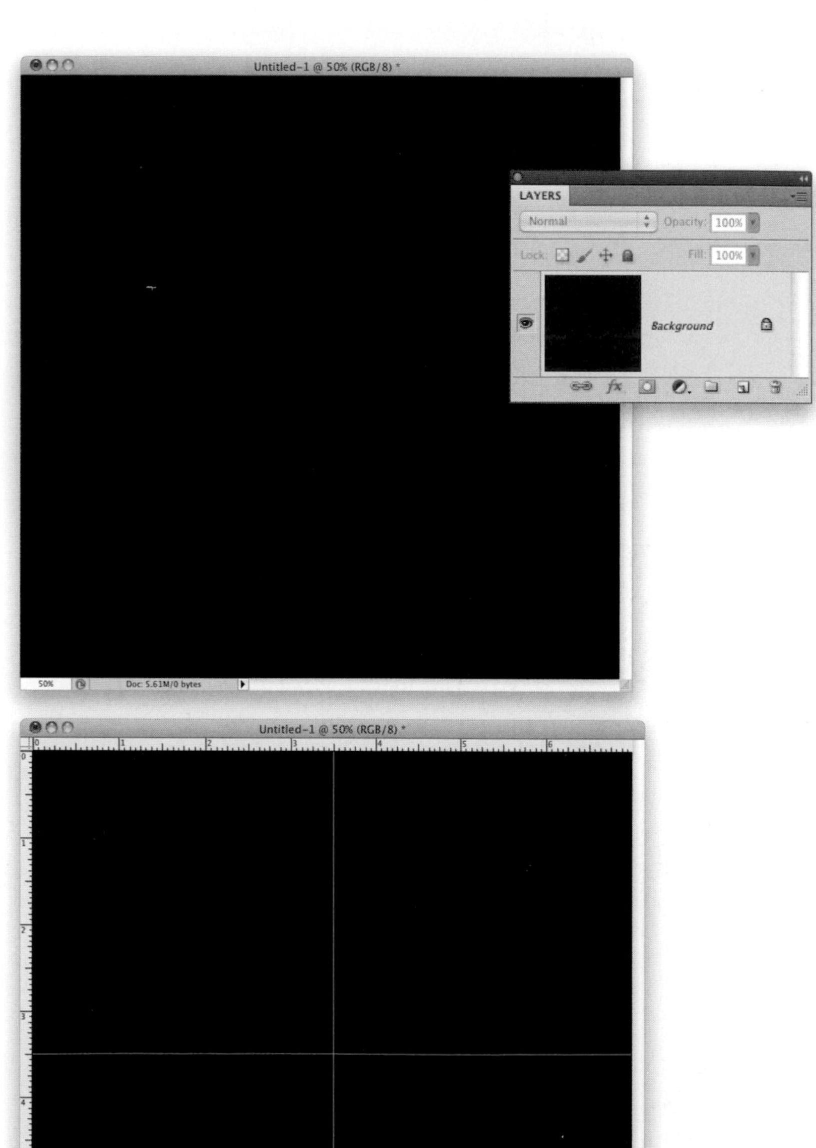

STEP TWO:

Make the rulers visible by pressing **Command-R (PC: Ctrl-R)**, then click inside the vertical ruler and drag out a guide to the center of the canvas (3.5"). Click inside the horizontal ruler and create a horizontal guide, as well. These will help us in creating the pattern.

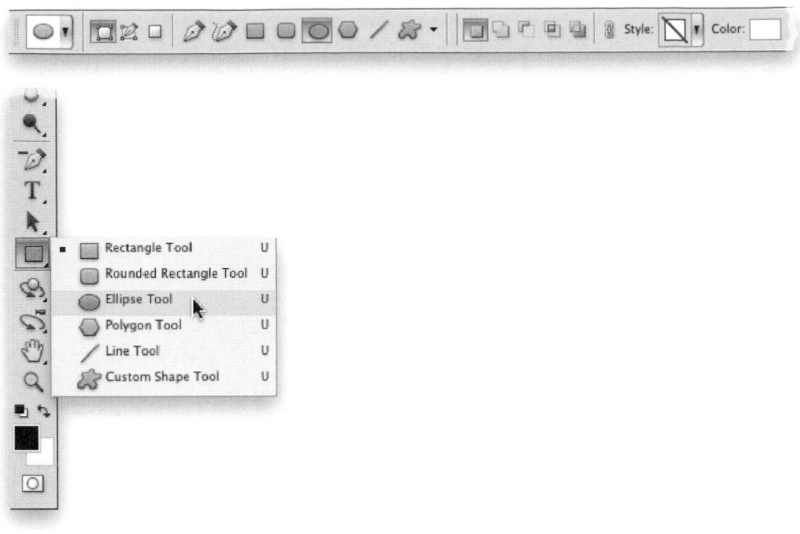

STEP THREE:

Click-and-hold on the Rectangle tool in the Toolbox and choose the Ellipse tool from the menu. Then, up in the Options Bar, make sure the Shape Layers icon is selected (the first one on the left next to the tool thumbnail), and make sure the Color is set to white.

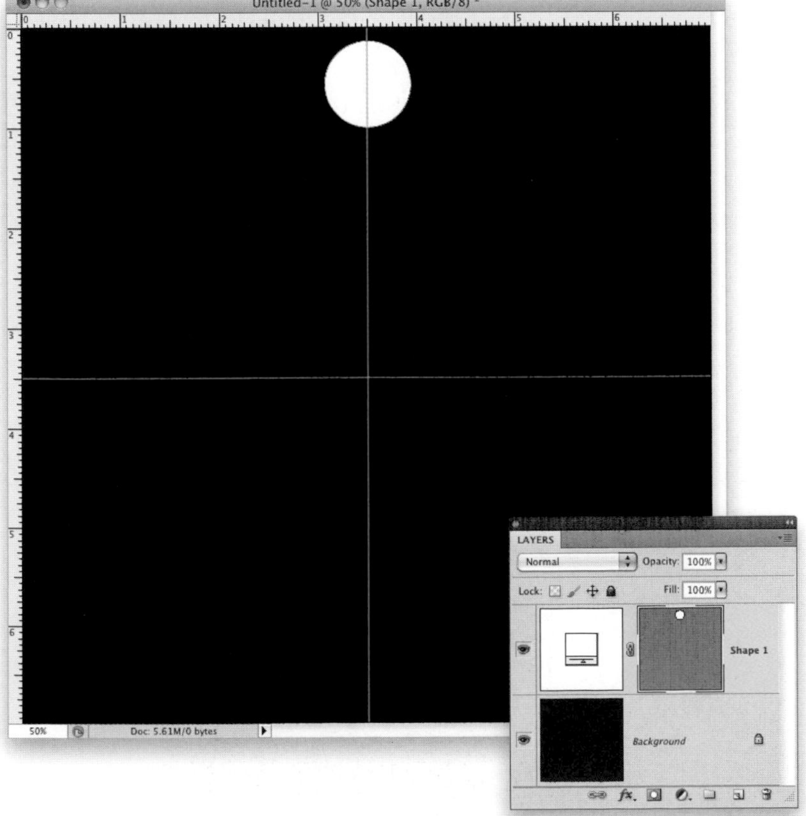

STEP FOUR:

Press-and-hold the Shift key and draw a small circle shape at the top of the canvas area, making sure it's centered to the guide. It should snap to the guide (if it doesn't, go under the View menu, under Snap To, and choose Guides).

Continued

STEP FIVE:

Choose the Path Selection tool **(A)** from the Toolbox, make sure the Show Bounding Box checkbox in the Options Bar is turned off, and click on the shape to select it. Then, press-and-hold **Option-Shift (PC: Alt-Shift)** and click-and-drag a duplicate shape to the bottom of the canvas, keeping it aligned to the vertical guide.

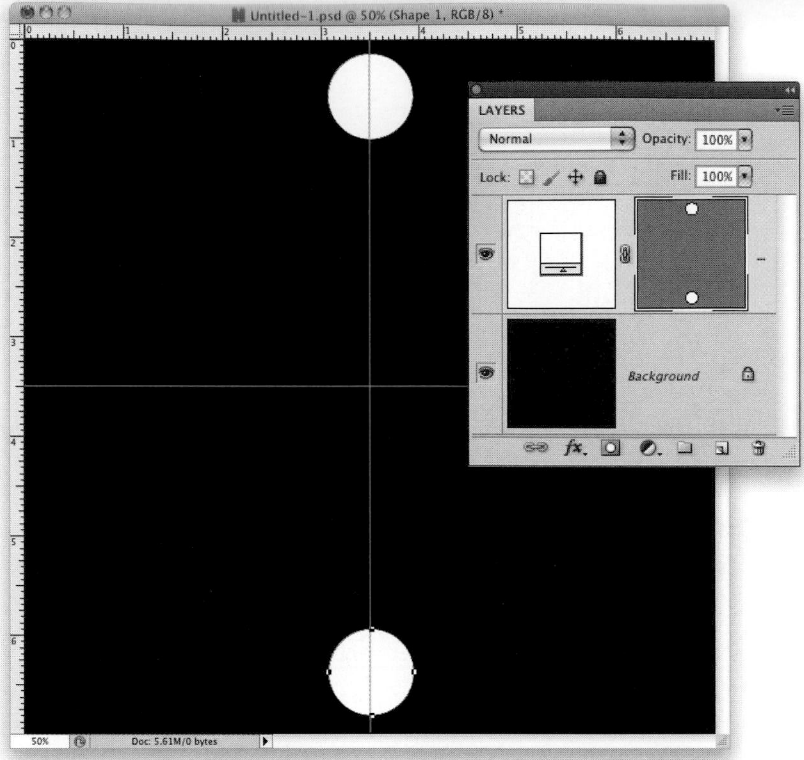

STEP SIX:

Now, to invoke step-and-repeat, Shift-click on the original shape to select both shapes and press **Command-Option-T (PC: Ctrl-Alt-T)**. This will place the shapes in a Free Transform bounding box. Press-and-hold the Shift key, move your cursor outside the bounding box, and click-and-drag to rotate the shapes clockwise. With the Shift key added, it will snap every 15 degrees. Just drag two stops to 30 degrees and press **Return (PC: Enter)**.

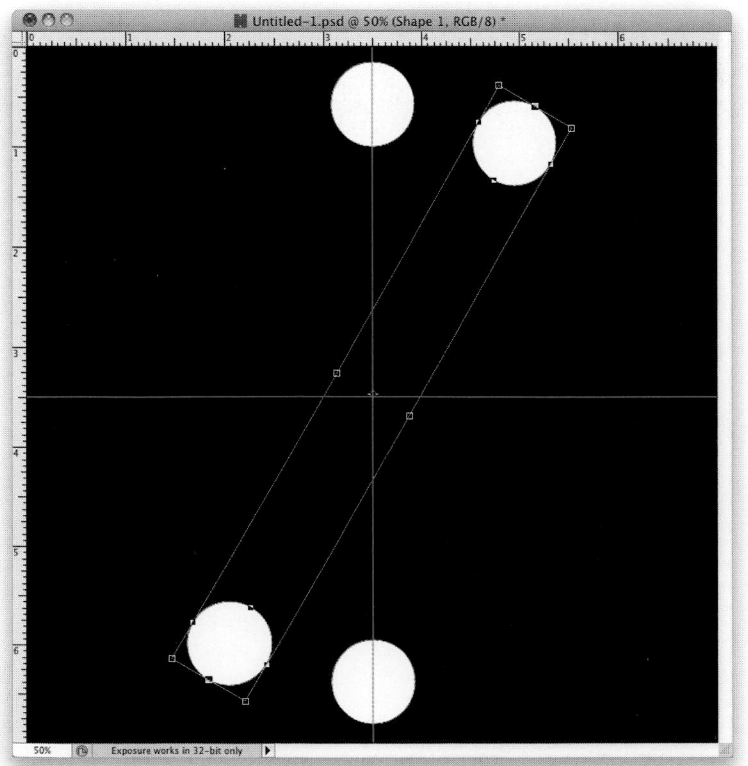

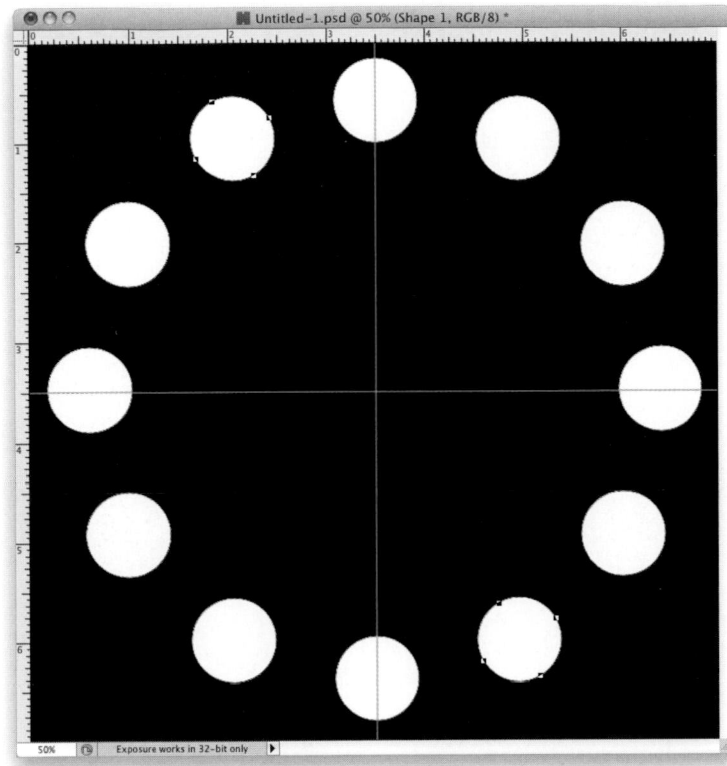

STEP SEVEN:

To complete the circle of circles, press-and-hold **Command-Option-Shift (PC: Ctrl-Alt-Shift)**, and press **T** four times.

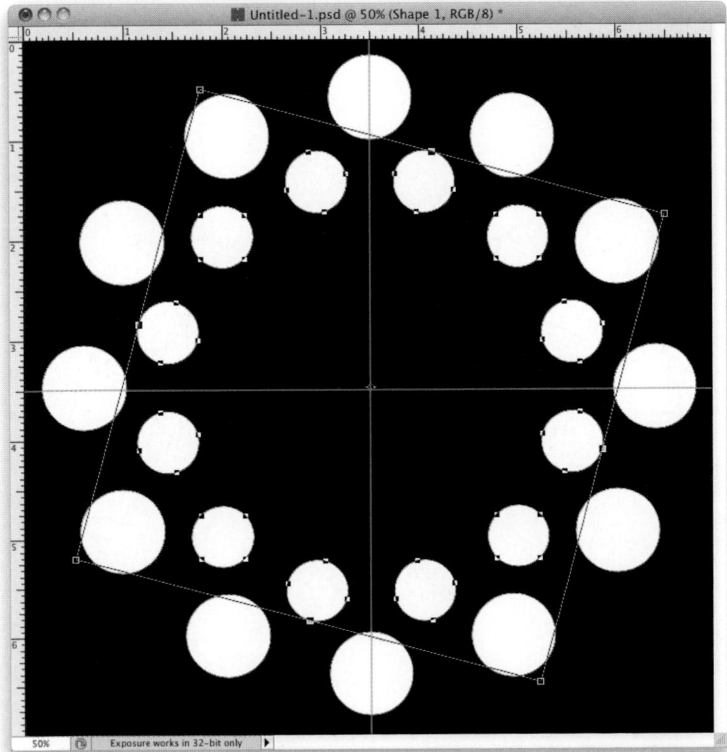

STEP EIGHT:

Once the circle is complete, use the Path Selection tool to select all the shapes in the circle (just click-and-drag a square that includes them all, and when you release the mouse button, they will all be selected). Press Command-Option-T to invoke step-and-repeat again. This time, press-and-hold the Shift key and just rotate it 15 degrees, then press-and-hold **Option-Shift (PC: Alt-Shift)**, grab a corner handle, and scale the shapes just inside the original shapes, like you see here, and press Return. If you can't see the corner handles to scale the shapes, press **Command-0** (zero; **PC: Ctrl-0**) to make the image window large enough to see them.

Continued

STEP NINE:

Once again, press-and-hold Command-Option-Shift (PC: Ctrl-Alt-Shift) and press T continuously to repeat the copying, rotation, and scaling (all three will happen every time you press T) into a receding pattern toward the center of the circle.

STEP 10:

Now, use the Path Selection tool to select all the circles again, and press Command-T (PC: Ctrl-T) to go into Free Transform mode. Press-and-hold Option-Shift (PC: Alt-Shift), grab a corner handle, and scale the pattern outward, so the shapes extend a little beyond the document edges.

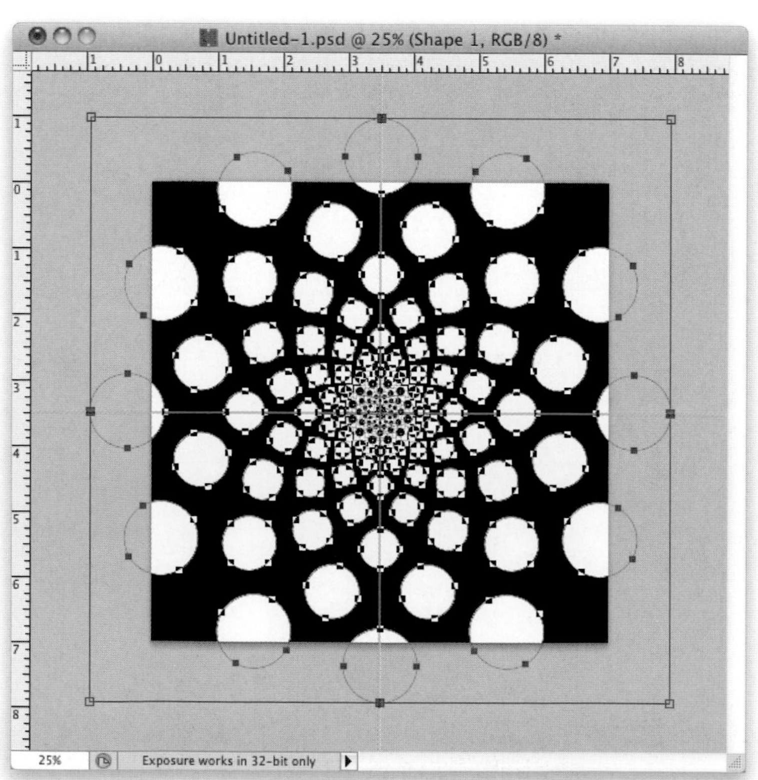

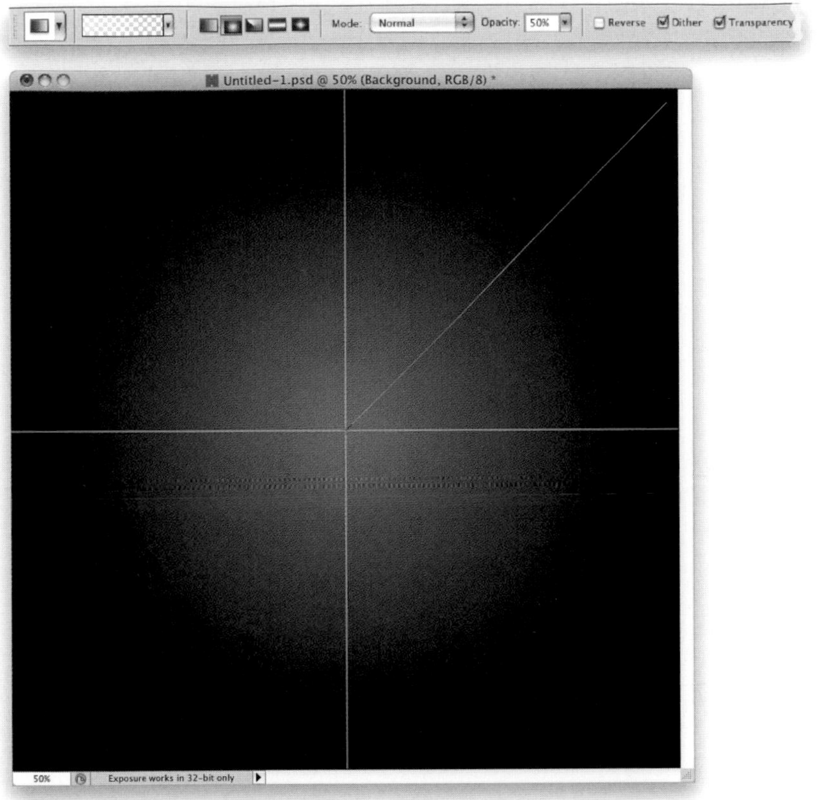

STEP 11:

Click on the Background layer that is filled with black. Get the Gradient tool **(G)** from the Toolbox, and click on the down-facing arrow next to the gradient thumbnail in the Options Bar to open the Gradient Picker. Make sure you are using the Foreground to Transparent gradient (the second one from the left in the top row), then click on the Radial Gradient icon (the second icon from the left to the right of the gradient thumbnail). Also, lower the Opacity to 50%. If your Foreground color isn't already set to white, press **D**, then **X** to make it white. Then, draw a light gradient out from the center of the canvas (here, I clicked on the Eye icon next to my Shape layer to turn it off).

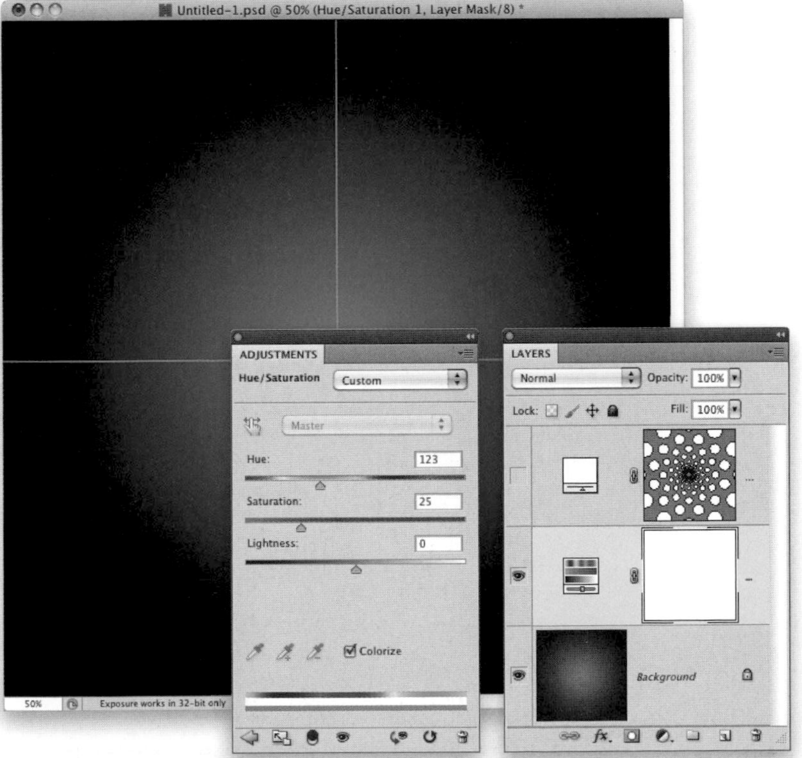

STEP 12:

Next, click on the Create New Adjustment Layer icon at the bottom of the Layers panel, and choose **Hue/Saturation** from the pop-up menu. Turn on the Colorize checkbox, and set the Hue to 123 and the Saturation to 25, which will give you a green background gradient. Obviously, you can experiment with these settings to get different colors—you can change the color at any time because it's an adjustment layer.

Continued

STEP 13:

Click back on the Shape layer and,z if you turned it off, click where the Eye icon used to be to turn it back on. Then, change the blend mode of the Shape layer to **Overlay** to make the white circles a lighter shade of your background color.

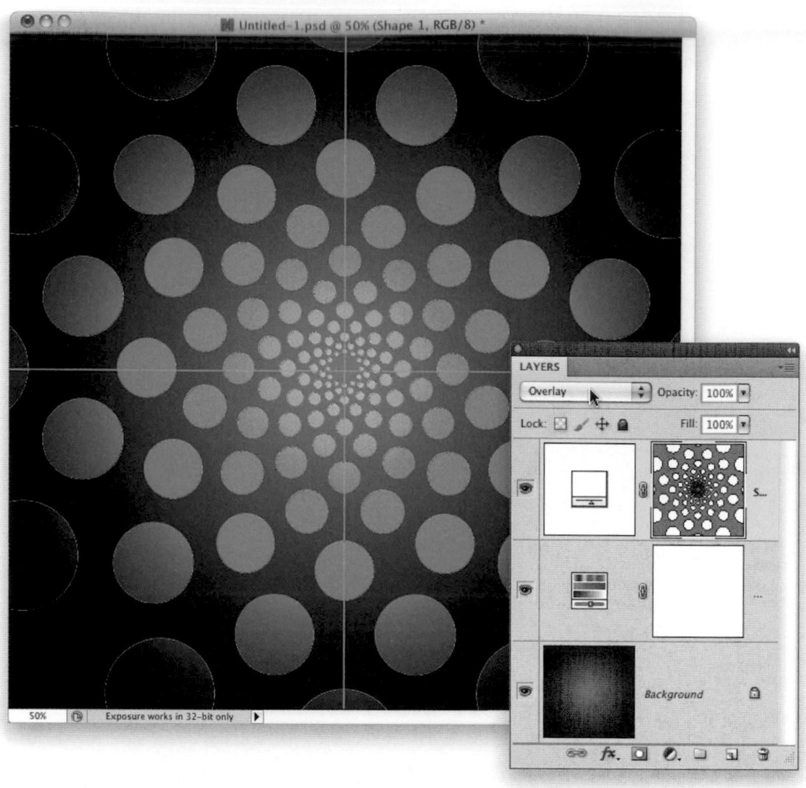

STEP 14:

Now, click on the Add Layer Mask icon at the bottom of the Layers panel to add a layer mask to your Shape layer. (Yes, you can have a layer mask and a vector mask on the same layer.) Using the Gradient tool again, with the same radial gradient from a few steps ago, raise the Opacity back to 100% and press D to change your Foreground color to black. Then, click-and-drag a gradient out from the center, like you did on the Background layer, only on the layer mask this time (and make it a little smaller). This will fade out the center of the pattern, as you see here.

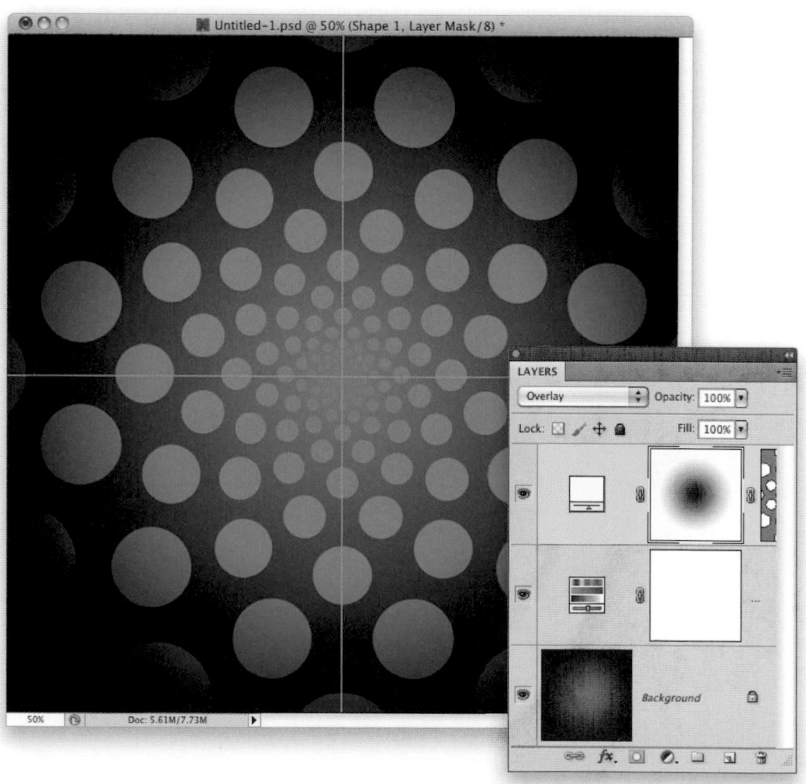

©ISTOCKPHOTO/ICONOGENIC

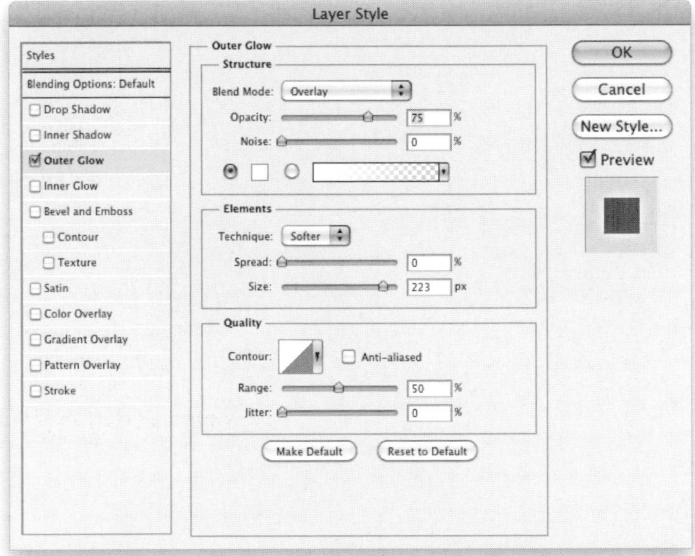

STEP 15:

The background is now ready for a foreground image. Here, I extracted a subject from her background, and dragged her into the step-and-repeat file, then added an Outer Glow layer style to her layer using the settings shown below. I could also copy this new pattern to other files as a multiple-use design element. This feature has a lot of potential, because you can experiment with different shapes and different patterns to get a myriad of different looks. The step-and-repeat feature can be applied to almost anything: shapes, images, text, etc.

Continued

Final Image

Compositing with Silhouettes

Here, we'll composite a photo inside the silhouette of another. This is an effect I've been seeing a lot lately, used everywhere from movies and TV to magazines and the Web. The reason, I think, is that it definitely can look pretty cool and is really not that hard of an effect to create if you have the right images.

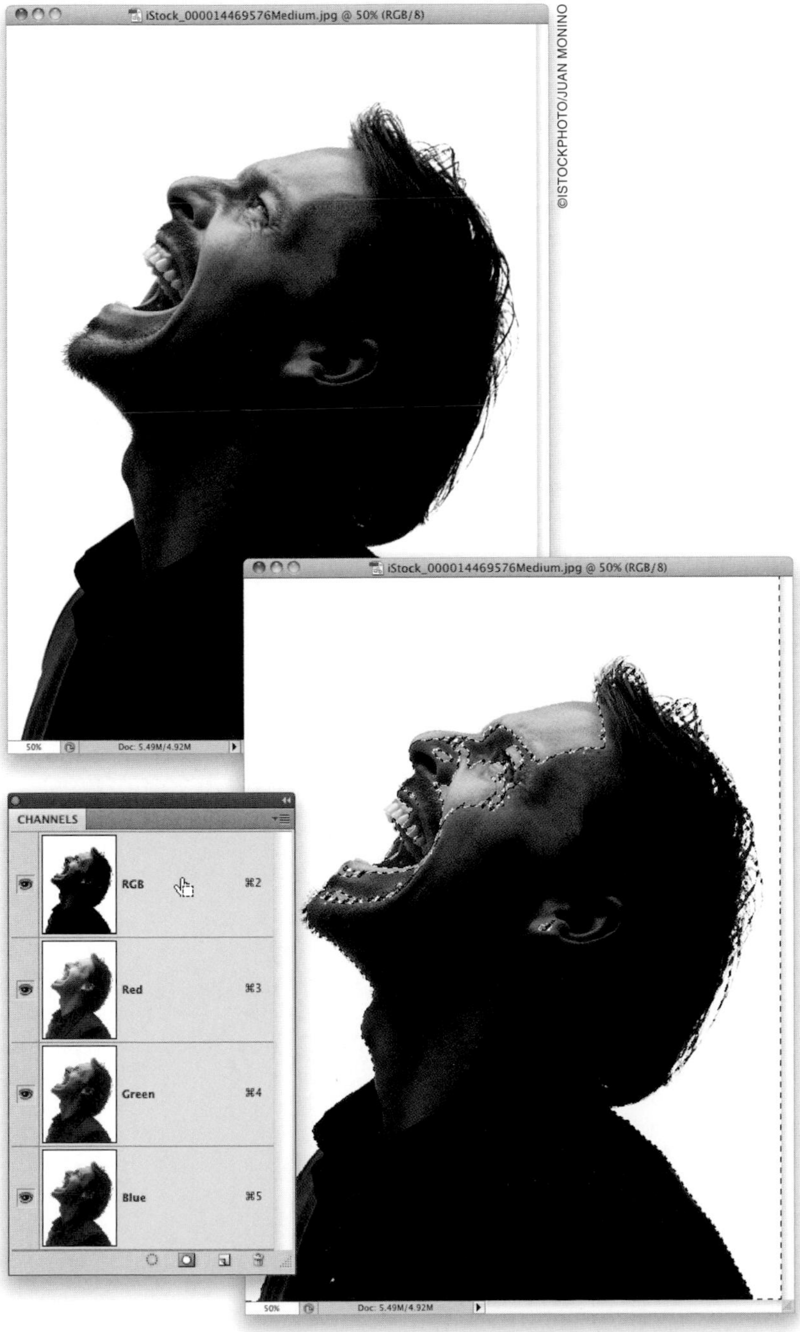

©ISTOCKPHOTO/JUAN MONINO

STEP ONE:

Start by opening the image we're going to build the silhouette from. Here's an image that has nice drama to it and has the subject on a white background, which will make it easier to extract the silhouette shape.

STEP TWO:

Open the Channels panel (found under the Window menu), press-and-hold the Command (PC: Ctrl) key, and click on the RGB channel to load the luminosity as a selection.

Continued

STEP THREE:

Create a new Alpha channel from this selection by clicking on the Create New Channel icon at the bottom of the Channels panel. Then, press **Shift-Delete (PC: Shift-Backspace)** and set the Fill dialog's Use pop-up menu to **White**. Click OK, then press **Command-D (PC: Ctrl-D)** to Deselect.

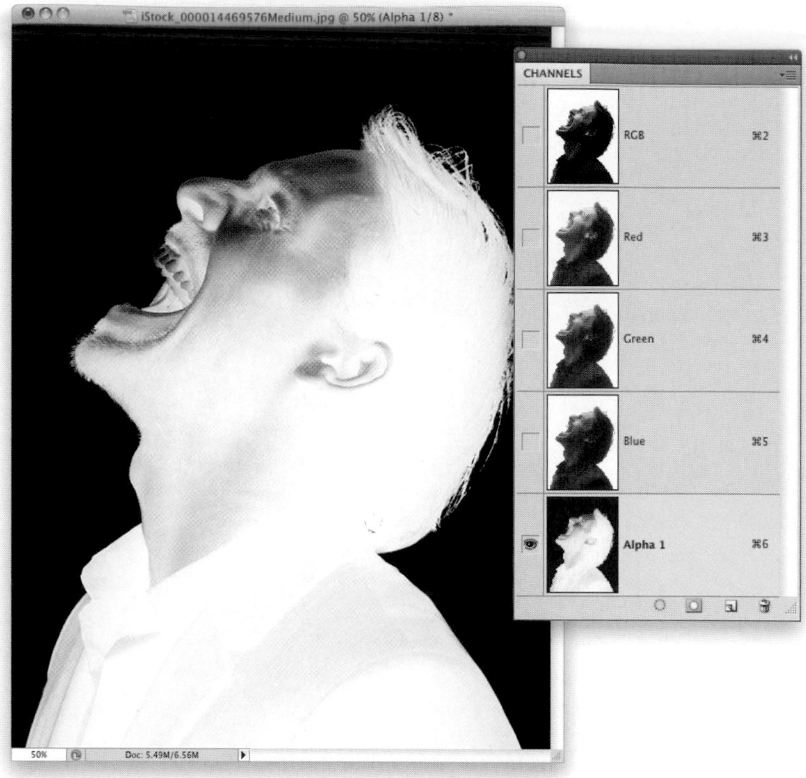

STEP FOUR:

Now press Shift-Delete again, leave the Use pop-up menu set to White, change the Blending Mode to **Overlay**, and click OK. This will make the white area even whiter, while leaving some subtle detail in the face area.

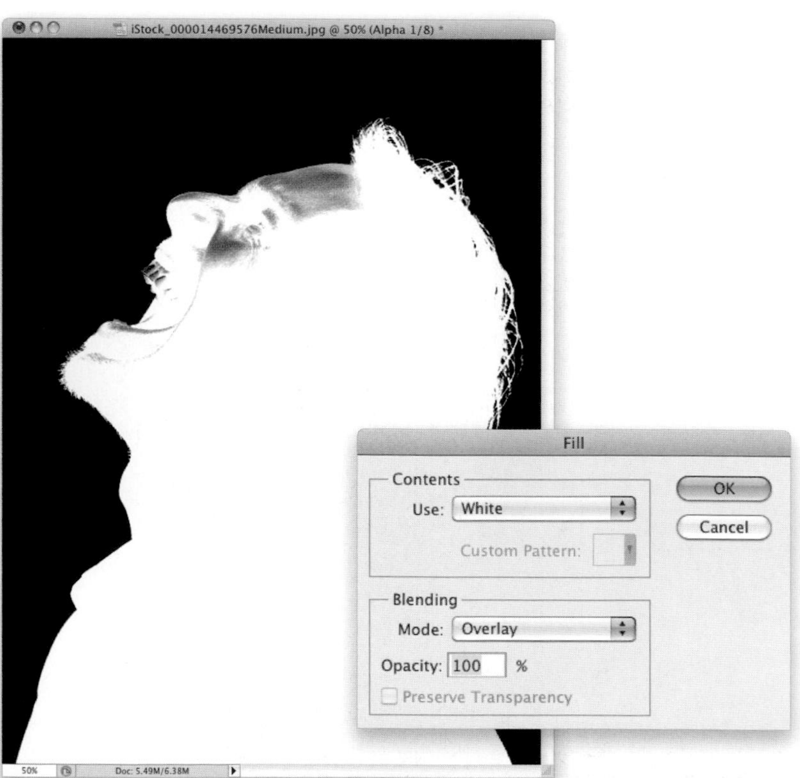

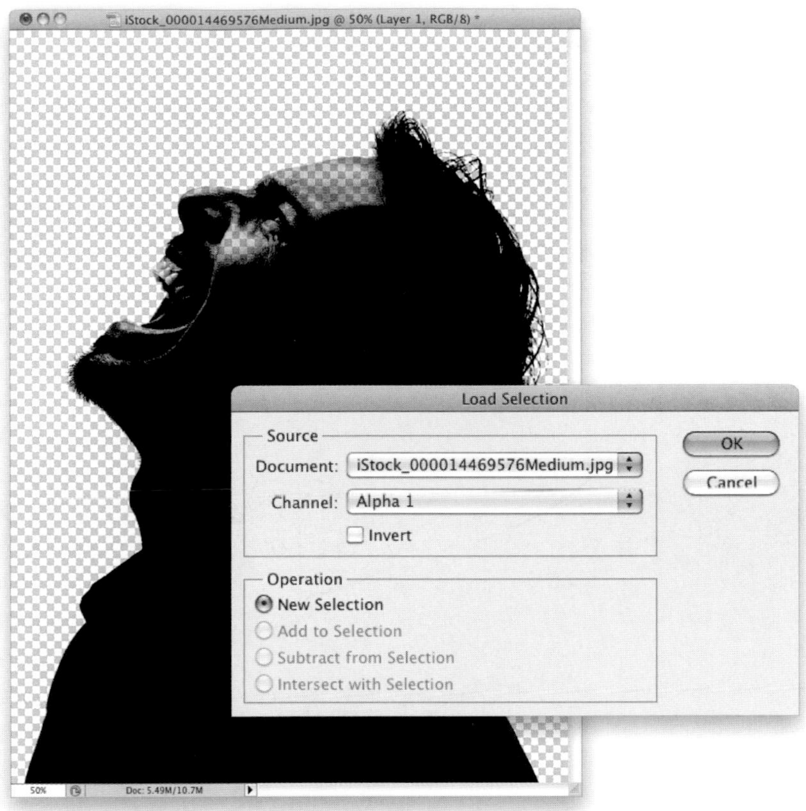

STEP FIVE:

Go back to the Layers panel and click on the Create a New Layer icon at the bottom of the panel. Then, go under the Select menu and choose **Load Selection**. Select **Alpha 1** from the Channel pop-up menu and click OK. Then, use the Fill dialog to fill this selected area with black to create the silhouette effect (I turned off the Background layer here, so you could see it better).

STEP SIX:

Now, open the padded room image that will be composited inside the silhouette. Currently, this image is not very menacing, so we need to make it unpleasant to go along with the theme of the image. So, click on the Create New Adjustment Layer icon at the bottom of the Layers panel and choose **Hue/Saturation** from the pop-up menu. Turn on the Colorize checkbox, and set the Hue to 190, the Saturation to 69, and the Lightness to –10. This will add a light blue cast to the image. We'll darken it (and make it more menacing) by changing the layer's blend mode to **Linear Burn**.

Continued

STEP SEVEN:

Let's apply a texture to grunge it up a little and make it even less pleasant (or as pleasant as a padded room can be). Open a rough texture file, like the one I have here, and use the Move tool **(V)** to drag it over to the padded room image.

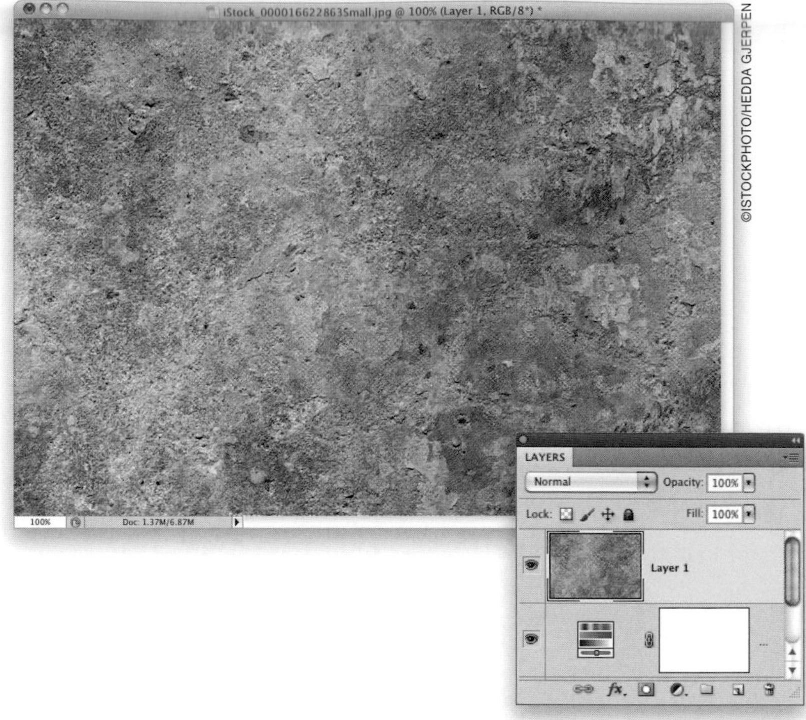

©ISTOCKPHOTO/HEDDA GJERPEN

STEP EIGHT:

Desaturate the color by pressing **Command-Shift-U (PC: Ctrl-Shift-U)**, as we're only interested in the texture and not the color. Change the layer's blend mode to **Overlay** to finish the effect. Then, create a merged copy of this image by pressing **Command-Option-Shift-E (PC: Ctrl-Alt-Shift-E)**.

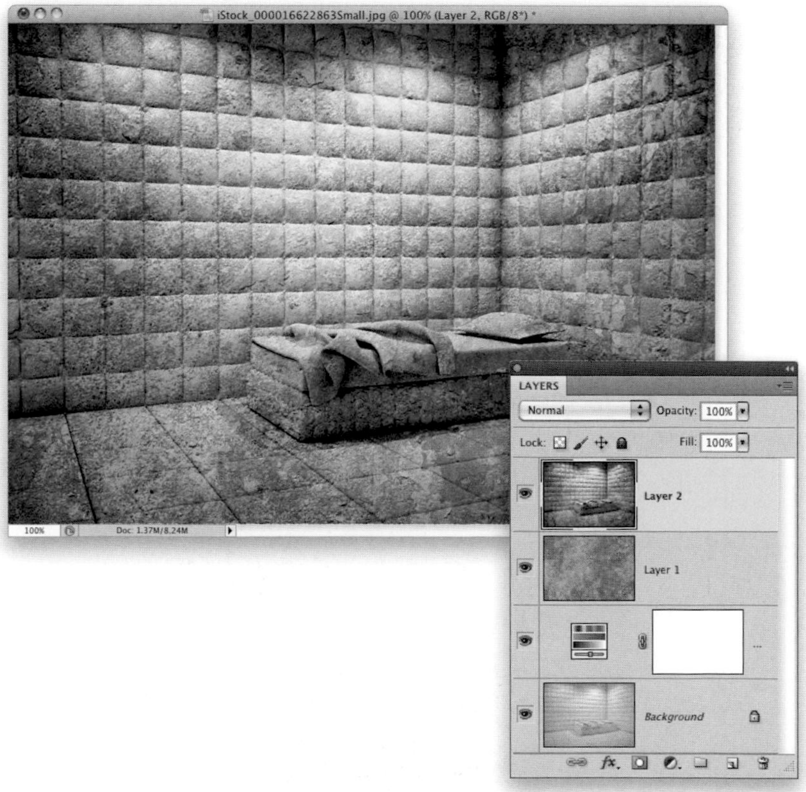

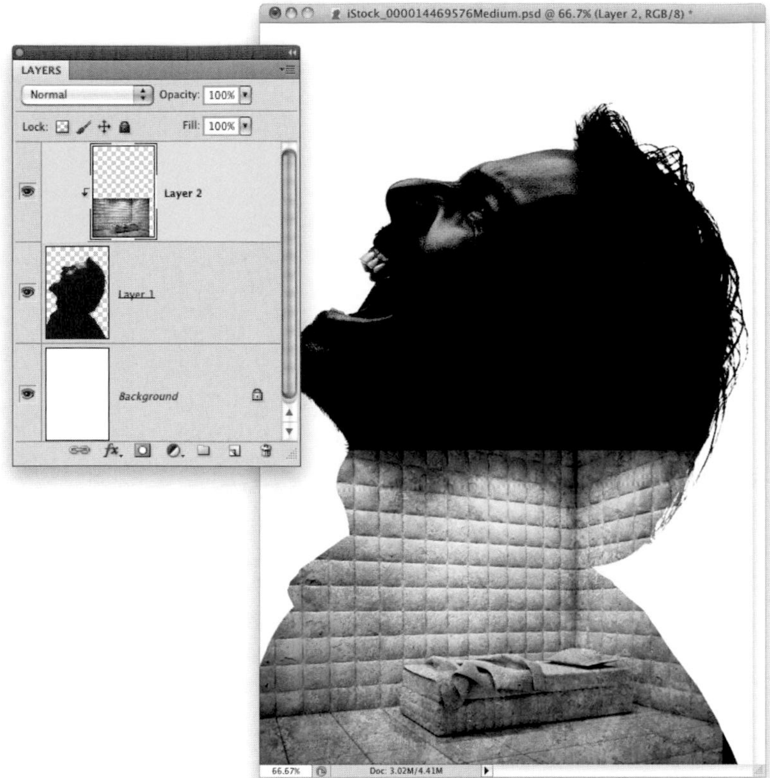

STEP NINE:

Now, use the Move tool to bring this merged layer into the silhouette layout. (I cropped it a little and filled the Background layer with white to give it more of a movie poster feel.) Position the padded room layer just above the silhouette layer and create a clipping group by pressing **Command-Option-G (PC: Ctrl-Alt-G)**. With the Move tool still active, move it around within the document, and position it wherever it looks best. If you need to, you can resize it by pressing **Command-T (PC: Ctrl-T)** to go into Free Transform. Press **Return (PC: Enter)** when you're done.

STEP 10:

Next, click on the Add Layer Mask icon at the bottom of the Layers panel to add a layer mask to the padded room layer. Then, get the Gradient tool **(G)** from the Toolbox, click on the down-facing arrow to the right of the gradient thumbnail in the Options Bar, and choose the Foreground to Transparent gradient in the Gradient Picker (the second one from the left in the top row). Click on the Linear Gradient icon (the first icon to the right of the gradient thumbnail), make sure the tool's Opacity is set to 100%, press **D**, then **X** to set your Foreground and Background colors to their defaults of black and white, and draw out several gradients to fade the image on all four sides, just like you see here.

Continued

STEP 11:

Now, let's add a text layer. Set your Foreground color to white, then get the Horizontal Type tool **(T)**. Here, I have "THE ASYLUM" set in a condensed bold Helvetica. Then, using the Character panel (found under the Window menu) and Free Transform, I scaled and positioned the text across the neck of the silhouette, with each end touching the white edge of the background around him, giving the symbolic effect of strangling the subject, which goes along with the whole theme of the design.

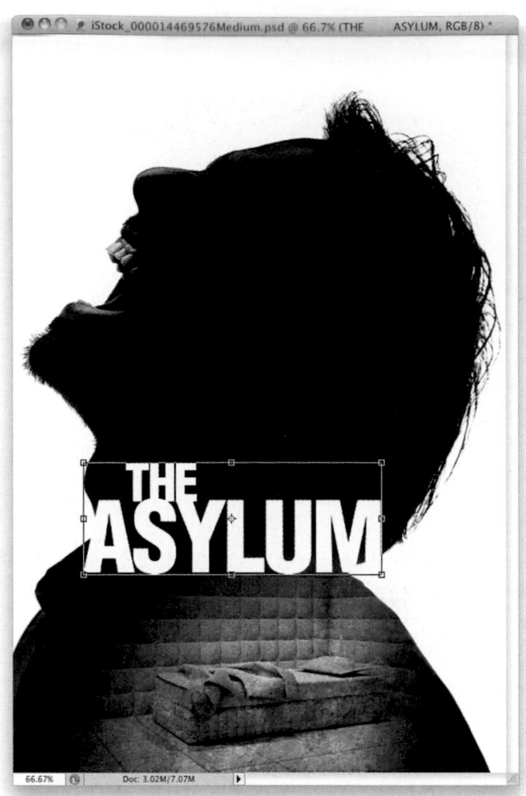

STEP 12:

Now, let's add one more design element. Go to the Toolbox, click-and-hold on the Rectangular Marquee tool to access the other tools beneath it, and choose the Single Row Marquee tool. Click on the Create a New Layer icon to create a new blank layer, then click at the top edge of the word "ASYLUM." This will load a selection across the width of the document that is only 1 pixel tall. Press **Option-Delete (PC: Alt-Backspace)** to fill the selection with your Foreground color (white), and then click to add another selection along the bottom of the text and fill it with white, as well.

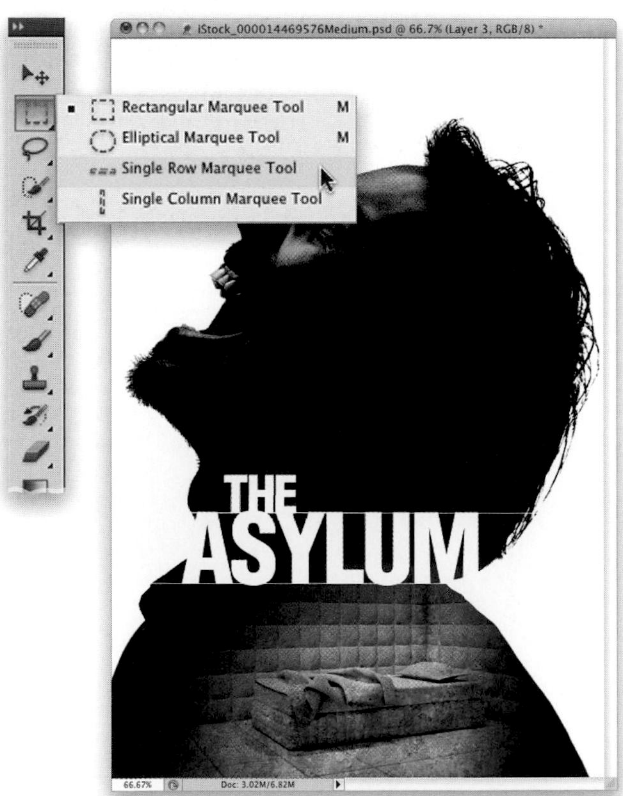

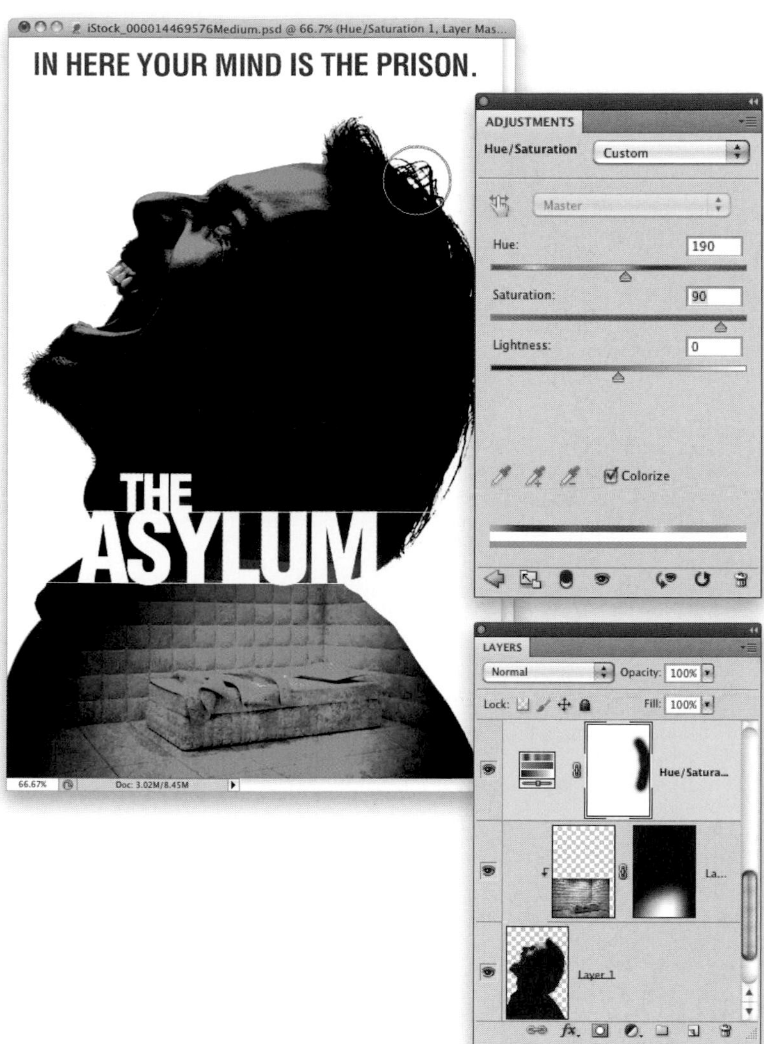

STEP 13:

We need a tagline, too, so we'll use a smaller bold condensed Helvetica. First, though, we'll change the font color to closer match the design, so click on the color swatch in the Options Bar and set it to R: 60, G: 83, B: 92. Now, click near the top of the document and start typing.

To give the little bit of detail in his face some color, go ahead and click on the padded room layer, and add a new Hue/Saturation adjustment layer. In the Adjustments panel, turn on the Colorize checkbox, set the Hue to 190, the Saturation to 90, and leave the Lightness set to 0. Some areas in the hair are picking up the blue color, and it looks kind of messy. So, to fix this, just click on the adjustment layer's mask to select it, then get the Brush tool **(B)**, and with a soft-edged round brush, paint with black in the area of the hair. This will mask away the color effect, keeping it only in the face area.

Continued

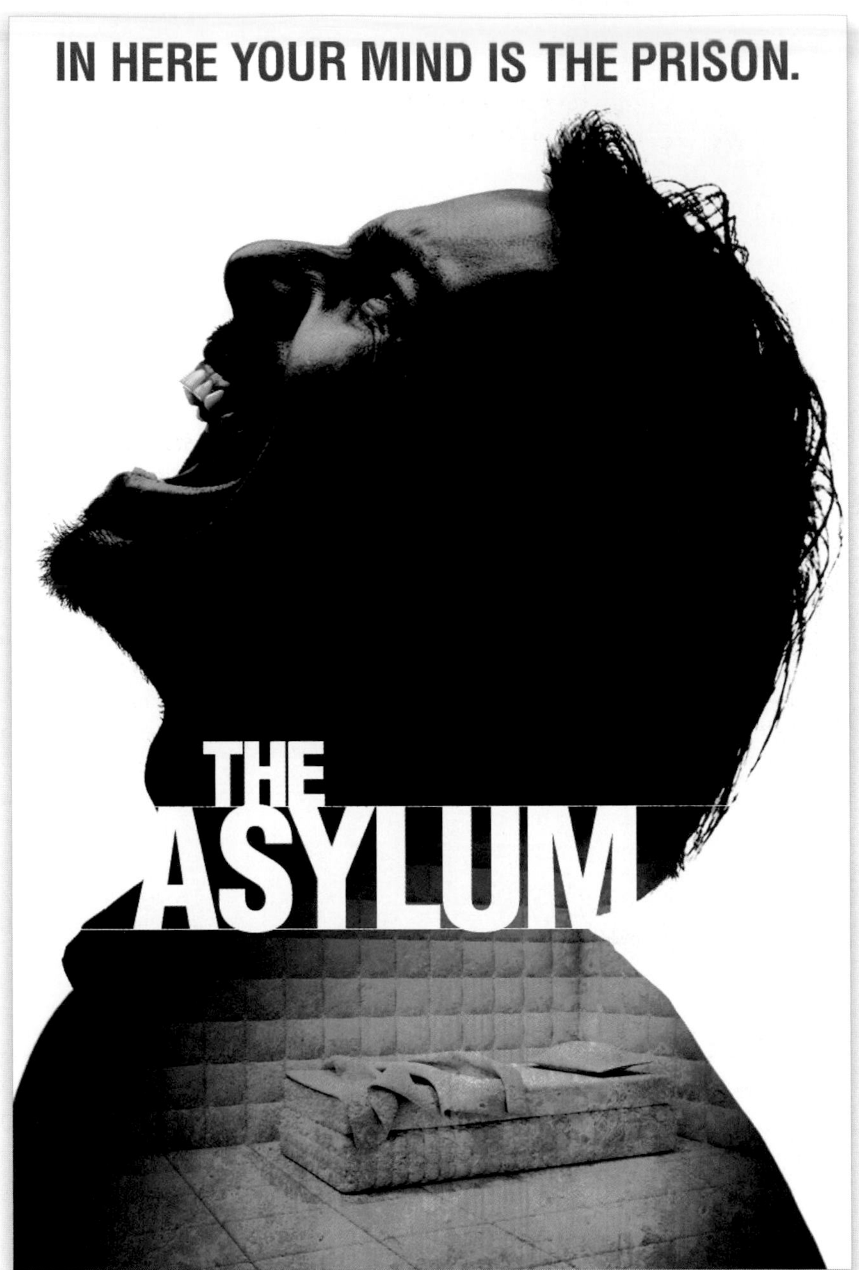
IN HERE YOUR MIND IS THE PRISON.
THE
ASYLUM

Final Image

Advanced Logo Design Effects

This project really gives you a good idea of how powerful Photoshop can be as a design tool for creating logos. With so few tutorials out there on creating complex logo effects, I felt it a necessary venture and found that re-creating the new Fiat logo was a great way to demonstrate what can be done using only Photoshop.

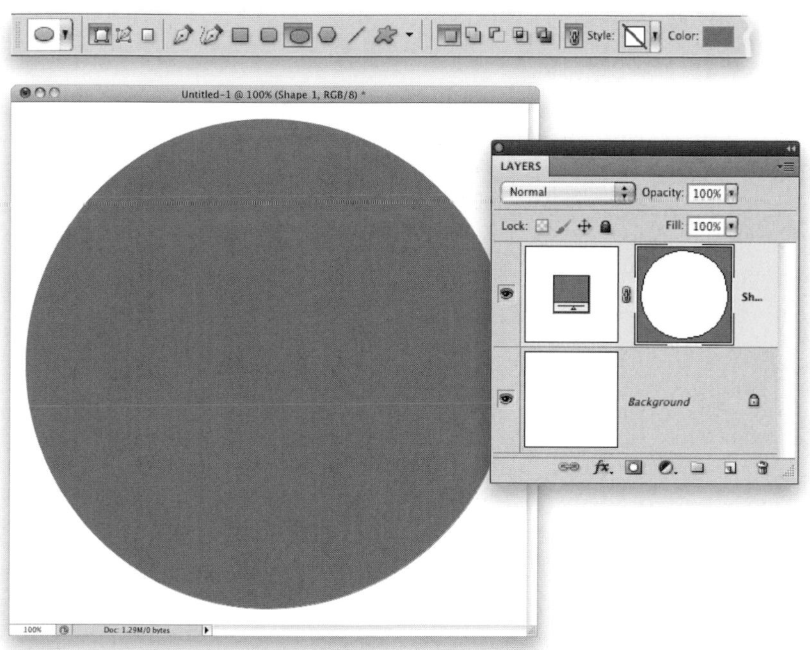

STEP ONE:

From the File menu, choose **New** and create a new document approximately 7 inches by 7 inches at 100 ppi, and set the Background Contents to **White**. Choose the Ellipse tool in the Toolbox (it's nested with the other Shape tools), and, in the Options Bar, click on the Shape Layers icon (the first icon on the left to the right of the tool thumbnail). Also, click on the color swatch (at the far-right end of the Options Bar) and set the color to a neutral gray. Then, press-and-hold the Shift key, and click-and-drag out a large circle shape that almost reaches the edges of the document.

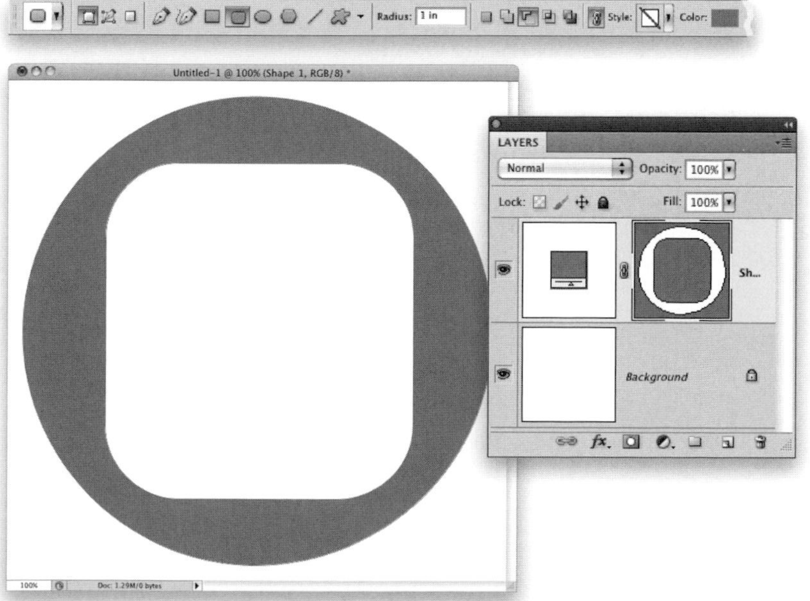

STEP TWO:

Next, choose the Rounded Rectangle tool (also nested with the other Shape tools) and, in the Options Bar, set the corner Radius to 1 inch and then click on the Subtract from Shape Area icon (the third icon to the right of the Radius field). Draw a rounded rectangle shape inside the circle shape.

Continued

STEP THREE:

Now, choose the Direct Selection tool (which is nested with the Path Selection tool) from the Toolbox and use it to select just the top control handles of the rounded rectangle. Just click-and-drag over the points to select them, or Shift-click on each one directly. The selected points are solid and the unselected points are hollow. With these top control points selected, press **Command-T (PC: Ctrl-T)** to put them in Free Transform mode. Then, press-and-hold the Option (PC: Alt) key while clicking on either one of the side handles and drag outward to make the shape a bit wider at the top than at the bottom. Press **Return (PC: Enter)** to lock in the transformation.

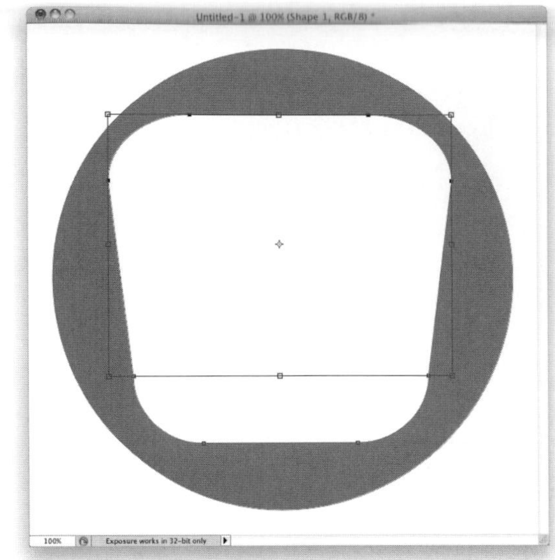

STEP FOUR:

Let's give the outer shape of the logo a little dimension with some creative layer style effects. Click on the Add a Layer Style icon at the bottom of the Layers panel and choose **Bevel and Emboss** from the pop-up menu. Keep the Style set to **Inner Bevel** and the Technique to **Smooth**. Increase the Depth to 600% and the Size to 100 px. Down in the Shading section, set the Angle to 126° and the Altitude to 42°.

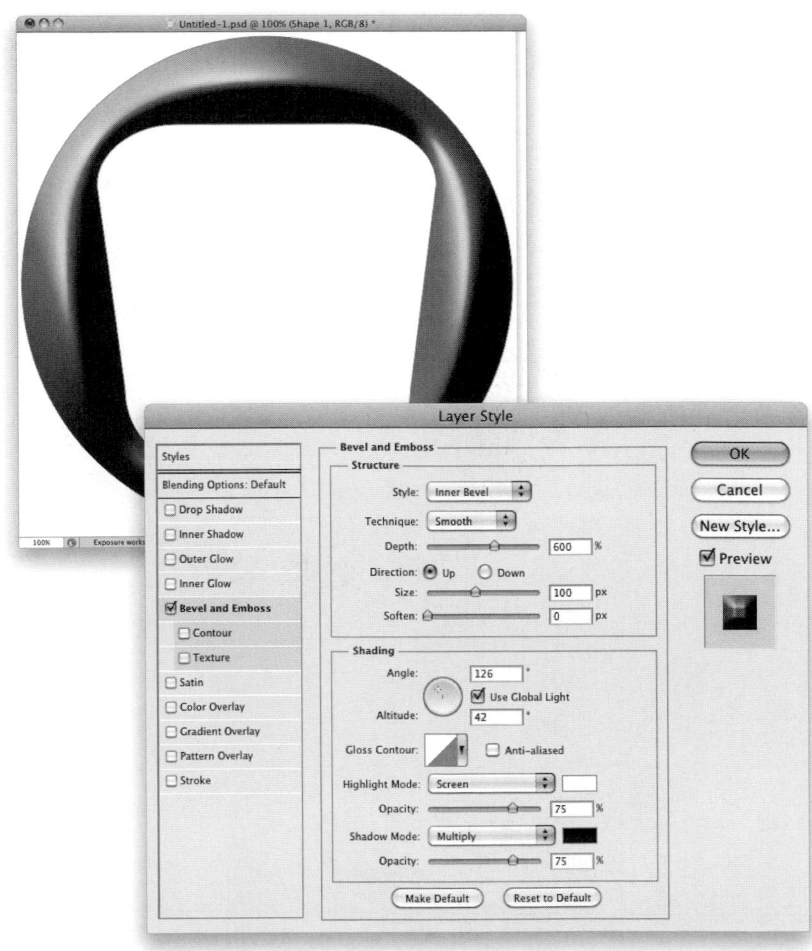

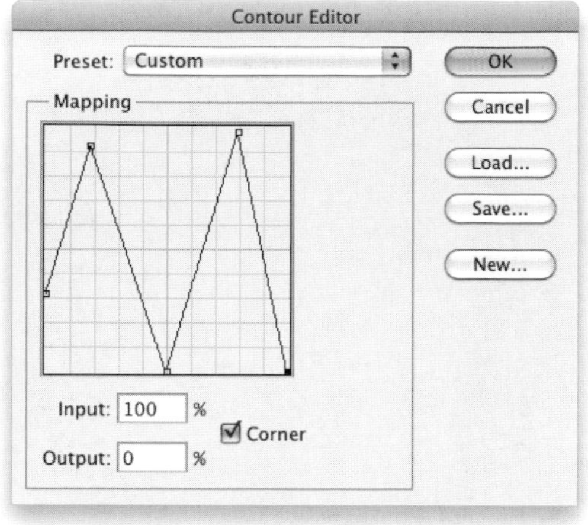

STEP FIVE:

Then, click on the Gloss Contour thumbnail to open the Contour Editor. Here, we can modify the curve of the contour by manipulating the control handles on the curve. You can add control points by clicking directly on the curve. Add the control points and position them as you see here, and make sure that the Corner checkbox is turned on for each control point, so that each one is a sharp corner rather than a curve. Click OK when you're done in the Contour Editor.

STEP SIX:

Now, back in the Bevel and Emboss options, set the Highlight Mode to **Hard Light**, keep the color white, and raise the Opacity to 100%. Then, for the Shadow Mode, just increase the Opacity to 100%. Don't click OK yet.

Continued

STEP SEVEN:

Next, click on Satin on the left side of the dialog to turn it on, and set the Blend Mode to **Screen**. Click on the color swatch and set the numeric value (below the RGB fields) to #bbe1ff. Click OK in the Color Picker to set the color. Then, set the Opacity to 75% and set the Angle to 129°. Increase the Distance to 209 px and the Size to 50 px. Don't click OK yet.

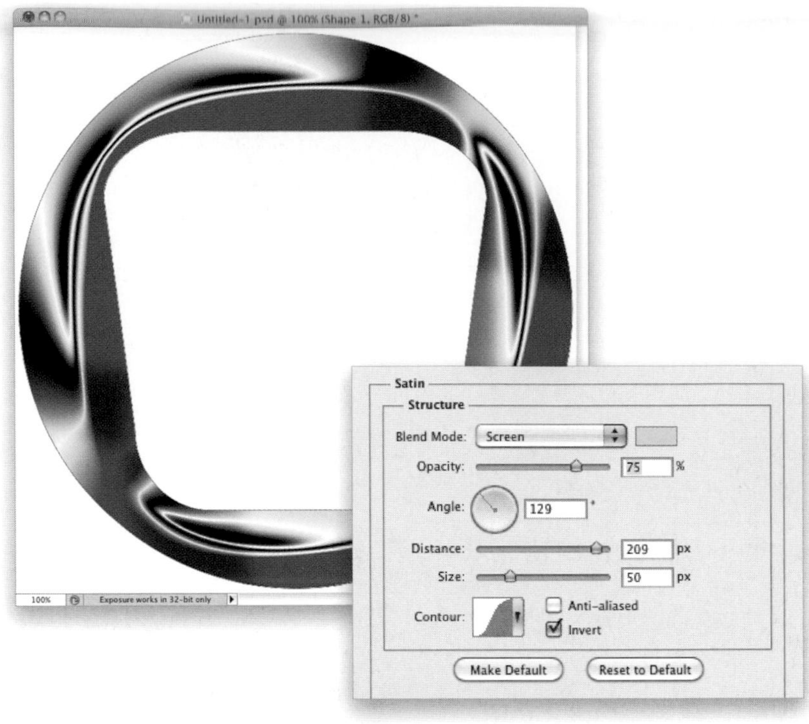

STEP EIGHT:

Lastly, click on Inner Glow on the left to turn it on, and set the Blend Mode here to **Screen**. Set the color to the same color blue we used for the Satin layer style. Then, set the Opacity to 75%, and set the Size to 49 px. Now click OK. You can see the result gives us a realistic chrome look, all with layer styles. Be sure to experiment with the layer styles because, like with brushes, they can be combined and mixed in ways you may have never even considered.

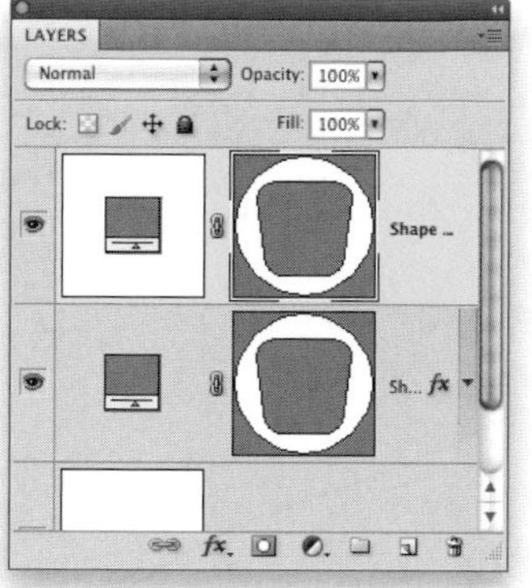

STEP NINE:

Now, we want to define the edge more with another bevel effect, but the Bevel and Emboss layer style is already in use. No problem, we'll just make a duplicate of this layer by pressing **Command-J (PC: Ctrl-J),** and delete the layer style on the duplicate layer by grabbing the *fx* icon on the layer and dragging it to the Trash icon at the bottom of the Layers panel.

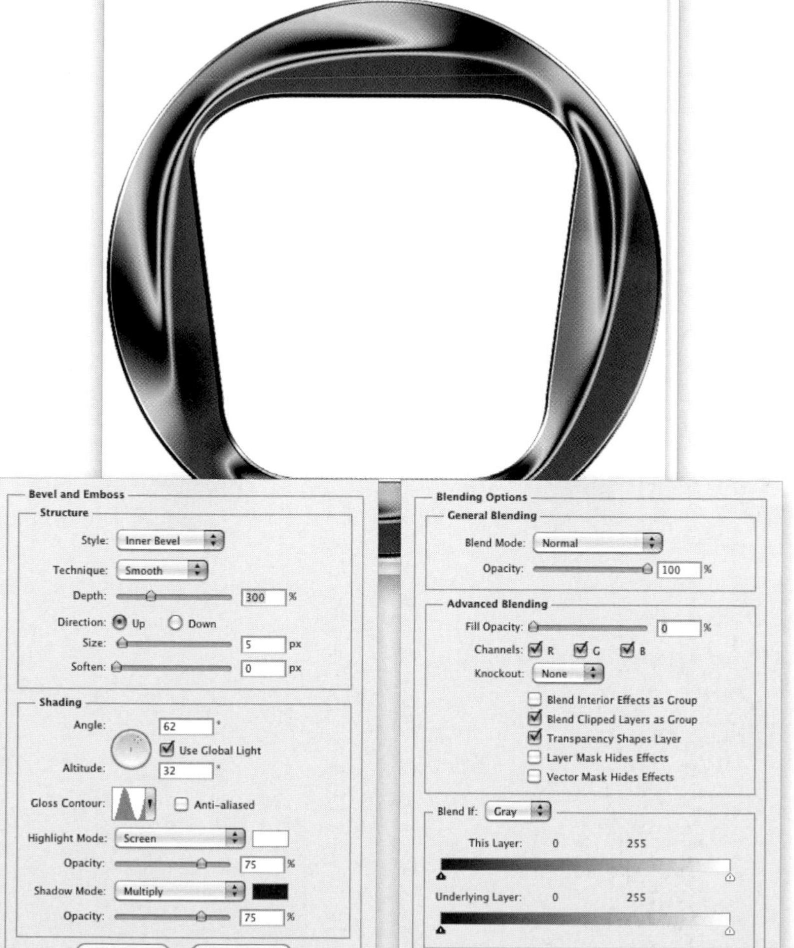

STEP 10:

Click on the Add a Layer Style icon once again, and choose **Bevel and Emboss** to add a new effect. Increase the Depth setting to 300% and set the size to 5 px. Then, go into the Shading section and set the Angle to 62° and Altitude to 32°. Next, click on the down-facing arrow next to the Gloss Contour thumbnail and choose Ring Contour (it's the second one in the second row). Now, to blend this bevel with the original shape, click on Blending Options at the top left and, under Advanced Blending, lower the Fill Opacity to 0%. This will make the duplicate gray shape invisible, leaving only the bevel effect, which now blends into the original shape.

Continued

STEP 11:

This would be a good time to save if you have not already! After that, create a duplicate of this file by choosing Image>**Duplicate**, because we'll need to create a displacement file out of the graphic up to this point. In the duplicate file, click on the Background layer to make it active, then press **Shift-Delete (PC: Shift-Backspace)**, and choose **50% Gray** from the Fill dialog's Use pop-up menu. Go to Layer>**Flatten Image** and flatten the image. Save this file to your desktop as a PSD file, so we can load it as a displacement map.

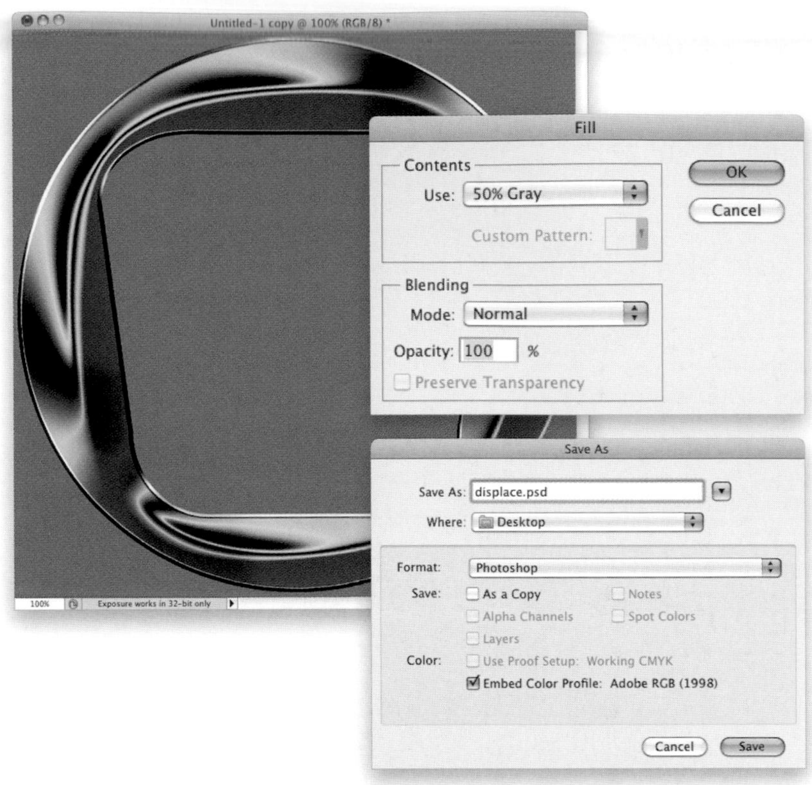

STEP 12:

Now, here, we have a simple beach image that we'll use as the reflected image on the chrome surface. Press **Command-Shift-U (PC: Ctrl-Shift-U)** to remove the color, then use the Move tool **(V)** to bring it into your working logo file and place it at the top of the layer stack. Once there, use Free Transform (press Command-T [PC: Ctrl-T]) to scale it to cover the entire canvas area, press Return (PC: Enter), then press **Command-A (PC: Ctrl-A)** to select everything. Once the entire canvas is selected, go under the Image menu and choose **Crop** to get rid of any parts that extend beyond the edge, as this will affect the positioning of the displacement.

©ISTOCKPHOTO/IAKOV KALININ

STEP 13:

You might think we're going to apply the displacement map using the Displace filter. Nope! We're actually going to use the Glass filter. This will give a much smoother distortion. So, go under the Filter menu, under Distort, and choose **Glass**. In the Glass filter dialog, click on the small icon to the right of the Texture pop-up menu, and from the flyout menu, choose **Load Texture**. When the Load Texture dialog opens, locate the displacement map file, then click Load (PC: Open). Set the Distortion to 17 and the Smoothness to 3, then click OK.

STEP 14:

Now, Option-click-and-drag (PC: Alt-click-and-drag) the vector mask from the Shape layer just below the beach image layer up to the beach image layer, as seen here. This will copy the vector mask to the beach image, masking it just like the Shape layers. Finally, change the top layer's blend mode to **Overlay** to blend the image to the chrome effect.

Continued

STEP 15:

Okay, let's build the inside of the logo. Get the Direct Selection tool and click on the inside shape of any of the Shape layers. Open the Paths panel (Window> **Paths**) and click on the Load Path as a Selection icon (the third icon from the left) at the bottom of the panel to load this path as an active selection. Because this inner path was set to Subtract from Shape Area when it was created, the selection is inversed. Just press **Command-Shift-I (PC: Ctrl-Shit-I)** to Inverse the selection, so that the inside of the logo is selected.

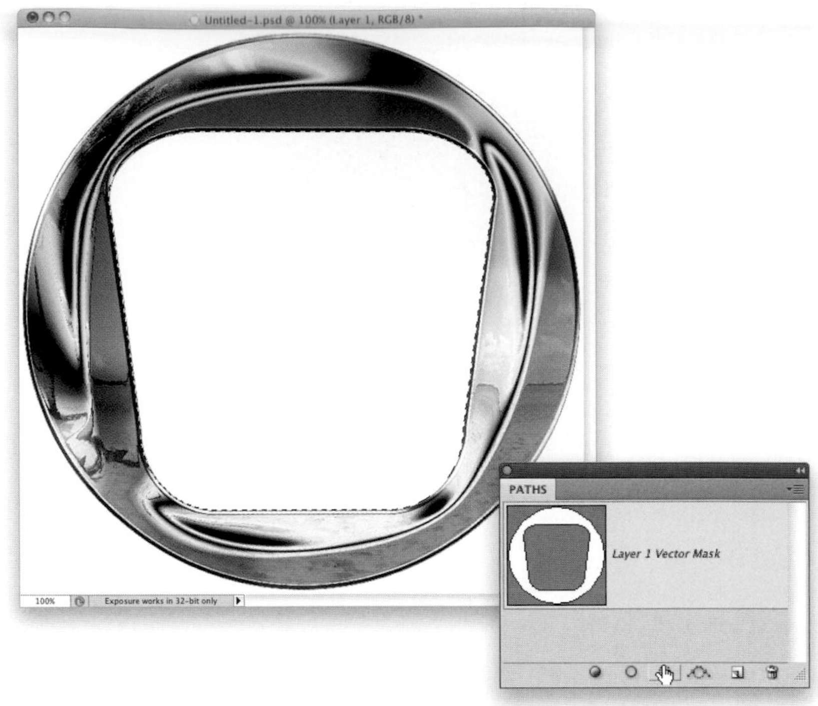

STEP 16:

Next, click on the Create a New Layer icon at the bottom of the Layers panel to create a new blank layer and make sure it appears at the top of your layer stack. Then, click on your Foreground color swatch and set it to a red (I used R: 103, G: 0, B: 0). Press **Option-Delete (PC: Alt-Backspace)** to fill the selection with your Foreground color, then **Command-D (PC: Ctrl-D)** to Deselect. Now, add an Inner Glow layer style, and set the Blend Mode to **Multiply** and the Opacity to 75%. Then, click on the color swatch and change the color to black. After that, go into the Elements section and set the Choke to 29% and the Size to 59 px, but don't click OK yet.

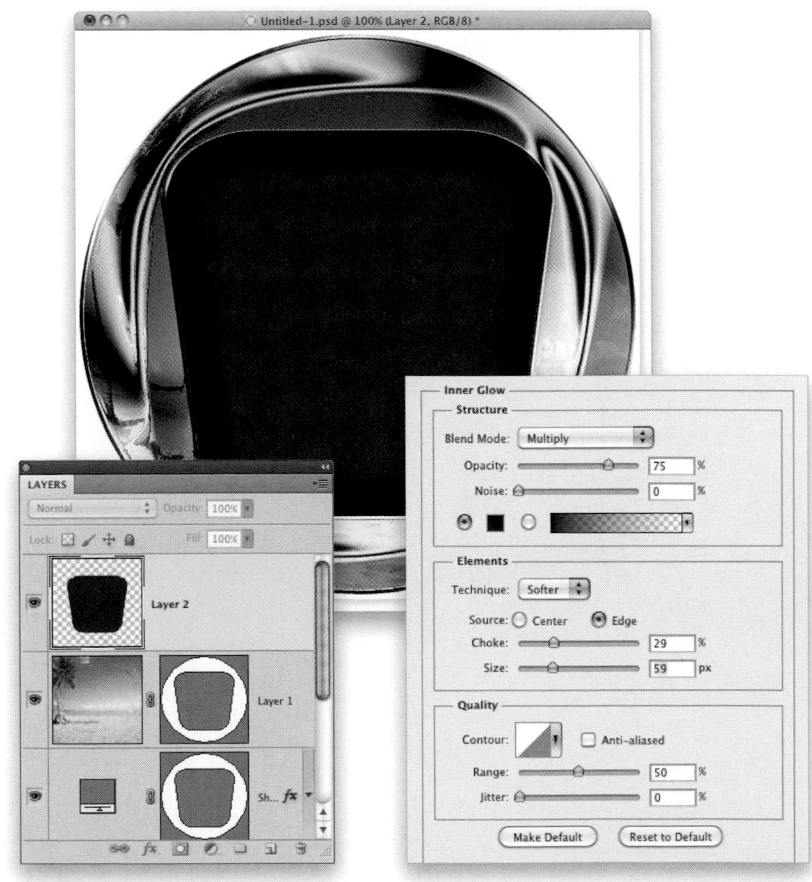

STEP 17:

Next, click on Satin on the left side of the Layer Style dialog to turn it on. Set the Blend Mode to **Color Dodge**, and click on the color swatch and choose a light pink color. Here, I used R: 247, G: 202, B: 202. Set the Opacity to 50%, the Angle to 105°, the Distance to 73 px, and the Size to 43 px. Click OK to set these layer styles.

STEP 18:

Lastly, add an Outer Glow layer style (we had to click OK in the last step to get our color set). Click on the color swatch here, and then click on the red area of the logo to sample it. Then, just increase the Size to 10 px and click OK. As you can see, the inner shape has some dimension now and has the appearance of reflecting the red on the edge of the chrome. All with layer styles!

Continued

STEP 19:

Now let's add a halftone line element to complete this center area. Press **D** to set your Foreground color to black, then create a new blank layer and fill it with 50% gray. Go under the Filter menu, under Sketch, and choose **Halftone Pattern**. Choose **Line** from the Pattern Type menu. Set the Size to 1 and the Contrast to 0, and click OK.

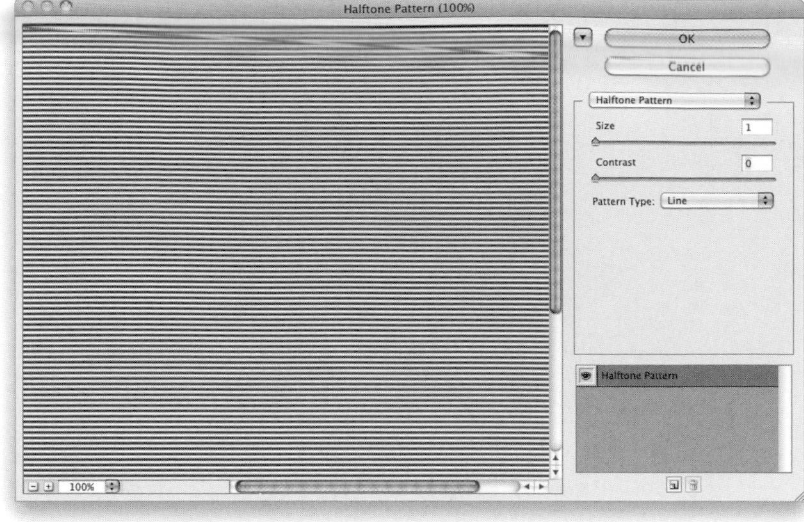

STEP 20:

By default, the Halftone Pattern filter applied the lines horizontally, so go under the Edit menu, under Transform, and choose **Rotate 90° CW**.

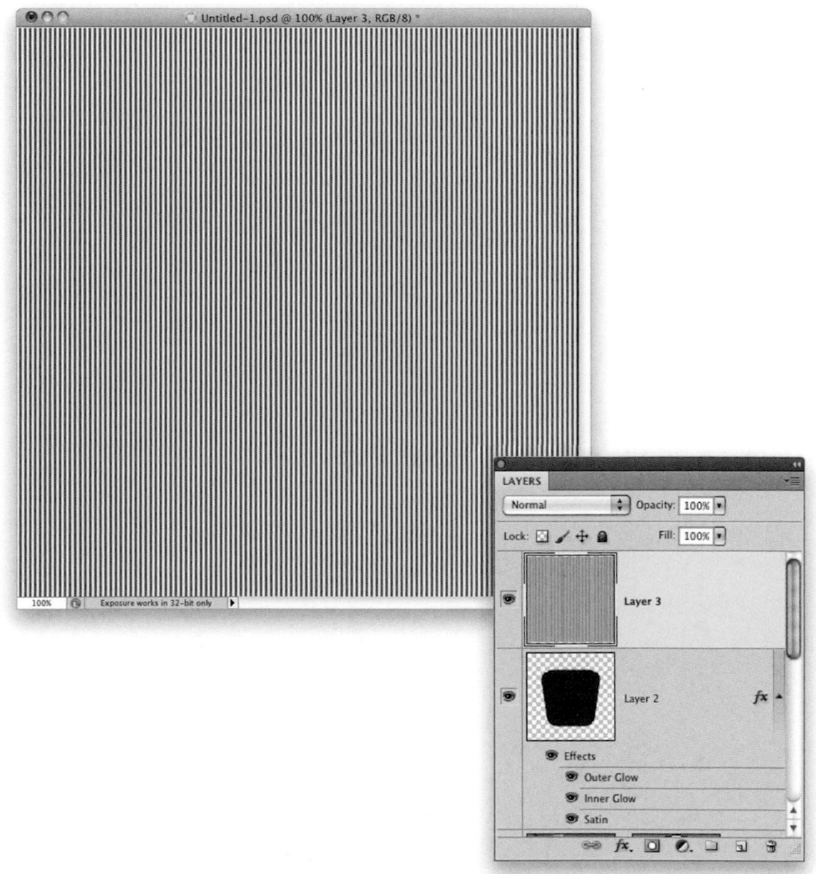

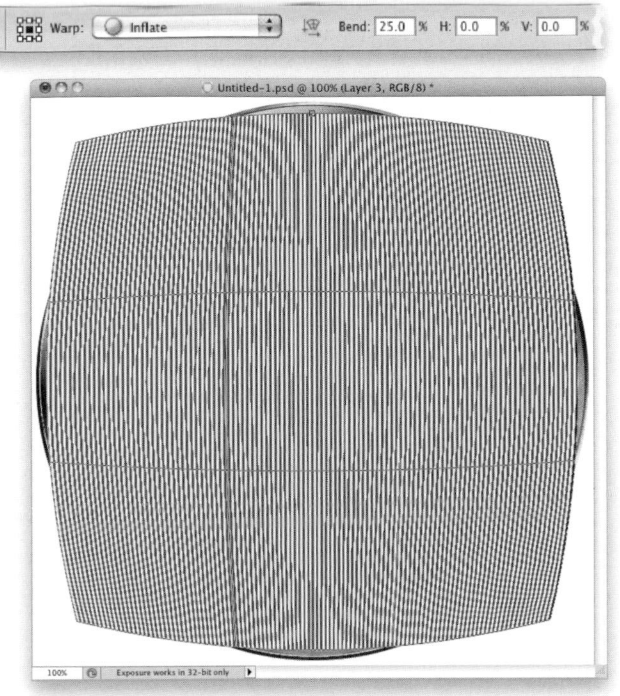

STEP 21:

Go into Free Transform, and scale the pattern down to where it's just a little bigger than the inner logo shape. Then Right-click on it while you're still in Free Transform mode, and choose **Warp**. In the Options Bar, go to the Warp pop-up menu and choose **Inflate**, and then drop the Bend down to 25%. Press **Return (PC: Enter)** to commit the change.

STEP 22:

Press-and-hold the Option (PC: Alt) key and click in between this layer and the layer below to clip the halftone pattern inside the red shape below (your cursor will change into overlapping black and white circles). Then, change the layer's blend mode to **Hard Light** and drop the Opacity to down to 25%.

Continued

STEP 23:

Now let's add one final light effect to the logo. Choose the Elliptical Marquee tool from the Toolbox (or press **Shift-M** until you have it), and draw an oversized selection, positioned slightly off-center, just below the top edge of the chrome, like you see here. Then set your Foreground color to white, and get the Gradient tool **(G)** from the Toolbox. Click on the down-facing arrow next to the gradient thumbnail in the Options Bar to open the Gradient Picker, choose the Foreground to Transparent gradient (the second gradient from the left in the top row), and then click on the Linear Gradient icon (the first icon to the right of the gradient thumbnail). Create a new blank layer, then click to start the gradient just a little bit above the top edge of the active selection and drag the gradient down.

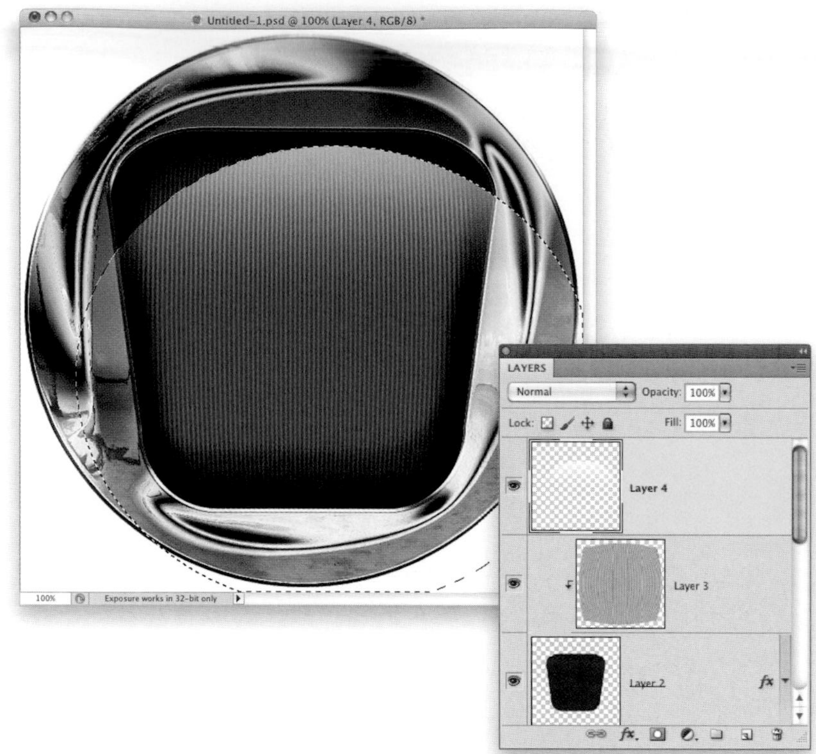

STEP 24:

Deselect, then click on the Add Layer Mask icon at the bottom of the Layers panel to add a white layer mask to this gradient layer. Make sure your Foreground color is now black, and draw a gradient on the left and right edges, so the white gradient doesn't creep into the chrome area. This adds much more dimension to the overall look.

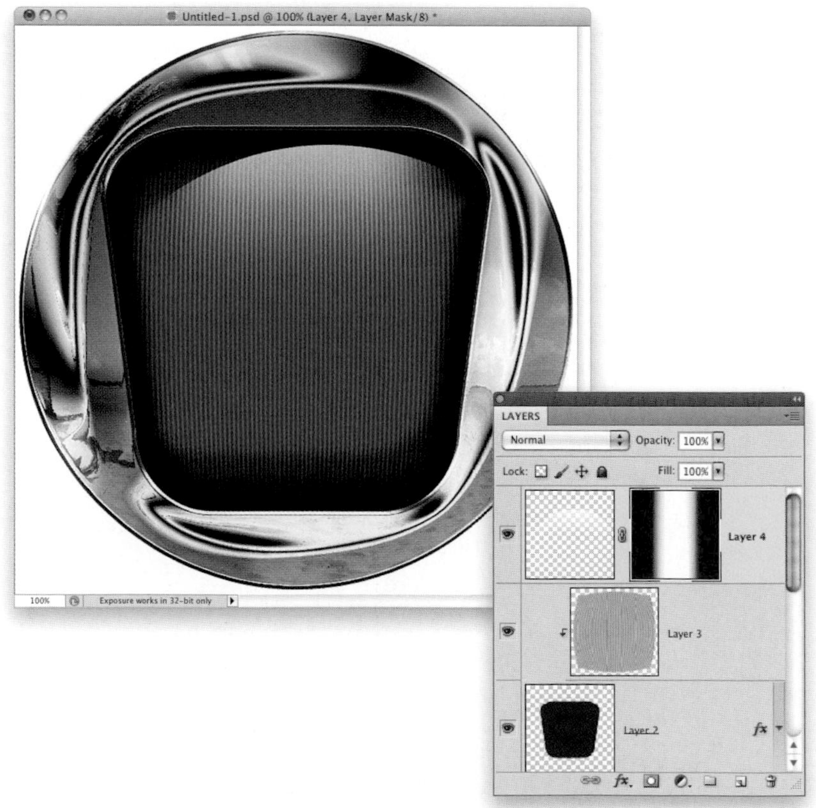

STEP 25:
Finally, let's add the text to the center area. Here, I have set text in a font called Industria, however, almost any condensed font will do.

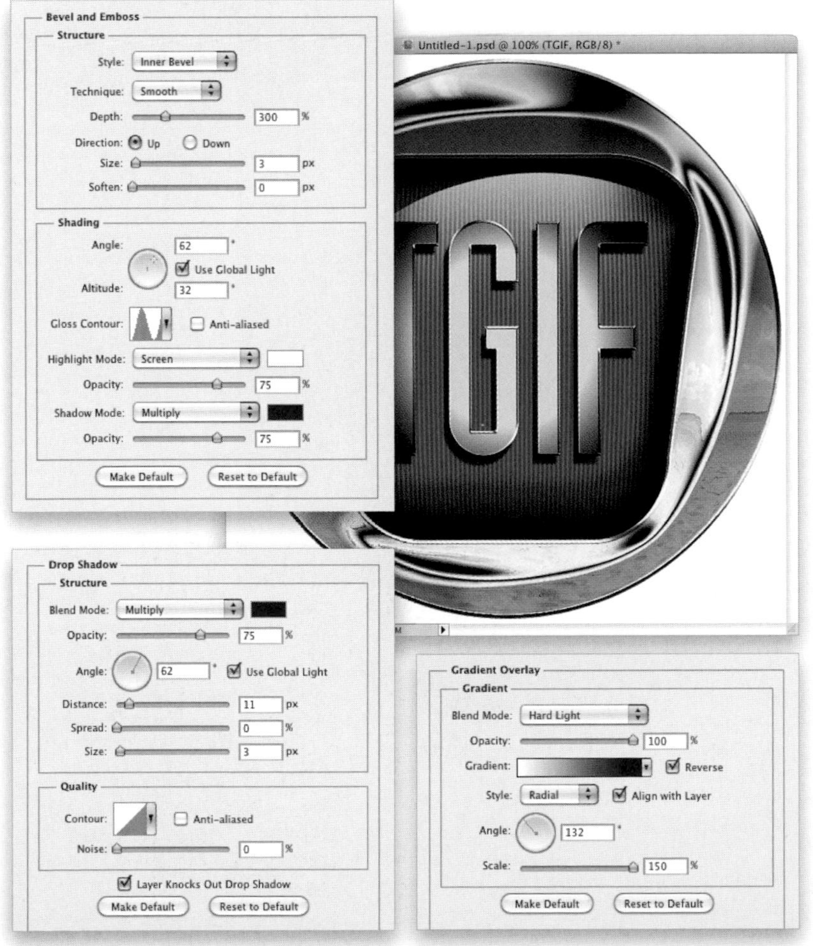

STEP 26:
Now, remember the Bevel and Emboss layer style we added to the second Shape layer earlier to give the chrome a more defined edge? Go and copy that layer style to this text layer (Option-click-and-drag it from the Shape layer). Once it is applied, double-click on the layer style's name to open the Layer Style dialog to tweak the settings. In the Bevel and Emboss options, change the Size to 3 px. Next, click on Drop Shadow on the left to turn it on, and set the Distance to 11 px and the Size to 3 px. Then, click on Gradient Overlay on the left to turn it on. Set the Blend Mode to **Hard Light** and set the Opacity to 100%. Change the gradient Style to **Radial**, set the Angle to 132°, turn on the Reverse checkbox, and increase the Scale all the way to 150%. Click OK.

Continued

STEP 27:

We're gonna want to bring this logo onto another layout, ideally without having to flatten the image in case we need to make changes. So, go ahead and click on the Eye icon to the left of the Background layer to turn it off, then Command-click (PC: Ctrl-click) on all of the layers that make up the logo to select them. Right-click on one of the layers and choose **Convert to Smart Object** to embed them all into a smart object. This will put everything into one layer, but still maintain the layers (you can double-click on the Smart Object thumbnail to open the layered file).

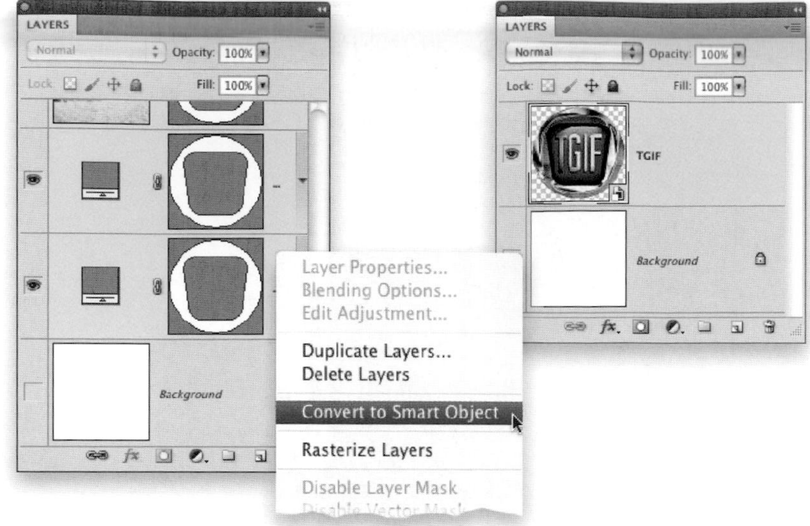

STEP 28:

Let's add the logo to a realistic background to finish the effect. We have a leather background image here that will work perfectly.

©ISTOCKPHOTO/DIANA WALTERS

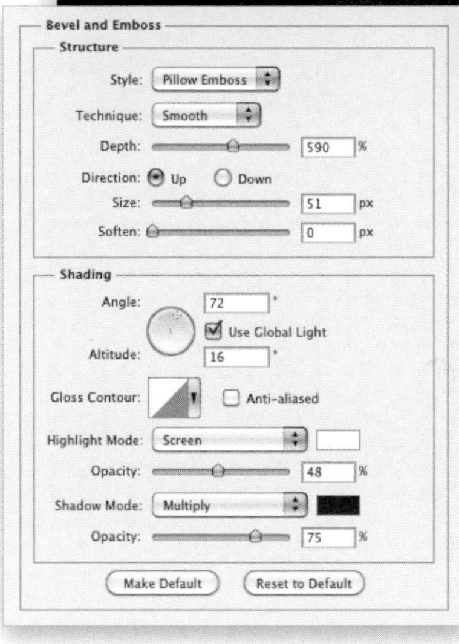

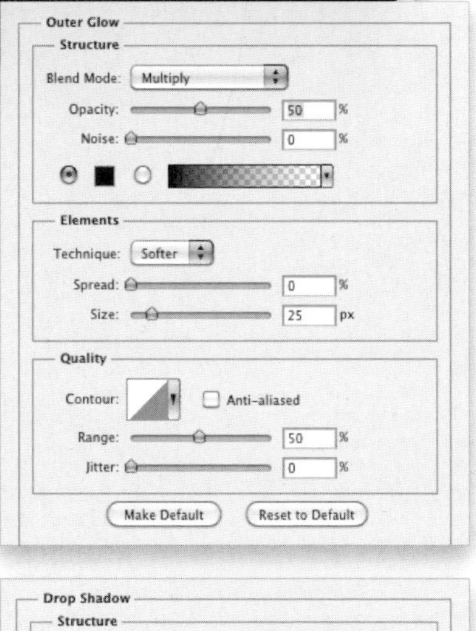

STEP 29:

Go ahead and bring the finished logo smart object into this leather background image, and use Free Transform to scale it down, if you need to. Then, add a Bevel and Emboss layer style. Use the settings here to make it look like the logo is embedded in the leather texture. Next, add an Outer Glow layer style with the settings shown here. Lastly, click on Drop Shadow on the left and make the shadow less strong by dropping the Opacity to 50%, and increasing the size to around 25 px. Turn off the Use Global Light checkbox and click in the image to manually reposition the shadow to the lower left area. Click OK.

Now, at this point it is just nitpicky stuff, as the job is basically done, but if you become an obsessive designer like me, you can fine-tune all day. At some point, you have to find a place to stop. I considered adding a tiny flare using the brush from Chapter 1, but decided it didn't add anything to the image and I should just stop here.

Continued

Final Image

A Word from Our Sponsor

commercial effects

Many designers refer to commercial design work as the type that pays the bills, meaning it's the work you do for commercial clients that doesn't always lend itself to creative work. You are often limited by assets, time, and sometimes input from the client. They always seem to know what they don't want, but never what they actually do want. However, it is under these conditions that you can really test your creativity. My first job out of design school was as an ad creator for a newspaper. Notice the title: Ad Creator, not Graphic Designer. The title alone limited my creativity, but I had to start somewhere. I pressed on to do the best I could and learned a lot. For one thing, I learned the value of speed. Because of daily deadlines, I was constantly in a pinch. As stressful as this sounds, I received more assignments beyond the scope of an ad creator because I showed higher proficiency. As a result, today I am able to infuse my own design style and still turn around projects, like commercial work, really quickly. So, don't look at commercial work as a burden on your creativity. Use it to challenge your imagination to come up with creative solutions.

Design with Grid Elements

I actually saw this effect in a movie poster, but it definitely has a number of uses. Once the base grid is created, you can add just about any image for any purpose. While we're creating the effect, try to be open-minded as to different ways of using this technique for different types of design scenarios.

STEP ONE:

Go under the File menu, choose **New**, and create a new document that's 9 inches wide by 12 inches tall at 125 ppi, and make sure the Background Contents pop-up menu is set to **White**.

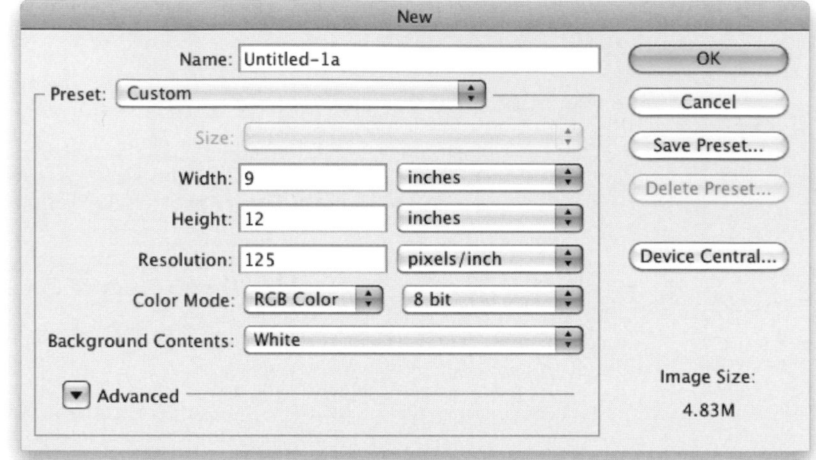

STEP TWO:

Go under the Photoshop (PC: Edit) menu, under Preferences, and choose **Guides, Grid, & Slices**. Since we want to create four squares across, in the Grid section, enter 2.25 in the Gridline Every field and leave its pop-up menu set to **Inches**. Then, enter 1 in the Subdivisions field below. The default gray color to the right would work fine, but I prefer something more visible. So, click on the color swatch and choose a different color. Here, I've chosen a shade of green. Click OK when you're done.

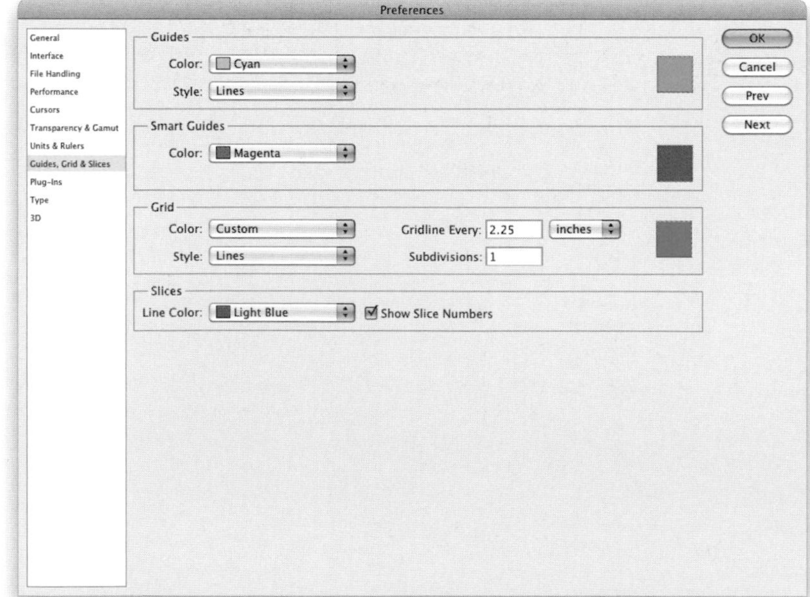

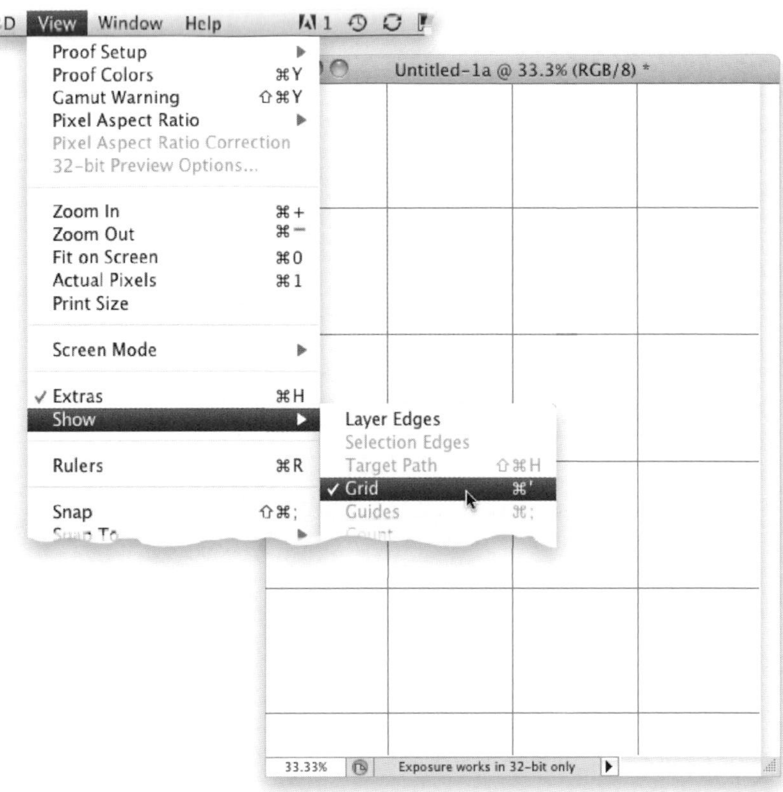

STEP THREE:

Go under the View menu, under Show, and choose **Grid**. In your image window, you should now see a 4-column grid going across the canvas.

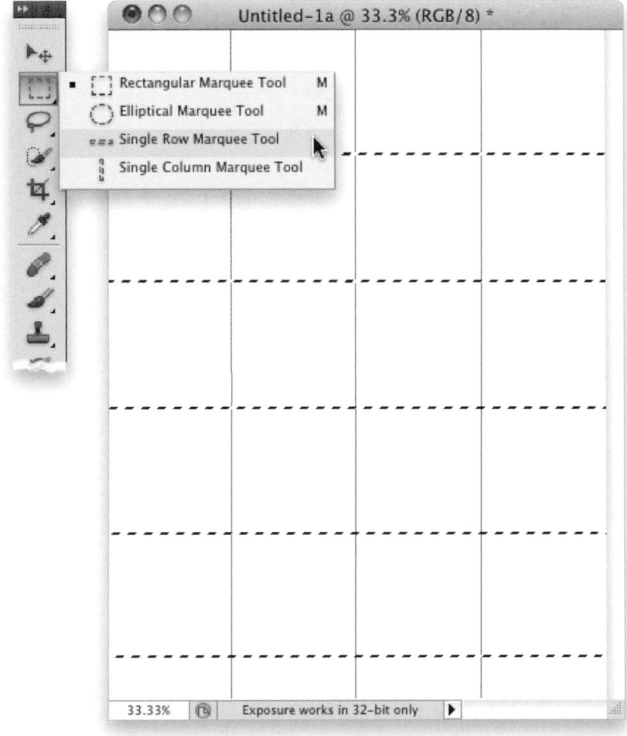

STEP FOUR:

In the Toolbox, click-and-hold on the Rectangular Marquee tool, and choose the Single Row Marquee tool. Click on the first horizontal grid line at the top of the document and it will add a selection 1-pixel high and the width of the document, snapping to the grid line. Then press-and-hold the Shift key (to add to the existing selection) and click on the other horizontal grid lines to add selections to them.

Continued

STEP FIVE:

Next, go into the Toolbox and grab the Single Column Marquee tool (also nested beneath the Rectangular Marquee tool) and use the same process to add selections to the vertical grid lines (remember to press-and-hold the Shift key to add to the existing selection). Once the selections are made, click on the Create a New Layer icon at the bottom of the Layers panel to create a new blank layer. Press **D** to set your Foreground and Background colors to their defaults of black and white, and then press **Command-Delete (PC: Ctrl-Backspace)** to fill the selections with white. Press **Command-D (PC: Ctrl-D)** to Deselect and then press **Command-'** (apostrophe; **PC: Ctrl-'**) to turn off the grid.

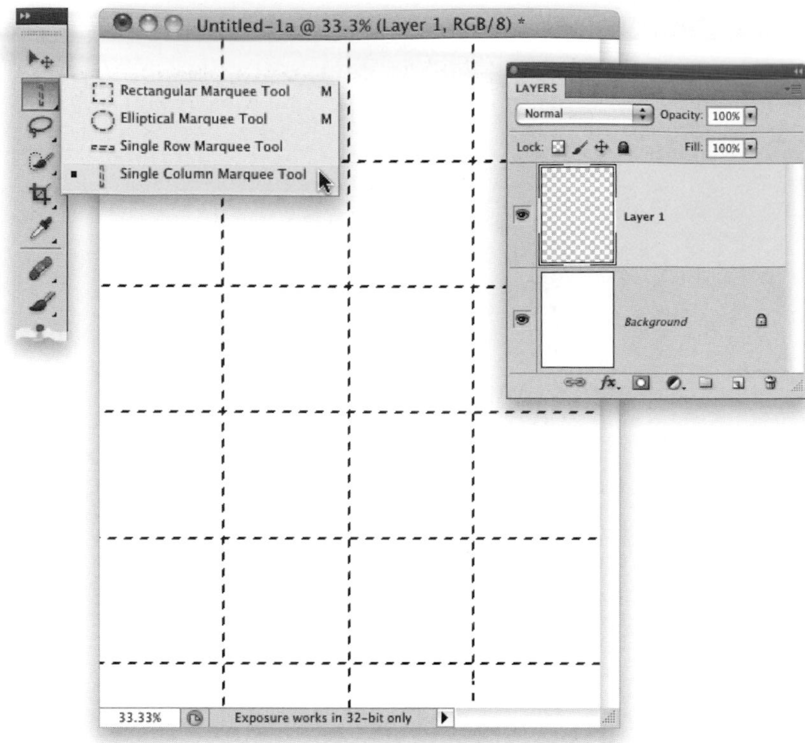

STEP SIX:

Open the model shot we're going to use in the design (or whatever image you might want to use). I liked this image, because of the lighting and the positioning of the model in the composition. Switch to the Move tool **(V)** and click-and-drag (or copy-and-paste) this image into the grid layout file.

STEP SEVEN:

Click-and-drag this image layer beneath the grid layer in the Layers panel. Then, position the image at the top edge of the canvas, like you see here.

STEP EIGHT:

Click on the Add Layer Mask icon at the bottom of the Layers panel to add a layer mask to the model layer and then select the Gradient tool **(G)** from the Toolbox. In the Options Bar, click on the down-facing arrow to the right of the gradient thumbnail and choose the Foreground to Transparent gradient (the second gradient from the left in the top row), and then click on the Linear Gradient icon to the right of the gradient thumbnail. Press **X** to set your Foreground color to black, and then click-and-drag the gradient up just a little bit, starting at the bottom edge of the photo, to fade the image into the white background.

Continued

STEP NINE:

Now, to make the grid lines a little thicker, we'll use a simple layer style. Click on your grid layer (Layer 1) to make it active, then click on the Add a Layer Style icon at the bottom of the Layers panel and choose **Stroke**. Click on the Color swatch and set the color to white. Then, set the Size to 2 px and make sure the Position pop-up menu is set to **Outside**. Click OK.

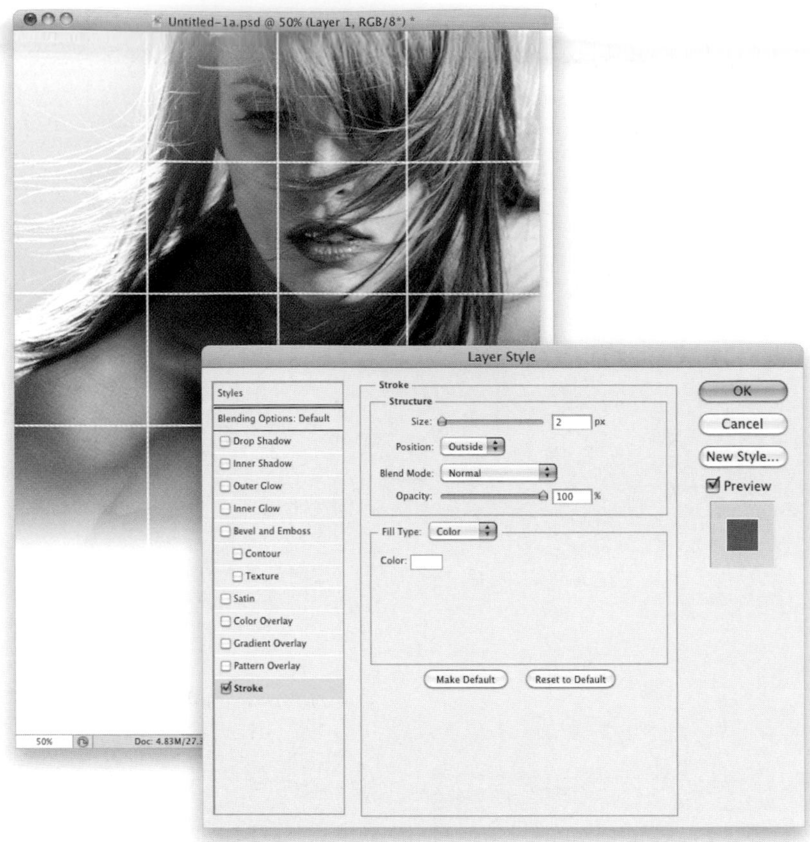

STEP 10:

Now, click back on the layer of the model to make it active and press **Command-J (PC: Ctrl-J)** to make a duplicate of it. Then, press **Command-Shift-U (PC: Ctrl-Shift-U)** to remove the color from this duplicate layer. Go under the Filter menu, under Distort, and choose **Diffuse Glow**. Set the Graininess to 3, the Glow Amount to 5, and the Clear Amount to 10. This will blow out the highlights a bit and give us a stylish grain over the whole image. Click OK. (*Note:* These settings will vary with different images, so be sure to experiment with other settings to get the look you want.)

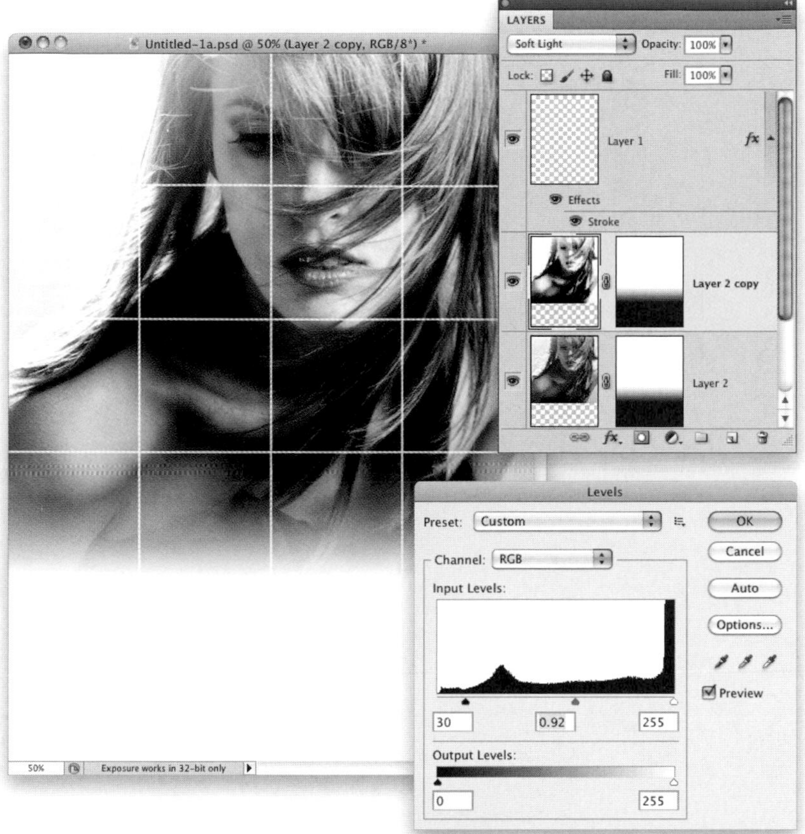

STEP 11:

As a result of the Diffuse Glow filter, the image is left a little flat. However, you can tighten up the contrast a bit by pressing **Command-L (PC: Ctrl-L)** and running a simple Levels adjustment. You can see here, I've adjusted the Input Levels shadows (black) and midtones (gray) sliders to darken the shadow areas. Next, change the layer's blend mode to **Soft Light**, which will add some stylish contrast to the image.

STEP 12:

Now, back to the grid layer. Click on it to activate it again, then select the Magic Wand tool from the Toolbox (or press **Shift-W** until you have it), and click inside one of the squares. Press-and-hold the Shift key and select two other squares (like you see here or however many you'd like). Once the selections are made, create a new blank layer, fill the square selections with white, and then deselect.

Continued

STEP 13:

Click back on the grid layer and use the Magic Wand tool, once again, to select three more squares. Then, with your Foreground and Background colors set to their defaults of black and white, click on the Create New Adjustment Layer icon at the bottom of the Layers panel and choose **Gradient Map**. This will make the selected grid squares black and white like you see here, giving us a very cool finished effect. Feel free to play around with other adjustments or colors to get different results.

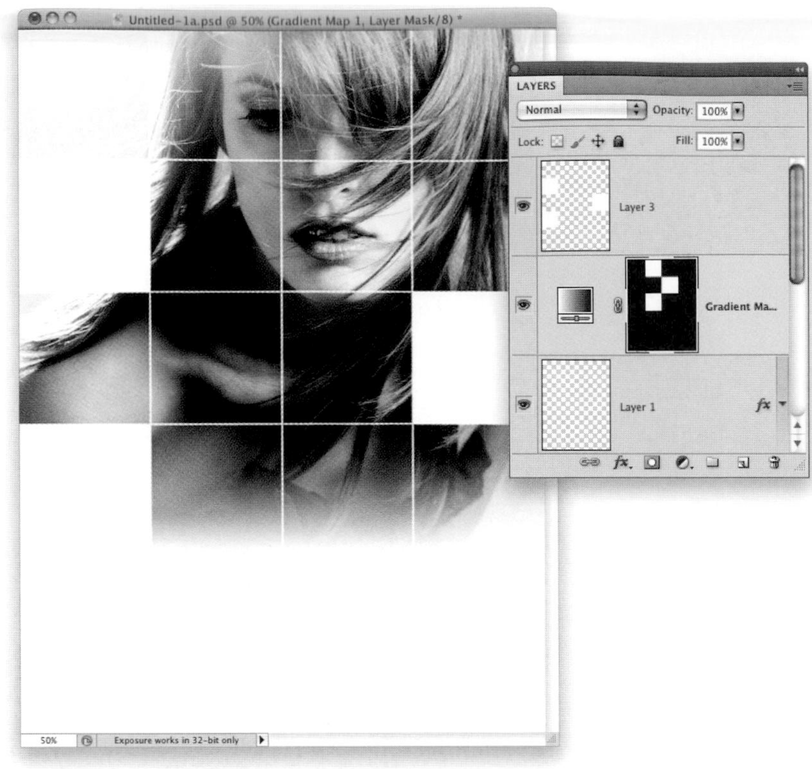

STEP 14:

Finally, just drop in some text (here, I used different styles of the Futura font) and you have a finished layout. You can see here how I used the white squares to act as frames for the text.

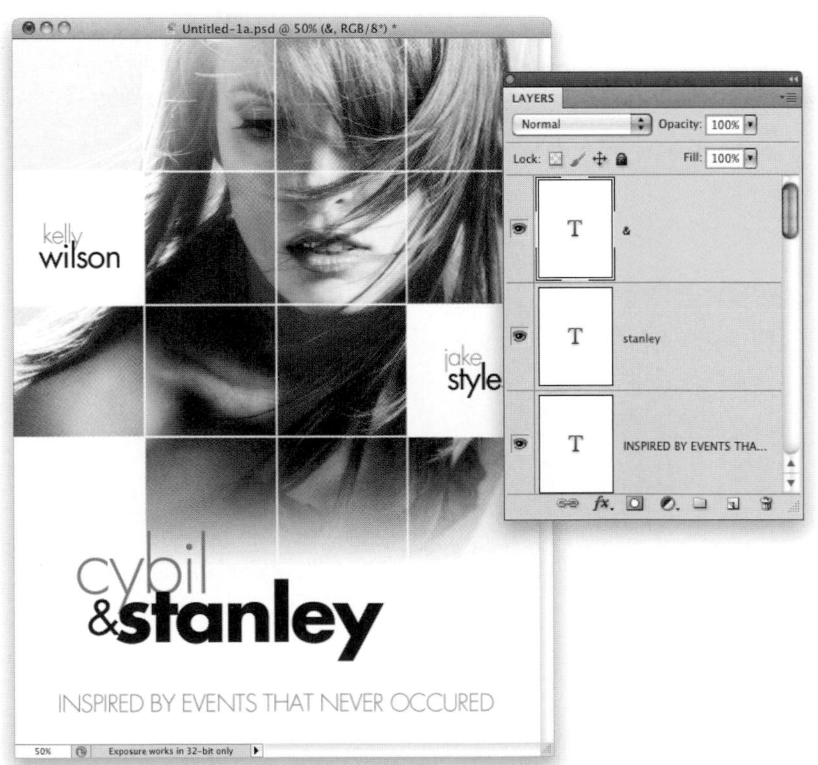

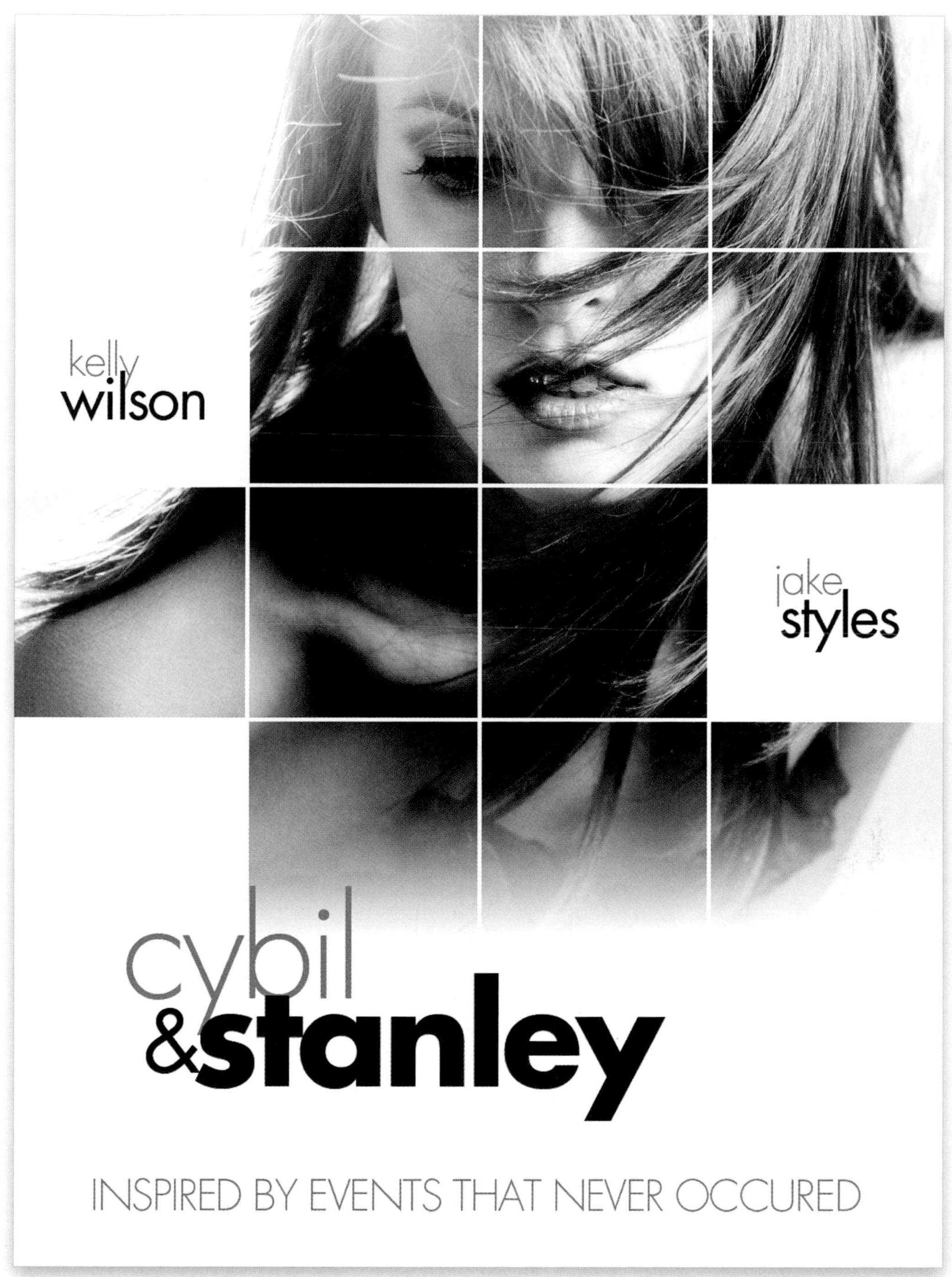
kelly
wilson
jake
styles
cybil
&stanley
INSPIRED BY EVENTS THAT NEVER OCCURED

Final Image

Halftone Image Effect

Halftone effects are certainly nothing new—designers have been using them for years—yet they never seem to go out of style. I saw this effect in a magazine and thought it had a cool look to it. Building on a technique I did a while back, I've added a couple new things to spice it up a bit.

STEP ONE:

Open the image of the model. Notice it was shot on a green screen. We won't need to extract the subject here, because we'll be working close enough in on the face that the green screen will not be seen anyway. So, press **Command-A (PC: Ctrl-A)** to select the entire image and then press **Command-C (PC: Ctrl-C)** to Copy it.

STEP TWO:

Press **Command-N (PC: Ctrl-N)** and create a new document that's 9 inches wide by 12 inches tall at 100 ppi. Click on your Foreground color swatch and set your Foreground color to a light beige (I chose R: 186, G: 179, B: 160) and then press **Option-Delete (PC: Alt-Backspace)** to fill the Background layer with this color.

STEP THREE:

Press **Command-V (PC: Ctrl-V)** to Paste the high-res model shot in the new document. It will appear very large, because the new document itself is a much smaller resolution than the image. This actually is okay, though, because we want the image big anyway. In fact, as you can see here, the face fills the canvas, leaving none of the green screen visible. Go into Free Transform (press **Command-T [PC: Ctrl-T]**) and, while pressing-and-holding the Shift key, click-and-drag a corner point inward to bring more of her face into the image, then move your cursor outside the bounding box, and rotate it just slightly to the left to make the subject more balanced in the composition. Once the image is in place, press **Return (PC: Enter)** to commit the transformation.

STEP FOUR:

Now, we don't need this image to be in color, so we'll convert it to black and white. While there are numerous methods for doing this, I like to use the Gradient Map adjustment, because it leaves the image with a fair bit of contrast. (If I were just creating a black-and-white photo, then I would probably use Camera Raw or the Black & White adjustment.) Press **D** to set your Foreground and Background colors to their defaults of black and white, then go under the Image menu, under Adjustments, and choose **Gradient Map**. Just click OK when the dialog opens.

Continued

STEP FIVE:

For the effect we're creating here, the subject is a little dark. However, rather than run a Levels adjustment, which will affect the whole image, I'd prefer to lighten the image in specific areas. So, click on the Create a New Layer icon at the bottom of the Layers panel to create a new blank layer above the model layer, then select the Gradient tool **(G)** from the Toolbox. In the Options Bar, click on the down-facing arrow to the right of the gradient thumbnail and choose the Foreground to Transparent gradient (the second one from the left in the top row) in the Gradient Picker, and then click on the Radial Gradient icon (the second icon to the right of the gradient thumbnail). Set your Foreground color to white by pressing **X**, then change the layer's blend mode to **Soft Light**, and click-and-drag the gradient in the dark areas of the image to lighten them (here, I mainly lightened her hair, the left side of her face, and her neck). This will show more of the halftone effect in a moment.

STEP SIX:

With this gradient layer active in the Layers panel, Command-click (PC: Ctrl-click) on the model layer beneath it to select them both. Then, Right-click on one of the layers and choose **Convert to Smart Object** from the pop-up menu.

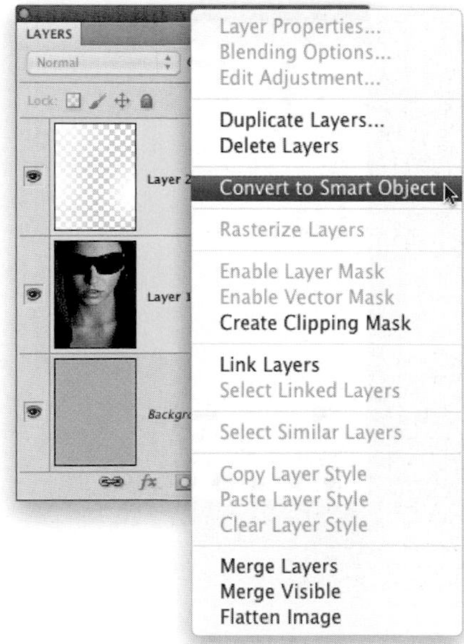

STEP SEVEN:

Now, press D to set your Foreground color to black, then, from the Filter menu, under Sketch, choose **Halftone Pattern**. From the Pattern Type pop-up menu, choose **Dot**, then set the Size to 2 and the Contrast to 0. Click OK.

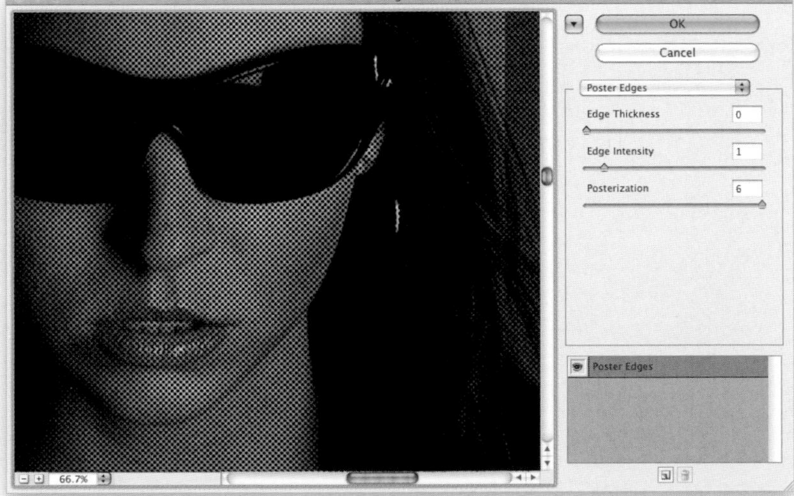

STEP EIGHT:

Go back under the Filter menu, again, this time under Artistic, and choose **Poster Edges**. Set the Edge Thickness to 0, the Edge Intensity to 1, and the Posterization to 6. Click OK. This will intensify the halftone effect quite a bit, but it could stand a little bit more contrast.

Continued

STEP NINE:

Here's a pretty cool trick to enhance the contrast a bit more: With the layer being a smart object, it automatically applies the filters as smart filters, allowing you to modify their appearance without having to reapply them. So, in the Layers panel, double-click on the icon to the right of the Halftone Pattern filter to open the filter's Blending Options. This dialog allows you to modify the opacity and blend mode of just this filter effect. In this case, change the blend Mode to **Hard Light** and you can see the halftone effect become a little more clearly defined—just through a single blend mode. Click OK when you're done.

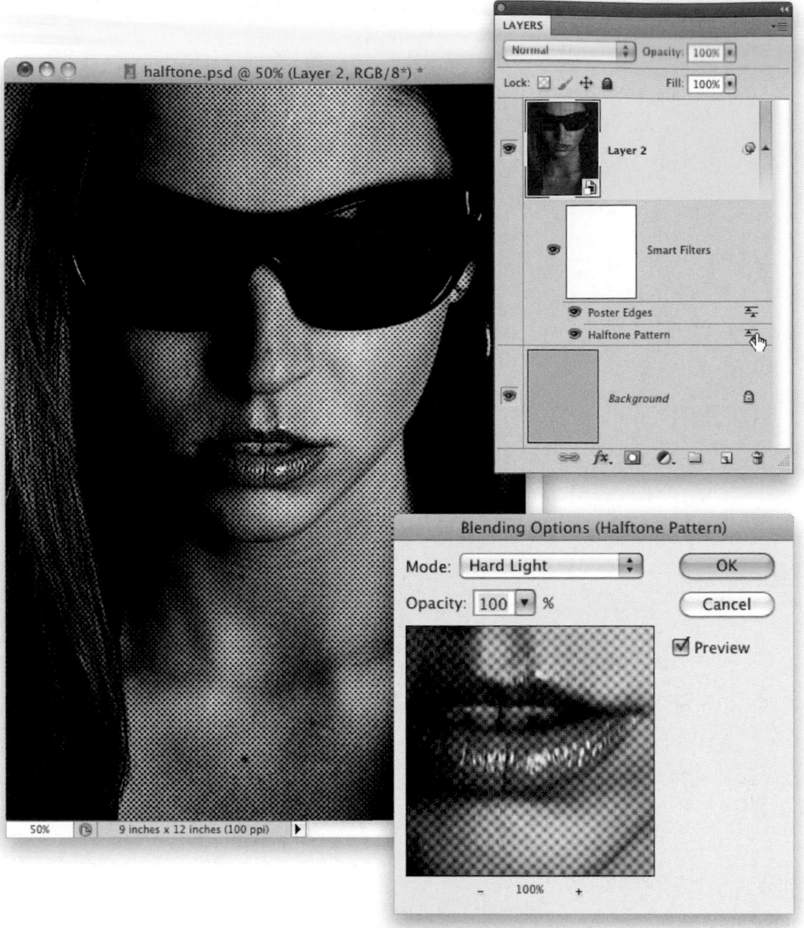

STEP 10:

Now, change the layer's blend mode to **Multiply** to blend the color of the Background layer with the halftone layer. By using Multiply, the dark areas remain, while the lighter areas are letting the Background layer color show through. Then, drop the layer's Opacity down to 90%.

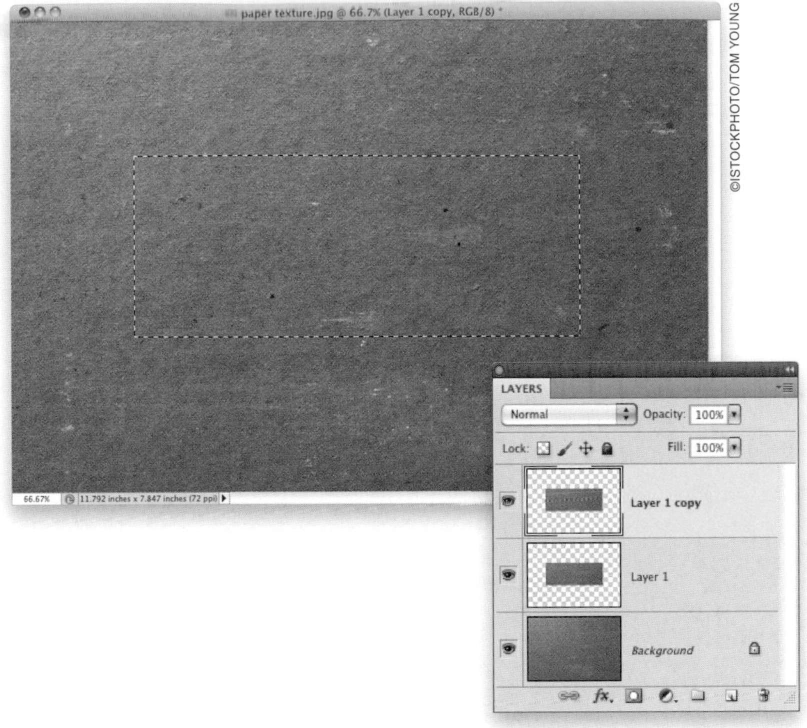

STEP 11:

Let's add a cool text element to finish the design. Open the file of the paper texture. Then get the Rectangular Marquee tool **(M)** from the Toolbox and draw a horizontal rectangle in the middle of the canvas, like you see here. Press **Command-J (PC: Ctrl-J)** two times to create two layers of the selected area.

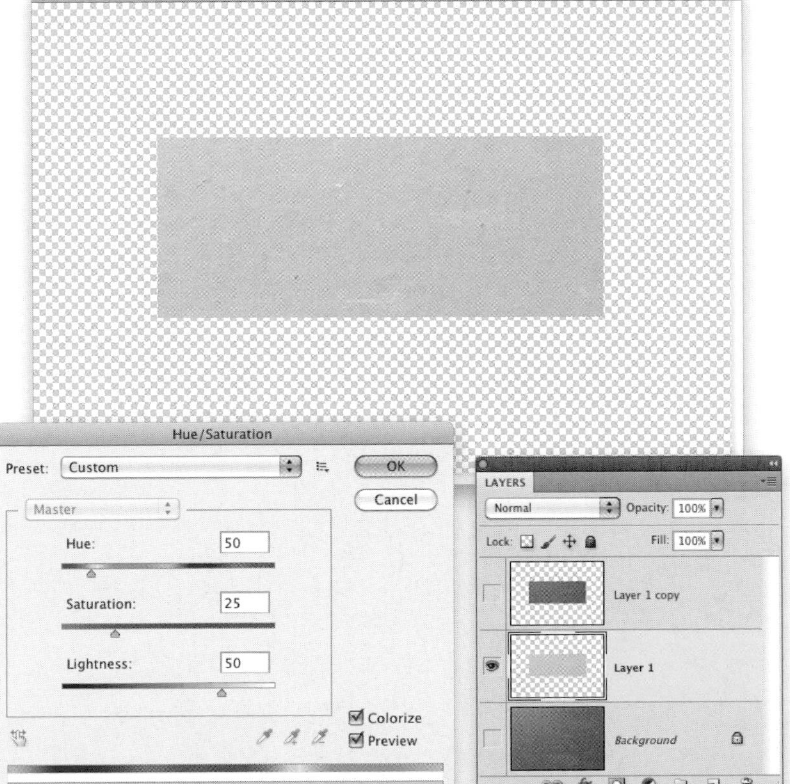

STEP 12:

Click on the Eye icons to the left of the Background layer and the top copy layer (Layer 1 copy) to turn them off, leaving just the bottom copy layer (Layer 1) visible. Then, click on the bottom copy layer to make it active. Press **Command-U (PC: Ctrl-U)** to open the Hue/Saturation dialog and turn on the Colorize checkbox. Set the Hue to 50, the Saturation to 25, and the Lightness to 50. This will give the texture an off-white color. Click OK.

Continued

STEP 13:

Next, turn the top copy layer (Layer 1 copy) back on, and then click on it to make it active. Press Command-U (PC: Ctrl-U) again to bring up the Hue/Saturation dialog and, this time, set the Hue to 23, the Saturation to 49, and the Lightness to –3 (don't forget to turn on the Colorize checkbox, again, as well). This will add a subtle orange hue to the texture.

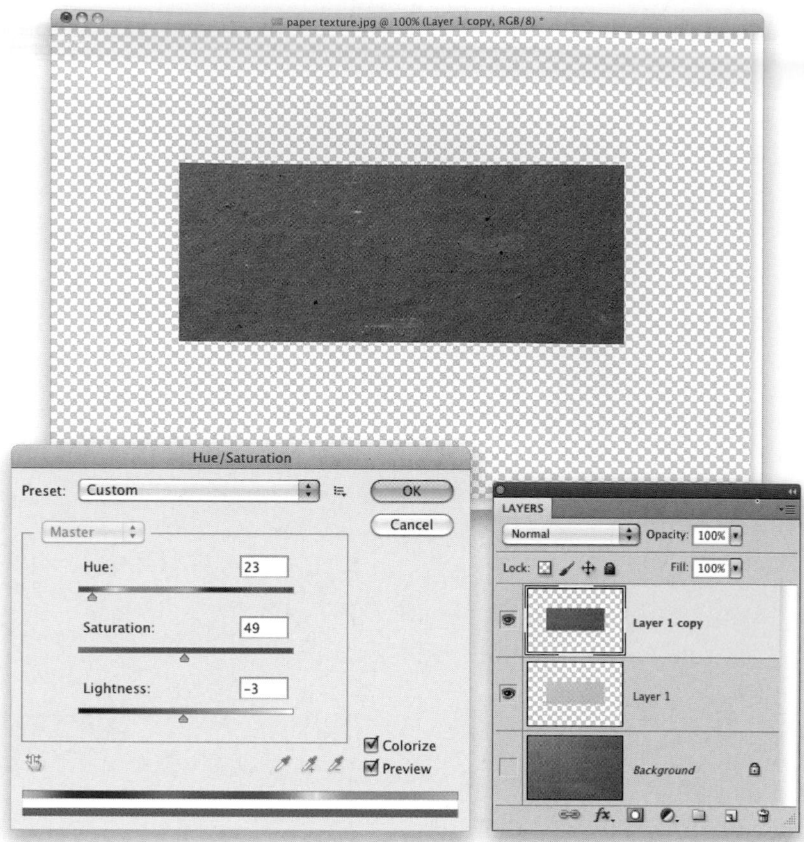

STEP 14:

Get the Polygonal Lasso tool from the Toolbox (or press **Shift-L** until you have it) and click in the top-left corner of the top texture layer, just a little inside the outer edge. Then, continue the selection around the rectangle just clicking in a random spot in each corner making the selection uneven all the way around. Press **Command-Shift-I (PC: Ctrl-Shift-I)** to Inverse the selection, then press **Delete (PC: Backspace)** to reveal the texture layer below around the edge, creating a border effect. Press **Command-D (PC: Ctrl-D)** to Deselect.

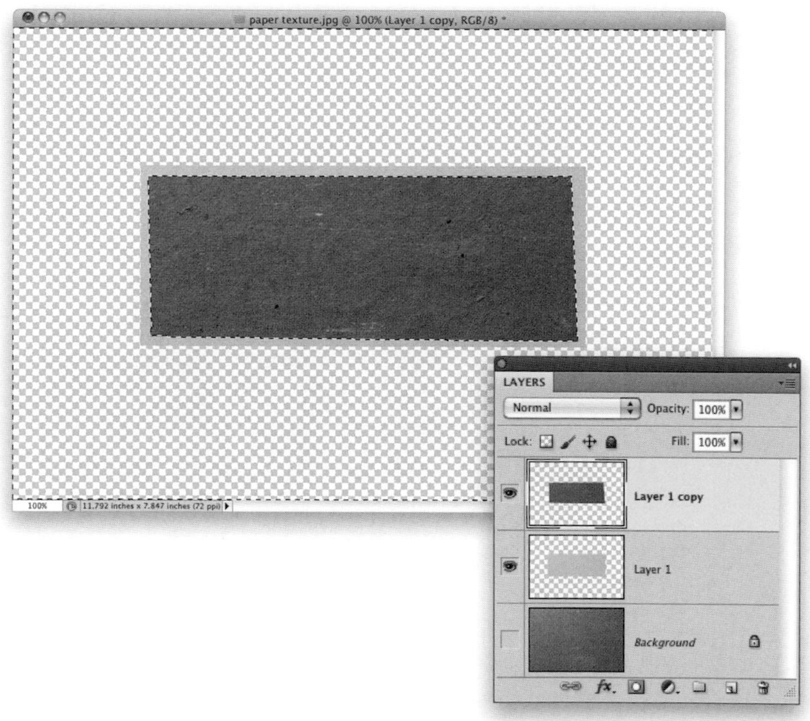

STEP 15:
Now get the Horizontal Type tool **(T)** from the Toolbox and click on the canvas to create a text layer. Here, I typed the word "TABS" in Helvetica Black Oblique and set the font size to occupy a large area of the texture. Next, select the text by Command-clicking (PC: Ctrl-clicking) on the text layer's thumbnail in the Layers panel. Then, click on the top texture layer to make it active and press Delete. Turn off the text layer and you'll be able to see through the text to the bottom texture layer below. You can now deselect.

STEP 16:
To give this top texture layer a sense of separation from the texture layer below, let's add a Drop Shadow layer style. Click on the Add a Layer Style icon at the bottom of the Layers panel and choose **Drop Shadow**. Feel free to change the angle of the shadow, if you like (I changed it to 30°, but the other default settings will work fine here), and click OK.

Continued

STEP 17:

Finally, Command-click (PC: Ctrl-click) on the bottom texture layer to select both texture layers. Then, Right-click on one of the layers and choose **Convert to Smart Object** to convert these layers into a smart object to bring over to our halftone image.

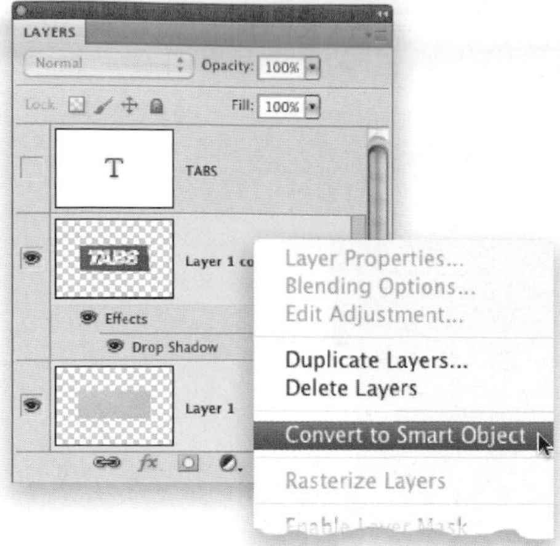

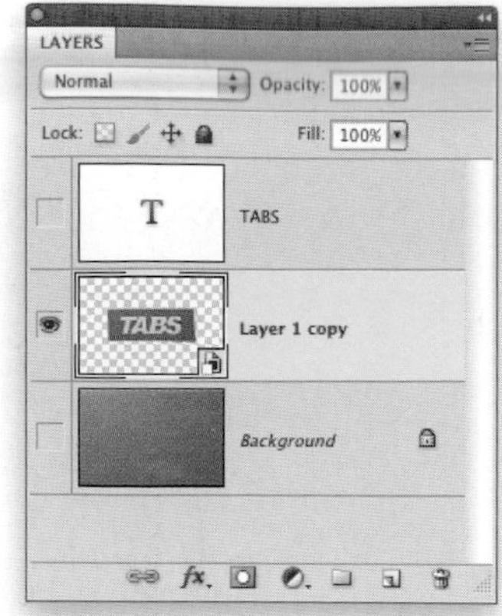

STEP 18:

Go back to the halftone image and, using the Move tool **(V),** drag-and-drop this text graphic onto the layout. Position it at the bottom of the image and there you have it!

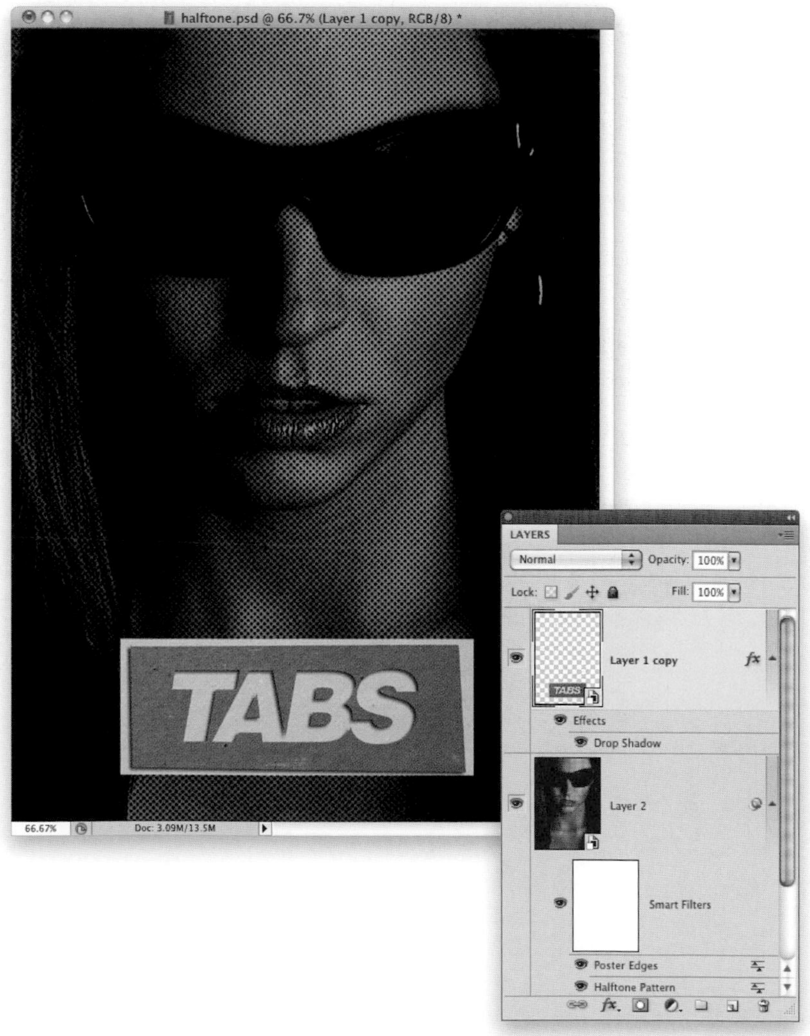

Final Image

Cool Watch Ad

If you've ever flipped through some of the high-end fashion magazines, there are always a few of those classy watch ads. I like them because they have a very sleek look to them. Here, I thought we would take a different approach and create a watch ad that gives an underwater perspective.

STEP ONE:

We'll start with this underwater image I downloaded from iStockphoto (www.istockphoto.com). It seems to fit with what we're going for here, so we'll start building the design around this image.

©ISTOCKPHOTO/SEBASTIAN MECKELMANN

STEP TWO:

Now press **Command-N (PC: Ctrl-N)** and create a new blank document measuring 12 inches wide by 8 inches tall at 100 ppi. Press **D** to set your Foreground color to black, and then press **Option-Delete (PC: Alt-Backspace)** to fill the Background layer with black. Then, use the Move tool **(V)** to click-and-drag the underwater image into this new document. Position it so the light beams are just coming in at the top-left edge of the canvas area, like you see here, and use Free Transform (press **Command-T [PC: Ctrl-T]**) to increase the size of the beams a bit. Press **Return (PC: Enter)** when you're done.

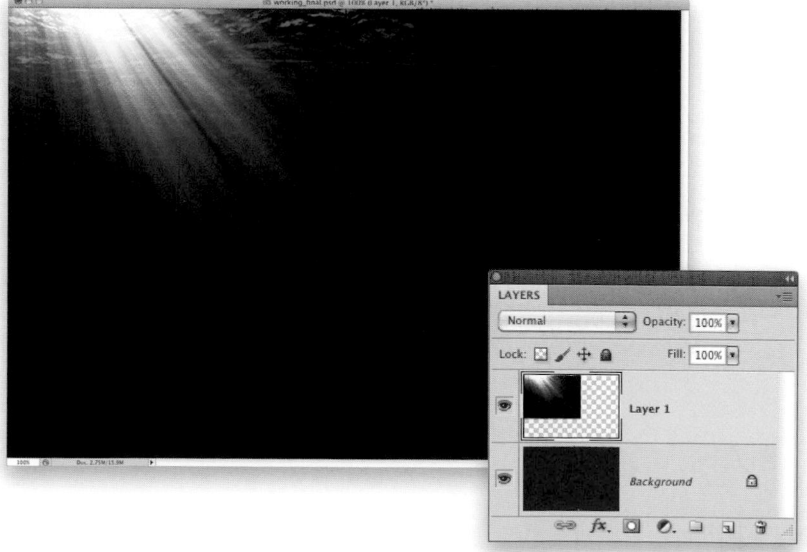

STEP THREE:
Next, click on the Add Layer Mask icon at the bottom of the Layers panel to add a layer mask. Then, get the Gradient tool **(G)** from the Toolbox and, in the Options Bar, click on the down-facing arrow to the right of the gradient thumbnail and choose the Foreground to Transparent gradient (the second gradient from the left in the top row). With your Foreground color set to black, click-and-drag from outside the underwater image to just over the edge of it to fade it into the black background on the bottom and right side.

©ISTOCKPHOTO/MOREPIXELS

STEP FOUR:
Now, open the image of the watch. Here, we have one that is on a black background and already has a reflection that we can work with. Since the overall composition is going to be mostly black, it will be easy to blend. So, go ahead and click-and-drag or copy-and-paste this image into the working layout.

Continued

STEP FIVE:

Position the watch in the lower-right area of the composition, like you see here, and use Free Transform to make it a little bigger. Change the layer's blend mode to **Screen** to make the watch's black background blend into the working background. Then, add a layer mask and use the Foreground to Transparent gradient again to fade the reflection a little bit (click at the bottom of the reflection and drag up).

STEP SIX:

Now, we need to create a more visible surface for the watch to sit on. True, there is a reflection, which helps, but it's not enough. I really want to see the refracted light reflection on the same surface the watch seems to sit on. For that I am going to use an old trick from years ago that will work great here. Make sure your Foreground and Background colors are the default black and white, and then click on the Create a New Layer icon at the bottom of the Layers panel to create a new blank layer. Next, go under the Filter menu, under Render, and choose **Clouds**. There's no dialog for this filter—its results will just reflect in your image window (as shown here).

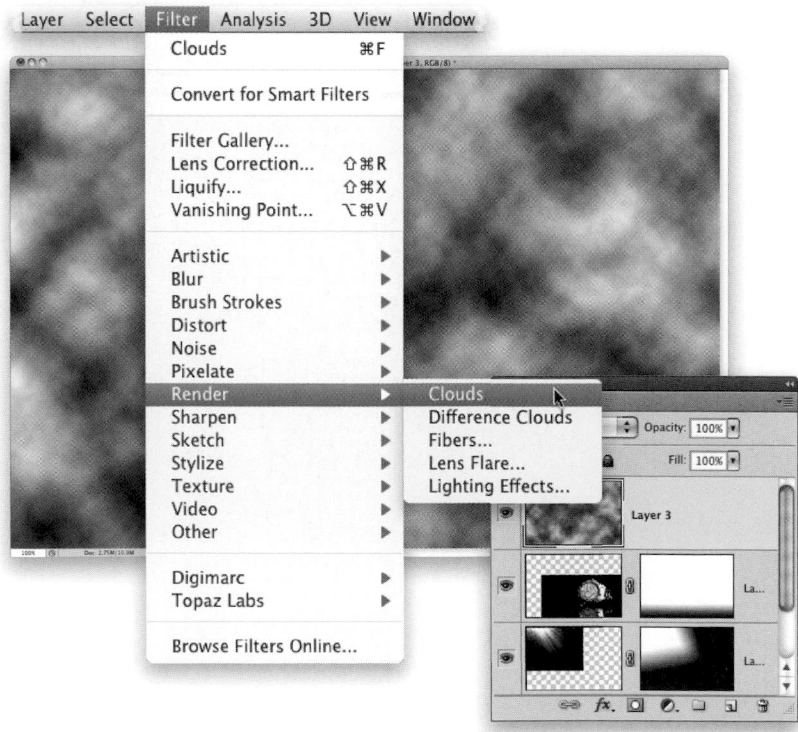

STEP SEVEN:

Go under the Filter menu, once again, this time under Blur, and choose **Gaussian Blur**. Set the Radius to 10 pixels and click OK.

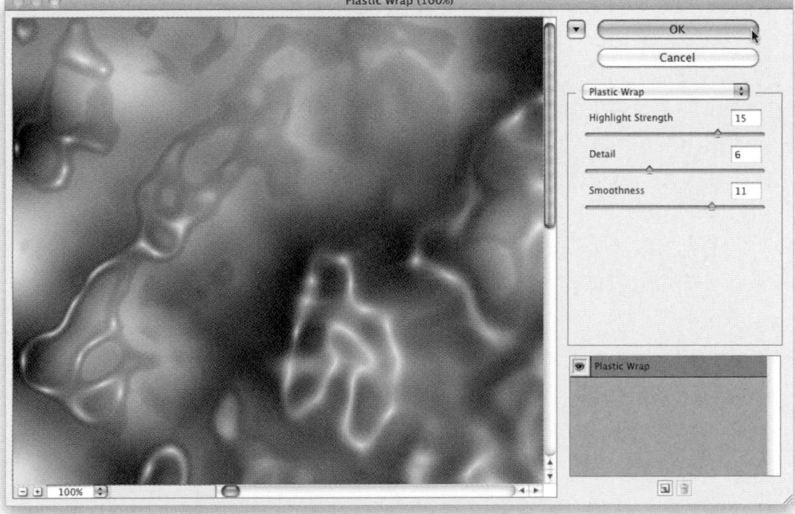

STEP EIGHT:

Again, go under the Filter menu, this time under Artistic, and choose **Plastic Wrap**. Set the Highlight Strength to 15, the Detail to 6, and the Smoothness to 11. You can see the effect starting to take shape at this point. Click OK when you're done.

Continued

STEP NINE:
Now, let's change the color of this texture layer to better match our background image. Press **Command-U (PC: Ctrl-U)** to open the Hue/Saturation dialog. Turn on the Colorize checkbox and increase the Hue to 190, and then click OK.

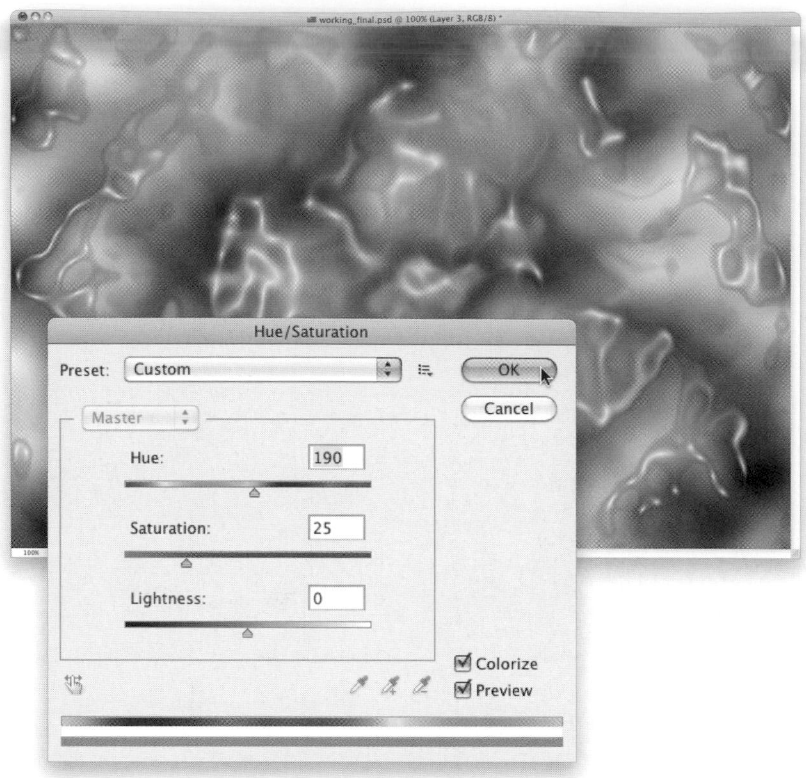

STEP 10:
Now, in the Layers panel, click-and-drag this texture layer just above the Background layer. Then, go into Free Transform mode and click-and-drag the top-middle control handle down to the bottom edge of the watch. Press Return (PC: Enter) to lock in your transformation.

STEP 11:
Press **Command-L (PC: Ctrl-L)** to open the Levels dialog and move the Input Levels shadows (black) and midtones (gray) sliders to the right to boost the contrast, making it look more like light reflecting on the ocean floor. Click OK.

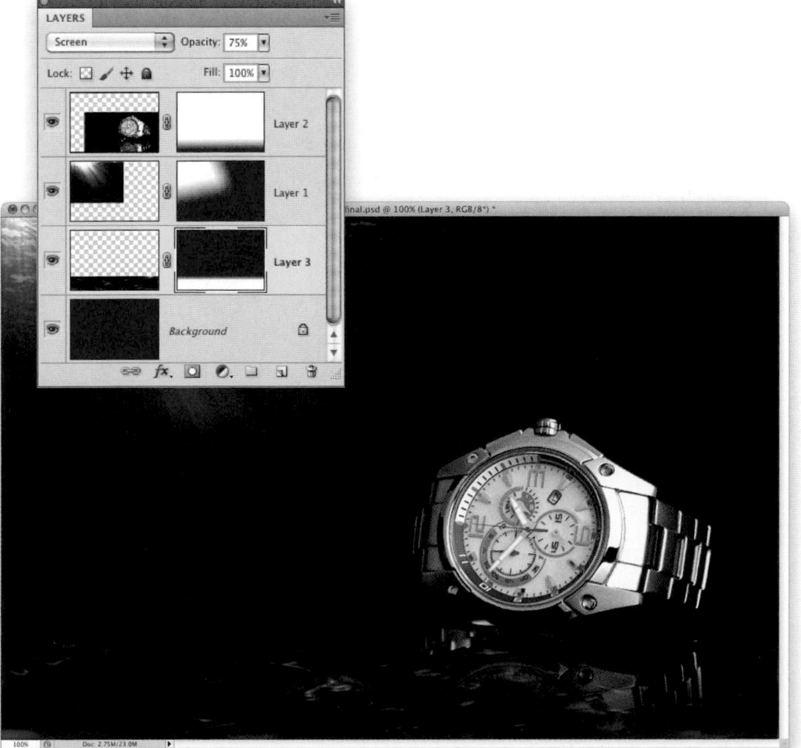

STEP 12:
Change the layer's blend mode to **Screen** and lower its Opacity to 75%. Then, add a layer mask and blend the hard edge at the top of the texture layer into the background with a Foreground to Transparent gradient (like we did with the watch reflection, but this time, dragging from above the texture layer downward).

Continued

STEP 13:

Now, with the floor texture in place, I can see that the area around the base of the watch could use a subtle light enhancement to bring out the reflection a bit more. Command-click (PC: Ctrl-click) on the Create a New Layer icon at the bottom of the Layers panel to place a new layer under the currently active one. Get the Eyedropper tool **(I)** from the Toolbox and click in the light beam area of the image to sample the teal color, making it your Foreground color. Then, get the Elliptical Marquee tool (press **Shift-M** until you have it), draw a long oval selection just below the watch, and press **Option-Delete (PC: Alt-Backspace)** to fill the selection with the sampled Foreground color.

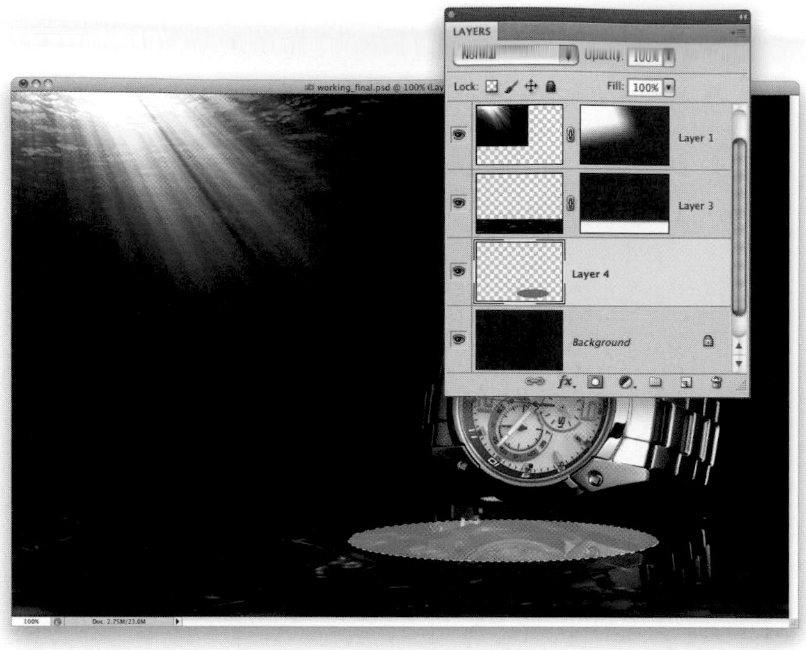

STEP 14:

Press **Command-D (PC: Ctrl-D)** to Deselect. Then, go under the Filter menu, under Blur, and choose **Gaussian Blur**. Set the Radius to 30 pixels and click OK. Next, just drop the layer's Opacity down to 75% and, as you can see, we have a nice, subtle light effect that blends with the background quite nicely.

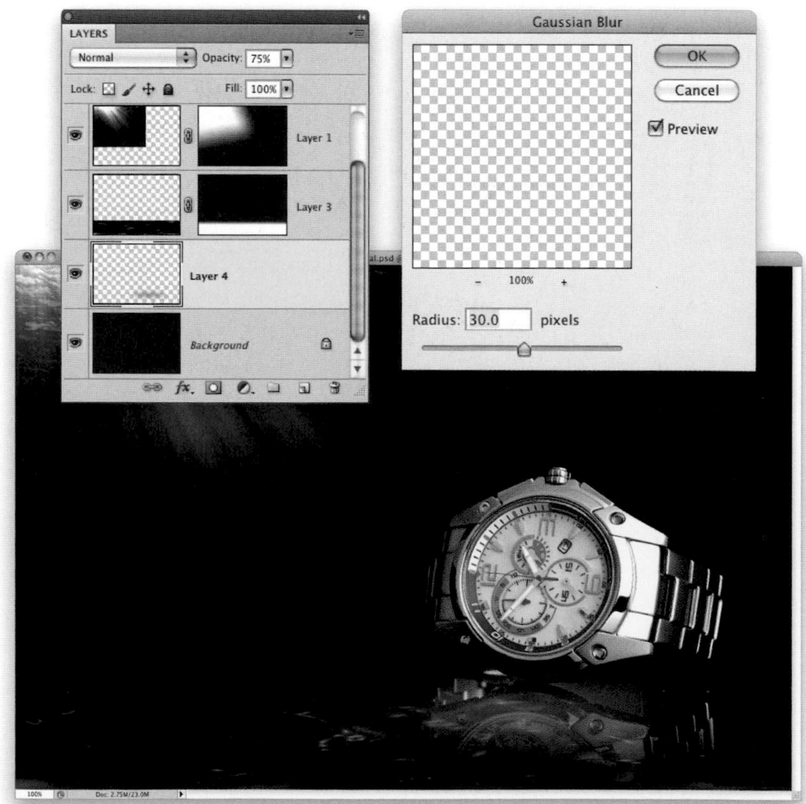

STEP 15:

Now let's add some more of that teal color to the surrounding area to get more of that aquatic underwater feel. Create a new blank layer at the top of the layer stack, then get the Gradient tool with the Foreground to Transparent gradient again, but this time, click on the Radial Gradient icon in the Options Bar (the second icon to the right of the gradient thumbnail). With your Foreground color still set to the same teal color we used a moment ago, click-and-drag a couple of gradients in the upper-right and bottom-left corners. Then, lower the layer's Opacity to 75%.

STEP 16:

Next, let's add a diver in the background. Since it will merely be a silhouette, a simple graphic of a diver will do fine. Here, I found a set of diver images at iStockphoto. This way, I have a set I can choose from for future use. Get the Lasso tool **(L)** from the Toolbox and draw a selection around the diver in the upper-right corner, then press **Command-C (PC: Ctrl-C)** to Copy the selected graphic.

Continued

STEP 17:
Press **Command-V (PC: Ctrl-V)** to Paste the diver into your working layout, then go into Free Transform, press-and-hold the Shift key, and decrease the size of the diver (press **Command-0** [zero; **PC: Ctrl-0**] to reach the corner handles). Press **Return (PC: Enter)** to lock in your transformation. In the Layers panel, position this layer under the gradient layer we just created back in Step 15. Then, use the Move tool to move the diver in the middle of the light beams. To get rid of the white background area, just change the layer's blend mode to **Multiply** and drop its Opacity to 60%.

STEP 18:
Now, because the diver is underwater and is in the distance, the edge detail would not realistically be as sharp. So, go under the Filter menu, under Blur, and choose **Gaussian Blur**. Set the Radius to 1 pixel and click OK.

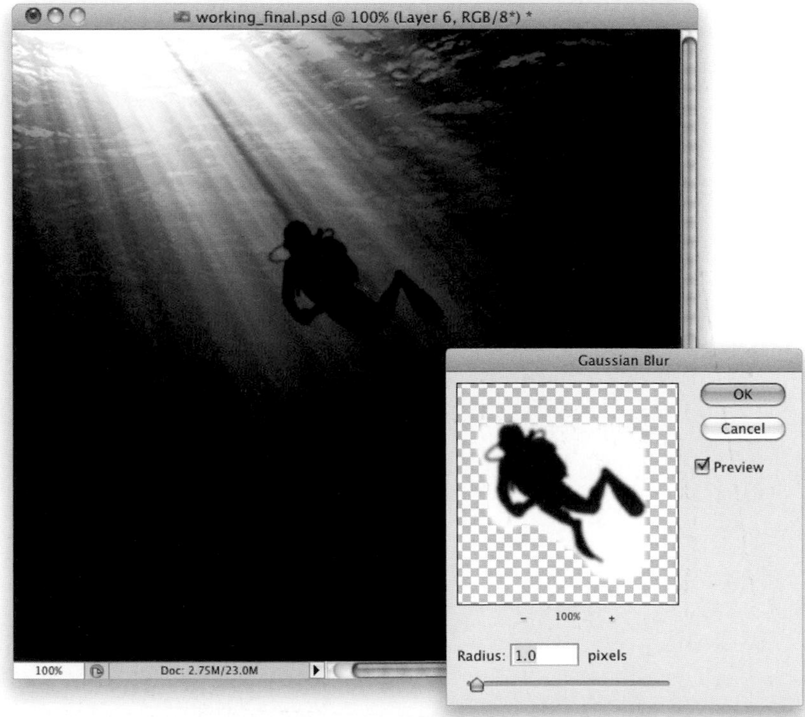

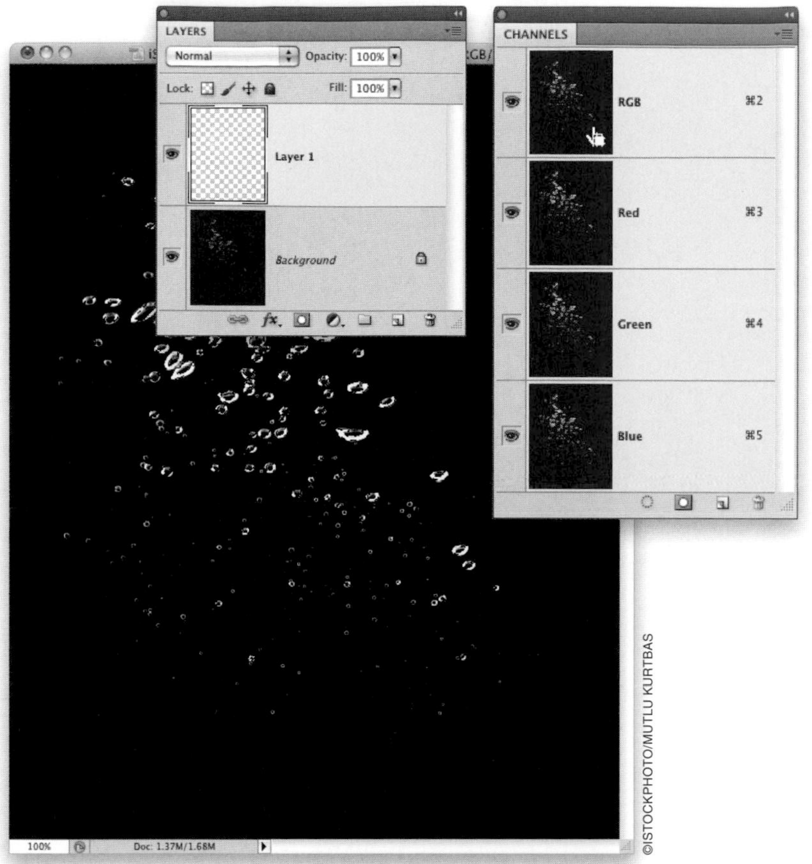

©ISTOCKPHOTO/MUTLU KURTBAS

STEP 19:

Let's add a bubble effect to finish off the diver in the water. Here, we have a simple image of bubbles on a white background. To quickly extract them, create a selection by pressing **Command-I (PC: Ctrl-I)** to Invert the image, then go into the Channels panel (Window>**Channels**) and Command-click (PC: Ctrl-click) on the RGB channel. Go to the Layers panel and create a new blank layer. Press **D**, then **X** to set your Foreground color to white, and press Option-Delete (PC: Alt-Backspace) to fill the selection with white. Press Command-D (PC: Ctrl-D) to Deselect.

STEP 20:

Next, click-and-drag or copy-and-paste the selected bubble layer into the working layout and place it above the diver layer in the Layers panel. Go into Free Transform mode and scale and position the bubbles just above the diver, like I have them here. Finally, change the layer's blend mode to **Overlay**.

Continued

STEP 21:

Okay, we are almost done. Looking at the overall layout, I can see that the upper-right corner area could use a little something. To go along with the whole diving theme, we have a cool nautical map to add as another background element. Open the nautical map image and remove the color by pressing **Command-Shift-U (PC: Ctrl-Shift-U)**. Then, invert the image, like we did with the bubbles.

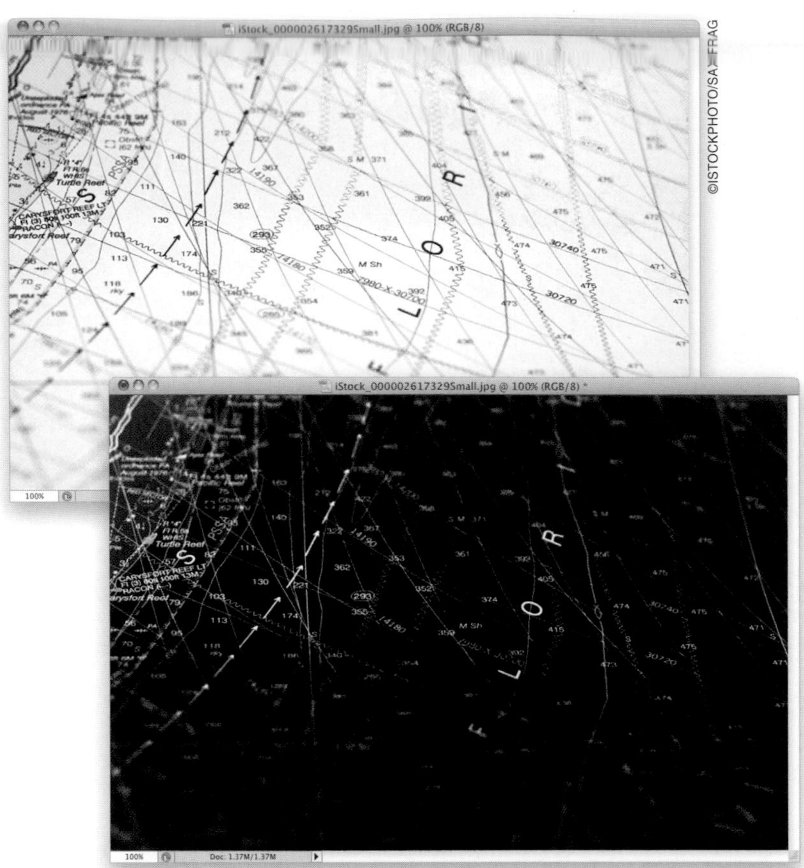

©ISTOCKPHOTO/SAJFRAG

STEP 22:

Now, go ahead and click-and-drag or copy-and-paste the map image into the working layout, and use the Move tool to position it in the upper-right corner, making sure its layer appears below the teal radial gradient layer in the Layers panel. Then, add a layer mask, get the Gradient tool, with the Foreground to Transparent Linear gradient again, and with your Foreground set to black, fade the edges of the map image. Change the blend mode to **Linear Dodge (Add)**, and then lastly, to soften the effect, drop the layer's Opacity down to 50%. This will subtly blend the map graphic into the background.

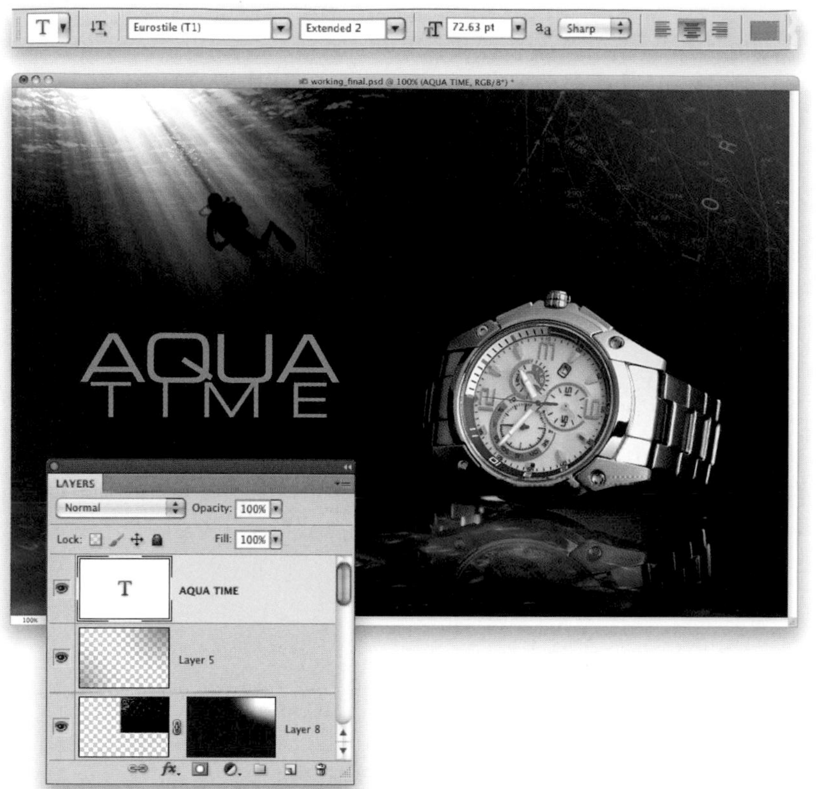

STEP 23:

Let's finish the whole design off with some text. Start by selecting the Horizontal Type tool **(T)** from the Toolbox and creating a text layer. Click on the color swatch in the Options Bar and enter R: 224, G: 146, B: 47 in the Color Picker. Here, I stacked the words "AQUA TIME" in Eurostile (T1) Extended 2 at almost 73 points for AQUA and at almost 53 points for TIME.

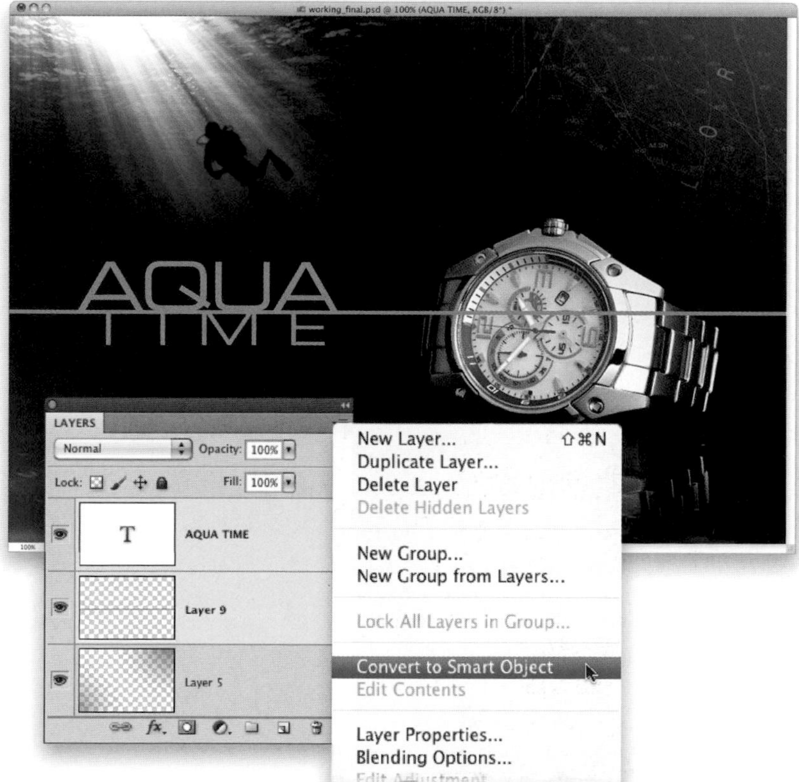

STEP 24:

Create a new blank layer below the text layer. Get the Rectangular Marquee tool **(M)**, and draw a thin-line selection across the document, in between the lines of text. Set your Foreground color to the same color used for the text and then press Option-Delete (PC: Alt-Backspace) to fill the line with that color, then deselect. (*Note:* To get both words to line up with the line you just created, use the Move tool to move the bottom of AQUA onto the line and then select TIME with the Horizontal Type tool, and press **Option-Up Arrow key (PC: Alt-Up Arrow key)** to bring the top of it up to the line.) Now, Command-click (PC: Ctrl-click) on both the line and text layers so both are selected, and then from the Layers panel's flyout menu, choose **Convert to Smart Object** to convert them into a single Smart Object layer.

Continued

STEP 25:

Now, let's dress up the text with layer styles. With the Smart Object layer active in the Layers panel, click on the Add a Layer Style icon at the bottom of the panel and choose **Inner Shadow**. Use the settings shown here to add some depth to the text.

STEP 26:

Next, click on Gradient Overlay on the left side of the dialog to turn it on, and just change the Blend Mode to **Soft Light**.

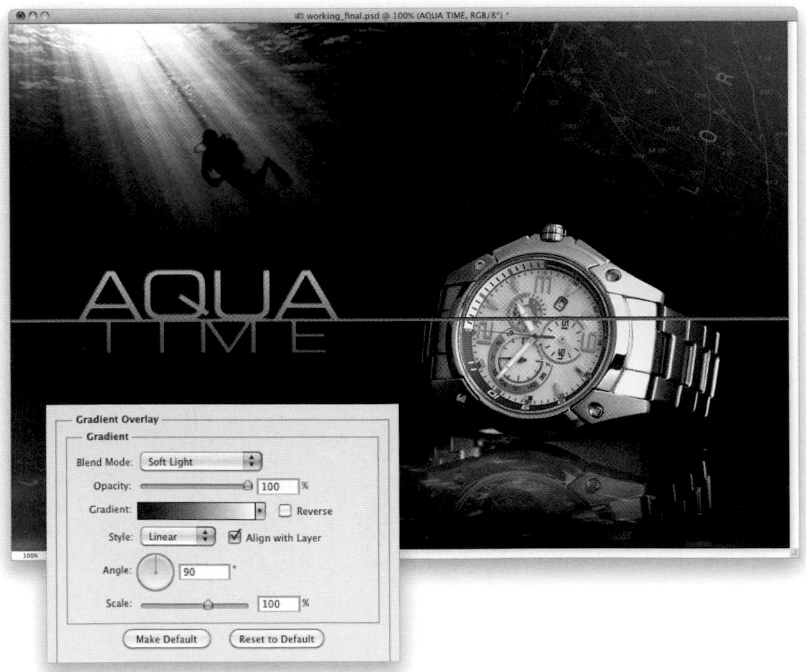

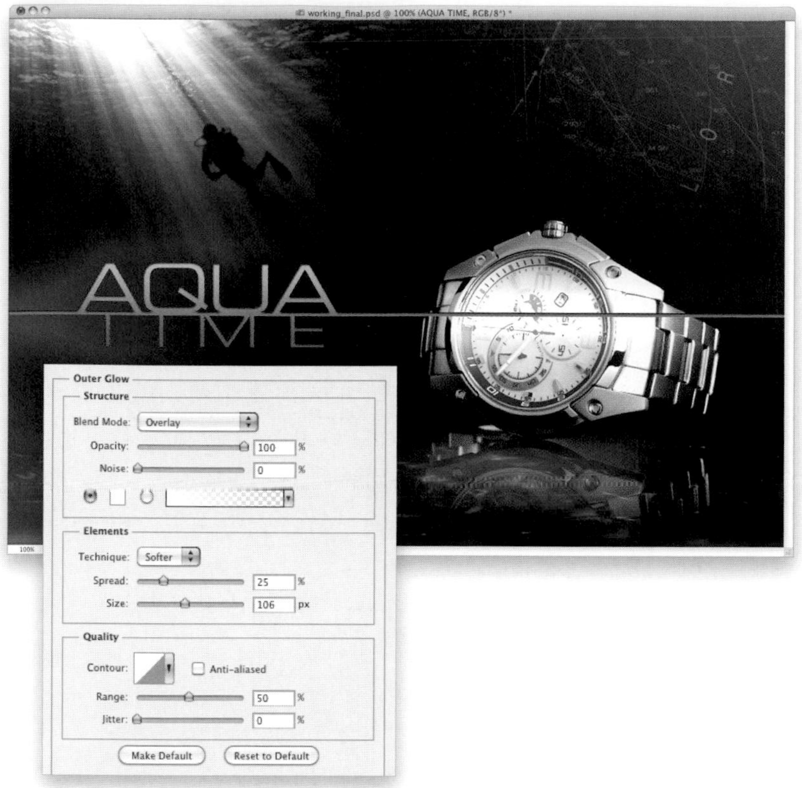

STEP 27:

Lastly, click on Outer Glow on the left to turn it on, and set this Blend Mode to **Overlay** and the Opacity to 100%. Click on the color swatch and change the color to white. Then, down in the Elements section, increase the Spread to 25% and set the Size to around 105 px. This will give the glow a subtle halo effect. Click OK.

STEP 28:

Now we need to mask the line where it goes over the watch. So, get the Elliptical Marquee tool (press **Shift-M** until you have it) and draw a long oval selection over the line where it goes over the watch.

Continued

STEP 29:

Press **Q** to put the selection in Quick Mask mode. (*Note:* If the masked area is in red, rather than the selection, double-click on the Quick Mask icon at the bottom of the Toolbox to open the Quick Mask Options dialog and change Color Indicated to Selected Areas.) Go under the Filter menu, under Blur, and choose **Gaussian Blur**. Set the Radius to 5 pixels and click OK.

STEP 30:

Press Q again to go back to the marching ants selection, then Option-click (PC: Alt-click) on the Add Layer Mask icon at the bottom of the Layers panel. This will give the illusion that the line goes behind the watch.

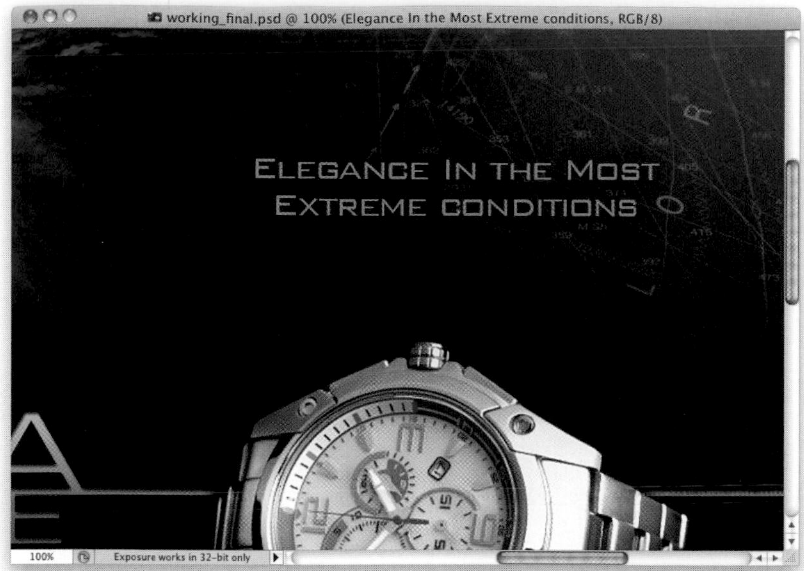

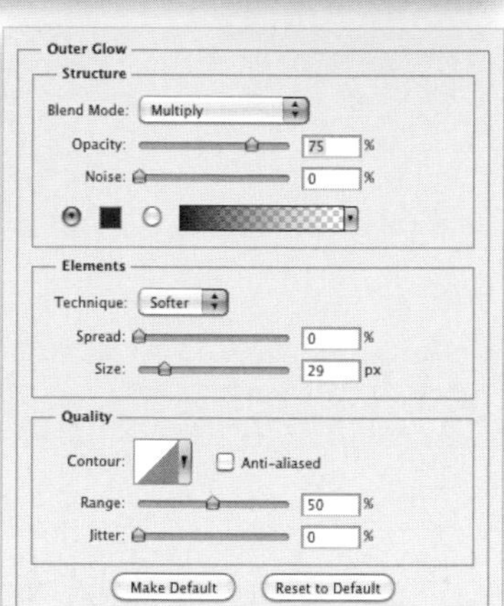

STEP 31:
Finish off the image by adding some more text in the top right. Here, I set some in Bank Gothic Light, and then added a black Outer Glow layer style with the settings shown here.

Continued

ELEGANCE IN THE MOST
EXTREME CONDITIONS
AQUA
TIME

Final Image

Wood Frame Surf Ad

This effect I saw, once again, in a magazine ad. It was an advertisement for beach sandals. I was really drawn to the wood frame effect and liked the whole surfer feel of the ad. Once you see how easy it is to create this effect, you'll really see how much fun you can have configuring the wood frame in different ways. Plus, it just looks cool!

©ISTOCKPHOTO/JAN RIHAK

STEP ONE:

To start building the wood frame, we'll use a stock image of some wood planks that have a sort of aged look that will work perfectly for this design. Plus, there are several planks, which will give us some variation. Start by getting the Rectangular Marquee tool **(M)** from the Toolbox. Then, draw a selection over any one of the planks in the image. Here, I chose the fourth one from the left. Once the selection is made, press **Command-C (PC: Ctrl-C)** to Copy it.

STEP TWO:

Press **Command-N (PC: Ctrl-N)** and create a new document that is 14 inches wide by 7 inches tall at 125 ppi. Then, press **Command-V (PC: Ctrl-V)** to Paste the wood plank selection in the new document. Press **Command-T (PC: Ctrl-T)** to go into Free Transform mode, Right-click inside the bounding box, and choose **Rotate 90° CW** to rotate the plank, making it horizontal.

Continued

STEP THREE:

Move the plank to the top edge of the canvas, then press-and-hold the Option (PC: Alt) key (to scale the object from the center), click on the right-middle control handle, and drag to stretch the plank to the right edge of the canvas. The left side will scale at the same time. Then, release the Option key, click on the bottom-middle control handle, and drag it up slightly to make the wood plank a little thinner. Press **Return (PC: Enter)** to lock in your transformation.

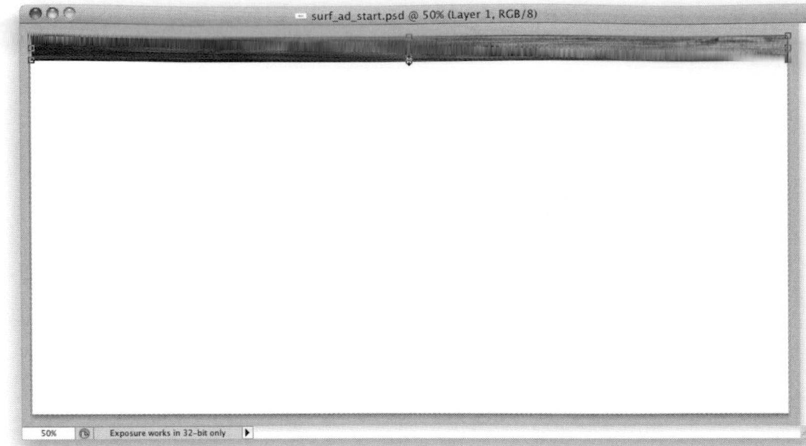

STEP FOUR:

Now, repeat the last few steps to add a different plank from the source file to the bottom of the working layout, like I have here.

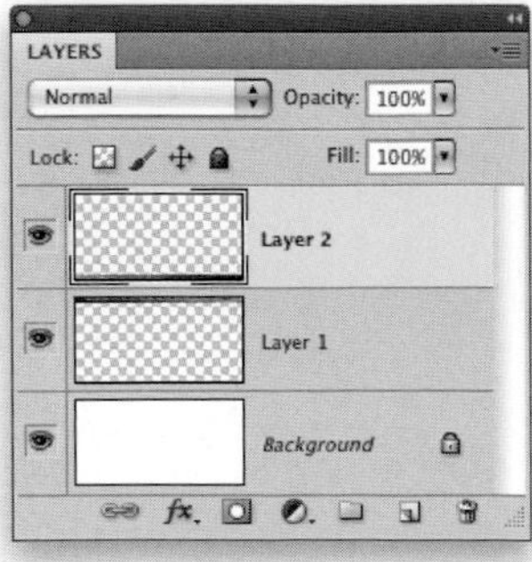

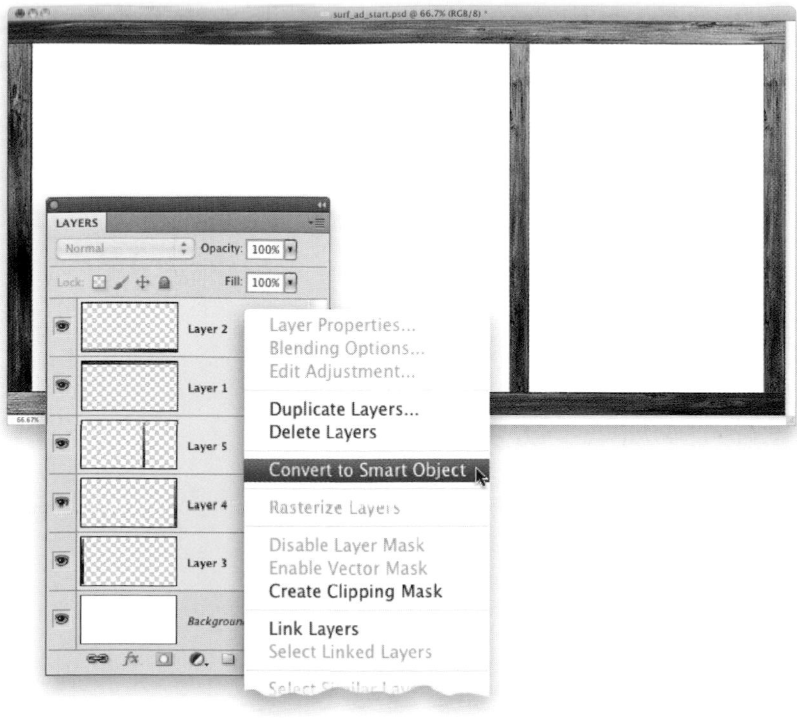

STEP FIVE:

Use the same process to add three more different vertical planks to the layout—one on each end and another about 9 inches from the left side. In the Layers panel, move the vertical plank layers beneath the horizontal plank layers. When all the planks are in place, Command-click (PC: Ctrl-click) on each plank layer to select them all, then Right-click on one of the layers and choose **Convert to Smart Object** from the pop-up menu to merge them all into a smart object.

STEP SIX:

Now open the other wood grain file (shown here), press **Command-A (PC: Ctrl-A)** to select the entire image, then copy-and-paste it into the working layout. Once it's there, move its layer beneath the wood plank Smart Object layer, and then position this wood grain in the rectangle area on the right side of the image. Go into Free Transform mode and scale it, if necessary, to fit it in the area.

Continued

STEP SEVEN:

Let's apply a color effect to the wood grain with a simple layer style. Click on the Add a Layer Style icon at the bottom of the Layers panel and choose **Color Overlay**. Click on the color swatch, choose R: 36, G: 79, B: 63, and click OK in the Color Picker to get a cool green color. Then, set the Blend Mode to **Color** and click OK.

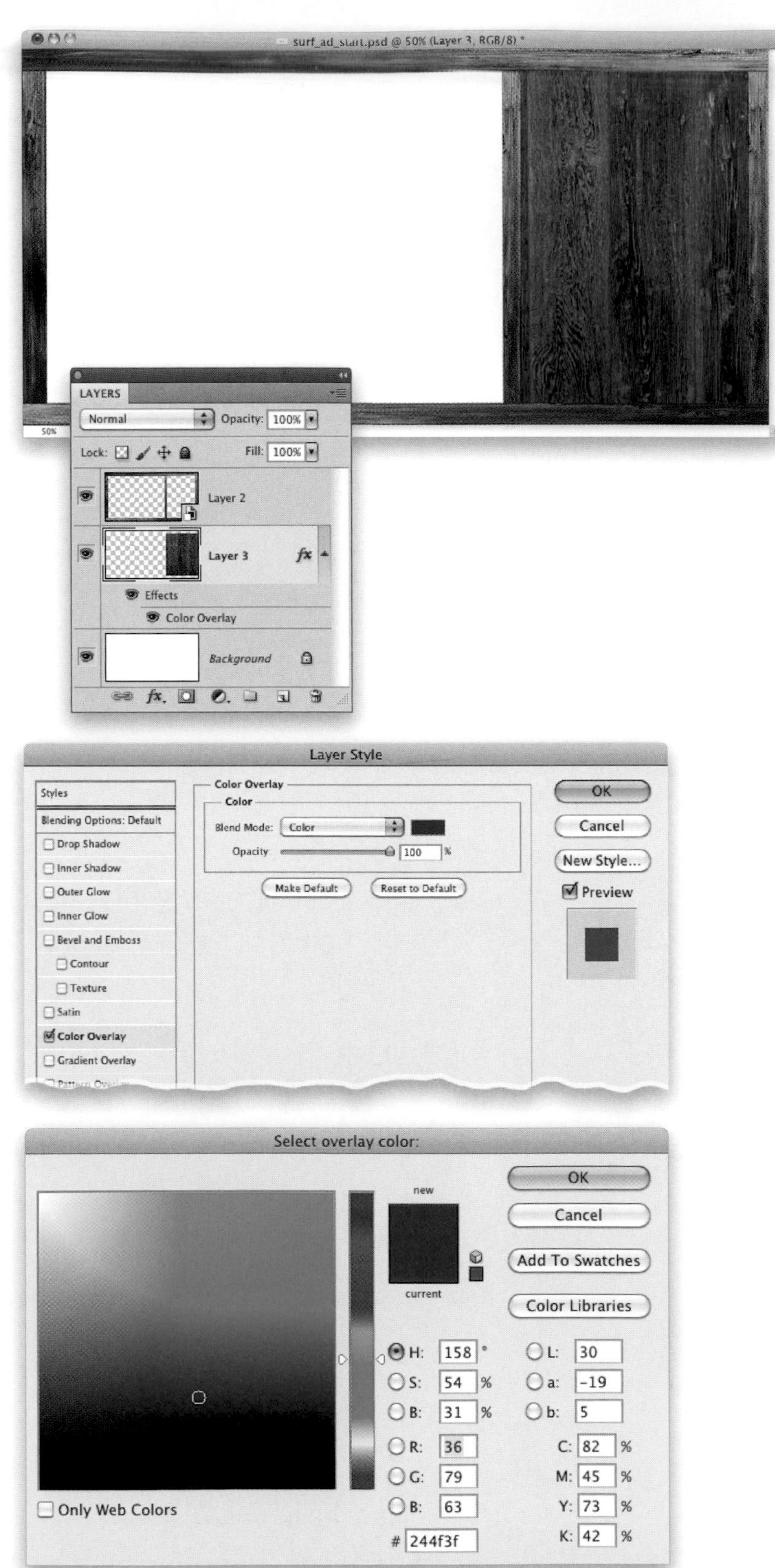

©ISTOCKPHOTO/BOBBY SCHUTZ

STEP EIGHT:

Open the surfer image, which we'll add to the other side of the layout. Copy-and-paste the image into your working layout and, in the Layers panel, move the surfer layer beneath the wood grain layer. Go into Free Transform, if needed, and scale and position it within the frame on the left side as I have here.

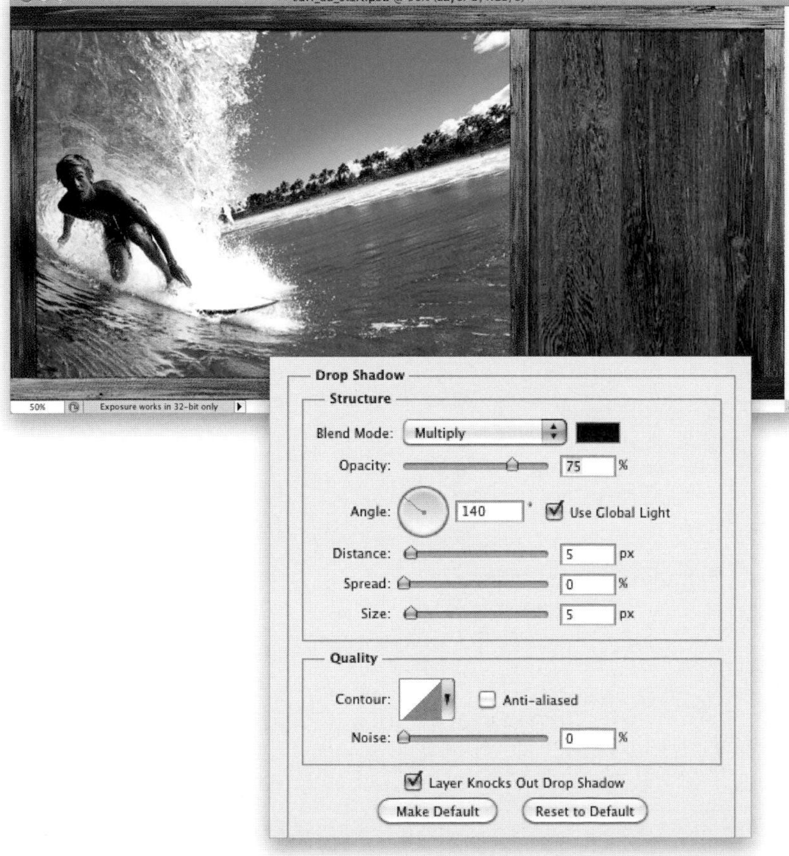

STEP NINE:

Let's create some depth between the surfer and wood grain images and the wood plank frame by adding a basic Drop Shadow layer style. Click back on the wood plank Smart Object layer in the Layers panel, then click on the Add a Layer Style icon and choose **Drop Shadow**. Use the settings shown here and click OK.

Continued

STEP 10:

Using the same process we used for the initial wood plank frame, follow the first few steps of this project again to create another wood plank frame element, like I have here. Then, just like before, convert it to a smart object and position it over the surfer image to the left of the green wood grain area (but make sure it appears beneath the original wood plank and wood grain layers in the Layers panel). This is going to contain the product logo. (*Note:* I included the wood grain layer this time, which I added a black Color Overlay layer style to, when I converted the wood plank layers into a smart object.) To finish this new element off, add the same Drop Shadow layer style that we just added to the wood plank frame by **Option-clicking (PC: Alt-clicking)** on the Drop Shadow layer style beneath the original wood plank frame layer and dragging it to the new frame layer. This will copy it to the new frame layer.

STEP 11:

Now we are ready to add the product for our ad. Since we're creating a surf-style ad, it seems like the right setting for some beach footwear. Here, we'll use a generic product shot of a pair of flip-flops, which will work well for this layout. Select the flip-flops by getting the Quick Selection tool **(W)** from the Toolbox and then painting over them. Once they're selected, press **Command-J (PC: Ctrl-J)** to copy the selection up onto a new layer. Extracting from a white background like this will often leave little artifacts around the edges. To get rid of them, just go under the Layer menu, to the very bottom, under Matting, and choose **Defringe**. You really don't need to set the Width to anything more than 1 or 2, but go ahead and enter 3 for good measure and click OK.

STEP 12:

Press Command-J again to duplicate this layer, and then remove the color by pressing **Command-Shift-U (PC: Ctrl-Shift-U)**. Change the desaturated layer's blend mode to **Soft Light** and drop the Opacity to 75%. This will boost the contrast and make the colors pop a little more.

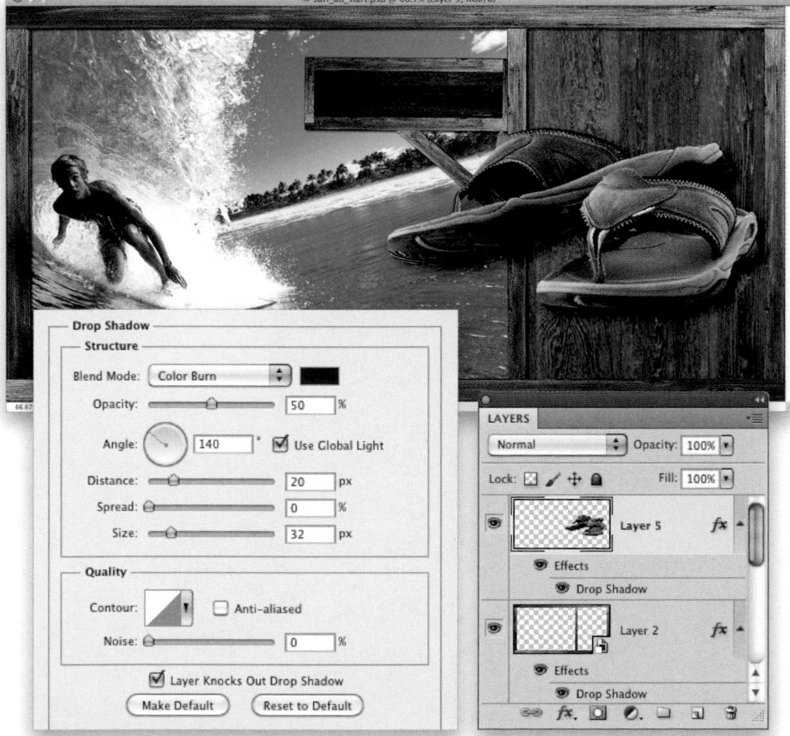

STEP 13:

Press **Command-E (PC: Ctrl-E)** to merge this layer with the original beneath it. Then, Command-click (PC: Ctrl-click) on the merged layer's thumbnail to select it, and copy-and-paste this layer into the working layout. Place the product image at the top of the layer stack and use Free Transform to decrease its size, as you see here, then add a Drop Shadow layer style using the settings shown here as a finishing touch. Notice that I have the Drop Shadow Blend Mode set to **Color Burn**, which greatly saturates the colors in the shadow, giving it a more stylized look.

Continued

STEP 14:
Now, let's add a couple more planks to finish off the design. Go back to the original wood plank image we started with and grab the Rectangular Marquee tool again. Draw a selection over the second plank from the right and then press **Command-C (PC: Ctrl-C)** to Copy the selected area.

STEP 15:
Go to the Channels panel (under the Window menu) and click on the Create New Channel icon at the bottom of the panel. With the selection still active, press **Command-V (PC: Ctrl-V)** to Paste the selection into the channel, then press **Command-D (PC: Ctrl-D)** to Deselect.

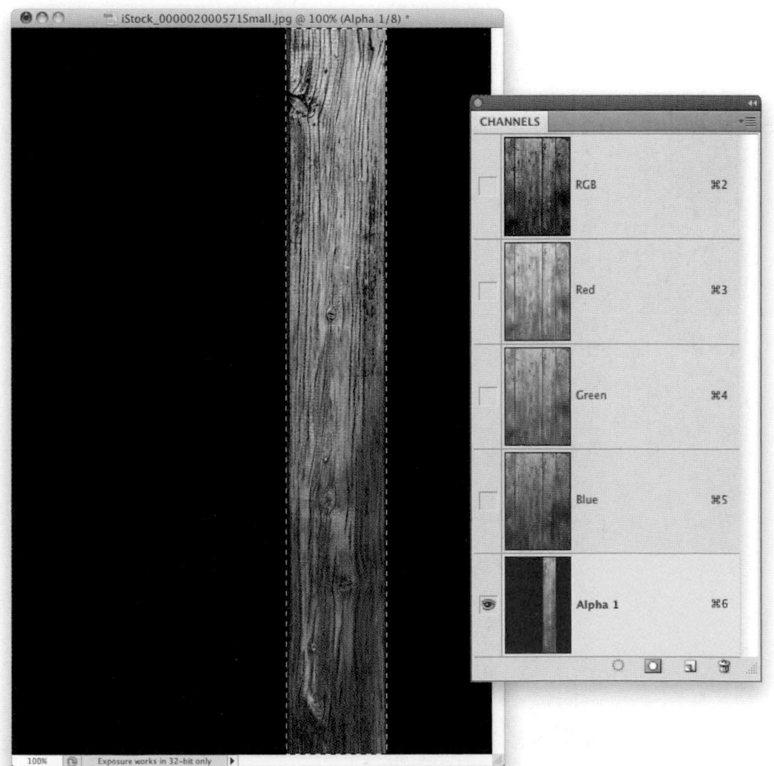

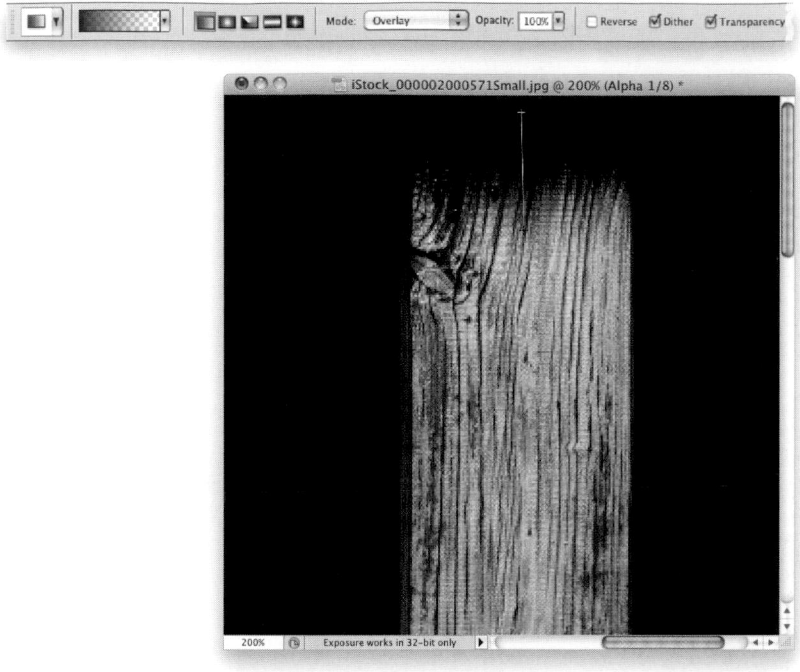

STEP 16:

Now, get the Gradient tool **(G)** from the Toolbox and then, in the Options Bar, click on the down-facing arrow next to the gradient thumbnail and choose the Foreground to Transparent gradient (the second gradient from the left in the top row) from the Gradient Picker. Make sure the Linear Gradient icon is selected (the first icon to the right of the gradient thumbnail) and change the blend Mode to **Overlay**. With your Foreground color set to black, starting at the top of the plank, click-and-drag the gradient down just a little bit. With the Gradient tool in Overlay mode, the edge will have more contrast than normal. Click-and-drag two or three more times to increase the contrast, making the edge more frayed. Do this same thing to the bottom edge of the plank, as well.

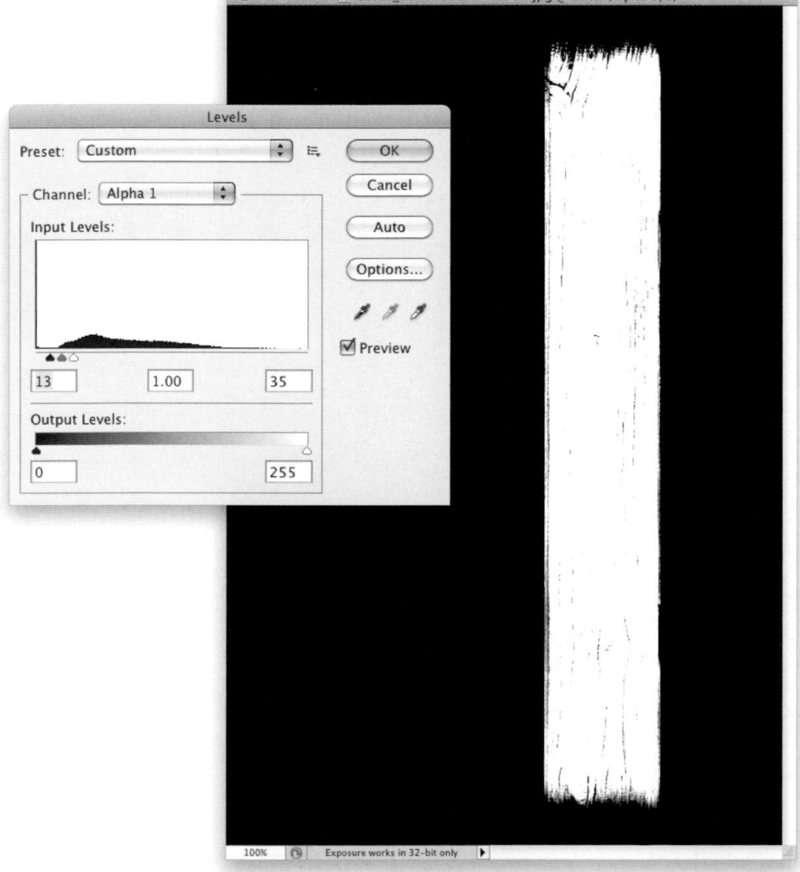

STEP 17:

Next, open the Levels dialog by pressing **Command-L (PC: Ctrl-L)**, then raise the contrast so much that it forces the plank to mostly white. Here, I dragged the Input Levels highlights (white) slider all the way to the left and dragged the Input Levels shadows (black) slider just a little bit to the right. Pay close attention to the top and bottom edges of the plank—you should see them get sharper. There might be some small black lines that appear on the plank, but they are not a big deal.

Continued

STEP 18:

Click on the RGB composite channel at the top of the Channels panel, then from the Select menu, choose **Load Selection**. Make sure the **Alpha 1** channel we just created is selected in the Channel pop-up menu and click OK.

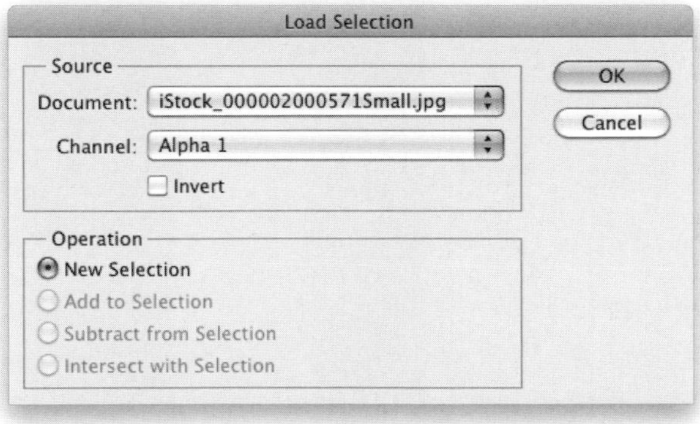

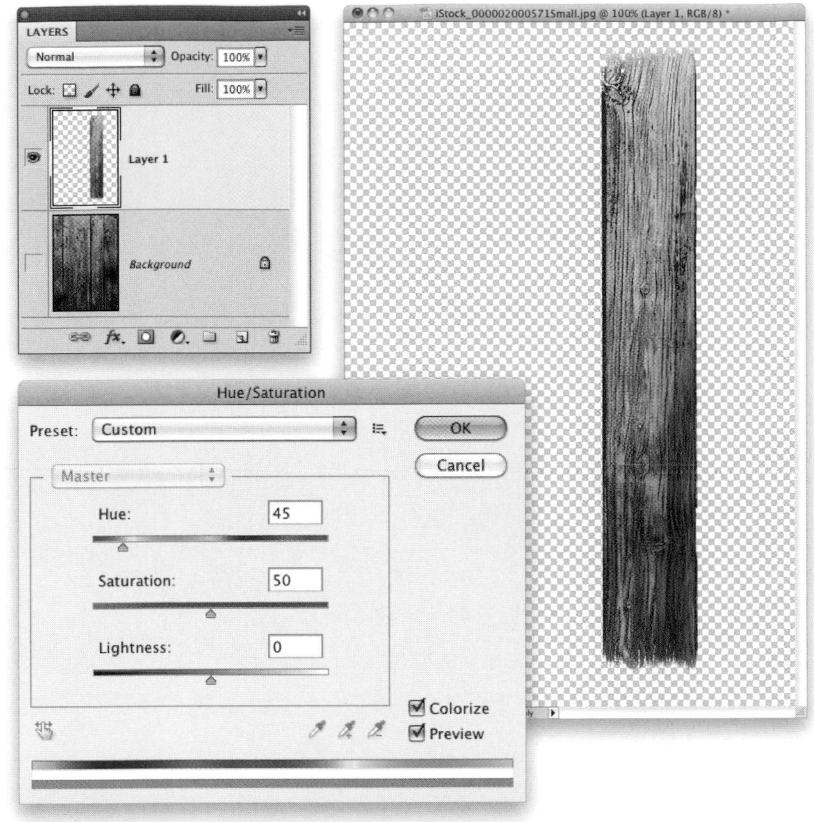

STEP 19:

Press Command-J (PC: Ctrl-J) to copy the selected area to a new layer. Then, click on the Eye icon to the left of the Background layer to turn it off and see the new plank with frayed edges. If necessary, you can increase the density by duplicating the layer two or three times, then merging them all back together into one layer. To give the plank a different color, open the Hue/Saturation dialog by pressing **Command-U (PC: Ctrl-U)**. Turn on the Colorize checkbox, set the Hue to 45 and the Saturation to 50, and click OK.

STEP 20:

Now, bring this new element into the layout, go into Free Transform, resize it, rotate it, and use it as a surface for the text to sit on. I simply used the same element in both cases here, by making a duplicate of the layer and rotating it just slightly for variation. Then, I added a Drop Shadow layer style to them using the settings shown here. Finally, I added a logo and some text to finish it off, as you'll see in the final image. (I used the fonts Futura, Myriad Pro, and Mama Regular. Oh, and in case you were wondering, "Sörf" is Turkish for "Surf".)

Continued

Final Image

Video Game Cover Design

One of the best places to find inspiration, aside from movie posters and magazines, is video game covers. In this project, we'll combine a number of different effects from several video game covers that I really like. It really demonstrates well how you can combine images with text elements in a non-destructive way with smart objects.

©ISTOCKPHOTO/MARK EVANS

STEP ONE:

As usual, we'll start our video game cover design with the background image. Open the car image shown here. It's a great shot, but we need to spice it up a little bit. First, let's get it into the layout by pressing **Command-A (PC: Ctrl-A)** to Select All, then **Command-C (PC: Ctrl-C)** to Copy it to the clipboard.

STEP TWO:

Press **Command-N (PC: Ctrl-N)** to create a new document, and make it 7 inches wide by 10 inches tall at 100 ppi. Then, paste the car image into the new document by pressing **Command-V (PC: Ctrl-V)**. Press **Command-T (PC: Ctrl-T)** to go into Free Transform mode, press-and-hold the Shift key, and click-and-drag a corner point to resize the image. Then, position it in the composition like you see here. Press **Return (PC: Enter)** to lock in your transformation.

Continued

STEP THREE:

Here's another cool trick for boosting the contrast of an image: click on the Create New Adjustment Layer icon at the bottom of the Layers panel and choose **Levels**. Do not make a single change in the Adjustments panel. Just change the Levels adjustment layer's blend mode to **Overlay**. This alone will make the colors really pop. I don't really know why, but hey, it works for me.

STEP FOUR:

To go along with the whole racing theme of the video game cover we're creating, open the checkered flag image and use the Move tool **(V)** to drag it or copy-and-paste it (the way we did with the background image) into the working layout. Position it in the top left of the layout (as shown here).

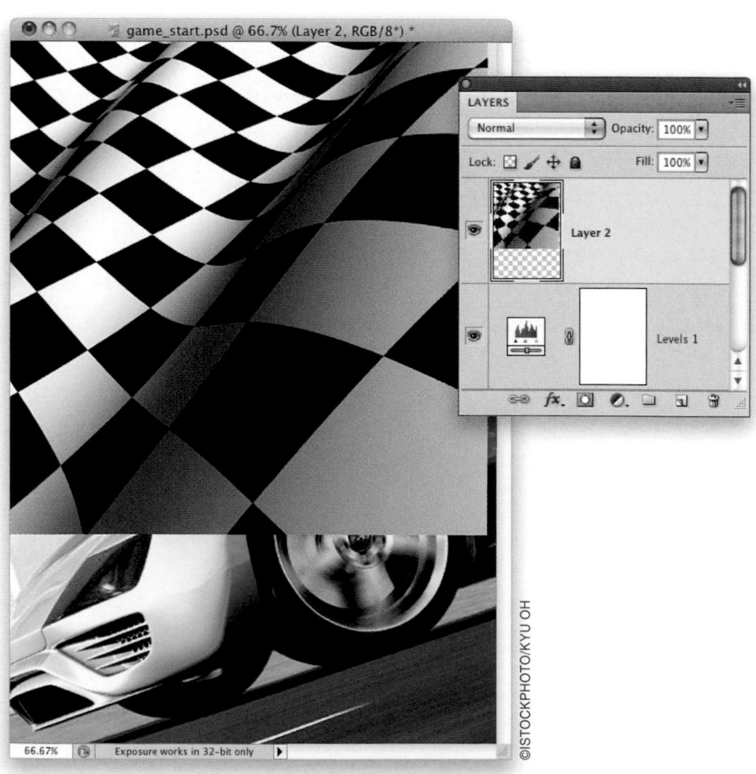

©ISTOCKPHOTO/KYU OH

STEP FIVE:

Add a layer mask to the checkered flag layer by clicking on the Add Layer Mask icon at the bottom of the Layers panel. Then, get the Gradient tool **(G)** from the Toolbox, click on the down-facing arrow to the right of the gradient thumbnail in the Options Bar, and choose the Foreground to Transparent gradient (the second gradient from the left in the top row). With your Foreground color set to black, click-and-drag diagonally from the bottom right to the top left to fade the checkered flag into the background, like I've done here.

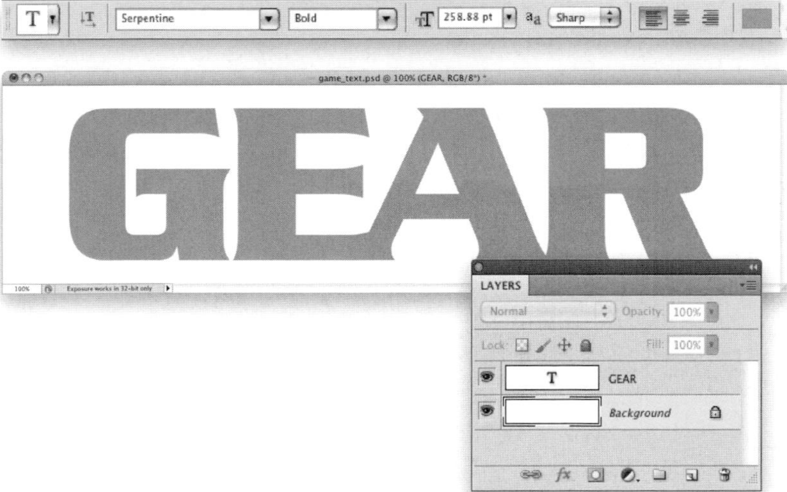

STEP SIX:

Now, on to the text objects. Create another new document that is 12 inches wide by 3 inches tall at 100 ppi. Grab the Horizontal Type tool **(T)** from the Toolbox and click in your new document to create a text layer. Here, I set the color to gray in the Options Bar, and typed the word "GEAR" using Serpentine Bold. Then, I went into Free Transform and scaled it to cover almost the entire image area.

Continued

STEP SEVEN:

Before we add some layer style effects to the text, we need to define a couple images as textures that we'll apply through layer styles. The first is this seamless carbon fiber pattern. Open the file, and then go under the Edit menu and choose **Define Pattern**. Give the pattern a name and click OK. We'll use this as a background element.

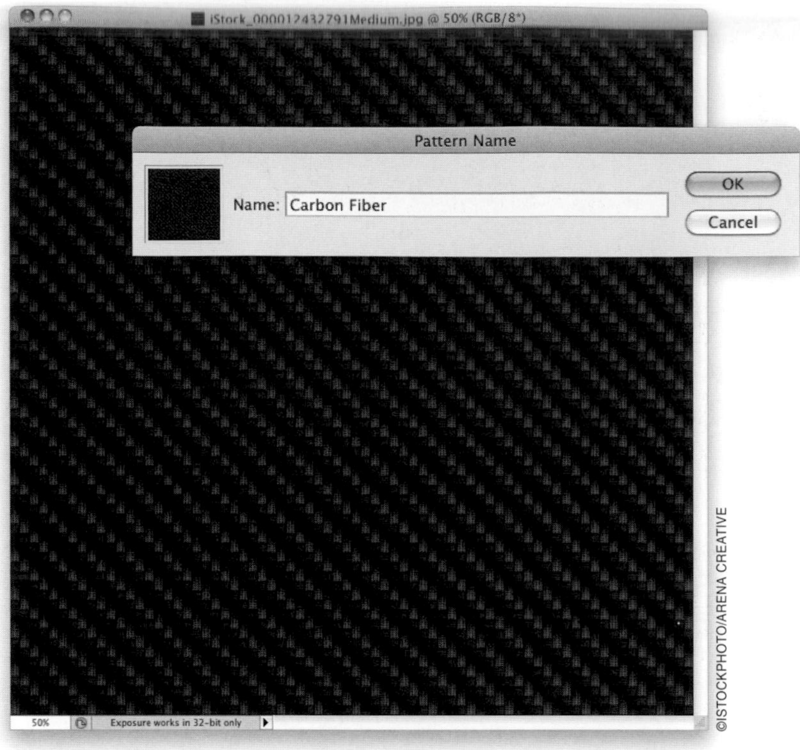

STEP EIGHT:

Next, open the other car image on the blue background and define it as a pattern, as well. We'll apply this image to the text through a layer style.

STEP NINE:

Now we have quite a collection of layer styles we're going to use to dress up this text graphic. First, in your text document, click on the Create a New Layer icon at the bottom of the Layers panel to create a new blank layer, and then move it below the text layer in the layer stack. Then, fill that layer with 50% gray by pressing **Shift-Delete (PC: Shift-Backspace)** and choosing **50% Gray** from the Use pop-up menu in the Fill dialog. Click OK.

STEP 10:

Click on the Add a Layer Style icon at the bottom of the Layers panel and choose **Pattern Overlay**. Then, click on the Pattern thumbnail, locate the Carbon Fiber pattern at the bottom of the Pattern Picker, and click on it to select it. Also, drop the Scale down to 50%.

Continued

STEP 11:

Click on Gradient Overlay on the left side of the dialog to turn it on. Use the default Black, White gradient, but change the Blend Mode to **Overlay**, turn on the Reverse checkbox, change the Style to **Radial**, the Angle to 180°, and the Scale to 150%. Remember, you can move the pattern around manually if you want by clicking in the image window and dragging it around. Click OK when you're done.

STEP 12:

Now, click on the text layer in the Layers panel to make it active, then click on the Add a Layer Style icon, choose **Bevel and Emboss**, and apply the settings you see here. For Gloss Contour, be sure to choose the Ring preset, which is the second icon in the second row in the Gloss Contour Picker.

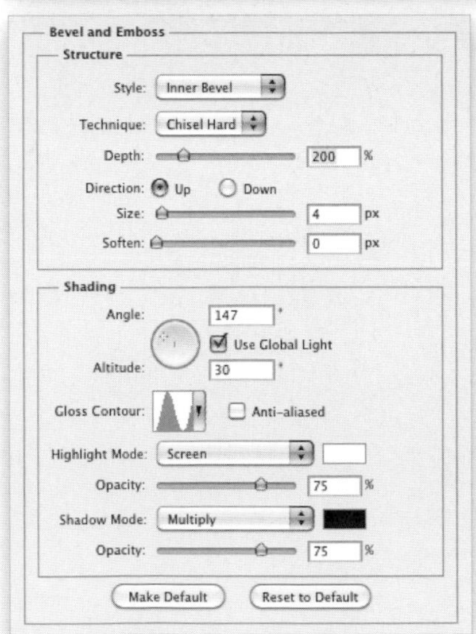

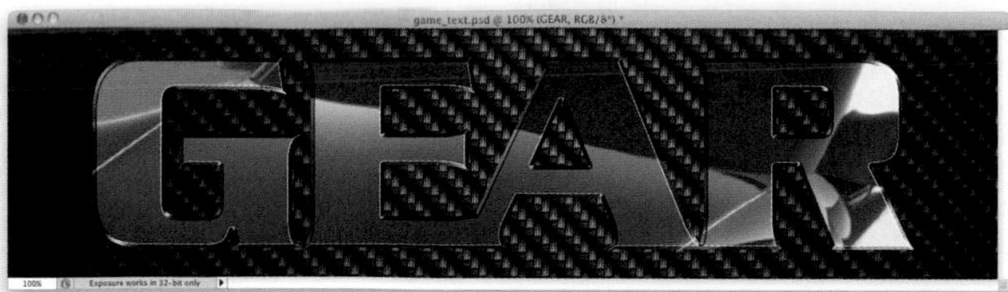

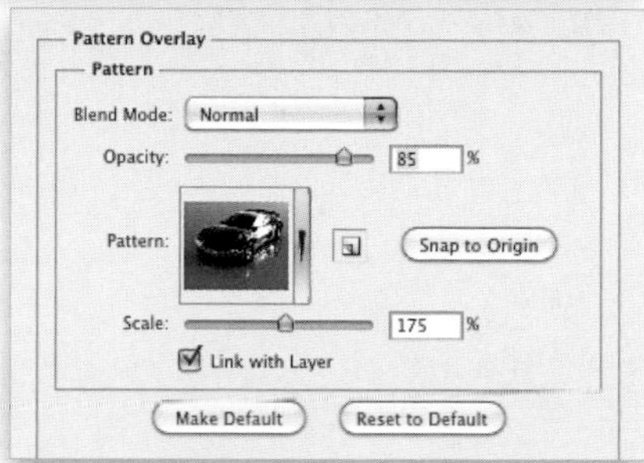

STEP 13:

Click on Pattern Overlay on the left to turn it on, then click on the Pattern thumbnail and, this time, locate the Car Pattern we defined earlier. Drop the Opacity down to 85% and increase the Scale to 175%. Then, move the Layer Style dialog aside and click-and-drag the pattern around in your image window, so you can see some of the reflective surface of the car inside the text.

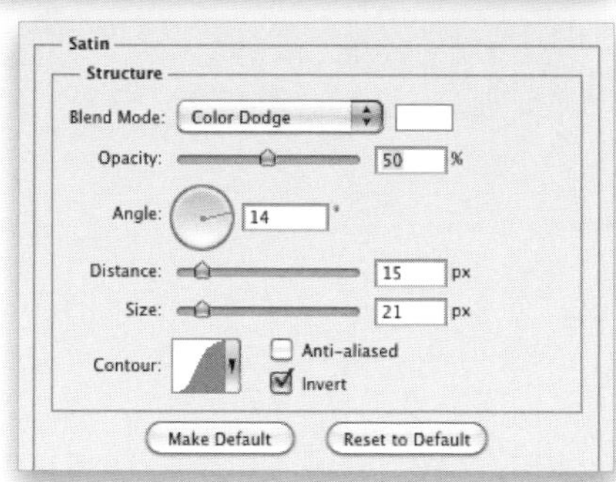

STEP 14:

Next, click on Satin on the left to turn it on, and then click on the color swatch to the right of the Blend Mode pop-up menu and choose white. Set the Blend Mode to **Color Dodge** and drop the Opacity to 50%. Set the Angle to 14°, the Distance to 15 px, and the Size to 21 px. You can also adjust the satin look manually by clicking in the image window and dragging it around, like we did with the Pattern Overlay layer style.

Continued

STEP 15:
Finally, click on Stroke on the left to turn it on. Keep the Color set to black, increase the Size to 10 px, and make sure the Position is set to **Outside**. Click OK when you're done.

STEP 16:
Now you can see, after all we've done, that we've dressed the text up quite nicely with layer styles. Before we bring the text into the working layout, though, Command-click (PC: Ctrl-click) on the carbon fiber layer (Layer 1), so that both it and the text layer are selected, then Right-click on either layer and choose **Convert to Smart Object**. Now, click-and-drag or copy-and-paste this smart object into the working layout.

STEP 17:
With the smart object in your working layout, go into Free Transform, press-and-hold the Shift key, and resize the layer, so that the text fits the width of the layout (and you don't see all the extra carbon fiber texture on either side). Press **Return (PC: Enter)** to lock in the transformation. Add a layer mask and then select the Rectangular Marquee tool **(M)** from the Toolbox. Create a selection along the top edge of the word, then press-and-hold the Shift key (to add to the selection) and create a selection right along the bottom edge of the text. With your Foreground color set to black, press **Option-Delete (PC: Alt-Backspace)** to fill these selected areas with black. This will hide the excess edge of the carbon fiber texture. Press **Command-D (PC: Ctrl-D)** to Deselect.

STEP 18:
Go into Free Transform mode again, and then Right-click inside the bounding box and choose **Skew**. Press-and-hold the Option (PC: Alt) key, then click-and-drag the right-middle control handle upward to skew the text object to match the angle of the car. Right-click inside the bounding box again, choose **Scale**, then press-and-hold the Shift key and click-and-drag the top-middle control handle up to increase the size of the text. Press Return when you're done.

Continued

STEP 19:

Now we need to add one more text element just above GEAR. Since we've already gone through the process of creating the GEAR text, we can just do this by making a duplicate of the Smart Object layer and modifying it. However, creating a regular duplicate will keep the contents of the Smart Object layer linked to the duplicate—meaning, if we change one, it will change the other. So, to make an unlinked copy of the Smart Object layer, Right-click on it and choose **New Smart Object via Copy**.

STEP 20:

Double-click on the duplicate Smart Object thumbnail to open it up. Using the Horizontal Type tool, highlight the text and type "MAXX." Then, move the text to fit in the canvas area. Lastly, click on the Eye icon to the left of the background carbon fiber layer to turn it off, press **Command-W (PC: Ctrl-W)** to close the document window, and save the changes when prompted. The new text will then be updated in the working layout.

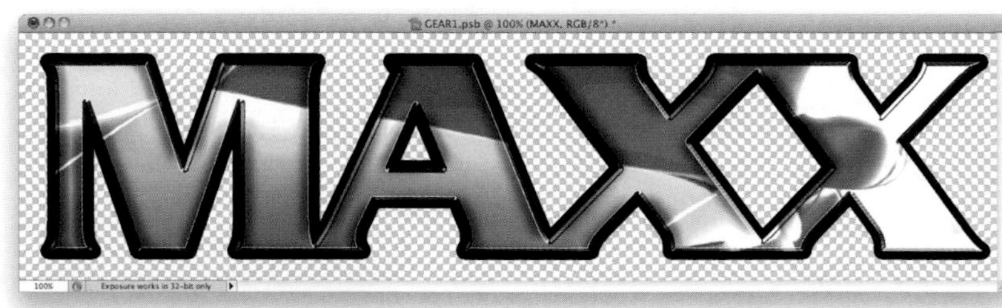

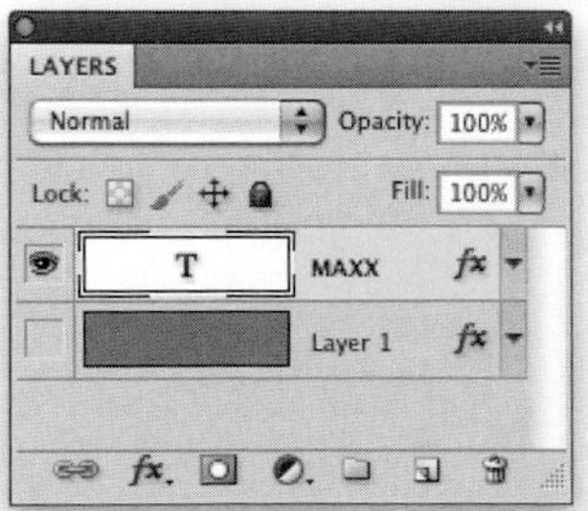

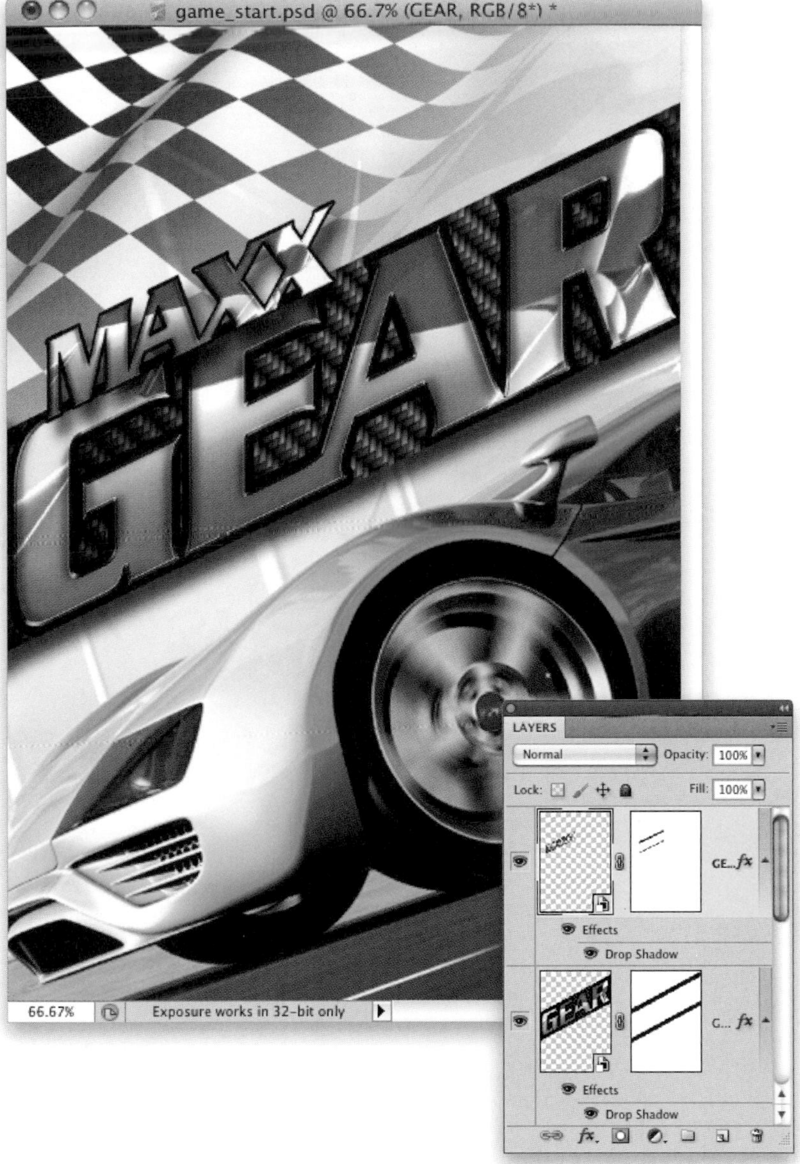

STEP 21:

Go into Free Transform again, and scale the MAXX text layer down and position it just above the GEAR text, so it overlaps slightly, like you see here. As an option, you can add a Drop Shadow layer style to both Smart Object layers to help give them a little more depth (as I've done with the settings shown here). And, as a final touch, you could use the flare brush from Chapter 1 and add it to the specular highlight on the car, as well as the text.

In the final image, you'll see I added some finishing elements to polish the effect. At the top, I created a fake version of the Xbox label, with a few tweaks of my own. I simply created a rectangle on a new layer and filled it with white. Then, I added the gradient element along the bottom of it and added the logo and text on top. I also threw in the fake rating graphic at the bottom. These finishing elements would normally be handled by the manufacturer, but as a designer, you must be aware of them and leave space in the design to accommodate them. Otherwise, critical parts of your design can be obstructed.

Continued

Use the Flare brush created in Chapter 1.

Use the Flare brush created in Chapter 1.

Final Image

Widen Your Gaze

photo effects

Look beyond the obvious. How many of us have a digital camera and find ourselves with a whole bunch of images that just take up space on the memory card? I think we all have at some point. So, one day, I decided that I would force my creative mind to make something out of nothing. As a designer, I use photography as a big part of my work. However, unlike a normal photographer, I look at things differently, as I encourage you to do. Change your perspective on the world and look at things differently. Notice textures, shapes, patterns, and even negative space, and grab them with whatever you have—your phone, a DSLR camera, or even a point-and-shoot. Whatever you have, you can make something extraordinary from it. Even looking through stock images, you can shift your thinking and look at different ways to use images as design elements. As you widen your gaze, you will start to see a world of ideas right before your very eyes!

Illustrated Photo Effect

Here, we'll explore a cool technique for making a photo look like an illustrated image. The really cool thing about this technique is that you can apply it to just about any photo and get something interesting. In fact, I've used it so many times that I set up an action for it, so I can have this effect on call whenever I need it.

STEP ONE:
Open the image you want to apply the effect to. Here, we have an image that just screams for this effect (you can download and use this image or use one of your own).

STEP TWO:
First, make a duplicate of the Background layer by pressing **Command-J (PC: Ctrl-J)**. Then, convert the image to black and white using the Gradient Map adjustment by pressing **D** to set your Foreground and Background colors to their defaults of black and white, then going under the Image menu, under Adjustments, and choosing **Gradient Map**. Just click OK in the Gradient Map dialog.

STEP THREE:

Now, make a duplicate of this black-and-white layer and change the duplicate layer's blend mode to **Divide**. This will turn the entire image window white. To bring back detail, go under the Filter menu, under Blur, and choose **Gaussian Blur**. The Radius setting will vary on different images, but in this case, set it to 15 pixels and click OK. As you can see, the image now has a very stylish, almost illustrated, look, but we're not done yet.

STEP FOUR:

Press **Command-E (PC: Ctrl-E)** to merge the two duplicate layers together into one layer. Then, go under the Filter menu again, this time under Artistic, and choose **Poster Edges**. Again, these settings may vary with different images, but here, I set the Edge Thickness to 0, the Edge Intensity to 1, and the Posterization to 6. This will intensify the effect a bit more. Click OK.

Continued

STEP FIVE:

Now, open the texture file to add the illustrated effect to (you can see it here at the bottom of the Layers panel). Then, get the Move tool **(V)**, go back to the subject image, Command-click (PC: Ctrl-click) on the processed layer and the original color Background layer, so that they're both selected, and then drag them both onto the texture file. Keep them both selected, press **Command-T (PC: Ctrl-T)** to go into Free Transform, then press **Command-0** (zero; **Ctrl-0**), so that you can reach the control handles. Press-and-hold the Shift key and then click-and-drag a corner handle outward to increase their size a bit, so that they fit over the texture image.

STEP SIX:

Click on the black-and-white "illustrated" layer to make it active, then press **Command-U (PC: Ctrl-U)** to open the Hue/Saturation dialog. Turn on the Colorize checkbox, set the Hue to 35, the Saturation to 50, and leave the Lightness set to 0. Click OK. Now, change the blend mode of this top layer to **Multiply**. Click on the Eye icon to the left of the original color layer beneath the illustrated layer (Layer 1) to hide it and get a better look at how the effect is coming along.

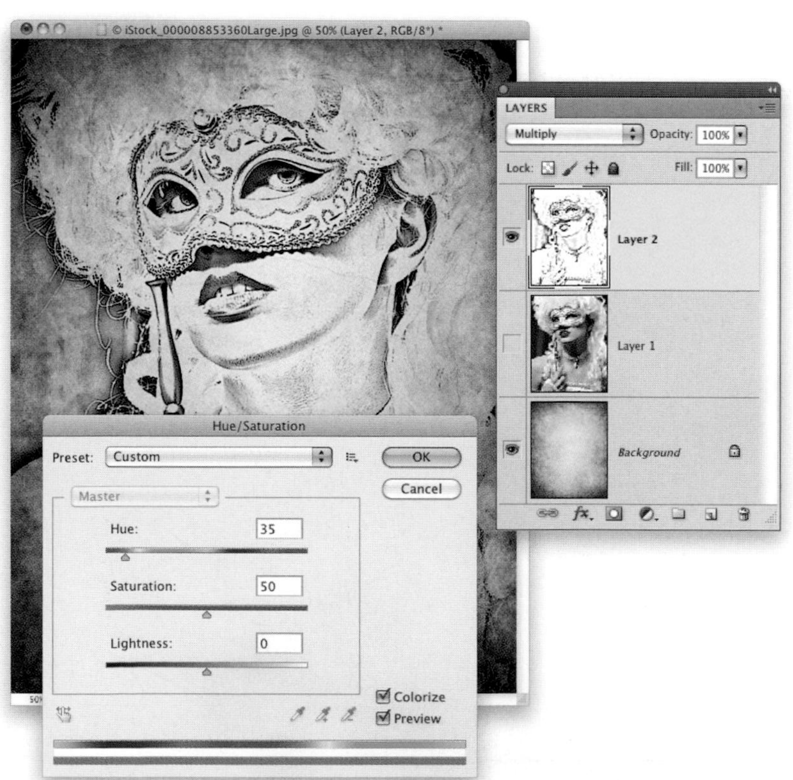

STEP SEVEN:

Now, make the original color layer visible again, and then click on it to make it active. Option-click (PC: Alt-click) on the Add Layer Mask icon at the bottom of the Layers panel to add a black layer mask. This will hide everything on the layer.

STEP EIGHT:

Get the Gradient tool **(G)** from the Toolbox, then in the Options Bar, click on the down-facing arrow to the right of the gradient thumbnail, choose the Foreground to Transparent gradient (the second one from the left in the top row), and then click on the Radial Gradient icon (the second icon to the right of the gradient thumbnail). Make sure the layer mask is selected in the Layers panel, press **X** to set your Foreground color to white, and then, starting in the middle of the face, click-and-drag outward. This will reveal some of the color image, giving the illustrated look some color. Continue to add more gradients around the image in areas you want to see some color. You can stylize the color effect a bit more by changing the layer blend mode to **Linear Burn** and dropping the Opacity down to about 75%.

Continued

STEP NINE:

Finally, I clicked on the Add Layer Mask icon again and added a white layer mask to the top illustrated layer. Then, I switched my Foreground color to black and used the Radial Gradient to fade the top corners to make them blend better.

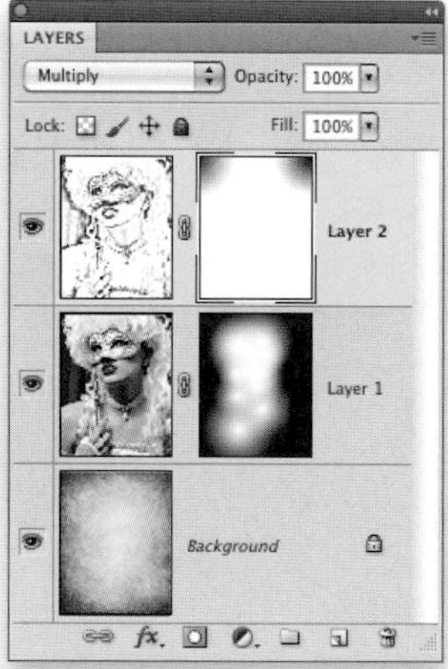

Final Image

Gritty Texture Composite

I'm a big fan of textures. I keep a folder of nothing but textures for any occasion. Whether they're from iStock-photo, my own camera, or even my phone, I always like to have a variety on hand. In this project, we'll use a simple texture file to add an element of grit and ruggedness to a photo. Textures can have so many uses beyond their face value; you just have to look at them a little differently.

STEP ONE:
Open the file of the rugged cowboy or any other photo you might like to apply this effect to.

©ISTOCKPHOTO/CAMERON WHITMAN

STEP TWO:
Next, open the texture file you see here. Again, I like to keep a folder of nothing but textures in the event that I need them for whatever reason. Get the Move tool **(V)** from the Toolbox and drag this texture into the cowboy image file. Center it over the cowboy image and, if needed, go into Free Transform **(Command-T [PC: Ctrl-T])**, adjust the size of it, and then press **Return (PC: Enter)**.

©ISTOCKPHOTO/EVA SERRABASSA

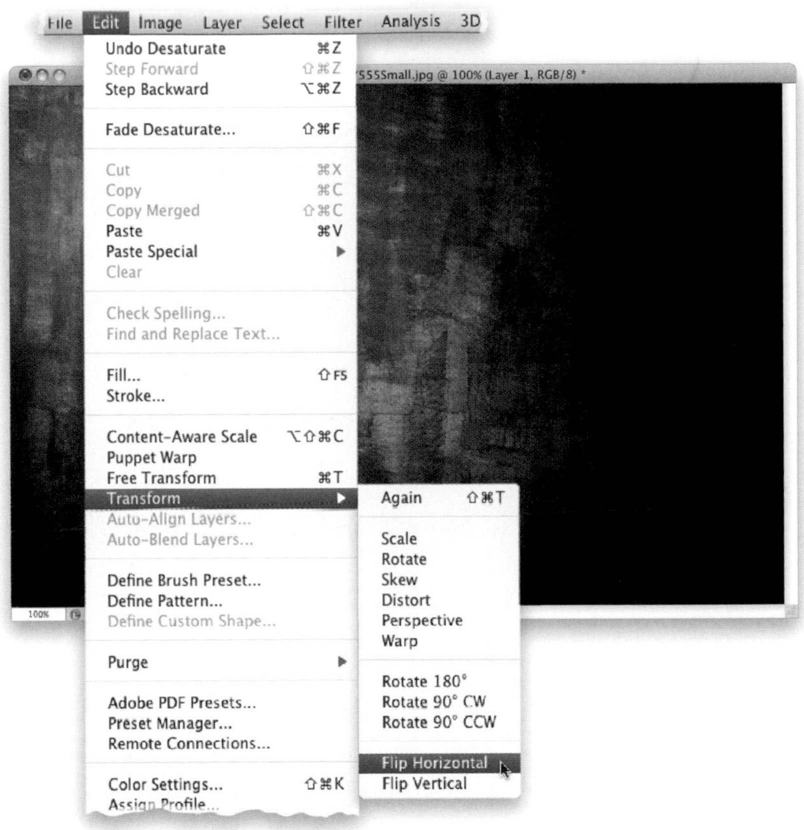

STEP THREE:

Now, first we need to remove the color from the texture image by pressing **Command-Shift-U (PC: Ctrl-Shift-U)**. Since the cowboy is on the left side of the image, we also need to flip the texture around, so the lighter side of it is on the left side, as well. So, go under the Edit menu, under Transform, and choose **Flip Horizontal**.

STEP FOUR:

Next, go under the Image menu, under Adjustments, and choose **Invert** to flip the image values. Change the layer's blend mode to **Screen**, making the black areas invisible and revealing the cowboy image below.

Continued

STEP FIVE:

Now, if the texture seems a little overbearing, then you can go under the Image menu, again under Adjustments, and this time choose **Levels**. Run a simple Levels adjustment, like you see here, to darken the black areas.

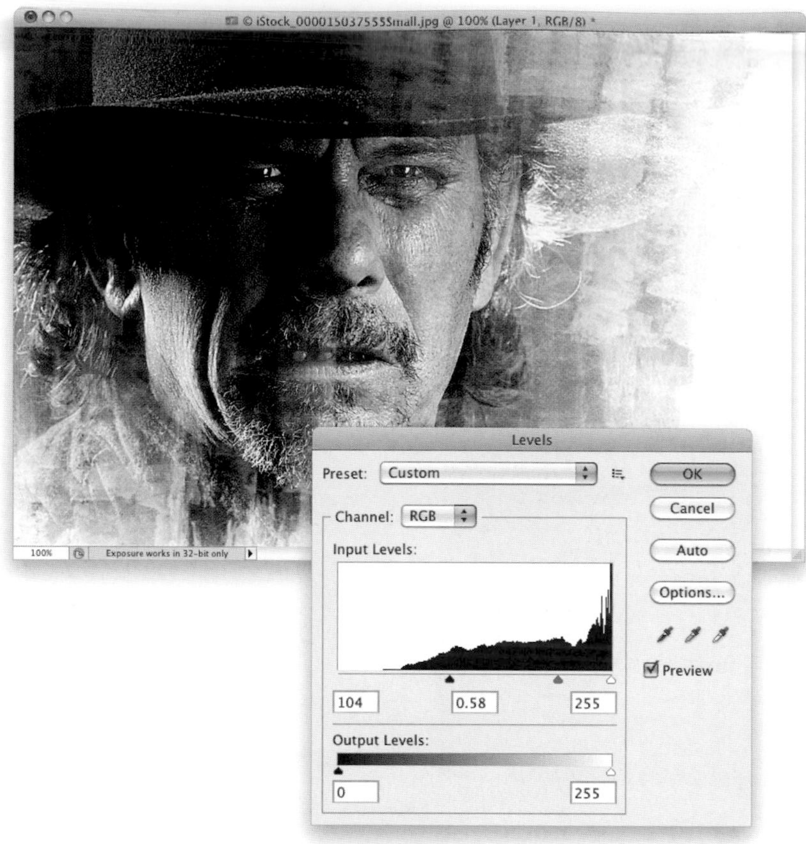

STEP SIX:

To add an extra element of grit to the cowboy image, click on the Background layer to make it active. Then, go under the Filter menu, under Sharpen, and choose **Smart Sharpen**. Set the Amount to 100%, the Radius to 1 px, and the Remove pop-up menu to **Gaussian Blur**. Click OK when you're done.

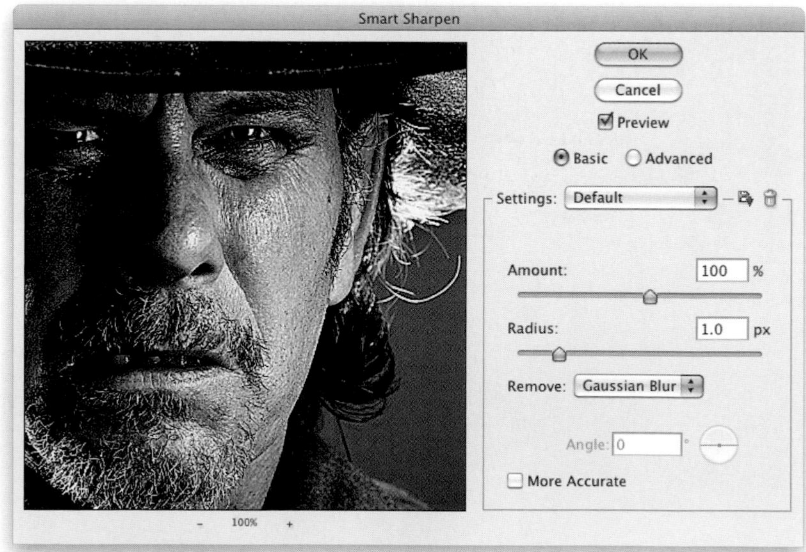

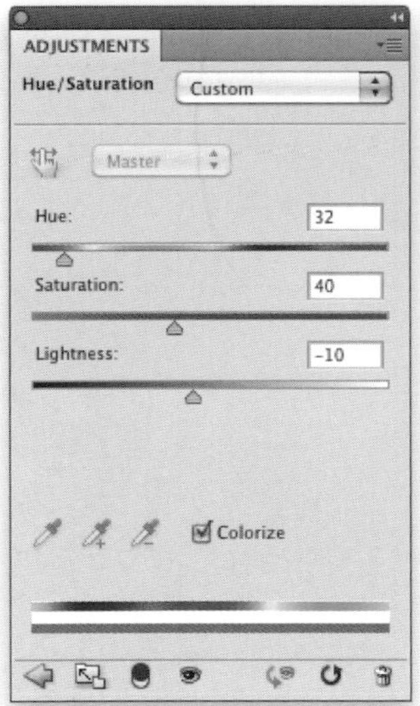

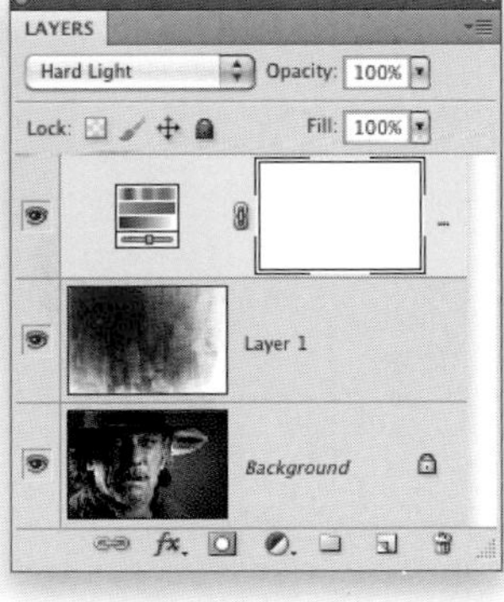

STEP SEVEN:

To finish this effect, click back on the texture layer in the Layers panel to make it active, then click on the Create New Adjustment Layer icon at the bottom of the panel and choose **Hue/Saturation**. In the Adjustments panel, turn on the Colorize checkbox, then set the Hue to 32, the Saturation to 40, and the Lightness to –10. This will give the image a vintage sepia look. Finally, change the adjustment layer's blend mode to **Hard Light** and, if needed, get the Crop tool **(C)** and crop the image slightly to remove some of the white background on the right (as you'll see I did in the Final Image).

That's pretty much it. As you play with this technique, be sure to try different textures and colors to get a variety of different looks.

TIP: Photograph Textures

Since textures are often very abstract images, you can use things like the camera on your phone to take pictures of textures when you're out and about. These days, camera phones take pretty decent pictures that you can work with.

Continued

Final Image

In this version, I used two copies of the texture file in different positions, and masked out part of each to cover the area I wanted to show. Then I merged all the layers into a new layer, changed the blend mode to Multiply, and added a new colored texture image below the merged layer.

Stylish High-Key Effect

This effect is definitely an oldie but goody. Stylized high-key effects are very common in high-fashion magazines, movies, and television. It has a very classy feel to it and is not that difficult of an effect to achieve with the right image. That doesn't mean it only works for certain images, though. You just never know until you try. I know that when I first learned this, I went crazy on almost every model shot I had!

©ISTOCKPHOTO/JULIA SAVCHENKO

STEP ONE:
Open the file of the model on the white background. While it's not entirely necessary for the subject to be on a white background, it does make the technique a little easier. I like this image especially, because it's pretty symmetrical and can be positioned in numerous ways once the effect is created.

STEP TWO:
Go to the Channels panel (under the Window menu), press-and-hold the Command (PC: Ctrl) key and click on the RGB channel to load the luminosity of the image as a selection.

Continued

STEP THREE:
Create a new Alpha channel by clicking on the Create New Channel icon at the bottom of the Channels panel. Then, fill the selection with white by pressing **Shift-Delete (PC: Shift-Backspace)** to open the Fill dialog, choosing **White** from the Use pop-up menu, and clicking OK.

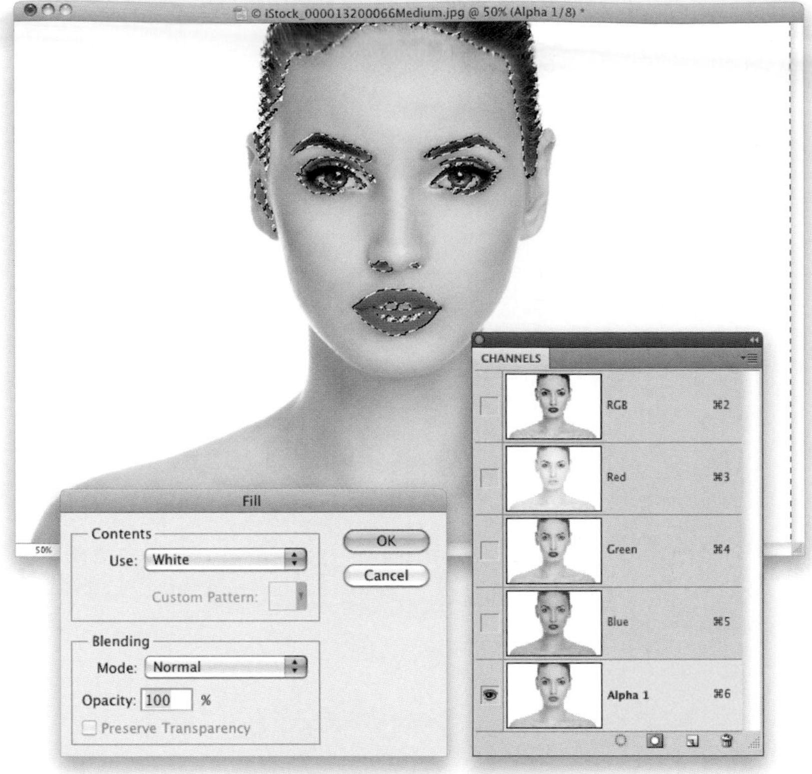

STEP FOUR:
Press **Command-Shift-I (PC: Ctrl-Shift-I)** to Inverse the selection, then press Shift-Delete to open the Fill dialog again, and this time, choose **Black** from the Use pop-up menu. This will darken the black areas a bit more. Do not deselect just yet.

STEP FIVE:

Now, press Command-Shift-I again, to invert the selection back around to the light areas. Then, fill the selection with white two times to blow out the detail in the face. However, even though we added more black, the dark areas are still a bit light. You can now press **Command-D (PC: Ctrl-D)** to Deselect.

STEP SIX:

To darken these areas, press Shift-Delete, once again, and choose Black from the Use pop-up menu, but this time, also change the Blending Mode to **Soft Light**. Do this once more and this will darken the black areas while leaving the lighter areas unaffected.

Continued

STEP SEVEN:

Now, this next step is optional, but does add a very stylish grain to the image and also puts a soft glow on the face. Go under the Filter menu, under Distort, and choose **Diffuse Glow**. Set the Graininess to 5, the Glow Amount to 3, and the Clear Amount to 10. Again, like other filters, these settings may vary depending on the image.

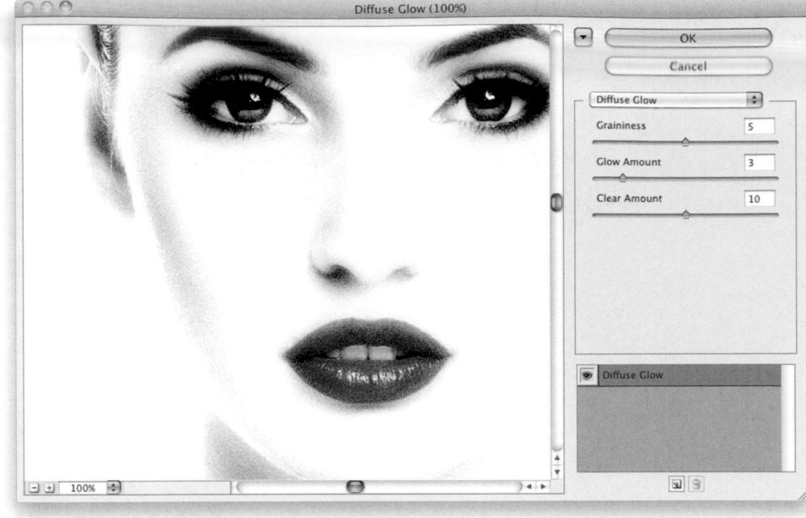

STEP EIGHT:

It may be necessary to darken specific areas of the image. Do this by selecting the Brush tool **(B)** from the Toolbox, then in the Options Bar, change the blend Mode to **Soft Light**. Click on the brush thumbnail, choose a large, soft-edged brush from the Brush Picker, and, with your Foreground color set to black, paint in the areas you want to darken. With the brush in Soft Light mode, it will ignore the light areas.

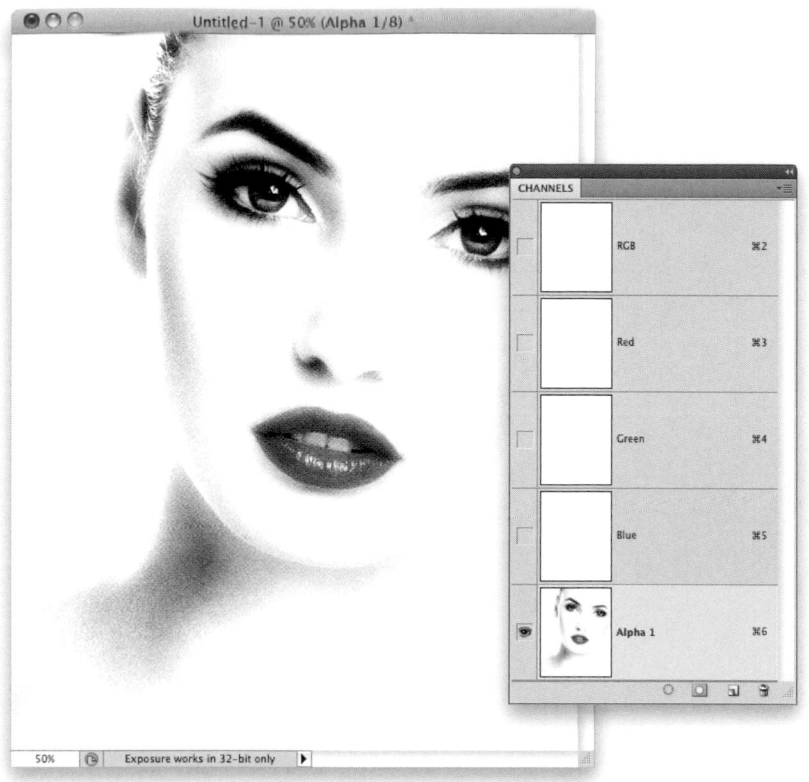

STEP NINE:

Next, from the File menu, choose **New,** and create a new document 8 inches wide by 10 inches tall at 125 ppi. Then, get the Move tool **(V)** from the Toolbox and drag the Alpha 1 channel to the new document, and it will automatically add it to the Channels panel. Press **Command-T (PC: Ctrl-T)** to put the channel into Free Transform mode, use the corner handles to scale the image outward, and then move your cursor outside the bounding box and click-and-drag to rotate it to fit the composition, like you see here. Press **Return (PC: Enter)** to lock in your transformation.

STEP 10:

Click on the Create a New Layer icon at the bottom of the Layers panel to create a new blank layer. Then, from the Select menu, choose **Load Selection**. From the Channel pop-up menu, choose **Alpha 1**, turn on the Invert checkbox, and then click OK. Once the selection is active, click on the Foreground color swatch at the bottom of the Toolbox and choose a color (I chose a purple color). Then, press **Option-Delete (PC: Alt-Backspace)** to fill the selection with this new color and deselect. How cool is that?

To finish up the design, you can add some text. You'll see in the final image on the next page, I just added one word to the bottom of the layout using Bank Gothic Light.

Continued

Final Image

In this alternate example, I did all the same steps using a different photo, merely changing the color and positioning of the subject. When scaled this close and this large, you can hide imperfections by duplicating the layer and changing the blend mode to Dissolve, and then creating a new blank layer below the duplicate layer. Merge the duplicate layer with the blank layer to lessen the Dissolve effect. You can back it off even more by dropping the layer opacity a bit.

Vintage Pinup-Girl Effect

An update to a technique I did on Planet Photoshop (www.planetphotoshop.com) a while back, this effect involves giving a model shot that vintage pinup-girl look. Now, this doesn't mean you only need a pinup-style shot for this effect to work. If you have one, great, but try it on other images and you might discover it gives you something you did not expect, and perhaps build on the effect to make it your own.

©ISTOCKPHOTO/UMBAR SHAKIR

STEP ONE:

To start this pinup effect, open an image you want to apply the effect to or use the one I have here. Make a duplicate of the Background layer by pressing **Command-J (PC: Ctrl-J)**.

STEP TWO:

Go under the Filter menu, under Blur, and choose **Surface Blur**. Set the Radius to 5 pixels and the Threshold to 10 levels. This will smooth out the image, while maintaining the edge detail. Click OK when you're done.

Continued

STEP THREE:
Now the skin area is nice and smooth, but the hair still looks a little too natural. To give it an illustrated look, get the Smudge tool from the Toolbox (it's nested with the Blur tool). Then, in the Options Bar, click on the brush thumbnail and choose a soft-edged brush around 40 pixels in size, then drop the Strength setting to 3%. Now, smudge the hair in the direction it flows, and it will smear slightly, giving it a painterly look.

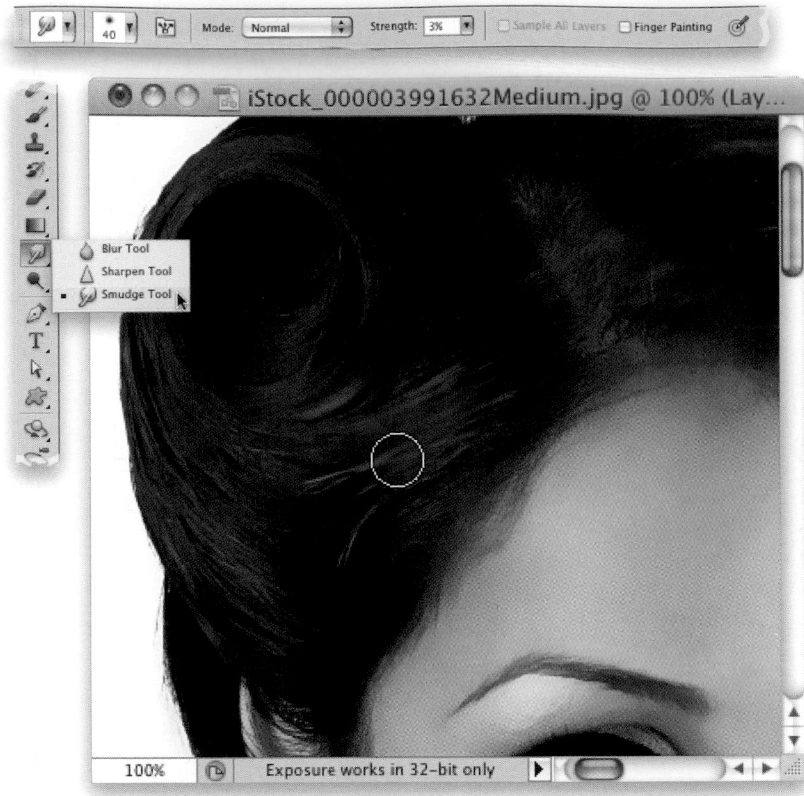

STEP FOUR:
Drop the brush size down just a bit and smudge the glare on the lips, just like the hair.

STEP FIVE:

Make a duplicate of this layer and change the blend mode to **Overlay** to boost the contrast and saturate the colors a little bit.

STEP SIX:

Go to the Channels panel (under the Window menu) and load the luminosity as a selection by Command-clicking (PC: Ctrl-clicking) on the RGB channel. Then, press **Command-Shift-I (PC: Ctrl-Shift-I)** to Inverse the selection.

Continued

STEP SEVEN:

Go back to the Layers panel and click on the Create a New Layer icon at the bottom of the panel to create a new blank layer. Press **Shift-Delete (PC: Shift-Backspace)** to bring up the Fill dialog, choose **White** from the Use pop-up menu, and click OK to fill the selection with white. Then, change the layer's blend mode to **Soft Light**. This will lighten the color slightly and brighten the darker areas, like the hair. Press **Command-D (PC: Ctrl-D)** to Deselect.

STEP EIGHT:

Now, create a merged copy of the image up this point by pressing **Command-Option-Shift-E (PC: Ctrl-Alt-Shift-E)**. Press **D** to set your Foreground and Background colors to their defaults of black and white, and then get the Eyedropper tool **(I)** from the Toolbox. Click on the red of the lips to set red as your Foreground color.

STEP NINE:
Go under the Filter menu, under Sketch, and choose **Photocopy**. Set the Detail to 3, the Darkness to 13, and then click OK.

STEP 10:
Now, change the blend mode of this layer to **Multiply**. This will give the edges of the image a more illustrated look. You can really see the difference if you click on the Eye icon to the left of the layer to turn it off, and then back on.

Continued

STEP 11:

Next, let's enhance the blush on the face a little bit. Create a new blank layer, change its blend mode to **Multiply**, and then get the Brush tool **(B)** from the Toolbox. In the Options Bar, click on the brush thumbnail and choose a soft-edged brush at around 125 pixels. Now, if you're using a Wacom pressure-sensitive tablet, you can go into the Brush panel (click on the icon to the right of the brush thumbnail to open it), click on Transfer on the left to turn it on, and set the Opacity Jitter Control pop-up menu to Pen Pressure. Otherwise, in the Options Bar, change the brush Opacity to 10%. Then, press-and-hold the Option (PC: Alt) key and click on the pinkish area in the lips to sample the color, and just paint a few strokes on the cheeks to build the blush effect. I also enhanced the areas below her eyebrows by decreasing the size of my brush, then sampling a color from the highlights in her hair, and painting below the eyebrows.

STEP 12:

Create another new blank layer, then press Shift-Delete (PC: Shift-Backspace) and choose **50% Gray** from the Fill dialog's Use pop-up menu to fill the layer with a medium gray. Go under the Filter menu, under Texture, and choose **Grain**. Set the Intensity to 30, the Contrast to 10, and for the Grain Type, choose **Enlarged**. Click OK.

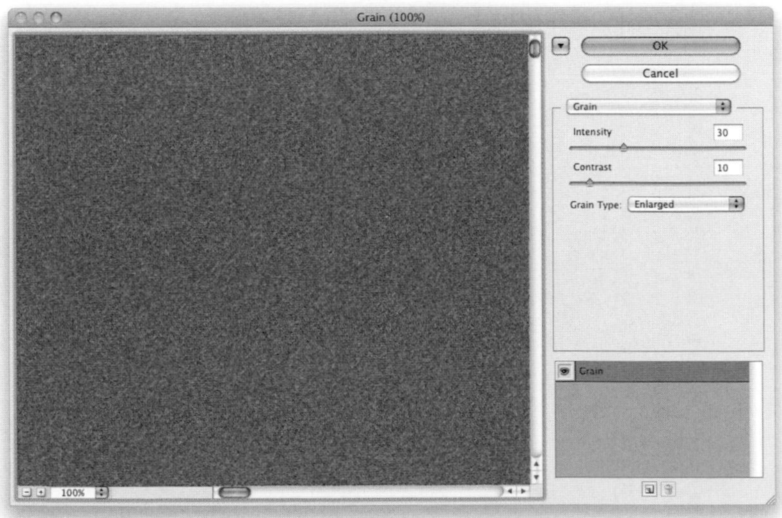

STEP 13:
Change the layer's blend mode to **Overlay** and then press Command-Option-Shift-E (PC: Ctrl-Alt-Shift-E) to create another merged copy of the file up to this point.

©ISTOCKPHOTO/PETER ZELEI

STEP 14:
Finally, open the old paper texture file and use the Move tool **(V)** to click-and-drag or copy-and-paste the pinup image into this file. Change the layer's blend mode to **Multiply**, which eliminates all the white areas and blends the image with the background texture, finishing the pinup look.

Now, not every project you do is going to call for a pinup effect, but as you experiment with this effect on different images, you'll see it gives you various results that you can use for numerous reasons. Just remember to have fun with it!

Continued

Final Image

ADAM ROHRMANN

In this example, you can see how this effect, with a little tweaking, can be applied to almost any photo. Here, I went through the same steps, only modifying the intensity or color of the effects where necessary. Experiment with your own images, and you'll find yourself trying it on every photo you have.

Themed Composite

Often, as designers, we love to see how a basic studio shot becomes a fully dressed Hollywood-style design. Here, we'll create a themed composite, starting with a basic studio shot of a subject in costume and taking it all the way through to a fully realized cinematic composite. Along the way, we'll use design elements from unusual sources.

©ISTOCKPHOTO/BAHADIR KUYUCU

STEP ONE:

Let's start by opening the gladiator image. You can see here it's a very basic studio shot, which is a great place to start.

STEP TWO:

The first thing we're going to do is grunge the image up with some HDR Toning. Make a duplicate of the image by going under the Image menu and choosing **Duplicate**. Then, go under the Image menu, under Adjustments, and choose **HDR Toning**. If you're using a different image, then you'll need to play around with the sliders a little bit here, but for this image, go ahead and use the settings I have here. Click OK when you're done.

Continued

STEP THREE:

Now, get the Move tool **(V)** from the Toolbox, press-and-hold the Shift key, and drag-and-drop the faux-HDR image into the original document (holding the Shift key will keep it aligned with the original). Once it's there, click on the Eye icon to the left of the faux-HDR layer to hide it for a moment.

STEP FOUR:

Click on the Background layer to make it active, then grab the Quick Selection tool **(W)** from the Toolbox, and paint over the gladiator to select him. Zoom in to make sure he's fully selected. Press-and-hold the **Option (PC: Alt) key** and paint to remove any areas from the selection that you don't want selected. Then, press **Command-J (PC: Ctrl-J)** to copy the selected area up to a new layer.

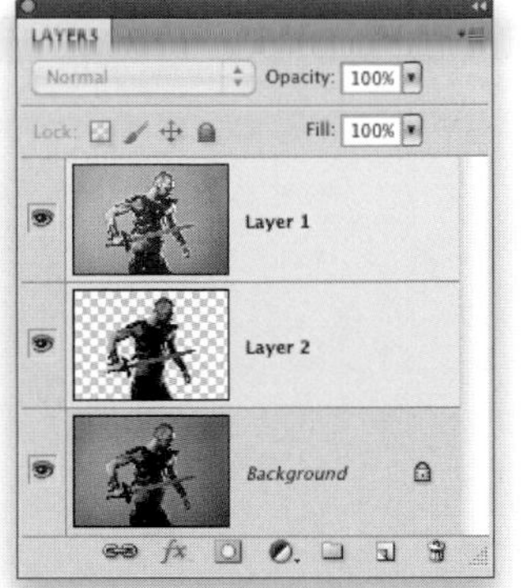

STEP FIVE:

Now, click where the Eye icon used to be to the left of the HDR-toned layer to make it visible again. Then, press-and-hold the Command (PC: Ctrl) key and click on the HDR-toned layer to select both it and the selected layer below.

STEP SIX:

From the File menu, choose **New** and create a new document that's 8 inches wide by 12 inches tall at 140 ppi. Switch back to the Move tool and drag-and-drop the two selected layers from the other file into this new document. Then, press **Command-T (PC: Ctrl-T)** to go into Free Transform, press-and-hold the Shift key, and click-and-drag a corner handle to scale the layers to fit in the layout the way you see here. Press **Return (PC: Enter)** to commit your transformation. Next, click on the HDR-toned layer in the Layers panel, so that only it is active, and then clip it inside the layer below by pressing **Command-Option-G (PC: Ctrl-Alt-G)**. Then, change the layer's blend mode to **Overlay**.

Continued

STEP SEVEN:

Open the background texture file. The texture looks okay, but seems a little flat. So, let's use the HDR Toning feature again to tighten up the contrast and sharpen the detail. You can see the difference here after using these settings. When you're done, bring the texture into the design file and move its layer beneath the gladiator layers.

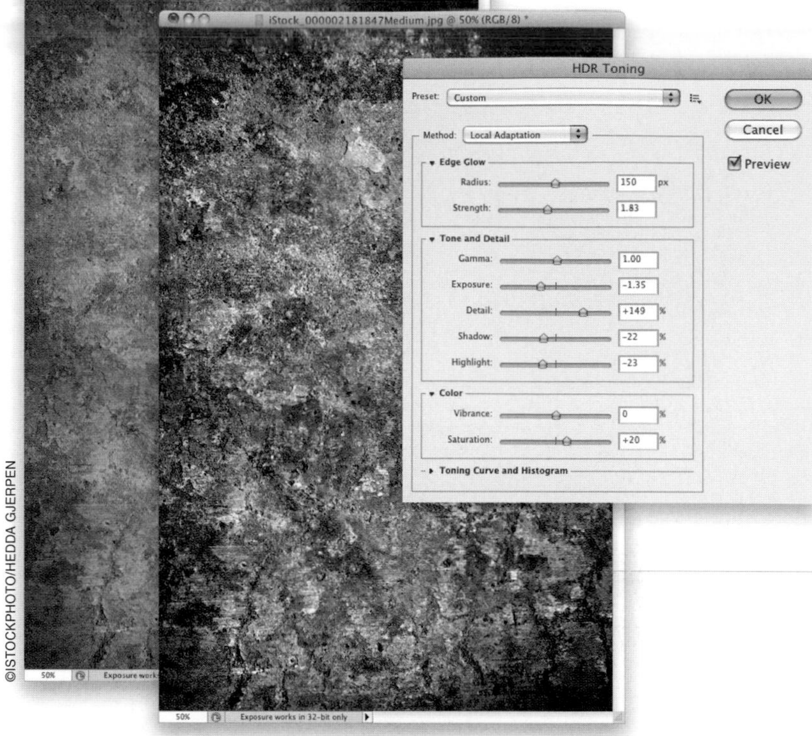

©ISTOCKPHOTO/HEDDA GJERPEN

STEP EIGHT:

Now, we're going to add a color effect to help blend the images together a bit more. Click on the Create a New Layer icon at the bottom of the Layers panel to create a new blank layer, and move it to the top of the layer stack. Then, click on the Foreground color swatch at the bottom of the Toolbox, and, in the Color Picker, set the color to R: 224, G: 146, B: 46. Click OK. Press **Option-Delete (PC: Alt-Backspace)** to fill the new layer with this color and then change its blend mode to **Soft Light**.

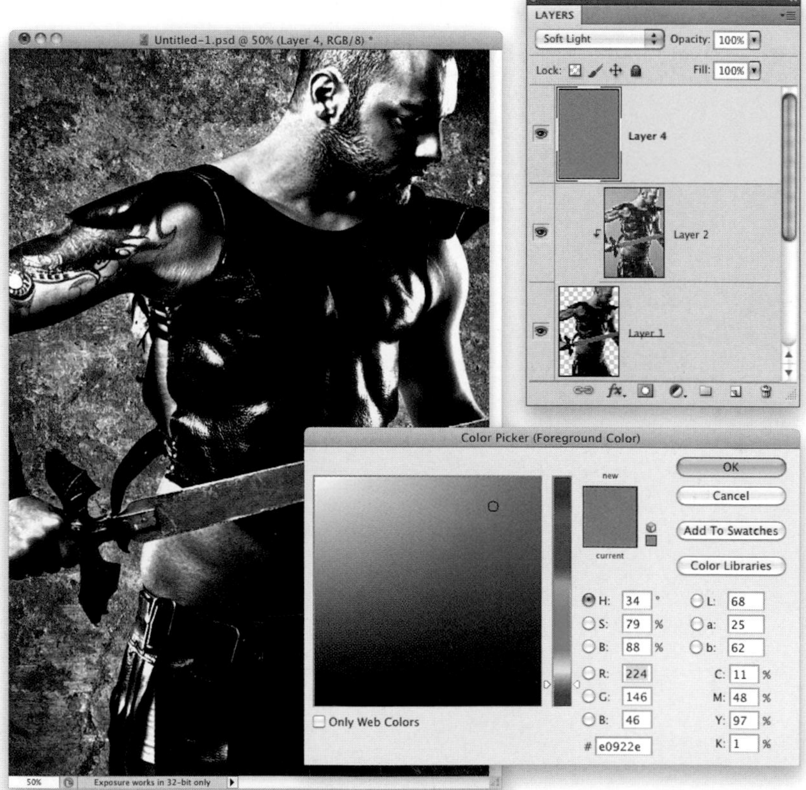

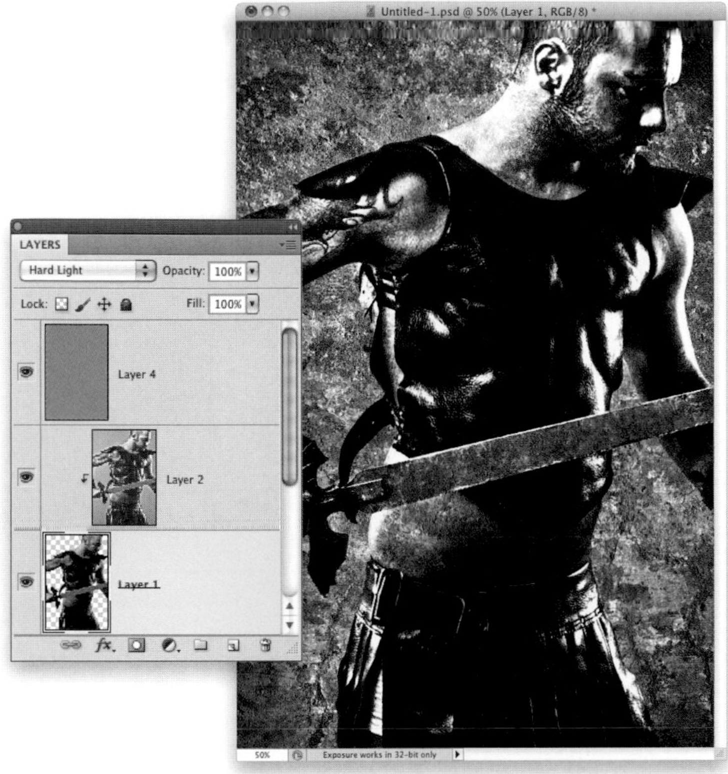

STEP NINE:

To help the gladiator blend better with the background, click on the bottom (color) gladiator layer and change its blend mode to **Hard Light**.

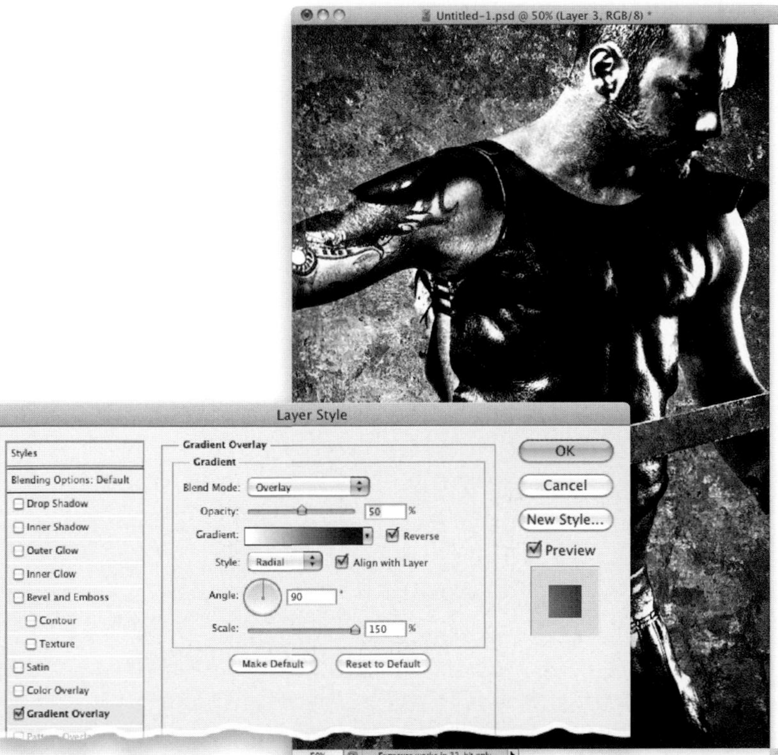

STEP 10:

Now, click on the texture layer in the Layers panel to make it active, and then click on the Add a Layer Style icon at the bottom of the panel and choose **Gradient Overlay**. Using the default Black, White gradient, turn on the Reverse checkbox, change the Blend Mode to **Overlay**, drop the Opacity to 50%, change the Style to **Radial**, and increase the Scale to 150%. Then, move the Layer Style dialog to the side and, in the image window, move the gradient around and you'll see it gives it a somewhat dramatic light effect. Position the center of the gradient just to the left of the subject. Click OK.

Continued

STEP 11:

We're going to add an element of dirt particles flying across the bottom, but we need to darken the bottom area a bit first, so we can actually see it. Create a new blank layer and move it below the color layer in the layer stack. Choose the Gradient tool **(G)** from the Toolbox and then press **D** to set your Foreground color to black. In the Options Bar, click on the down-facing arrow to the right of the gradient thumbnail and choose the Foreground to Transparent gradient (the second one from the left in the top row). Then, click on the Linear Gradient icon (to the right of the gradient thumbnail), and create two or three gradients at the bottom of the image to darken it, setting up the layout for the particle effect.

STEP 12:

For the particle effect itself, we're going to use a new method. You can certainly use a still image to create the particle effect, but I found it difficult to find a stock image of just flying dirt. Apart from shooting it yourself, here's an alternative if you have Photoshop Extended: Here, I have a video clip of someone off-camera just throwing dirt into the frame (I actually did find this video clip on iStockphoto's website). Open the video clip inside Photoshop. Then, open the Animation panel (found under the Window menu), grab the Current Time Indicator, and move through the clip to find a frame that has a good amount of flying particles.

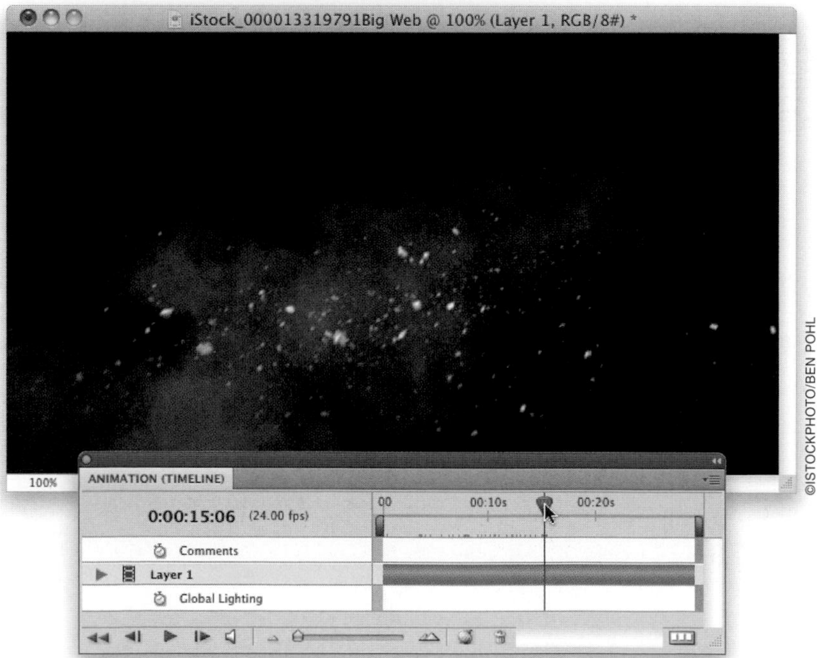

©ISTOCKPHOTO/BEN POHL

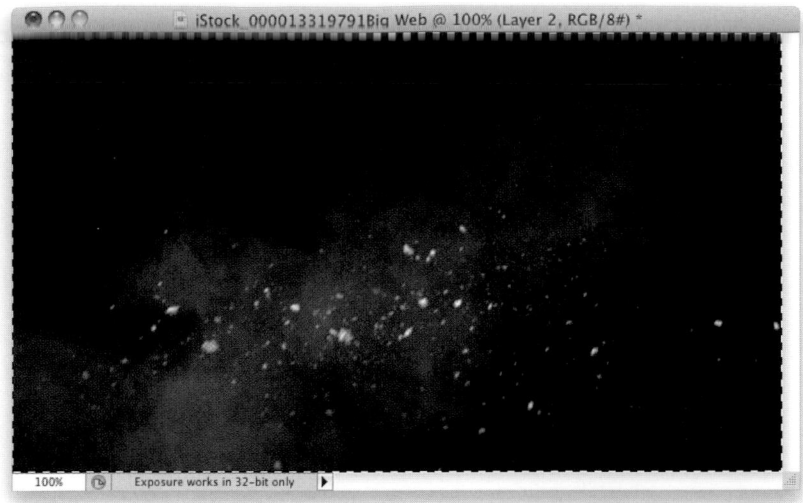

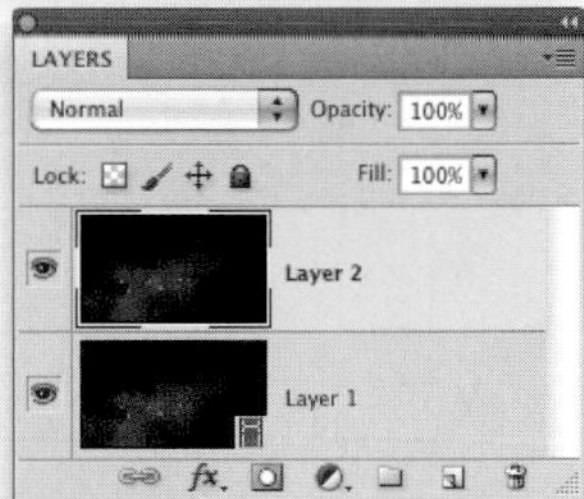

STEP 13:

Press **Command-A (PC: Ctrl-A)** to select the entire frame, then press Command-J (PC: Ctrl-J) to copy the selected frame to a new layer. It's now a static image. Go ahead and use the Move tool to click-and-drag, or just copy-and-paste, this layer into the design layout. The cool thing here is that you have several choices of frames to use, rather than a single image, which only gives you one option.

STEP 14:

Now, make sure this layer is also beneath the color layer in the Layers panel, so it picks up the orange hue. Then, press Command-T (PC: Ctrl-T) to go into Free Transform and scale-and-position this particle layer at the bottom of the image, just above where the black gradients are. Press Return (PC: Enter).

Continued

STEP 15:
Next, change the layer's blend mode to **Screen** to make the black areas invisible, leaving only the dirt particle effect.

STEP 16:
Now, at this point, the particles look good and we could be done, but I wanted to show you one more trick: To get some more variation to the particle effect, go under the Edit menu, under Transform, and choose **Warp**. Click-and-drag the control handles to distort the shape of the particle layer to get more of a sense of movement, as the warping will stretch the pixels, making it look like a motion blur. Press **Return (PC: Enter)** when you're done. As an option, repeat this process and add another particle layer to the top left of the layout (I did this for the final image).

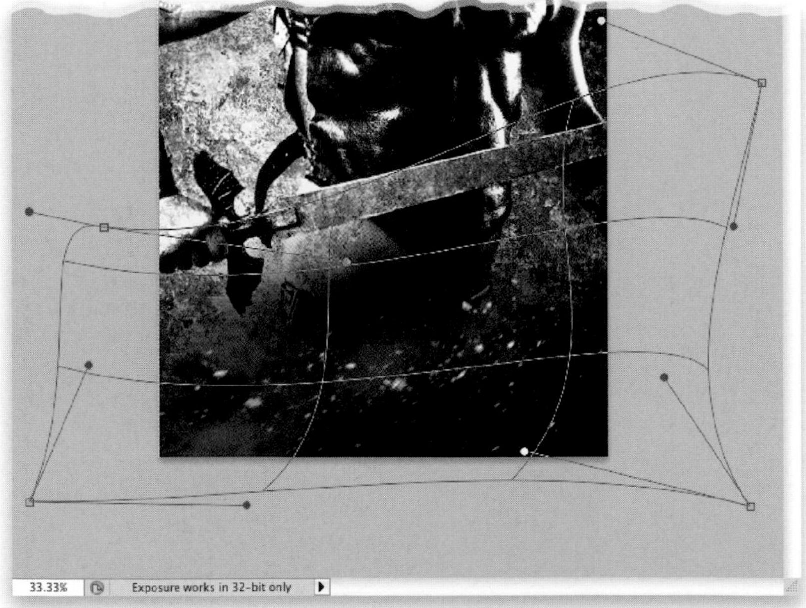

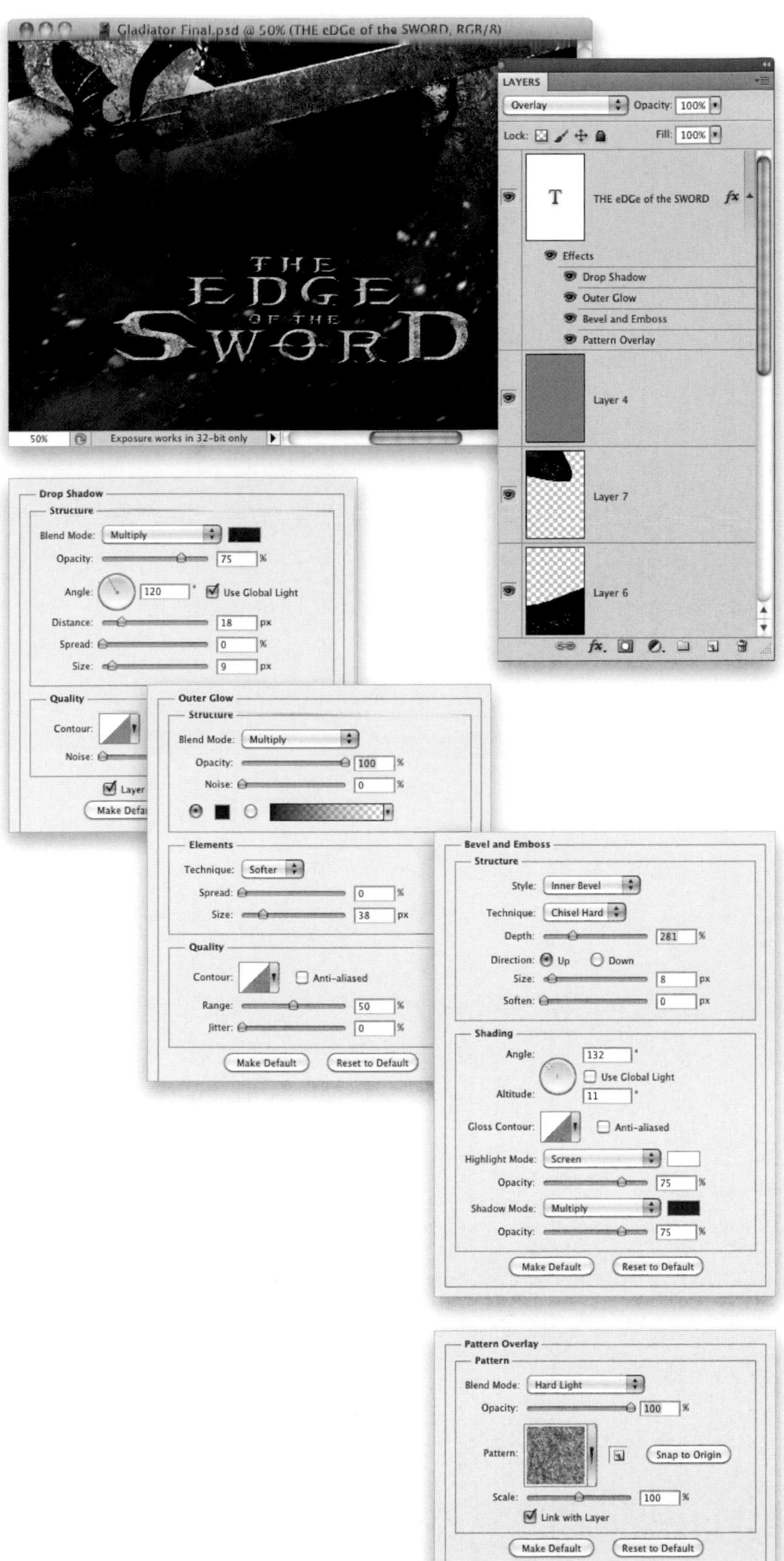

STEP 17:

Finally, add some text. I used VTCBelialsBladeRegular with Drop Shadow, Outer Glow, Bevel and Emboss, and Pattern Overlay layer styles, using the settings shown here.

Continued

Final Image

Refine Edge Border Trick

There are a myriad of ways to create cool border effects in Photoshop, but I bet you never thought of this method. The updated Refine Edge feature in Photoshop CS5 is remarkable for making more accurate selections, but is that all it can do? Nope! Here we'll take a look at how we can take advantage of this cool feature to create interesting border elements from just about any photo. No kidding! Once you learn this, you'll try it on almost every photo you have, and even try it on different parts of the same image.

©ISTOCKPHOTO/ISGABY

STEP ONE:

Now, the really cool part about this little trick is that you can try it on just about any image and you'll get something pretty interesting. Images of textures are always fun, because they can be so abstract. Here, we have a simple wood texture. Start by grabbing the Rectangular Marquee tool **(M)** from the Toolbox, and then draw a selection over the center area of the wood texture.

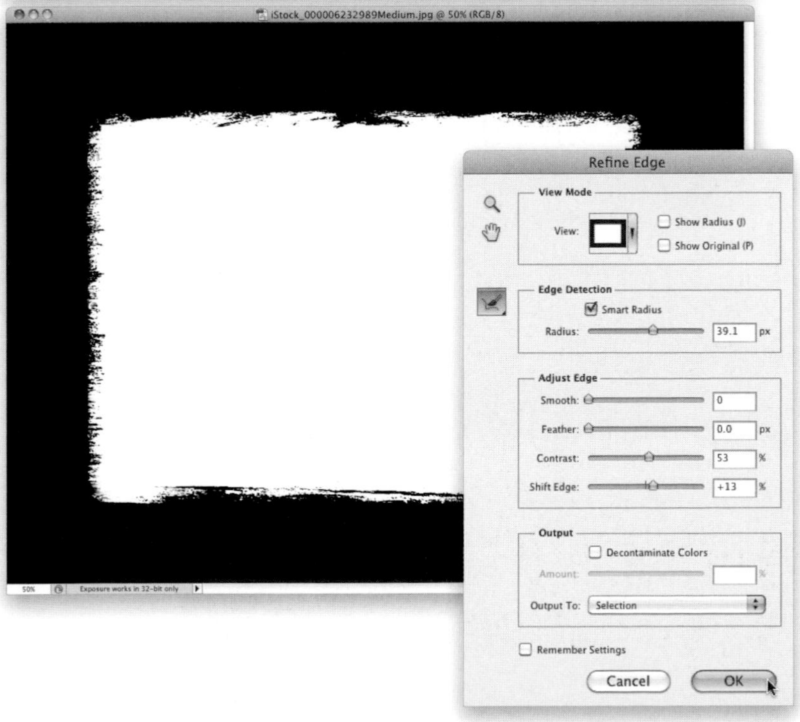

STEP TWO:

Now, just click on the Refine Edge button in the Options Bar to open the Refine Edge dialog. From the View menu, choose **Black & White**. Then, in the Edge Detection section, turn on the Smart Radius checkbox and move the Radius slider to around 40 px. Next, go down to the Contrast slider, and move it to around 50%, and push Shift Edge up to +13%. These settings will, of course, vary on different images, so remember to experiment. Finally, choose **Selection** from the Output To pop-up menu and click OK.

Continued

STEP THREE:

Click on the Create a New Layer icon at the bottom of the Layers panel to create a new blank layer. Then, fill the active selection with black by pressing **Shift-Delete (PC: Shift-Backspace)**, choosing **Black** from the Use pop-up menu in the Fill dialog, and clicking OK. Now we have a shape we can generate a selection from, or even clip an image into (I turned off the Background layer here, so you could see the shape better). Press **Command-D (PC: Ctrl-D)** to Deselect.

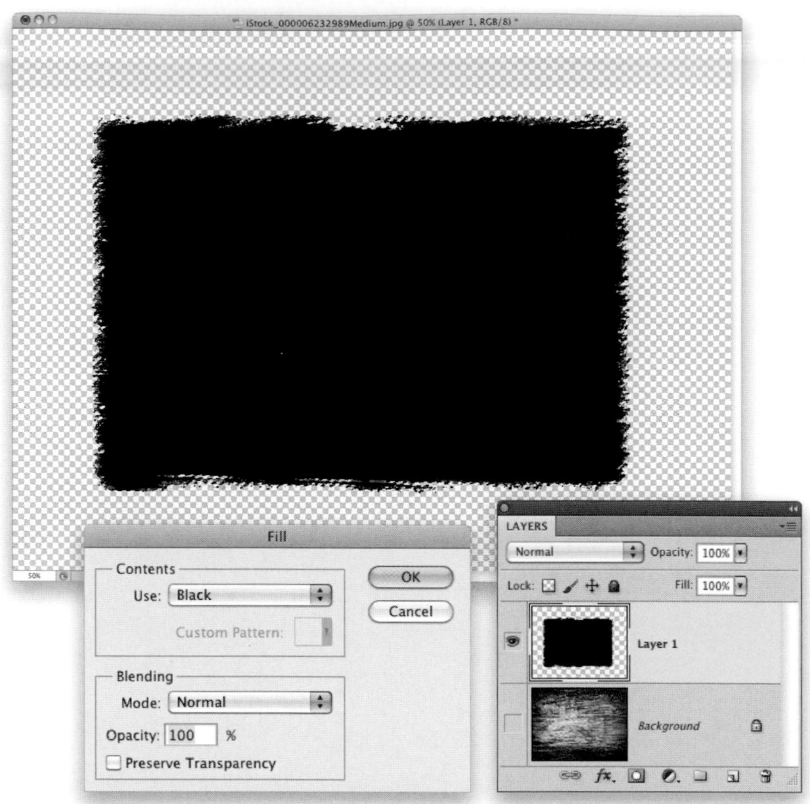

STEP FOUR:

Here, you can see I used this shape to create a border effect for this photo. Open the image you want to add the border effect to, then press **Command-N (PC: Ctrl-N)** to create a new document. In the New dialog, choose the name of your image file from the Preset pop-up menu to make the new document the same size. With the Move tool **(V)**, click-and-drag the frame layer into your new file, then drag the image file into your new file, and make sure it's above the frame layer in the Layers panel. With the image layer active, press **Command-Option-G (PC: Ctrl-Alt-G)** to clip it to the frame layer below. Now, click back on the frame layer, go into Free Transform (press **Command-T [PC: Ctrl-T]**), and resize the frame around the image. Press **Return (PC: Enter)** when you're done.

STEP FIVE:
Here's another example. Remember this wood plank image from Chapter 4? Open that file up and let's see what we might get out of this texture. Go ahead and use the Rectangular Marquee tool again to make a selection over most of the center area of the texture.

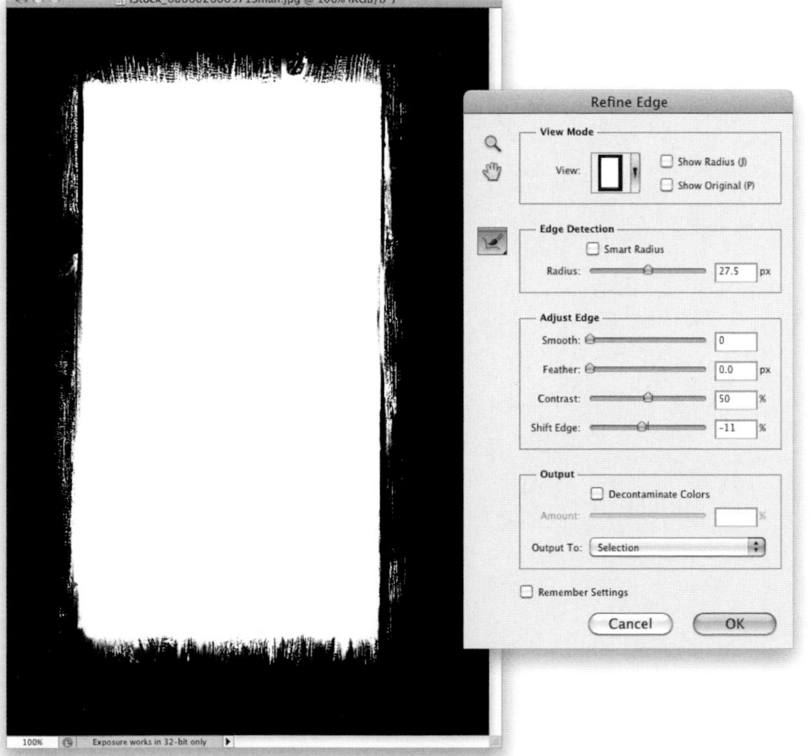

STEP SIX:
Now, click on the Refine Edge button and feel free to play around with the various settings to see what you might discover. You can see the settings I chose here are giving me a nice wood grain effect with some scattered elements—all from a simple selection. Go ahead and set the Output To pop-up menu to Selection and click OK.

Continued

STEP SEVEN:

Once again, create a new blank layer and fill the selection with black. We now have another interesting shape. Remember to save these files as you create these shapes, so you can use them again without having to re-create them. You can even define them as patterns (see more about defining patterns in Chapter 4, as well), or Command-click (PC: Ctrl-click) on the shape's thumbnail in the Layers panel to make a selection from it, and from the Paths panel's flyout menu (Window>**Paths**), choose **Make Work Path** to convert it to a path. Then, you can convert that path into a custom shape by going under the Edit menu and choosing **Define Custom Shape**. There are multiple options for having cool custom design elements on tap!

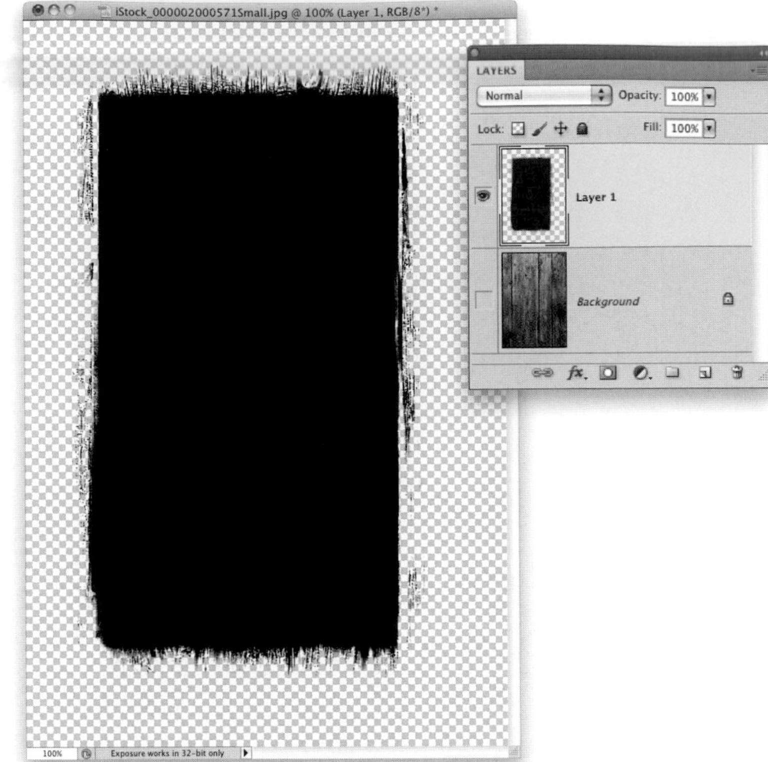

Final Image

In this alternate example, I used the surfer ad concept from Chapter 4 and clipped the image of the surfer in the shape created from the texture file, giving a rough, stylish edge effect.

Follow the White Rabbit

hollywood effects

It was certainly inevitable that I would have a chapter on Hollywood effects. I've been a movie fan since I was about 3 years old and, over the years, movies and television have played tremendous roles in my creative thought process. Things I see in trailers, TV ads, and even printed material, often inspire me and give me a spark of an idea. Sometimes, the mere act of re-creating an existing effect will not only fine-tune your Photoshop skills, but can lead you to an idea you can build on. So, bear in mind that while most of us are certainly not designing posters for the next big feature film, that doesn't mean we can't use what we learn through the process and repurpose it elsewhere. Think about it!

Hollywood Touch-Ups

There are a number of effects that designers use to add that final touch to their work. Some of the most common Hollywood touch-up effects I've seen are background elements, light effects, and sparks. There are a variety of ways to create these effects and, once you know how to create them, there are a variety of ways to use them.

STEP ONE:

Open the file of the mostly finished movie poster shown here. You can see it looks pretty good, but could use some finishing touches to spice it up a little. You can also see the Layers panel here and how the image was created up to this point.

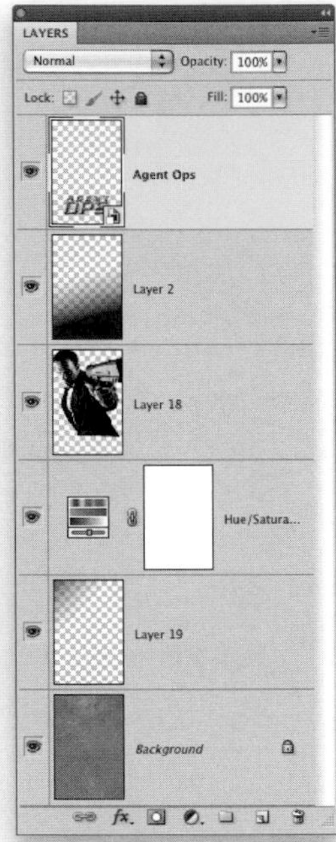

STEP TWO:

First, let's create a background element. Click on the text Smart Object layer and make a duplicate by pressing **Command-J (PC: Ctrl-J)**. Then, move this duplicate layer below the subject's layer. Go into Free Transform mode by pressing **Command-T (PC: Ctrl-T)**, press-and-hold the Shift key, and click-and-drag a corner point to scale the object really big in the background (drag your image window out larger, so you can continue to see the control handles). Then, move your cursor outside the bounding box and click-and-drag to rotate the text to roughly the same angle as the gunman. Press **Return (PC: Enter)** to lock in your changes. Change the layer's blend mode to **Hard Light** to let some of the background texture show through.

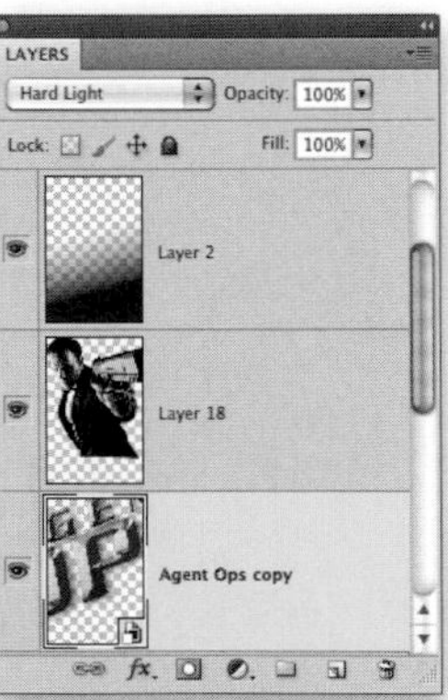

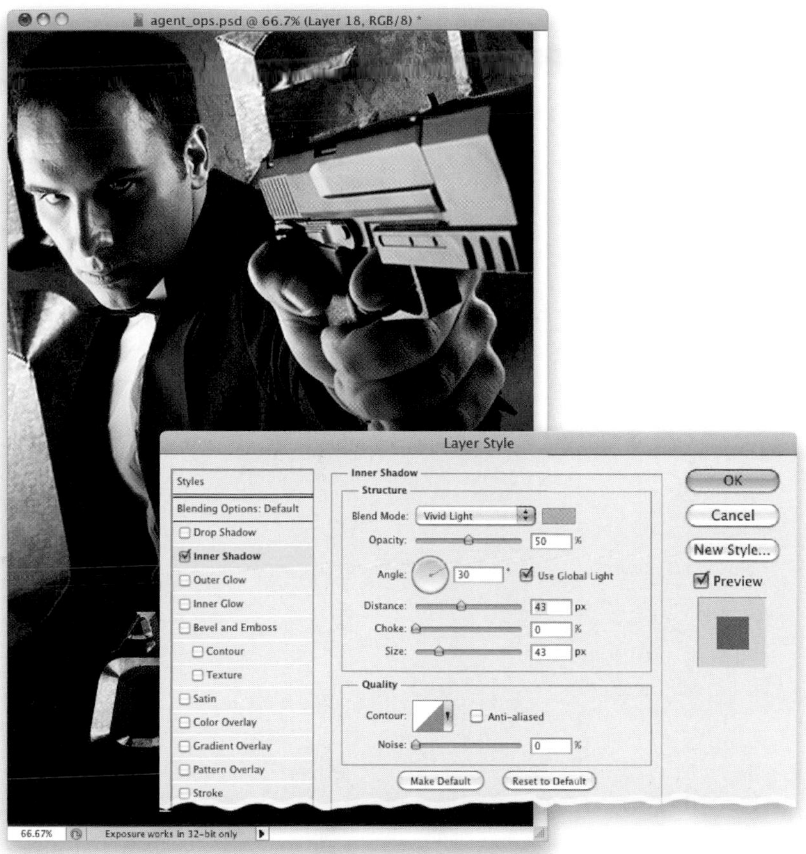

STEP THREE:

Now, we're going to add a warm light effect on the subject to contrast with the overall coolness of the image. We'll do this with a layer style. So, click on the layer with the guy, and then click on the Add a Layer Style icon at the bottom of the Layers panel and choose **Inner Shadow**. In the Layer Style dialog, click on the color swatch and choose a warm yellow/orange color. Then, change the Blend Mode to **Vivid Light**. Drop the Opacity down to 50%, and set the Angle to 30°, so the light appears as though it's coming from the upper right. Go down to Size and increase it to around 40 px. Then, for the Distance, you can either enter the number you see here, or move the Layer Style dialog to the side and manually move the effect to get the best placement. Click OK when you're done.

©ISTOCKPHOTO/DANE WIRTZFELD

STEP FOUR:

Next, we're going to add that cool spark effect you see in so many movie posters these days and I'm going to show you a couple of ways to achieve this effect. The first is from a stock image we have here of a fire element I found on iStockphoto's website. I like this image, not so much for the fire, but for the sparks that are flying out of it.

Continued

STEP FIVE:

Grab the Rectangular Marquee tool **(M)** from the Toolbox and select an area of sparks just above the flames, like I've done here. Then press **Command-C (PC: Ctrl-C)** to Copy this selected area.

STEP SIX:

Go back to your poster layout and, at the bottom of the Layers panel, click on the Create a New Layer icon and then drag this new layer right below the main text layer at the top of the layer stack. Press **Command-V (PC: Ctrl-V)** to Paste the sparks onto this layer. Use Free Transform to resize them, if you need to.

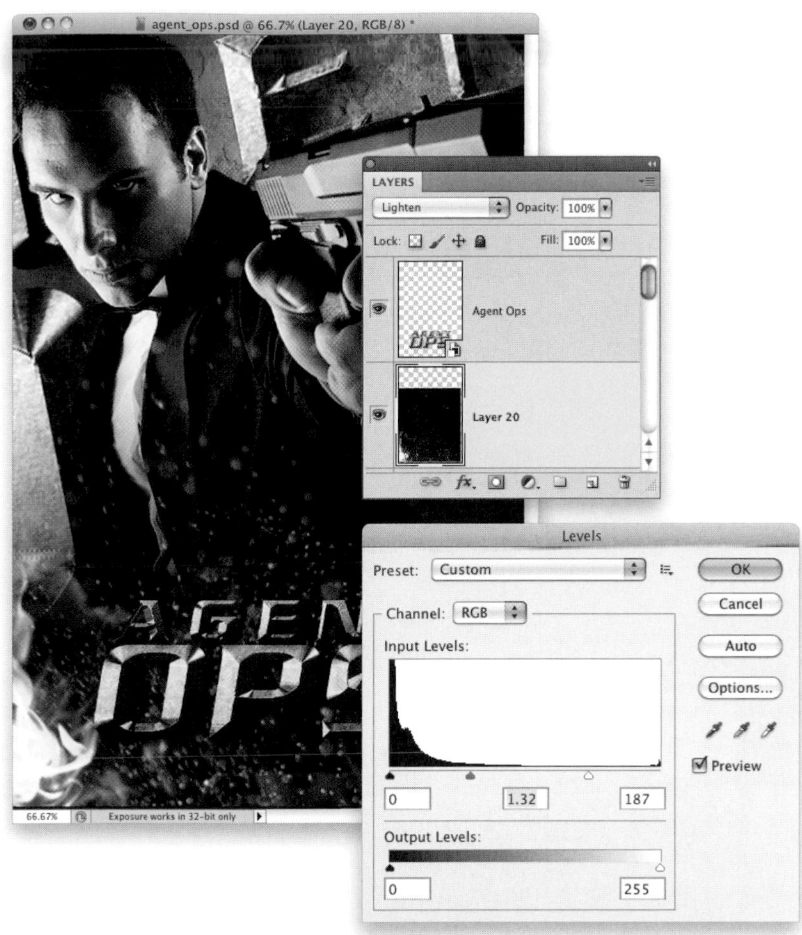

STEP SEVEN:

Change the layer's blend mode to **Lighten** and then press **Command-L (PC: Ctrl-L)** to open the Levels dialog. Drag the Input Levels highlights (white) and midtones (gray) sliders to the left to make the sparks a little brighter, increasing the saturation, as well. Click OK.

STEP EIGHT:

Now, go under the Edit menu, under Transform, and choose **Warp**. Grab the control handles and manually distort the sparks (similar to the way we did the dirt particle effect on the gladiator image in the last chapter). The stretching of the pixels will give the sparks a motion blur effect, giving more of a sense of motion.

Continued

STEP NINE:

Another method to add the spark effect involves using the video file of the dirt particles we used in the last chapter on that gladiator image. Open the QuickTime movie in Photoshop, and then open the Animation panel (Window>**Animation**). Grab the Current Time Indicator and scrub through the video to find a frame that shows a good amount of the particles. Press **Command-A (PC: Ctrl-A)** to select the frame, and then press Command-J (PC: Ctrl-J) to copy the selection to a new layer.

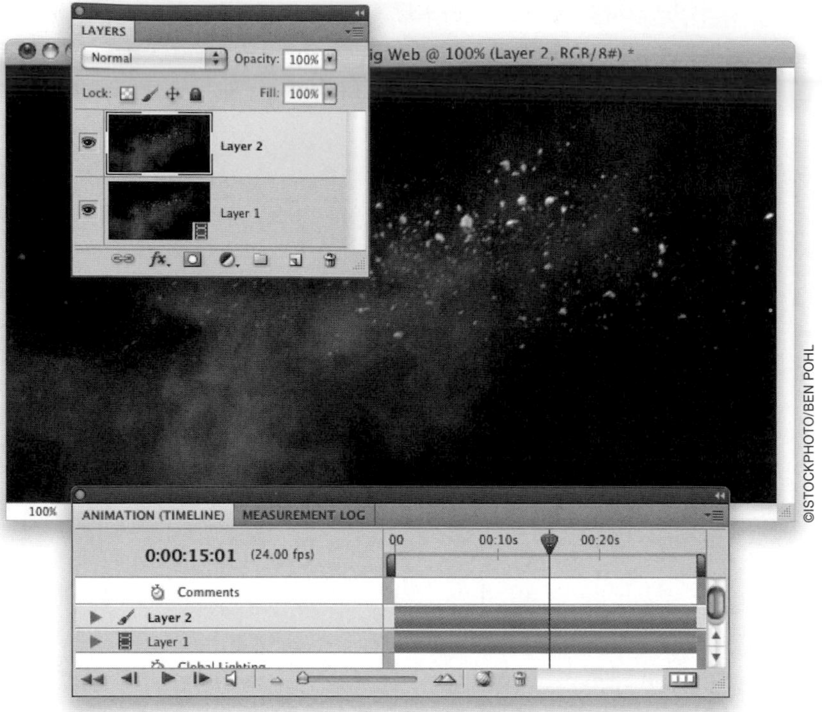

©ISTOCKPHOTO/BEN POHL

STEP 10:

To make these particles look like sparks, we need to add a color effect. So, press **Command-U (PC: Ctrl-U)** to open the Hue/Saturation dialog. Turn on the Colorize checkbox, and set the Hue to 25 and the Saturation to 50. Click OK.

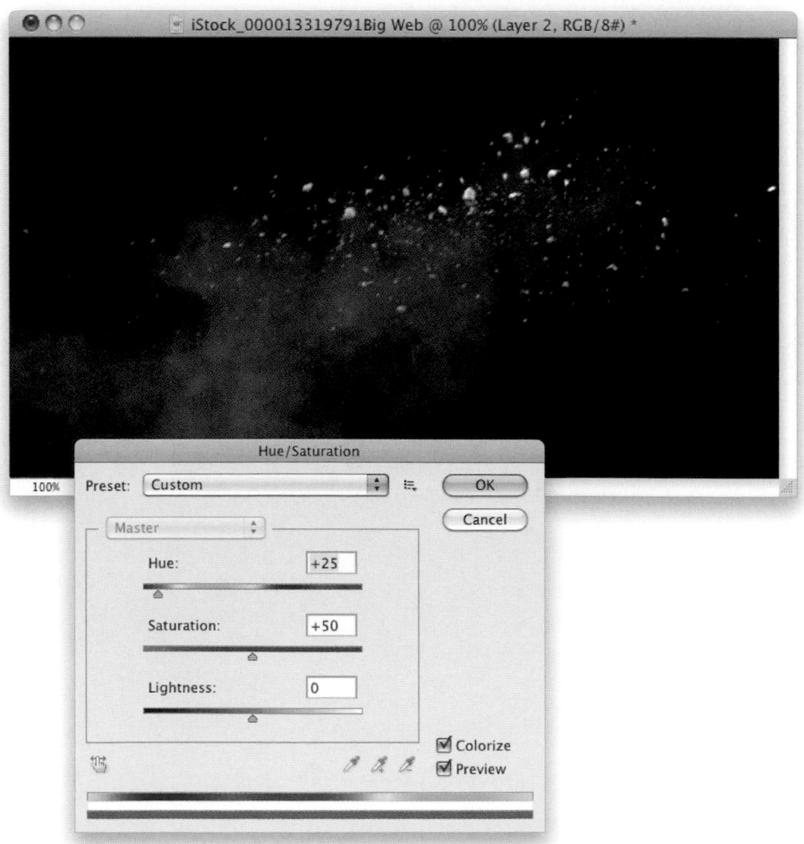

STEP 11:

Now copy-and-paste or use the Move tool **(V)** to click-and-drag this layer into the poster layout. Just like earlier, put the layer below the main text layer, and this time change the blend mode to **Screen**. Also like we did earlier, we're going to add a Levels adjustment to make the particles look brighter and more like sparks, so press Command-L (PC: Ctrl-L) to bring up the Levels dialog, and move the Input Levels shadows (black) and midtones (gray) sliders to the right a little. Even though the particles already have a sense of motion, because the image is from a video file, you can warp it like we did before (as I did here) to enhance the effect that much more.

Continued

Final Image with Flame Sparks

Final Image with Dirt Sparks

Dramatic Photo Special FX

This technique I learned from movie poster designer Tomasz Opasinski, who has worked on advertising materials for some of the biggest Hollywood films in recent years. He used this effect for the feature film *I Am Legend* with Will Smith, in which we take a basic photo of a building and make it seem as though it has deteriorated over time. Great technique, and surprisingly easier than you might think!

COFEY BARKER

STEP ONE:

Open the image of the buildings. I actually took this shot with a Canon point-and-shoot camera when I was in New York a while back. It was overcast that day, so I was able to get good detail in the buildings, however the sky was flat and boring. But, we'll fix that shortly. For now, select the Magic Wand tool in the Toolbox (or press **Shift-W** until you have it), and click on the sky area of the image. Then, Inverse the selection by pressing **Command-Shift-I (PC: Ctrl-Shift-I)**. With the buildings now selected, press **Command-C (PC: Ctrl-C)** to Copy them.

STEP TWO:

Now, press **Command-N (PC: Ctrl-N)** and create a new document that's 8 inches wide by 12 inches tall at 125 ppi. These dimensions are proportionate to an actual movie poster. Then, paste the image into the new document by pressing **Command-V (PC: Ctrl-V)**. Position the image so the building in the center will occupy most of the composition, as shown here. I also put the layer in Free Transform mode (by pressing **Command-T [PC: Ctrl-T]**) and scaled the building horizontally by Option-clicking (PC: Alt-clicking) on the middle-left control handle, and dragging inward to squeeze the image in a little bit (if you can't see the control handles, press **Comamnd-0** [zero; **PC: Ctrl-0**]). The result is that the building fills the image area better and you get the illusion that the building is a little taller than it actually is. Press **Return (PC: Enter)** to lock in your changes.

Continued

STEP THREE:

Next, let's fix that sky. It's easy enough to find an image of a sky, but we're gonna do something a bit different here. Like we did with the spark effect in the previous project, we're going to use a video clip to find a new sky. Here, I have a short video clip of a sunset sky with scattered clouds. Just open the Animation panel (Window>**Animation**) and use the Current Time Indicator to scrub through the video—you'll see that you have several choices of sky for this effect. Once you find a frame you like, just press **Command-A (PC: Ctrl-A)** to Select All and then press **Command-J (PC: Ctrl-J)** to copy the frame to a new layer. Copy-and-paste it, or use the Move tool **(V)** to click-and-drag it, into the buildings layout. With many DSLR cameras now shooting high-res video, you can see the advantage of using video frames as design elements.

©ISTOCKPHOTO/ULI HAMACHER

STEP FOUR:

Once the new sky is in the layout, click-and-drag its layer below the layer containing the buildings. Then, use Free Transform to scale it to cover the entire sky area. (I scaled it up, Right-clicked on it and chose **Flip Horizontal**, then pressed-and-held the Option key while dragging a side handle, like we did with the building.) Press Return (PC: Enter) when you're done. Then, press **Command-Shift-U (PC: Shift-Ctrl-U)** to remove the color from the sky layer.

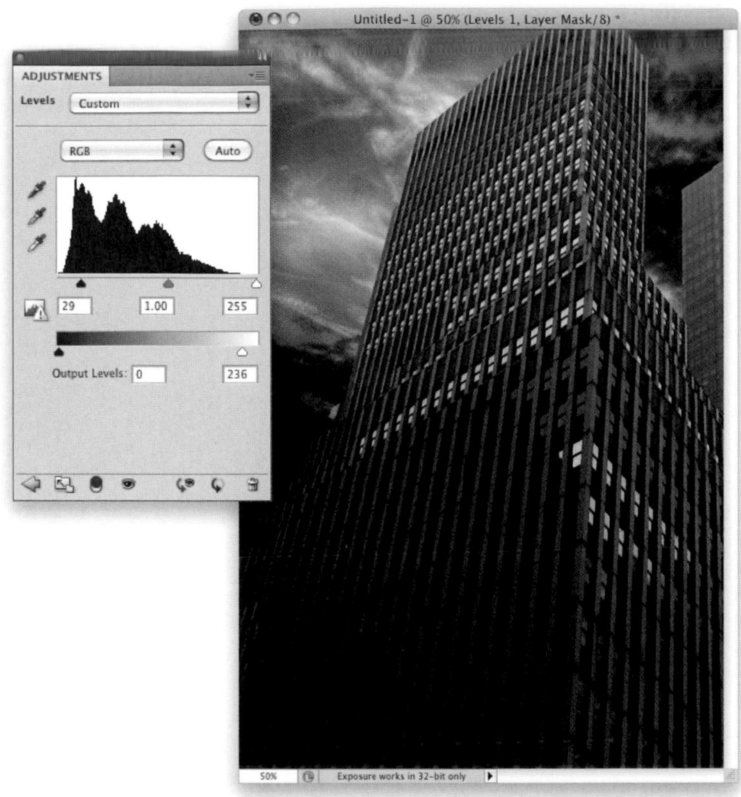

STEP FIVE:

In the Layers panel, click on the layer containing the buildings to make it active, and then click on the Create New Adjustment Layer icon at the bottom of the panel, and choose **Levels**. Move the shadows (black) slider below the histogram in to around 30, and then go to the Output Levels sliders and move the highlights (white) slider to around the 235 mark. This will darken the image a bit to make it more dramatic.

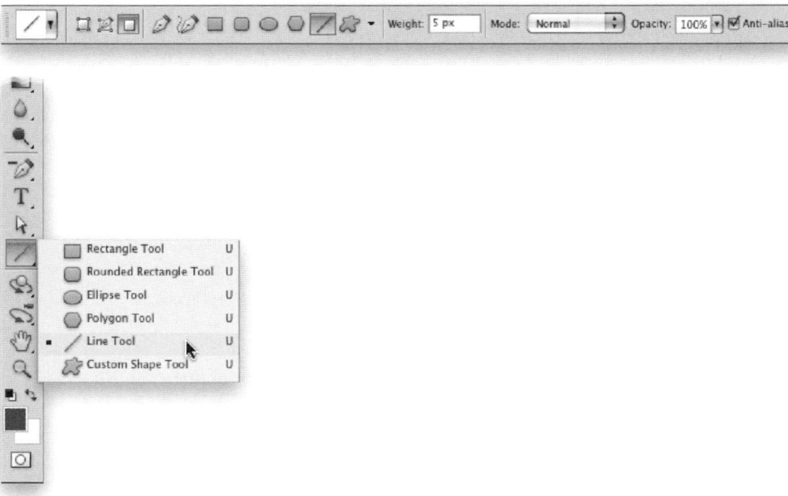

STEP SIX:

Now, we need to create some guidelines on the building, so we can get the perspective accurate for the next effect we're going to apply. Go into the Shape tools in the Toolbox and choose the Line tool (or press **Shift-U** until you have it). In the Options Bar, click on the Fill Pixels icon (the third icon to the right of the tool thumbnail) and then set the Weight to around 5 px. Set your Foreground color to something that will be really visible on the image (here, I chose red).

Continued

STEP SEVEN:

With the top layer active in the Layers panel, click on the Create a New Layer icon at the bottom of the panel to create a new blank layer to put these guidelines on. Click-and-drag with the Line tool to draw lines along the contours of the building, as you see here. Be sure to include enough horizontal and vertical guides to help line up the damaged effect.

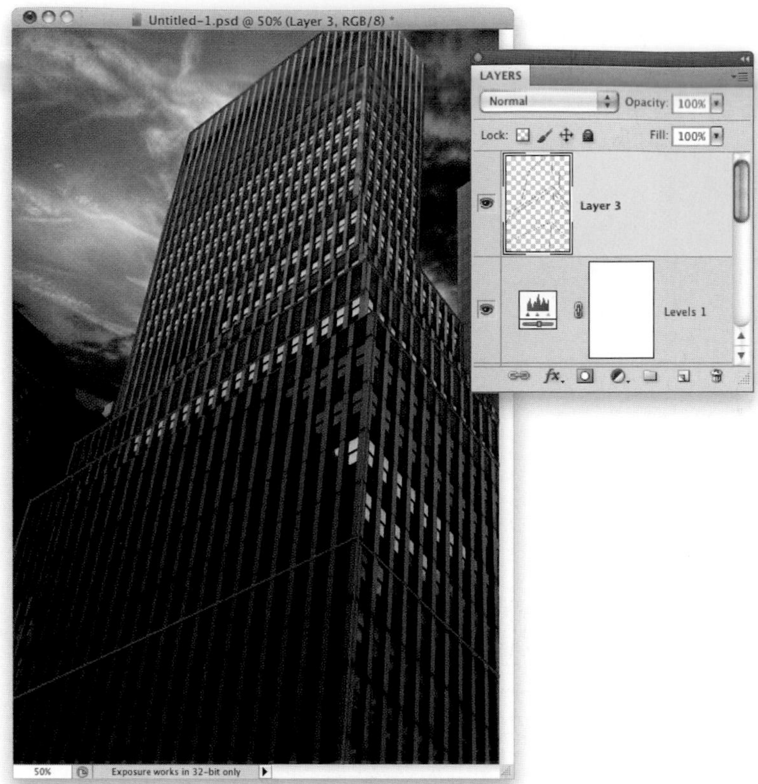

STEP EIGHT:

For the damaged effect, we're going to use a photo of a building that is already damaged. So, open this building image and use the Rectangular Marquee tool **(M)** to make a selection of just the damaged area of the building. Then, copy your selection to the clipboard by pressing Command-C (PC: Ctrl-C).

©ISTOCKPHOTO/PHOTOBVIOUS

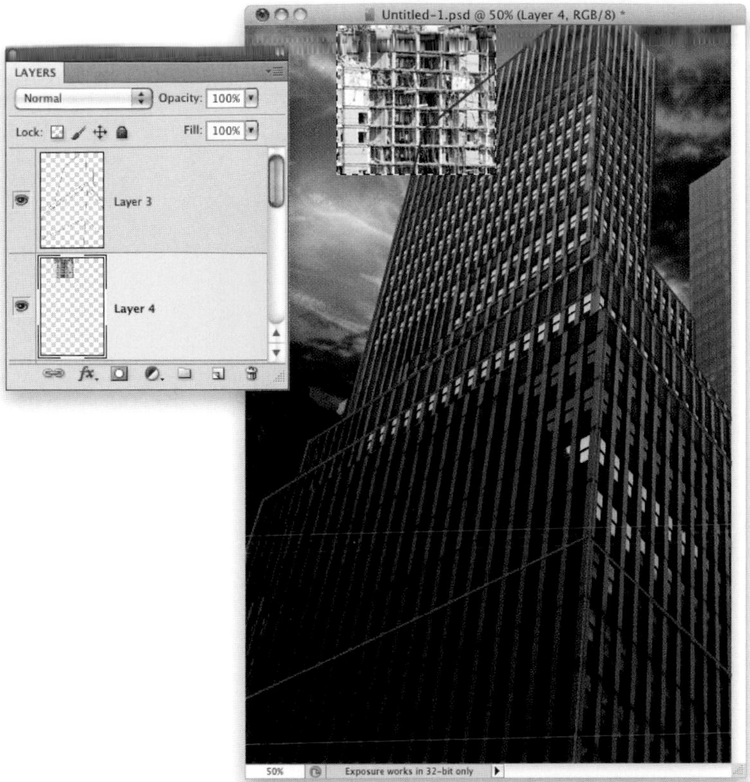

STEP NINE:

In your working layout, click on the layer below the guidelines, so you can still see them, then press Command-V (PC: Ctrl-V) to Paste the damaged building segment into your layout, and use the Move tool to position it at the top edge of the canvas. Use Free Transform to scale it smaller, so the window areas better match the size of the windows in our building. Then, press-and-hold the Command (PC: Ctrl) key, and click on the layer's thumbnail to load it as a selection in your layout (we're going to do a step-and-repeat effect, and if the object is not selected, it will create a new layer for each repeat).

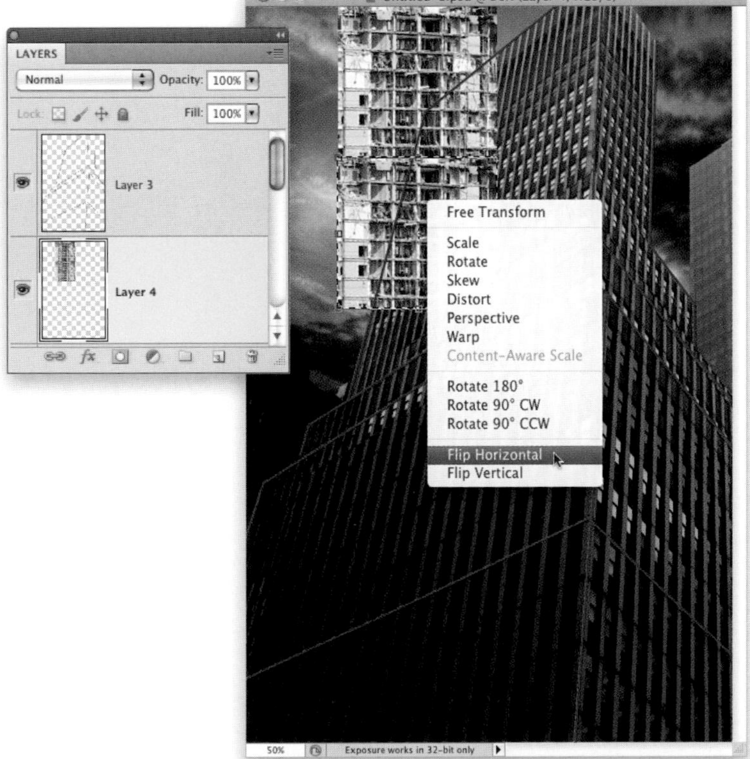

STEP 10:

Press **Command-Option-T (PC: Ctrl-Alt-T)** to invoke step-and-repeat. Click-and-drag the duplicate down to where its top edge meets the bottom of the original. Press-and-hold the Shift key as you drag to keep the object aligned. Also, to have more variation in the pattern, Right-click on this duplicate and choose **Flip Horizontal** from the pop-up menu. Press **Return (PC: Enter)** when you're done.

Continued

STEP 11:

Now, press-and-hold **Command-Option-Shift (PC: Ctrl-Alt-Shift)** and press **T** over and over until the pattern reaches the bottom edge of the canvas. It's okay if it goes beyond the edge a little bit. Press Return (PC: Enter) when you're done, and then press **Command-D (PC: Ctrl-D)** to Deselect.

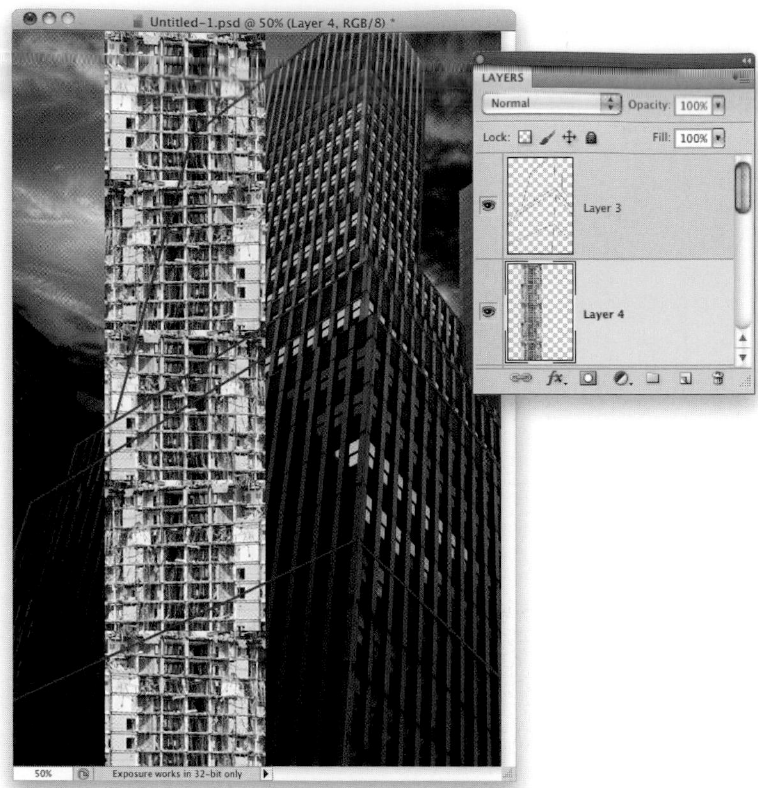

STEP 12:

Next, Command-click on the layer's thumbnail to select the entire column of damage. Then, press-and-hold **Option-Shift (PC: Alt-Shift)** as you click-and-drag with the Move tool to create a duplicate to the right, making the damaged area that much wider, and then deselect.

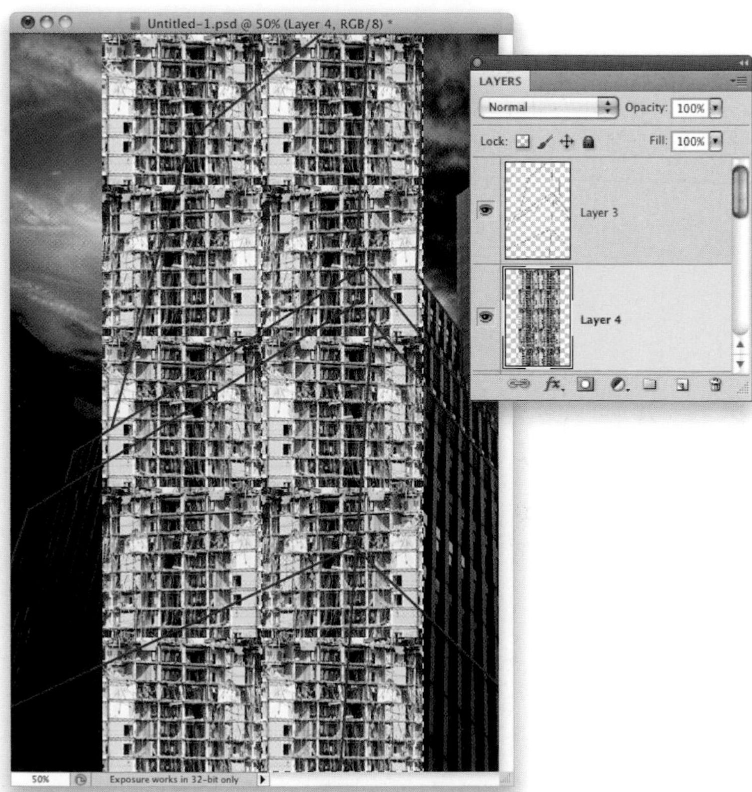

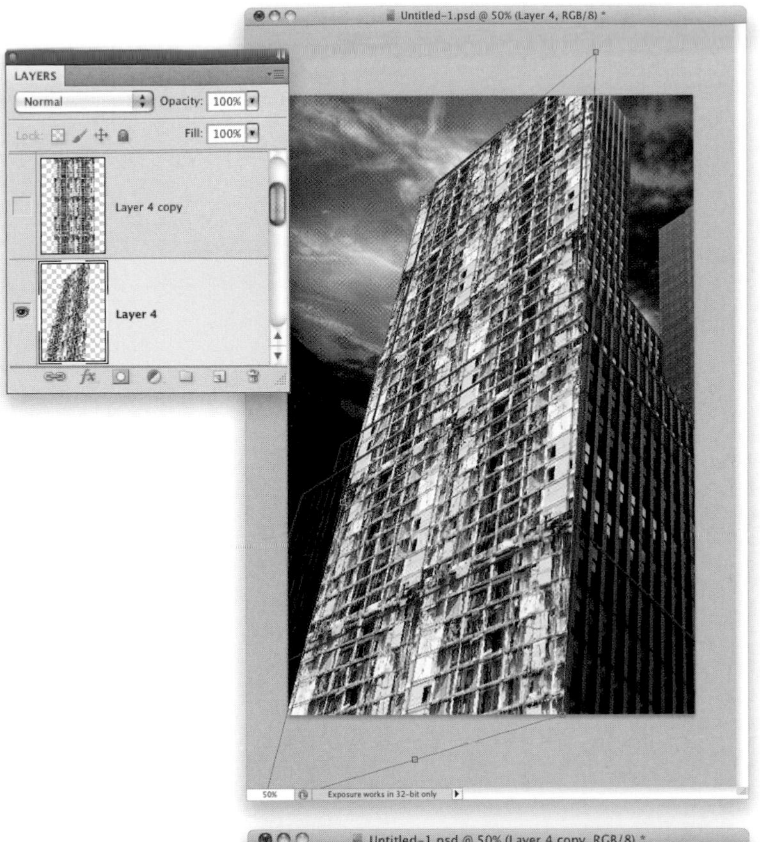

STEP 13:

This is where the red guidelines come in handy. We need to distort the damaged building layer to fit the area on the face of the building. First, press Command-J (PC: Ctrl-J) to make a duplicate of the damaged building layer, so we have one to apply to the side of the building, as well. Click on the Eye icon to the left of the duplicate layer's thumbnail to turn that layer off for the moment. Then, click back on the original damaged building layer, go under the Edit menu, under Transform, and choose **Distort**. Grab the corner handles and distort the image to conform to the guides. Use the vertical and horizontal lines to match the perspective of the damaged layer to the building. Press Return when you're done.

STEP 14:

Turn the duplicate layer back on by clicking where the Eye icon used to be, and then click on the layer to make it active. Now, distort it to the side of the building, like you see here. Then, merge these two layers into one by making sure the top one of the two is active, and pressing **Command-E (PC: Ctrl-E)**.

Continued

STEP 15:

Clearly, this damaged effect is way too bright for what we need here, so press **Command-L (PC: Ctrl-L)** to open the Levels dialog and darken the image by dragging the Input Levels midtones (gray) slider to the right to around 0.57, and the Output Levels highlights (white) slider to the left to around 167, then click OK.

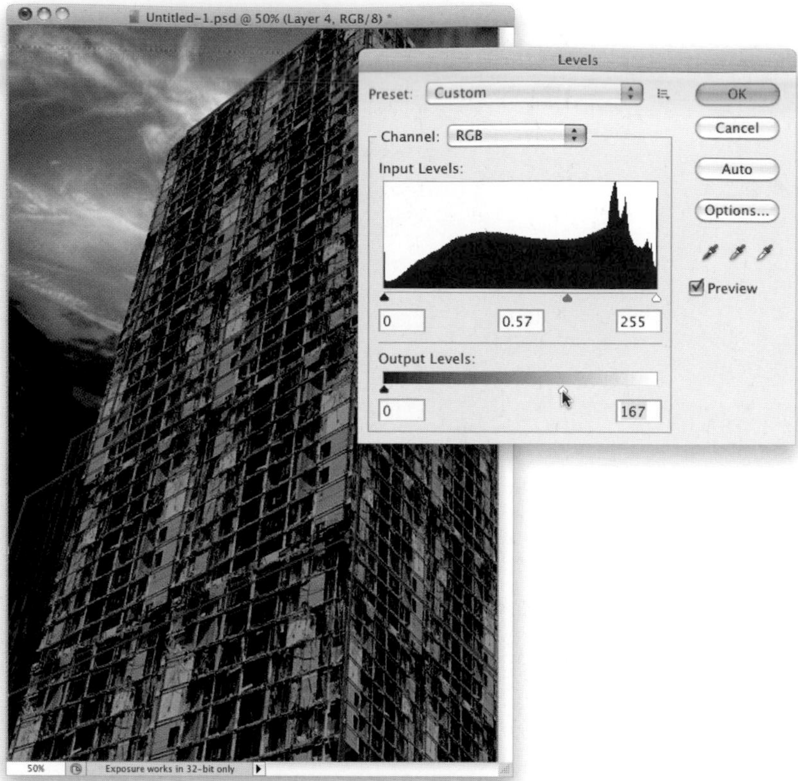

STEP 16:

Now, hide your guidelines layer by clicking on its Eye icon, then hide the damage layer with a black layer mask by pressing-and-holding the Option (PC: Alt) key while clicking on the Add Layer Mask icon at the bottom of the Layers panel.

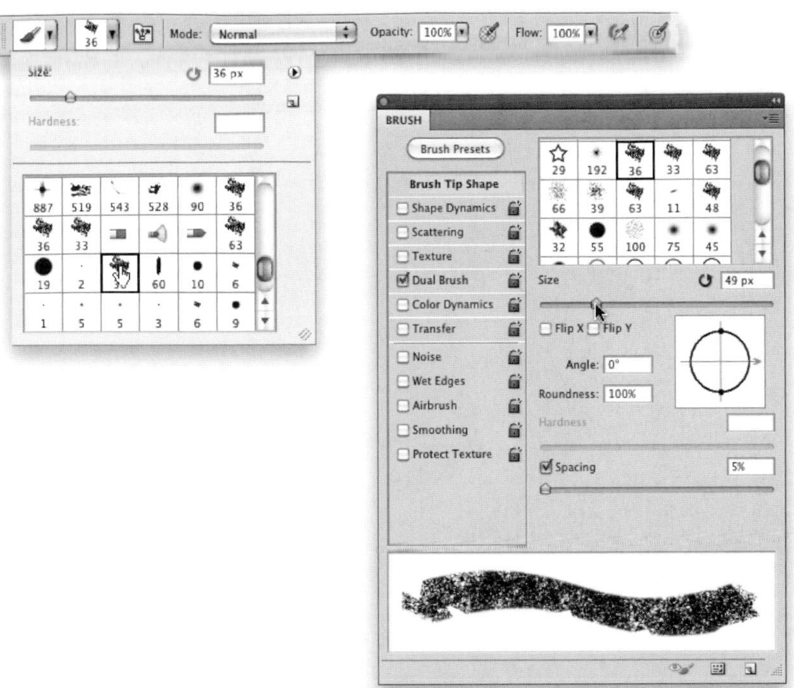

STEP 17:

Press **D** to set your Foreground and Background colors to their defaults of black and white, then go into the Toolbox and choose the Brush tool **(B)**. Click on the brush thumbnail in the Options Bar to open the Brush Picker, then click on the right-facing arrow in the top-right corner and choose **Dry Media Brushes**. In the dialog that appears, click Append, then scroll down in your Brush Picker and click on the Soft Oil Pastel brush tip to select it. Open the Brush panel (Window>**Brush**), and set the Size to around 50 px.

STEP 18:

Now, let's start modifying the behavior of the brush by first clicking on Shape Dynamics in the list on the left to turn it on. Set the Size Jitter to 100% and the Angle Jitter to 100%, as well.

Continued

STEP 19:
Next, click on Scattering on the left to turn it on. Turn on the Both Axes checkbox, and set the Scatter amount to around 290%.

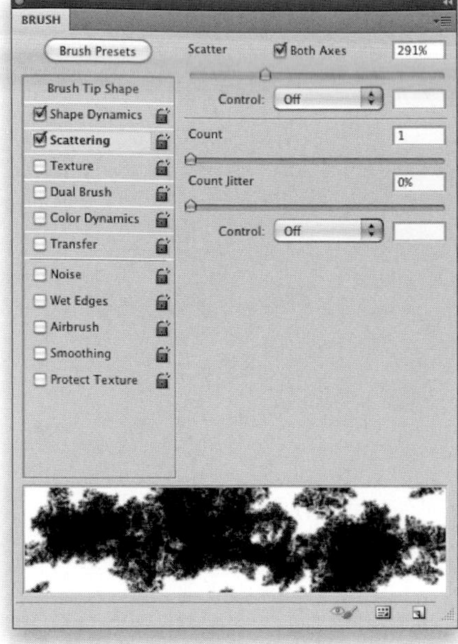

STEP 20:
Lastly, click on Transfer on the left to turn it on, and increase the Opacity Jitter to 100%. Also, set the Control pop-up menu to Pen Pressure if you are using a pressure-sensitive tablet. You can see down in the preview at the bottom what the brush effect will look like.

STEP 21:

Before we go and start brushing in the damaged effect, let's first apply a color effect to the image. Click on the Create New Adjustment Layer icon and choose **Hue/Saturation**. In the Adjustments panel, turn on the Colorize checkbox, and set the Hue to 28 and the Saturation to 19.

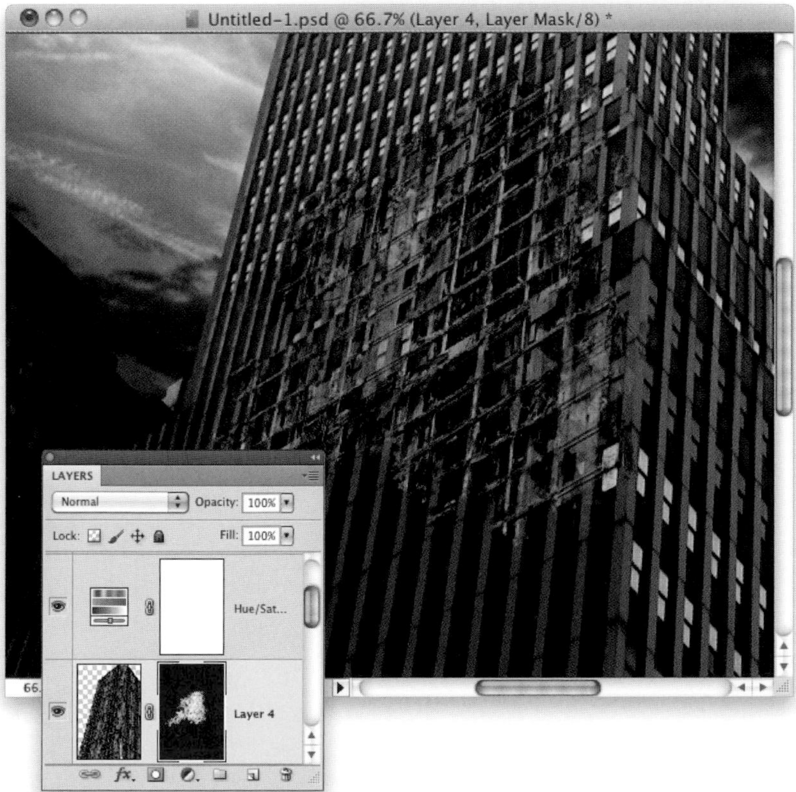

STEP 22:

Click on the layer mask we added to the damaged building layer. Then, make sure your Foreground color is set to white, and start painting in random areas of the building to reveal the damaged areas. As it blends with the original building, it will start to look like the building is really falling apart. Don't go too crazy, though. It's easy to get carried away with this effect.

Continued

STEP 23:

Now, for the building to really look damaged, we need to do more than just affect the inside area of the building—we need to make some of the edges seem like they're really falling apart. Click on the original building layer and then click on the Add Layer Mask icon to add a regular white (reveal all) layer mask. Then, use the same brush, but press **X** to change your Foreground color to black, and paint away some random areas of the edge of the building.

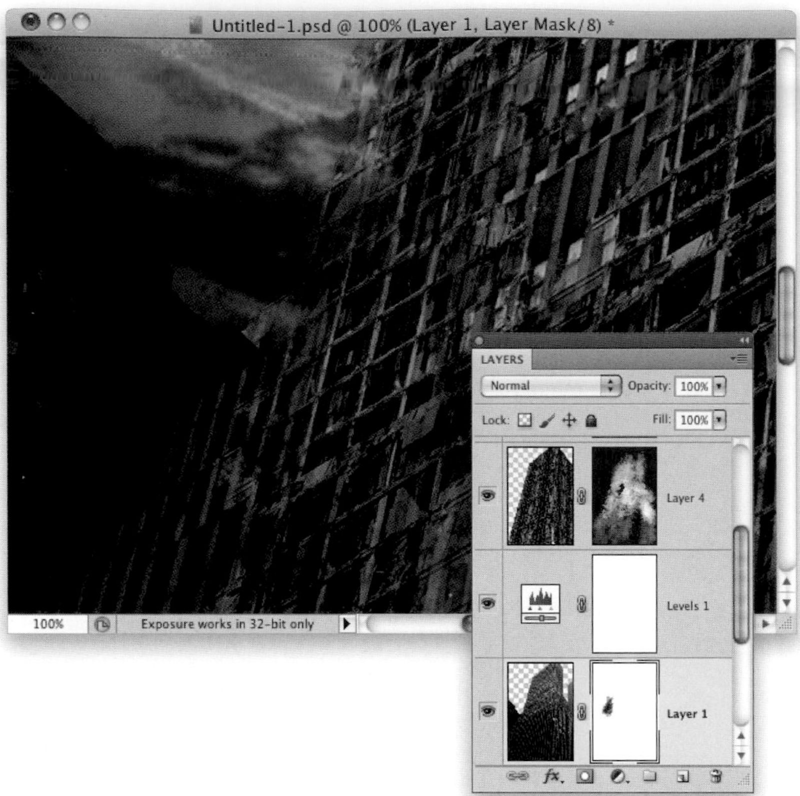

STEP 24:

Get the Gradient tool **(G)** from the Toolbox and, in the Options Bar, click on the down-facing arrow next to the gradient thumbnail to open the Gradient Picker. Choose the Foreground to Transparent gradient (the second one from the left in the top row), and then click on the Radial Gradient icon (the second icon to the right of the gradient thumbnail). Click on the damaged building layer, and then create a new blank layer above it. Press X to set your Foreground color to white, and then draw a gradient out from the center of the building almost to the edge of the document. Press **Command-T (PC: Ctrl-T)** to go into Free Transform and then scale the gradient vertically to cover more of the building, and change the layer's blend mode to **Overlay**. This will add a more enhanced light effect to the building face.

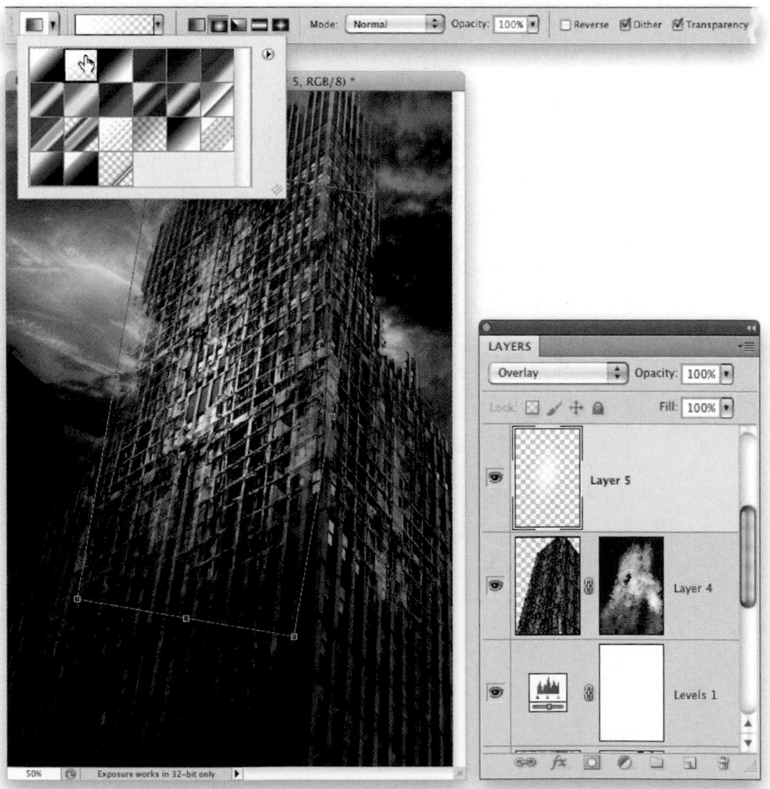

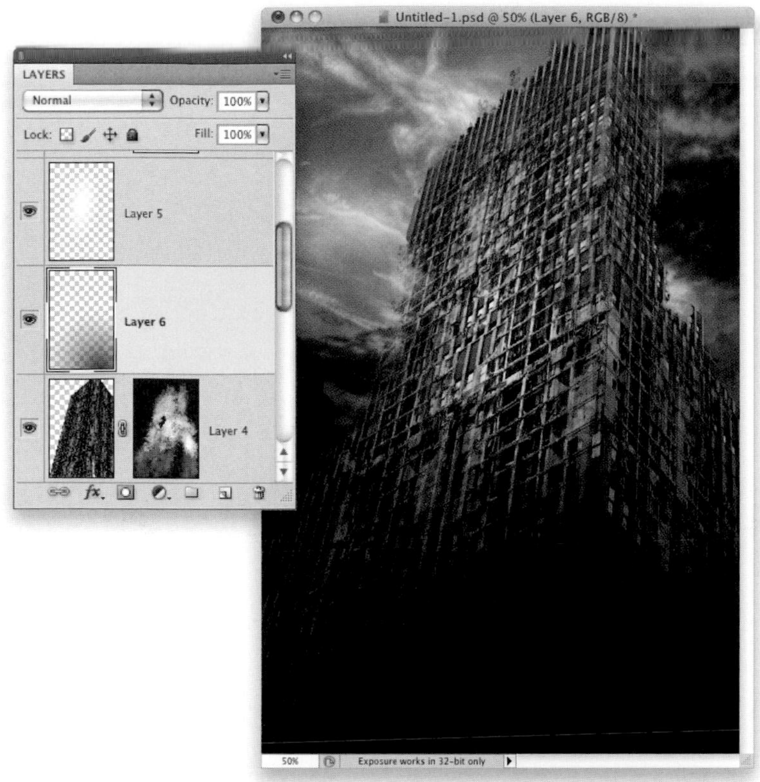

STEP 25:

Next, press D to set your Foreground color back to black, and create a new layer between the damaged building layer and the white gradient layer we just created. Then, use the same gradient to add some dark areas to the bottom of the image, like you see here. We'll be putting some text in that area, and this will help make it more readable.

©ISTOCKPHOTO/DMITRY MORDVINTSEV

STEP 26:

Now, the image feels like it needs something in the atmosphere—something like rain, or even nuclear fallout—to add to the desolate feel of the image. I searched on iStock-photo's website for dust particles, and found the image here. True, the color is not what we need, but the particle effect looks good.

Continued

STEP 27:

Go ahead and remove the color by pressing **Command-Shift-U (PC: Ctrl-Shift-U)**, then copy-and-paste or use the Move tool to click-and-drag this particle effect into the design layout. Use Free Transform to make it larger, so it covers the entire image.

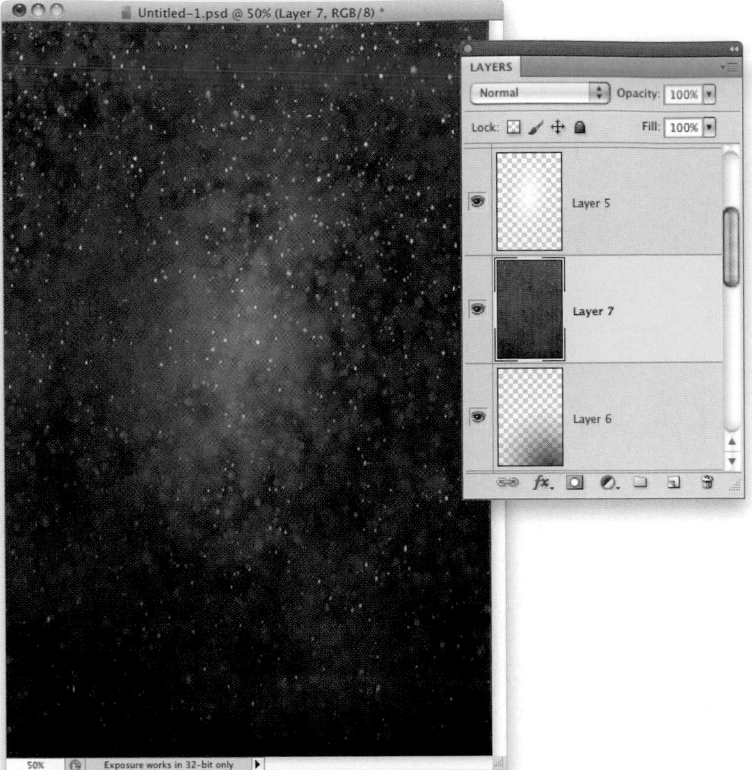

STEP 28:

In the Layers panel, drag this layer just above the original building layer and change its blend mode to **Screen**. The particle effect may still seem a little too much, so go ahead and run a quick Levels adjustment to make the image darker, making the particle effect that much less intense. You can also lower the layer's Opacity (here, I lowered it to 75%). Aside from some subtle tweaking of the image here and there, that pretty much completes the effect.

As you can see in the final image on the next page, all I did to finish it up was to add some text in Trajan Pro, with Drop Shadow and Gradient Overlay layer styles, at the bottom and there you have it!

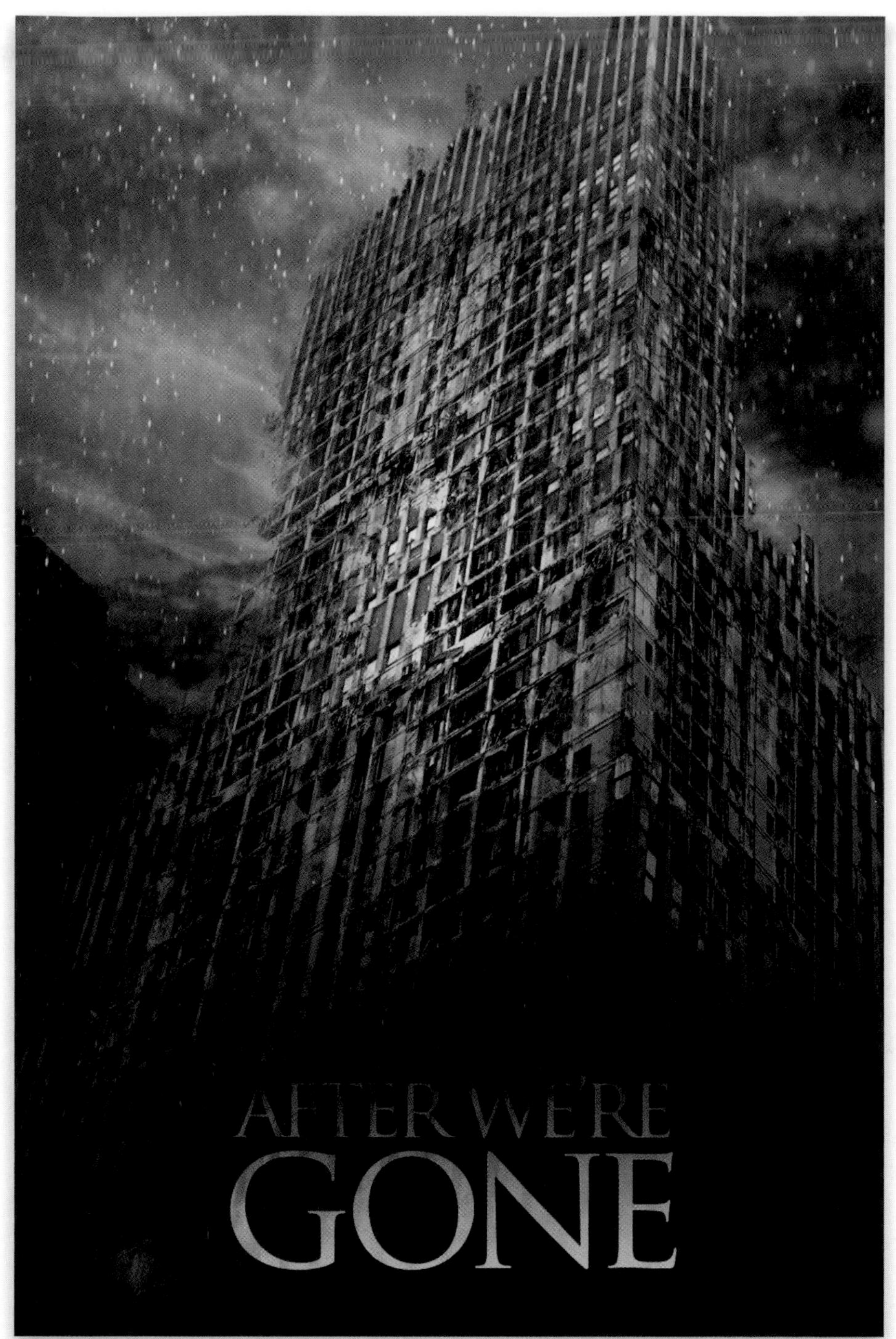
AFTER WE'RE
GONE

Final Image

Hi-Tech Effects

If you look at most sci-fi or action film posters these days, you'll see some common high-tech effects, like grids or random fields of code, combined with images and subtle light effects to add more interest and wow factor to a design. Here, I'm going to show you how you can set up these effects to use on the fly whenever you need them.

STEP ONE:

Start by opening the binary code file shown here, which is merely a bunch of random 1s and 0s. I created them as white text, and have them on a black Background layer just for the sake of visibility.

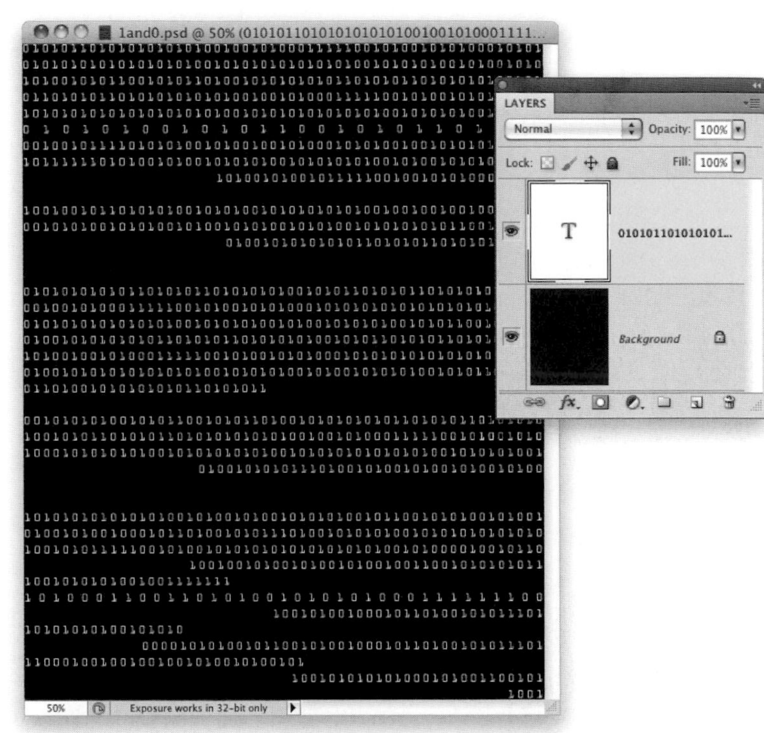

STEP TWO:

Turn off the Background layer by clicking on the Eye icon to the left of the layer's thumbnail, and make sure the text layer is active. Then, go under the Edit menu and choose **Define Pattern**. Give the new pattern a name, and click OK.

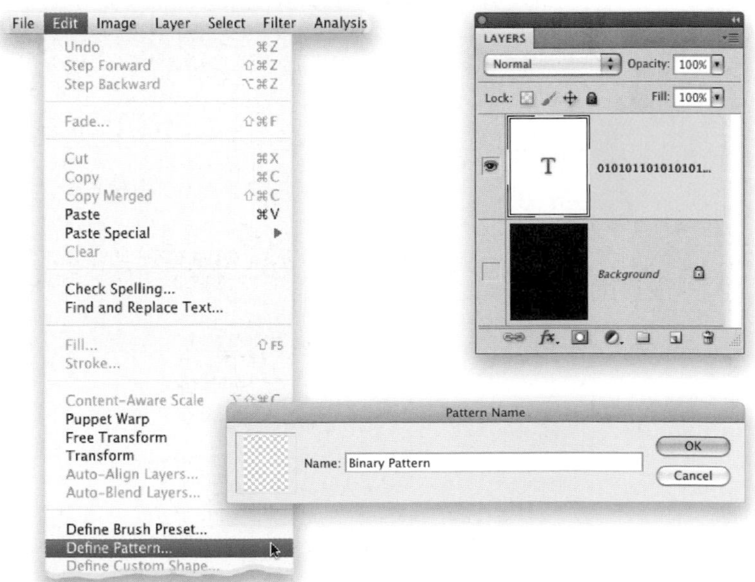

STEP THREE:

Now, open an image to apply the effect to. Here, we have a dark, dramatic shot of a man looking to the side, which could easily work for a movie or TV ad. Click on the Create New Adjustment Layer icon at the bottom of the Layers panel and choose **Hue/Saturation** from the pop-up menu. In the Adjustments panel, turn on the Colorize checkbox and set the Hue to 215 and the Saturation to 25. Leave the Lightness set to 0.

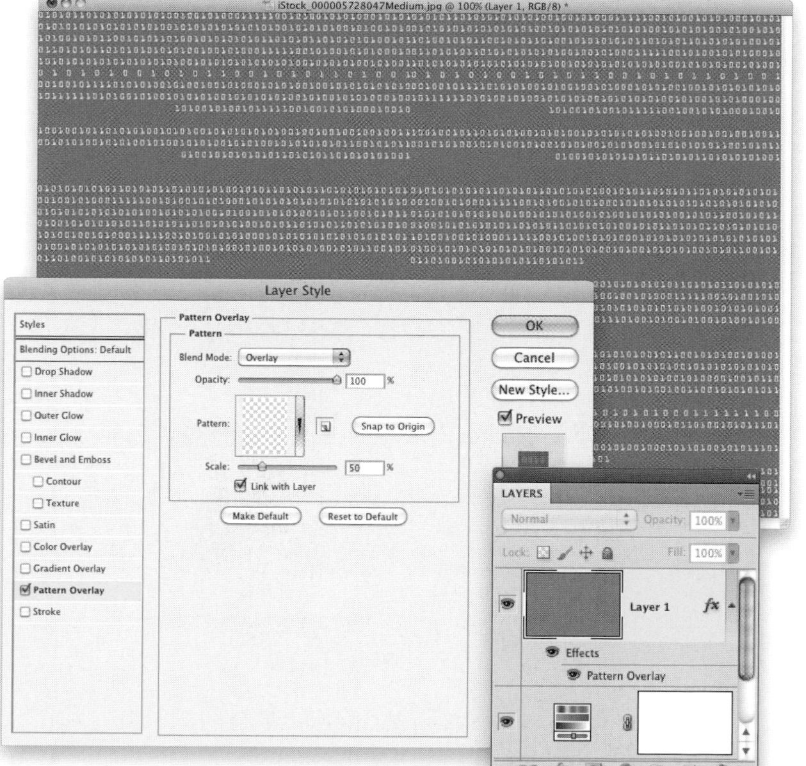

STEP FOUR:

Next, click on the Create a New Layer icon at the bottom of the Layers panel to create a new blank layer. Press **Shift-Delete (PC: Shift-Backspace)** to open the Fill dialog, then choose **50% Gray** from the Use pop-up menu, and click OK. Click on the Add a Layer Style icon at the bottom of the Layers panel and choose **Pattern Overlay**. Click on the Pattern thumbnail and select your newly defined binary pattern in the Pattern Picker (it should be at the bottom of the list). Then, change the Blend Mode to **Overlay** and set the Scale to 50%. Now, the cool part about this effect being applied as a layer style is that you have some flexibility with its look. You can move the pattern around manually and it will tile, which means you can also scale it and it will continue endlessly, no matter how small or large you make it. Plus, the pattern now lives in Photoshop, so you have it at your disposal pretty much whenever you need it.

Continued

STEP FIVE:

Now, you probably noticed that even with the Overlay blend mode, the gray background is still there. So, just click on Blending Options: Default at the top left of the Layer Style dialog, drop the Fill Opacity down to 0%, and click OK. This will leave the pattern, while making the gray layer pixels invisible. Isn't that cool?

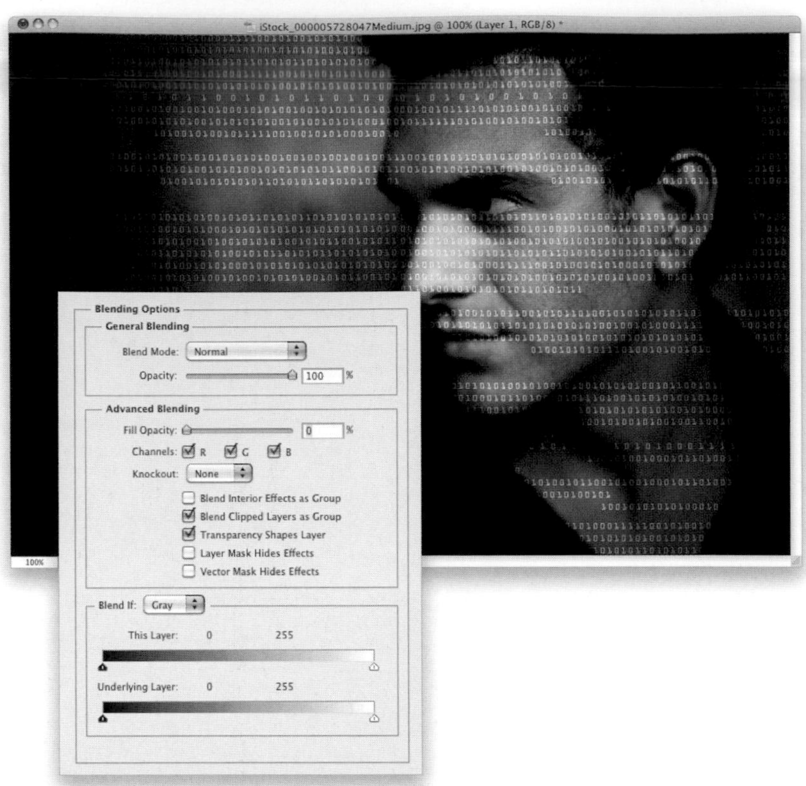

STEP SIX:

There may be some areas of the image where the code is a little overbearing, or perhaps you just want to vary the opacity. So, click on the Add Layer Mask icon at the bottom of the Layers panel to add a white mask to the layer. Then, get the Gradient tool **(G)** from the Toolbox and, up in the Options Bar, click on the down-facing arrow to the right of the gradient thumbnail to open the Gradient Picker, and choose the Foreground to Transparent gradient (the second one from the left in the top row). Click on the Radial Gradient icon (the second icon to the right of the gradient thumbnail), and then press **D** to set your Foreground color to black. Click-and-drag a couple of gradients around the face area to fade the binary pattern, like you see here.

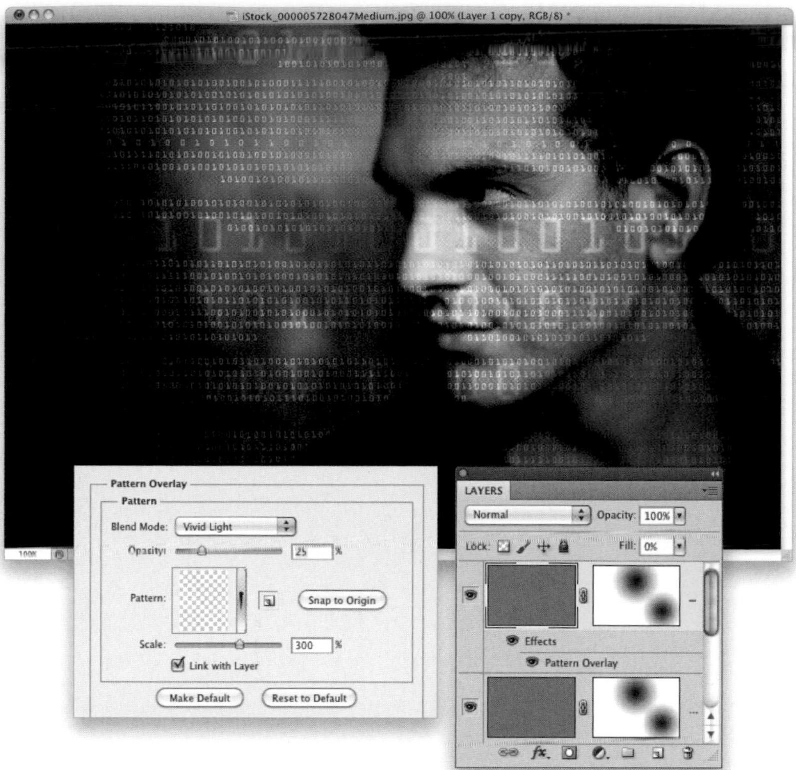

STEP SEVEN:

Just to show you how you can double up the effect, make a duplicate of this binary layer (press **Command-J [PC: Ctrl-J]**), and then double-click in the Layers panel on the Pattern Overlay layer style for this duplicate layer. Keep the pattern the same, but change the Blend Mode to **Vivid Light** and drop the Opacity to 25%. Then, increase the Scale to 300%, and click on the image and manually move the pattern around to where it interacts with the image best. Click OK when you're done.

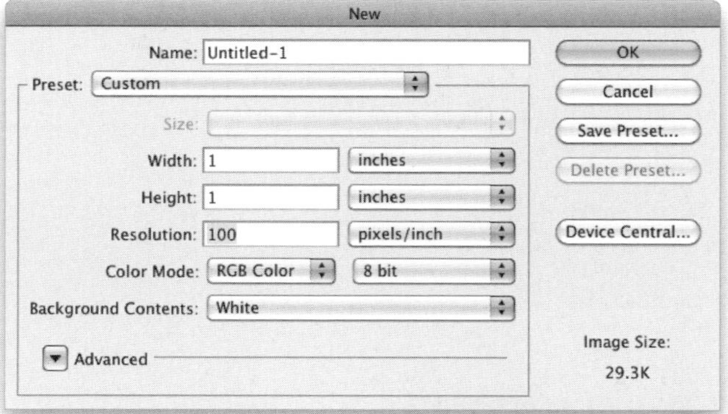

STEP EIGHT:

Now, another popular high-tech graphic element is a simple grid pattern. Again, we're going to create this effect and define it as a pattern that we can have on call whenever we need it. Press **Command-N (PC: Ctrl-N)** and create a new blank document measuring 1 inch by 1 inch at 100 ppi. Grab the padlock icon on the right side of the Background layer and drag it to the Trash icon at the bottom of the panel to unlock the layer.

Continued

STEP NINE:

Press **Command-A (PC: Ctrl-A)** to select the entire canvas. Then, make sure you have a selection tool chosen in the Toolbox, and press the **Right Arrow key** two times, then the **Down Arrow key** two times to nudge the selection a little bit. Press **Delete (PC: Backspace)**. This will leave a white line along both the top and left edge of the image. Press **Command-D (PC: Ctrl-D)** to Deselect. Now, like we did before, go under the Edit menu and choose Define Pattern. With this pattern defined, when we tile it in a layer style, it will create a grid.

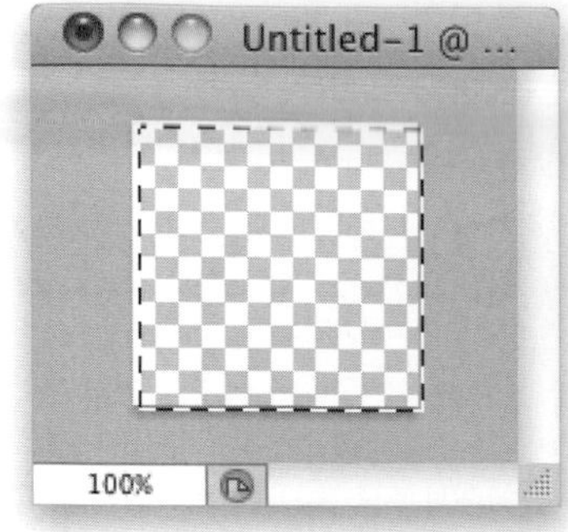

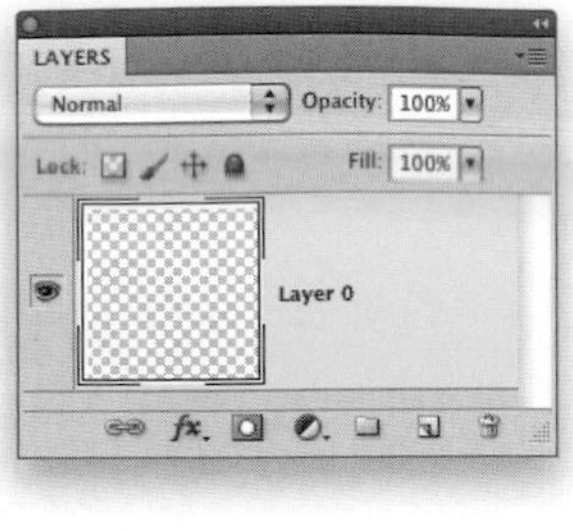

STEP 10:

Go back to your working layout and, just like before, create a new blank layer and fill it with 50% gray. Then, add a Pattern Overlay layer style. Click on the Pattern thumbnail and choose the grid element. Change the Blend Mode to **Overlay** and drop the Scale to around 50%. Click on the image and move the grid around, if needed. Don't forget to click on Blending Options and drop the Fill Opacity to 0%, so the grid will blend with the rest of the image. Click OK when you're done. Again, the beauty of these effects is that they are always available and can be tweaked to be whatever you need them to be without having to go and redefine them. Huge time saver!

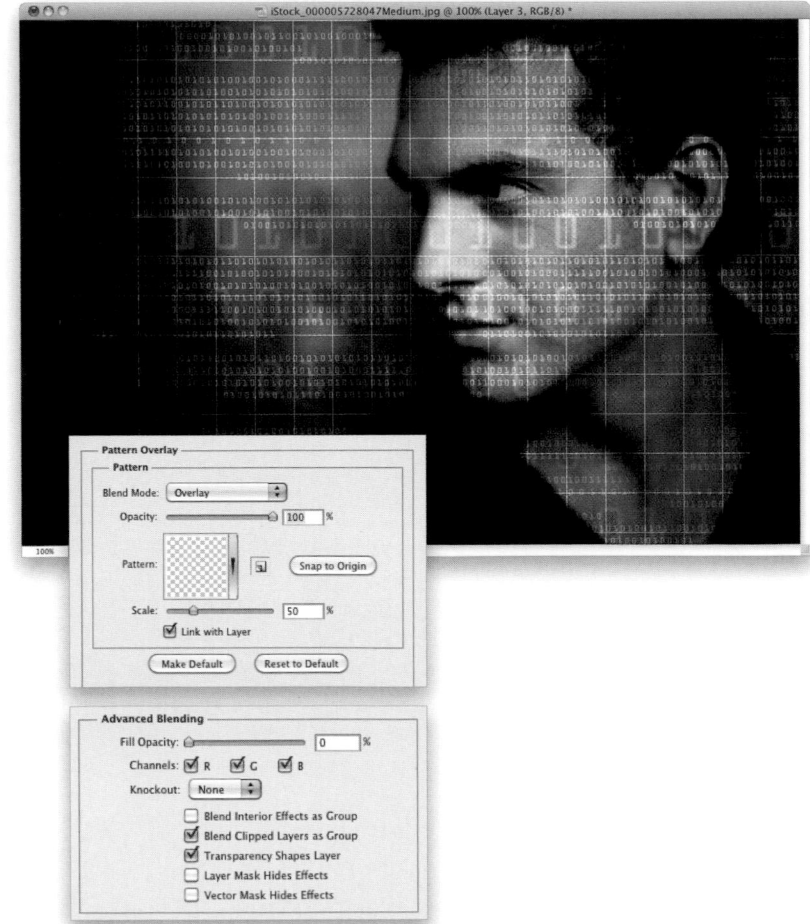

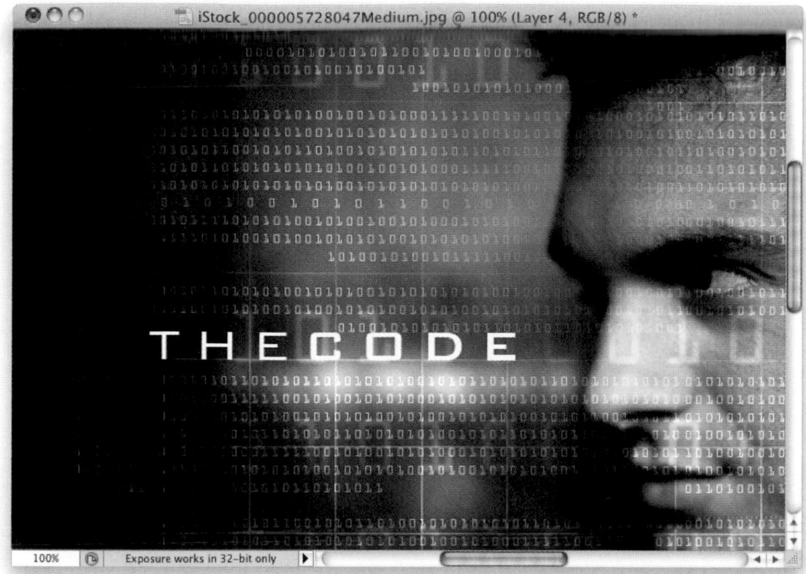

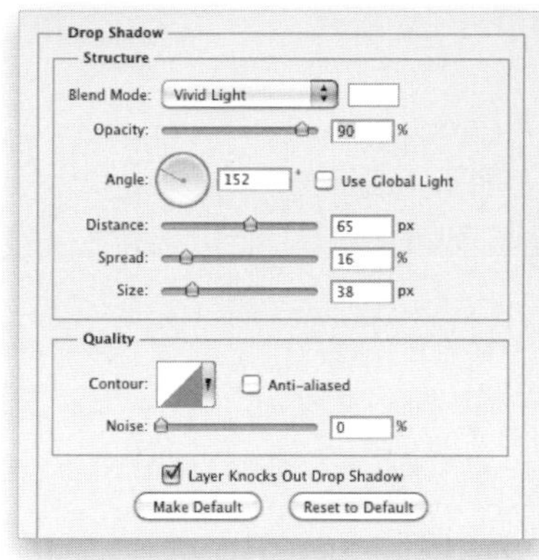

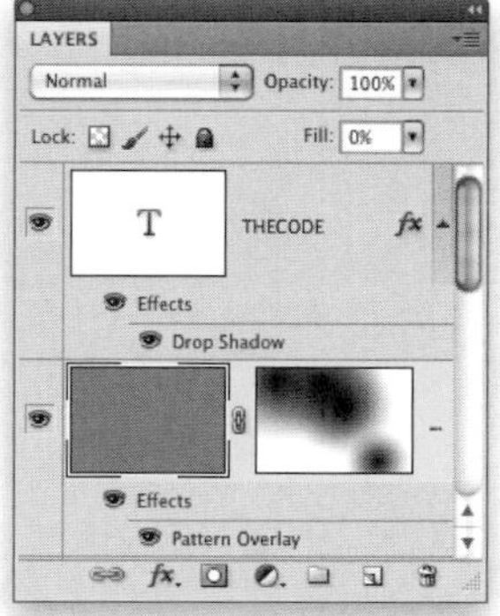

STEP 11:

Just like we did with the binary pattern layer, add a white layer mask and, with your Foreground color set to black, use the Foreground to Transparent radial gradient to hide parts of the grid pattern, like you see here. To finish it off, I added some text in white, using Bank Gothic Light and Bank Gothic Medium. Then, I created a flare below the text by adding a Drop Shadow layer style to it, using the settings seen here.

In the final image on the next page, I decided his neck area was too bright, so I added a blank layer above the Background layer and dragged out a small, black, Foreground to Transparent radial gradient in the bottom-right corner of the image.

Continued

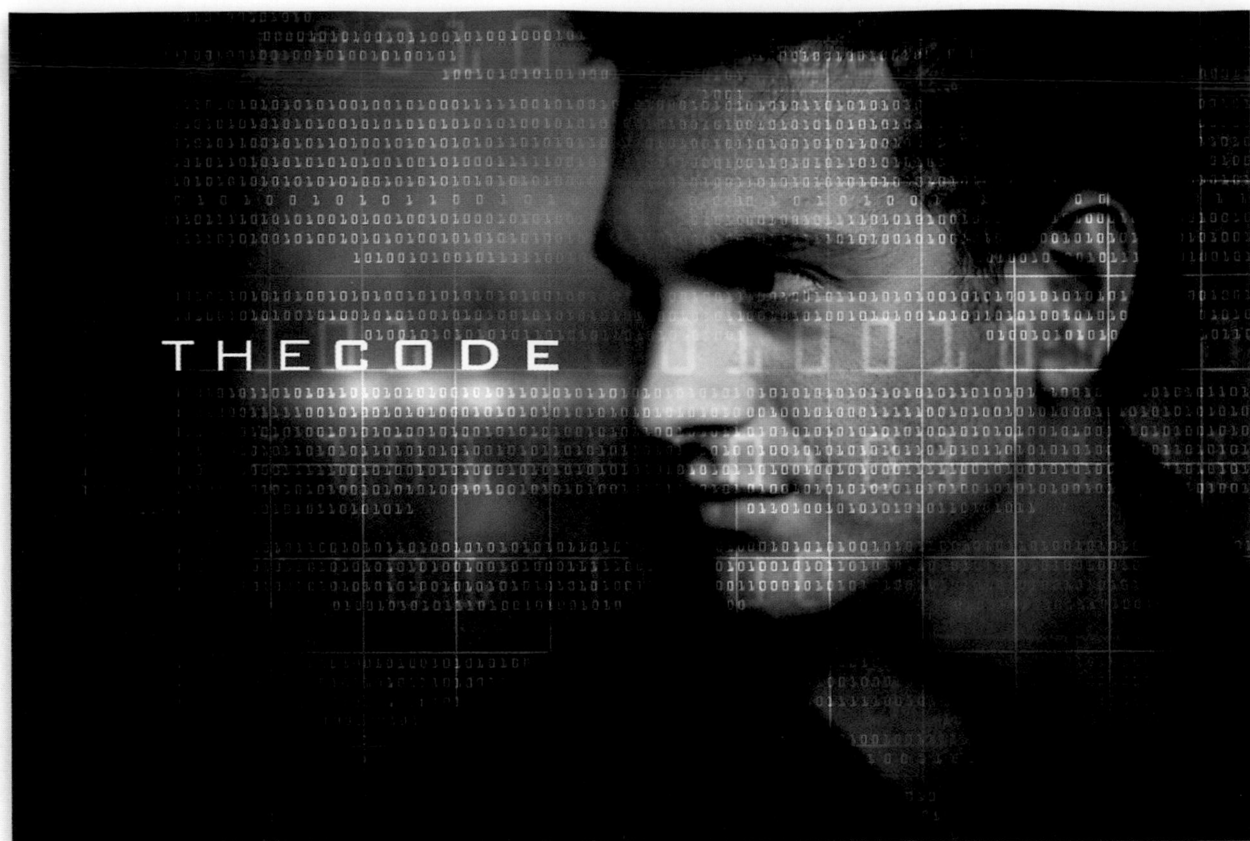

Final Image

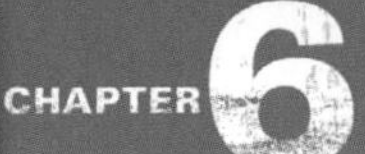

Hollywoodify That Photo!

For lack of a better title, this seems to sum up what's really going on here. We'll start with a very basic photo on a white background and, through some simple layer effects, we'll transform this image into a dramatic poster, complete with title and atmospheric effects that can be applied in numerous ways.

©ISTOCKPHOTO//THOMAS ECKSTADT

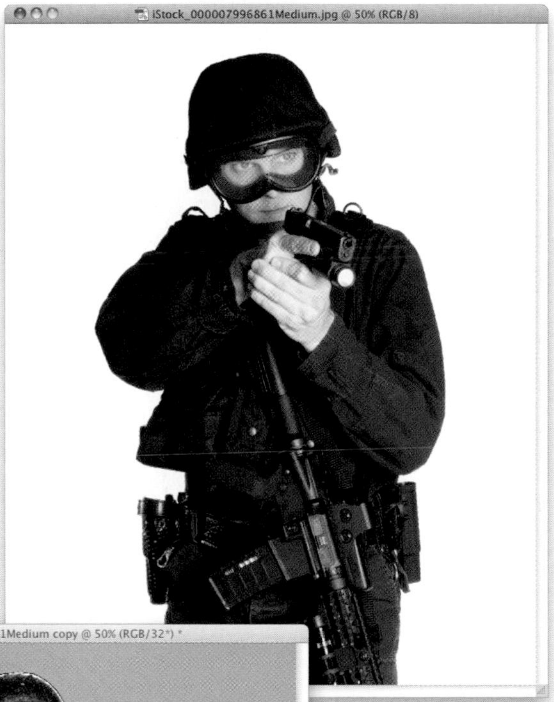

STEP ONE:

This effect starts with a stock image of a man in SWAT gear. The pose is right, but we'll need to do a little work here to make it work in our design.

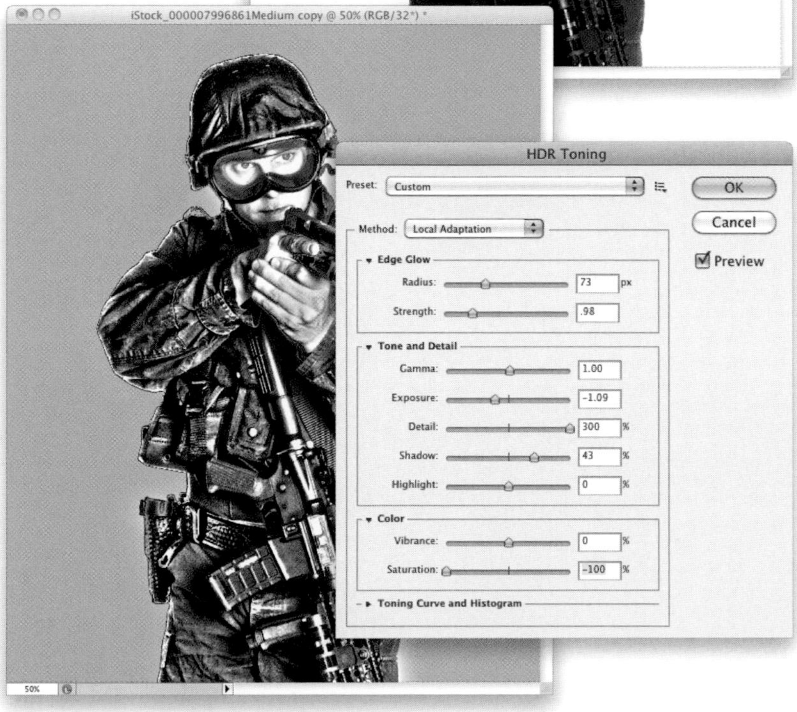

STEP TWO:

To start, let's darken and grunge the image up with some HDR Toning. Make a duplicate of the file by going under the Image menu and choosing **Duplicate**, and then go under the Image menu, under Adjustments, and choose **HDR Toning**. After experimenting with the sliders, I found that these settings really brought out the detail and boosted the contrast quite a bit. If you're using a different image, then you'll want to play around with the sliders and see what results you might get. This is just one of those features that does not have a real formula to it. It really depends on the image. Click OK when you're done.

Continued

STEP THREE:

Go back to the original image file and get the Quick Selection tool **(W)** from the Toolbox. Paint over the white background to select it, then press **Command-Shift-I (PC: Ctrl-Shift-I)** to Inverse the selection, so the SWAT guy is selected instead. Use the Zoom tool **(Z)** to zoom way in, press the **Left Bracket ([) key** to make your brush really small, then Option-click in the white areas under the loops on his shoulders and next to his chin strap to remove them from the selection. Press **Command-J (PC: Ctrl-J)** when you're done to copy the selected area to a new layer. Here, I've turned off the Background layer, so you can see the selection better.

STEP FOUR:

Get the Move tool **(V)** from the Toolbox, then press-and-hold the Shift key (to keep it lined up) and click-and-drag the HDR-toned image into this layout. With the HDR-toned layer still active, Command-click (PC: Ctrl-click) on the layer thumbnail of the extracted SWAT guy to load him as a selection. Inverse the selection and press **Delete (PC: Backspace)** to remove the HDR-toned background. Press **Command-D (PC: Ctrl-D)** to Deselect. Change the HDR-toned layer's blend mode to **Multiply** to apply it to the original SWAT guy, then press **Command-E (PC: Ctrl-E)** to merge this layer with the layer below, making the HDR effect permanent. Finally, click on the Background layer, and press **Shift-Delete (PC: Shift-Backspace)** to open the Fill dialog. Set the Use pop-up menu to **Black** and click OK.

©ISTOCKPHOTO/PLAINVIEW

STEP FIVE:

Now, open the smoke image. We'll use this to create a cool fire effect. Yes, we are going to make fire out of smoke. This will give you a good idea of how textures and other elements can be used for various effects.

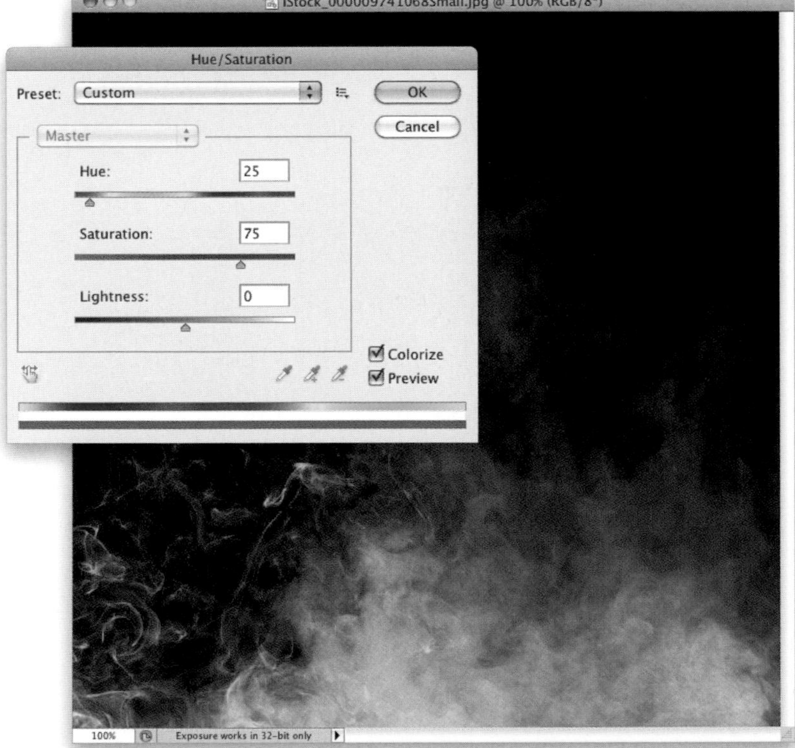

STEP SIX:

Press **Command-U (PC: Ctrl-U)** to open the Hue/Saturation dialog. Turn on the Colorize checkbox, and set the Hue to 25 and the Saturation to 75. This will start to warm up the image. Click OK when you're done.

Continued

STEP SEVEN:

Now, make a duplicate of this layer by pressing **Command-J (PC: Ctrl-J)** then change the duplicate layer's blend mode to **Overlay**. This will really make the colors pop, and it will almost start to look like fire. You could even go so far as to make a second duplicate layer to intensify the effect. When you're done, go under the Layer menu and choose **Flatten Image**.

STEP EIGHT:

After the image is flattened, use the Move tool to bring it into the file containing the SWAT guy and position this layer below the subject layer. Press **Command-T (PC: Ctrl-T)** to go into Free Transform mode, then press-and-hold the Shift key and click-and-drag a corner handle to scale it up. Right-click inside the bounding box and choose **Flip Horizontal**, then move it around behind the SWAT guy until it looks like what you see here. Press **Return (PC: Enter)** to lock in your changes.

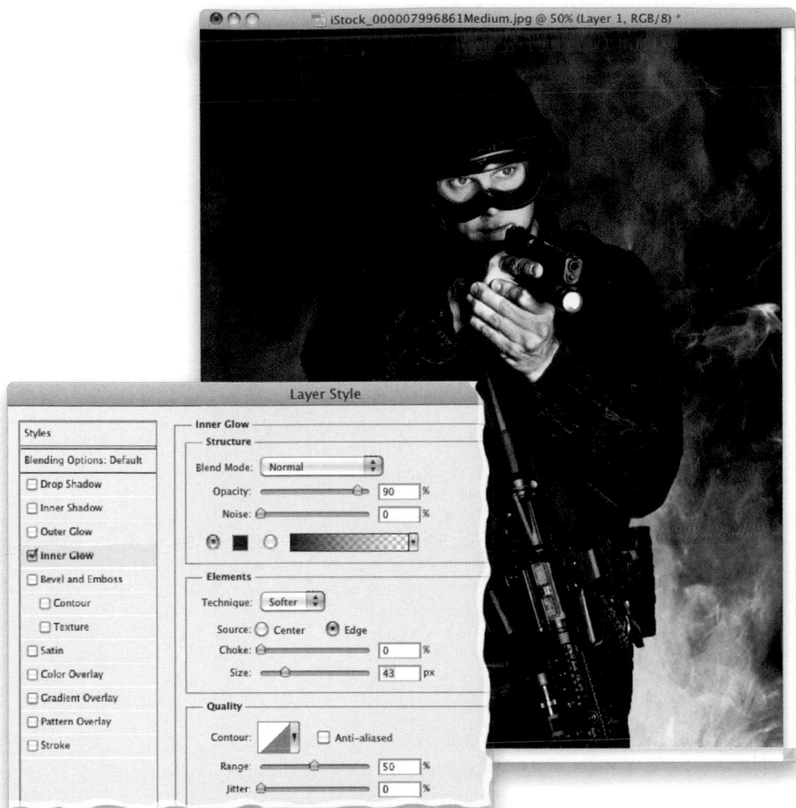

STEP NINE:

Now, we're going to use some layer styles to help the subject blend into the scene more. So, in the Layers panel, click on the SWAT guy's layer to make it active, then click on the Add a Layer Style icon and choose **Inner Glow** from the pop-up menu. Set the Blend Mode to **Normal** and the Opacity to 90%, then click on the color swatch, and choose black in the Color Picker. Then, increase the Size to 43 px. That eliminates the white fringe from his edges.

STEP 10:

Next, click on Color Overlay in the list on the left to turn it on. Click on the color swatch and, when the Color Picker opens, click on the background to sample a hot orange color. Then, change the Blend Mode to **Overlay** and drop the Opacity to 75%.

Continued

STEP 11:
Click on Inner Shadow on the left to turn it on and change the Blend Mode to **Vivid Light**. Then, click on the color swatch, sample a lighter orange color from the background, and drop the Opacity to 50%. Now, increase the Size to around 225 px, and as for the Distance and Angle, you can input the numbers you see here or click on the image and move the shadow around to wherever you like, then click OK. Notice that this shadow has become a hot glow from the fire, and watch how it affects the image when you move it around. The other effects have also darkened the edges and put a cast over the image that makes it blend with the background that much more.

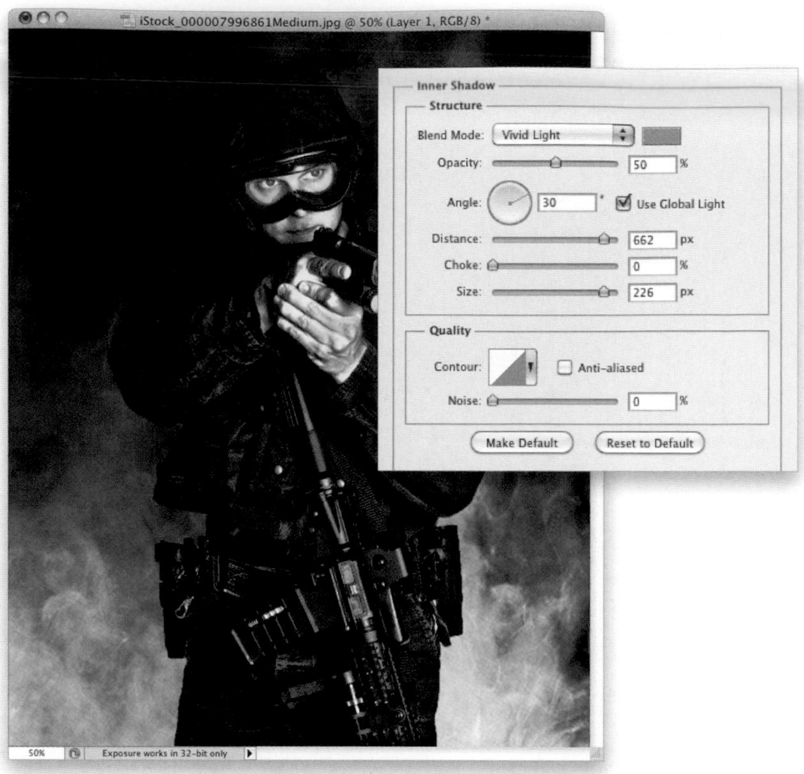

STEP 12:
At this point, the subject is blending better, but we can do one more thing to help make the effect wrap around the subject: Double-click on the SWAT guy's layer to go back into the Layer Style dialog to the Blending Options, then go down to the bottom of the dialog to the Blend If section. Go to the Underlying Layer slider and press-and-hold the Option (PC: Alt) key, while clicking-and-dragging the white slider, splitting the slider to allow the lightest area of the smoky fire layer to be more visible. This makes the subject appear as though the smoke is surrounding him.

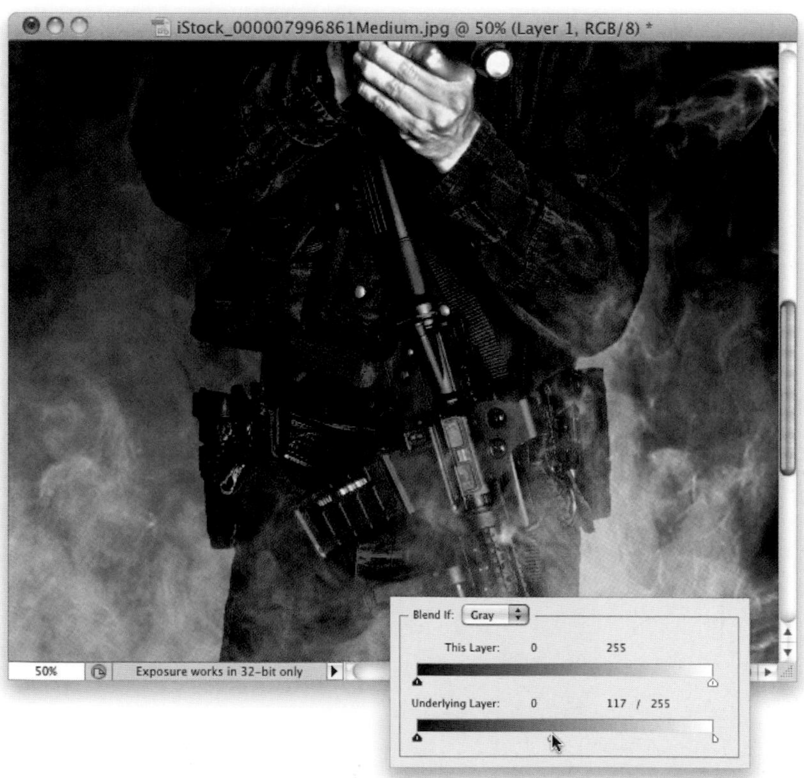

STEP 13:

Now, everything looks good except one thing: the subject's eyes need to be a bit more menacing. In fact, we should only barely see them at all. So, select the Pen tool **(P)** from the Toolbox and use it to draw a path around the area of the mask. Click to add a point and click-and-drag to create a curve. Option-click on the point after adjusting the curve to lock it into place and click back on your original point to complete your path.

STEP 14:

Once the path is created, press **Command-Return (PC: Ctrl-Enter)** to load the path as a selection. Click on the Create a New Layer icon at the bottom of the Layers panel to create a new blank layer, and then press Shift-Delete (PC: Shift-Backspace) to open the Fill dialog and fill the selection with black. Deselect, then drop the layer's Opacity down to 90%.

Continued

STEP 15:
Now, if the mask was really tinted this way, then it would reflect the fire in the glass. So, go back to the original smoke/fire document and use the Rectangular Marquee tool **(M)** to draw a selection around a small section of the fire effect, then press **Command-C (PC: Ctrl-C)** to Copy it.

STEP 16:
Switch back to your working layout, make sure the top layer is selected, and press **Command-V (PC: Ctrl-V)** to Paste the fire graphic into the design. Use the Move tool **(V)** to position it over the black mask area we just created. Use Free Transform to scale it, if necessary, and don't worry too much about quality loss. It's a subtle effect. Press **Command-Option-G (PC: Ctrl-Alt-G)** to clip the fire layer inside the mask tint layer. Then, drop the layer's Opacity to 35%.

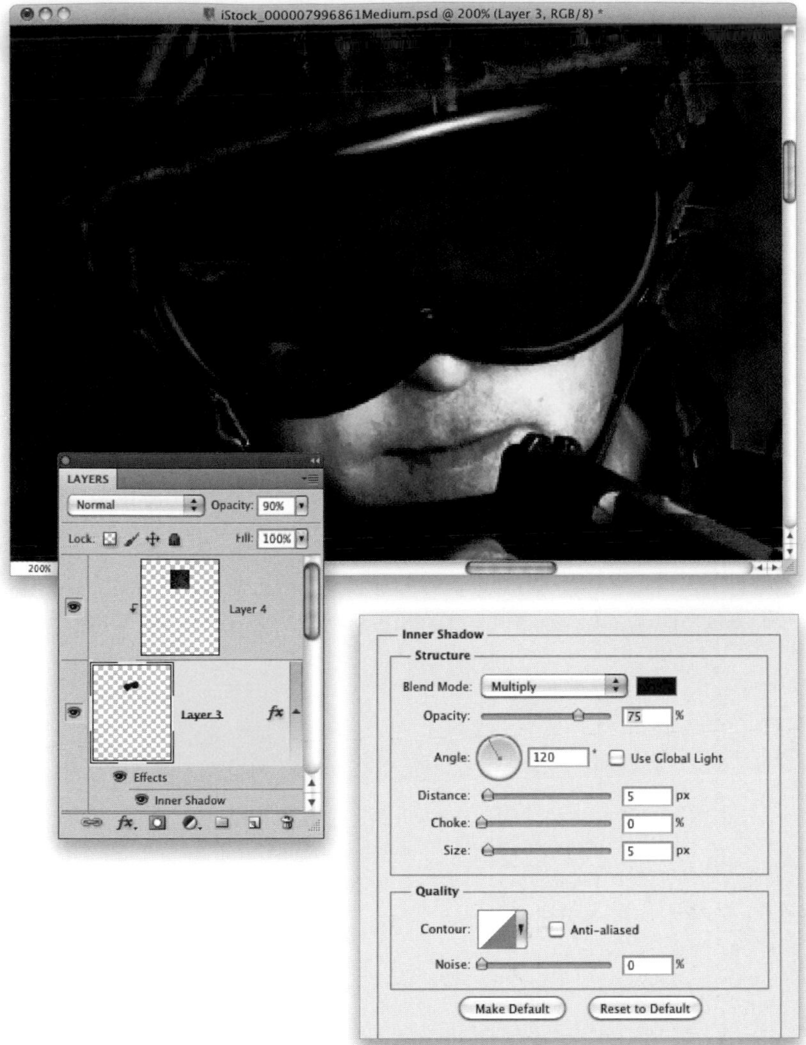

STEP 17:

Now, to add one last touch, click on the mask tint layer and add an Inner Shadow layer style. Use the settings here to create a subtle shadow being cast by the edge of the mask. As you can see, we have once again achieved a number of seemingly complex effects through the use of layer styles and layer effects.

For the final image, I added some text with a small Inner Shadow layer style, and clipped a texture file with a Gradient Overlay layer style inside the text to make it look like metal. Then on a new layer below the text layer, I created a rectangle, filled it with black, changed the blend mode to Multiply, and lowered the layer's opacity. I also used the flare brush from Chapter 1 to make it look like the metal was reflecting a light.

Continued

Use the Flare brush created in Chapter 1.

Final Image

Movie Poster Project

In this project, we will create a complete movie poster. Now, most of you aren't necessarily designing movie posters all the time, but that's not the point. By practicing on a project like this, you gain new insight into how you can get creative with photos, layer effects, and how powerful Photoshop really is as a designer's tool.

COREY BARKER

STEP ONE:

Let's start by creating the background. Here, we have a shot I took when I was in New York. I had no idea what I would use it for at the time—it just seemed like an interesting street downtown. Fortunately, this is perfect for the background for this movie poster concept.

STEP TWO:

The first thing is that we don't need this image in color, because we're going to add a color effect over the whole thing later. So, to make it black and white, press **D** to set your Foreground and Background colors to their defaults of black and white, then go under the Image menu, under Adjustments, and choose **Gradient Map.** Just click OK in the dialog and this will convert the image to a pretty crisp black-and-white image, which will work great for this effect.

Continued

STEP THREE:

Now, press **Command-N (PC: Ctrl-N)** to open the New dialog, and create a new document measuring 8 inches wide by 12 inches tall at 125 ppi. This is a proportional size to the industry standard. Once the file is created, go back to the street image and, using the Move tool **(V)**, click-and-drag it into your new document. Press **Command-T (PC: Ctrl-T)** to use Free Transform to scale and position the image as you see here. What we're concentrating on here is the right side of the image, because of the nice perspective angle of the building there. We're going to mirror this effect.

STEP FOUR:

Press **Command-R (PC: Ctrl-R)** to make the rulers visible, and then click on the vertical ruler and drag a guide to the center of the document. It should snap to it when you're close (if it doesn't, go under the View menu and choose **Snap**).

STEP FIVE:

Now, press **Command-J (PC: Ctrl-J)** to make a duplicate of this image layer, then go under the Edit menu, under Transform, and choose **Flip Horizontal**. With the Move tool still active, position this flipped duplicate so that it mirrors the positioning of the original. For instance, here I looked at the walkway in the upper corner and the number of windows to the edge.

STEP SIX:

Next, select the Rectangular Marquee tool **(M)** from the Toolbox and draw a selection over the entire left half of the document, until it snaps to the guide in the middle. Then, click on the Add Layer Mask icon at the bottom of the Layers panel to hide the opposite half of the photo. You can now see the mirror effect, and it creates an interesting result.

Continued

STEP SEVEN:

Press **Command-E (PC: Ctrl-E)** to merge these two layers together, because we have a few things to fix on this image before we go any further. Although they may only partially be there in the end, the JC Penney flags on the side of the building don't really go with our action/thriller concept. So, use the Zoom tool **(Z)** to zoom in a bit, then use the Rectangular Marquee tool to draw a selection over the flags on the left. Press-and-hold the Shift key to add to your selection, and draw a selection around the flags on the right. Press **Shift-Delete (PC: Shift-Backspace)** to open the Fill dialog, choose **Content-Aware** from the Use pop-up menu, and click OK. The flags are now gone, and while it's not perfect, it will do.

STEP EIGHT:

Now, one other spot in the new background that bothers me is the small gap of sky under the walkway. I tried Content-Aware Fill on this and did not like what I got, so I found another solution. Get the Patch tool from the Toolbox (it's nested beneath the Spot Healing Brush, or press **Shift-J** until you have it), make sure that, in the Options Bar, the Patch setting is set to Source, and then use it like the Lasso tool to draw a selection around the gap of sky (as you see here). Once you have your selection, move your cursor inside the selection, and drag straight down until you see the selection filled with the pattern below. Release the cursor and the change is applied. It probably could use some tweaks, but once the other effects are applied, this will barely be seen. So, don't waste time on parts of the image you know will not be seen or will be barely seen.

STEP NINE:

Press **Command-D (PC: Ctrl-D)** to Deselect. Then, press **Command-A (PC: Ctrl-A)** to select the entire image, go under the Image menu, and choose **Crop**. This will eliminate the excess image going beyond the image boundaries. Deselect, then turn off the rulers, and go under the View menu and choose **Clear Guides**.

STEP 10:

Go into Free Transform, and click-and-drag the top-center point up a little, because we are going to change the perspective, which makes the image squatter. Now, Right-click within the bounding box and choose **Perspective**. Click on the bottom-right corner of the image window and drag it out a bit, so you can see the edges of the bounding box. Then, grab either the left or right control handle at the top and drag outward just a little bit to alter the perspective of the street view. This just makes it more symmetrical and adds an interesting perspective to the overall background.

Continued

STEP 11:

Now, at this point, our city image is just way too clean and pretty for what we need, so we're going to use a texture to grunge it up. Here, we have an image of a wall I also shot in New York. Again, I had no idea what I might do with such an image, but you just never know. Turns out, it will work great for this poster.

STEP 12:

Press **D** to set your Foreground and Background colors to their defaults of black and white, then press **X** to swap the colors. Now, go under the Image menu, under Adjustments, and choose **Gradient Map**. You can see not only does it convert to black and white, but it also inverts the values. That's because we flipped the colors around. Click OK.

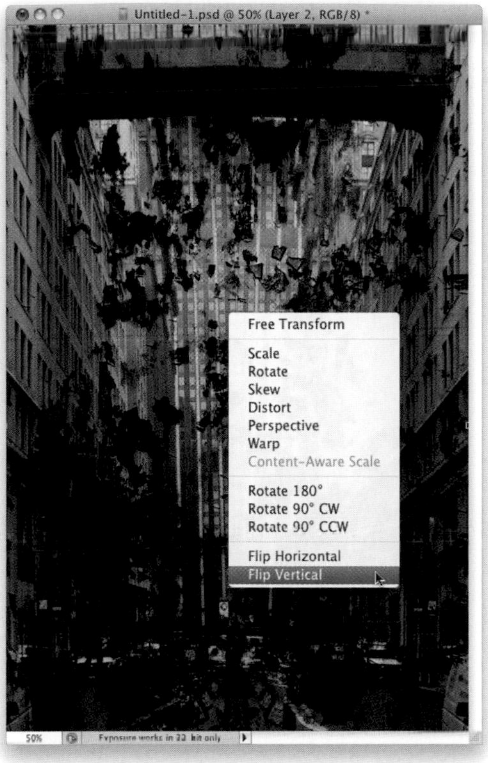

STEP 13:

Now, click-and-drag or copy-and-paste this file into your working layout, then press Command-T (PC: Ctrl-T) to go into Free Transform, and scale it to fit in the canvas area. I think the pattern looks better if the heavier black areas are closer to the bottom, so while you're in Free Transform, Right-click inside the bounding box and choose **Flip Vertical**. Press Return (PC: Enter) and then change the layer's blend mode to **Multiply**.

STEP 14:

Add a black (hide all) layer mask to this texture layer by pressing-and-holding the Option (PC: Alt) key and clicking on the Add Layer Mask icon at the bottom of the Layers panel. Then, select the Gradient tool **(G)** from the Toolbox. Click on the down-facing arrow to the right of the gradient thumbnail in the Options Bar to open the Gradient Picker, and choose the Foreground to Transparent gradient (the second from the left in the top row), and then click on the Radial Gradient icon (the second icon to the right of the gradient thumbnail). Finally, make sure your Foreground color is set to white. Now, draw a gradient out from roughly the lower-middle area of the city image. Then, draw another, smaller gradient at the top area of the image, as well. This will more subtly reveal the texture. If it still seems too dark, lower the layer's Opacity a little (here, I lowered mine to 75%).

Continued

STEP 15:
To fade out the bottom, just click on the Create a New Layer icon at the bottom of the Layers panel to add a new blank layer at the top of the layer stack. Then, use the same Gradient tool, but this time, click on the Linear Gradient icon (the first icon to the right of the gradient thumbnail) and set your Foreground color to black. Start at the bottom edge of the image, and click-and-drag the gradient up just a little.

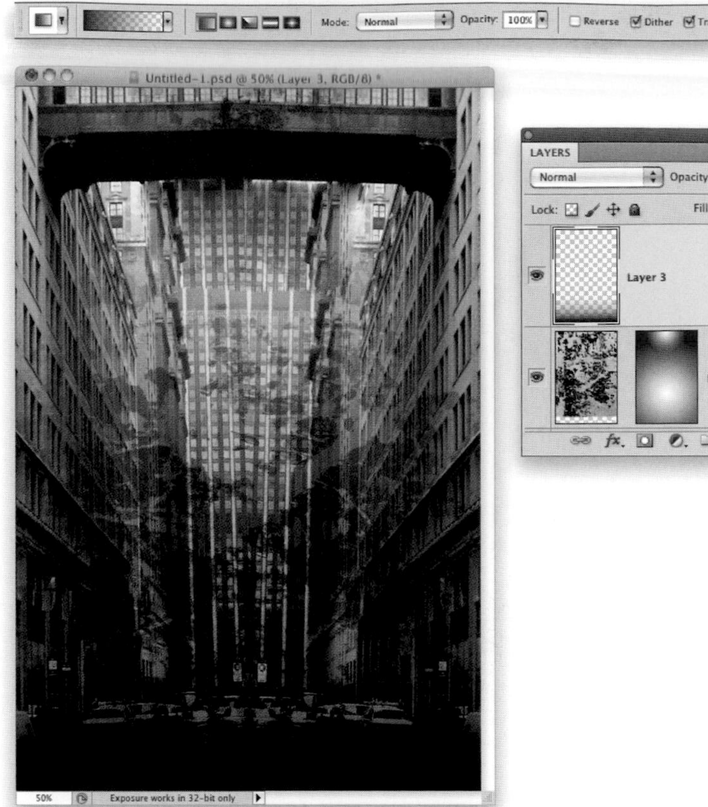

STEP 16:
Okay, so now we're ready to add the main subject. Open the file of the extracted sword assassin. I went ahead and extracted it for you, so you can just drop it into your working layout. Do this simply by dragging-and-dropping or copying-and-pasting it in.

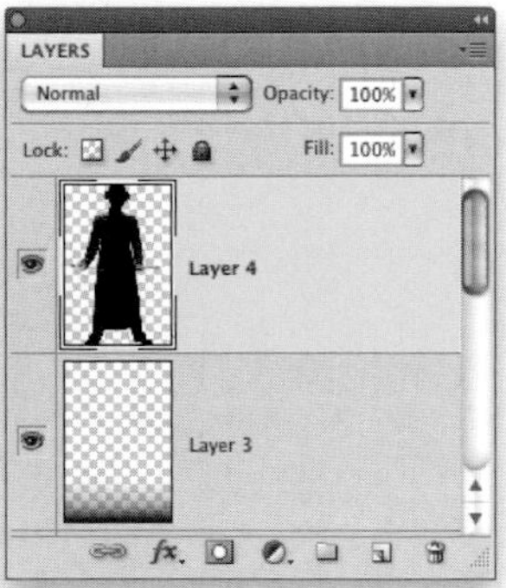

©ISTOCKPHOTO/DAN WILTON

STEP 17:

Once the subject is there, go ahead and center it in the middle of the background, just under the walkway area. Also, make sure this layer is at the top of the layer stack in the Layers panel.

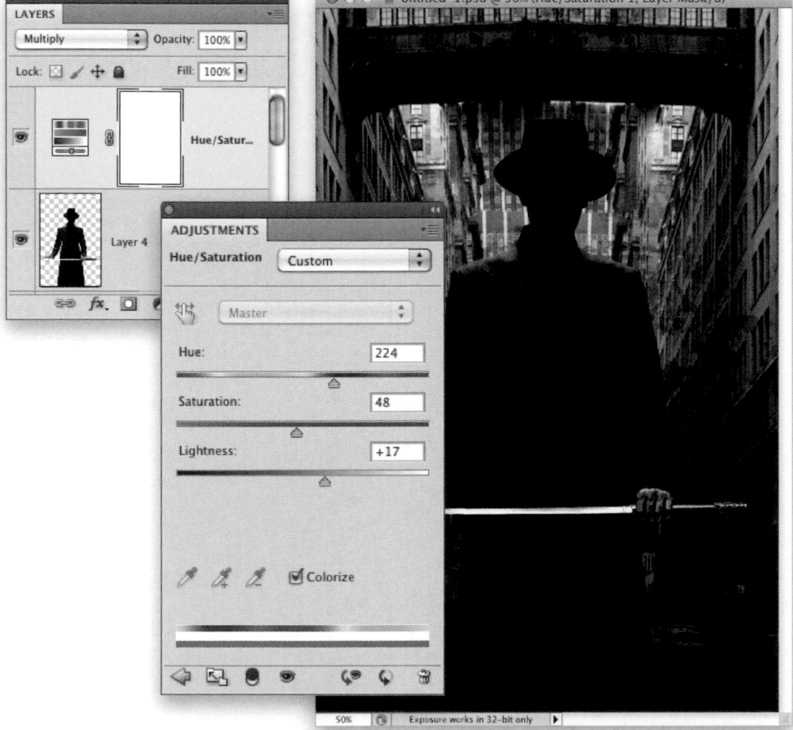

STEP 18:

Now, click on the Create New Adjustment Layer icon at the bottom of the Layers panel and choose **Hue/Saturation** from the pop-up menu. In the Adjustments panel, turn on the Colorize checkbox, and set the Hue to 224, the Saturation to 48, and the Lightness to +17. Then, change the adjustment layer's blend mode to **Multiply**. This will give you a high-contrast, dark blue cast over the image.

Continued

STEP 19:

I noticed that once the color effect was added, the background got a lot darker as a result, thus losing some detail. So, click on the street layer, press **Command-L (PC: Ctrl-L)** to open the Levels dialog, and move the Input Levels midtones (gray) slider to about the 1.40 mark to lighten the overall background a little bit. Click OK when you're done.

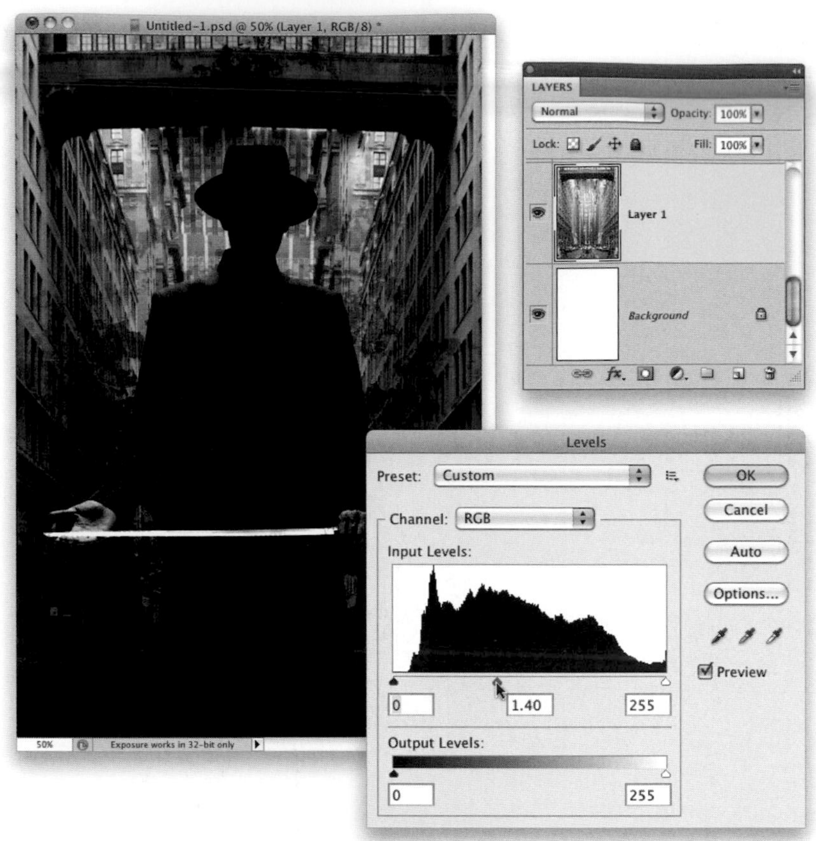

STEP 20:

Let's add an enhanced glow on the edge of the subject to help him blend in the background a bit more. We'll do this with a layer style. So, click on the subject's layer, then click on the Add a Layer Style icon at the bottom of the Layers panel, and choose **Inner Shadow**. In the Layer Style dialog, click on the color swatch and, when the Color Picker appears, move your cursor over the image and sample a light blue from the background. Click OK. Then, back in the Layer Style dialog, set the Blend Mode to **Screen** and set the Opacity to around 75%–85%. Increase the Size to around 25 px, then click inside the image and drag the effect around to position it so it looks like the light is coming from above. Click OK when you're done.

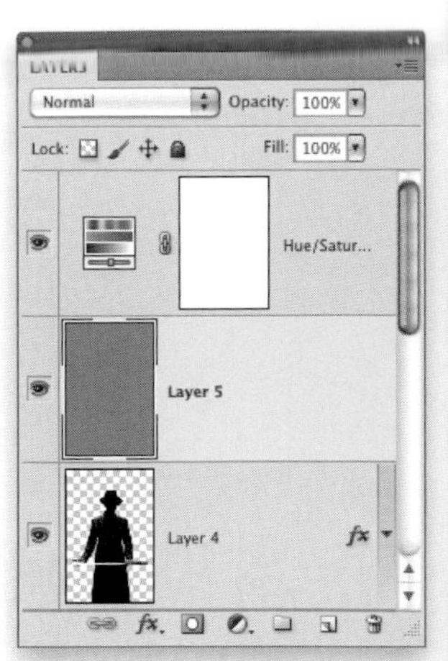

STEP 21:
Now, to finish creating drama in the image, let's add some rain. Create a new blank layer above the subject layer in the layer stack, then press Shift-Delete (PC: Shift-Backspace), and choose **50% Gray** from the Fill dialog's Use pop-up menu to fill the layer with a neutral gray. It will appear blue, because it's below the Hue/Saturation adjustment layer.

STEP 22:
Next, go to the Filter menu, under Noise, and choose **Add Noise**. Set the Amount to 400%, click on the Gaussian radio button, and turn on the Monochromatic checkbox. Click OK.

Continued

STEP 23:
Go under the Filter menu again, but this time, go under Blur and choose **Motion Blur.** Set the Angle to 72° and the Distance to 75 pixels. Click OK. Now, change the layer's blend mode to **Screen** and you'll see the rain effect take shape.

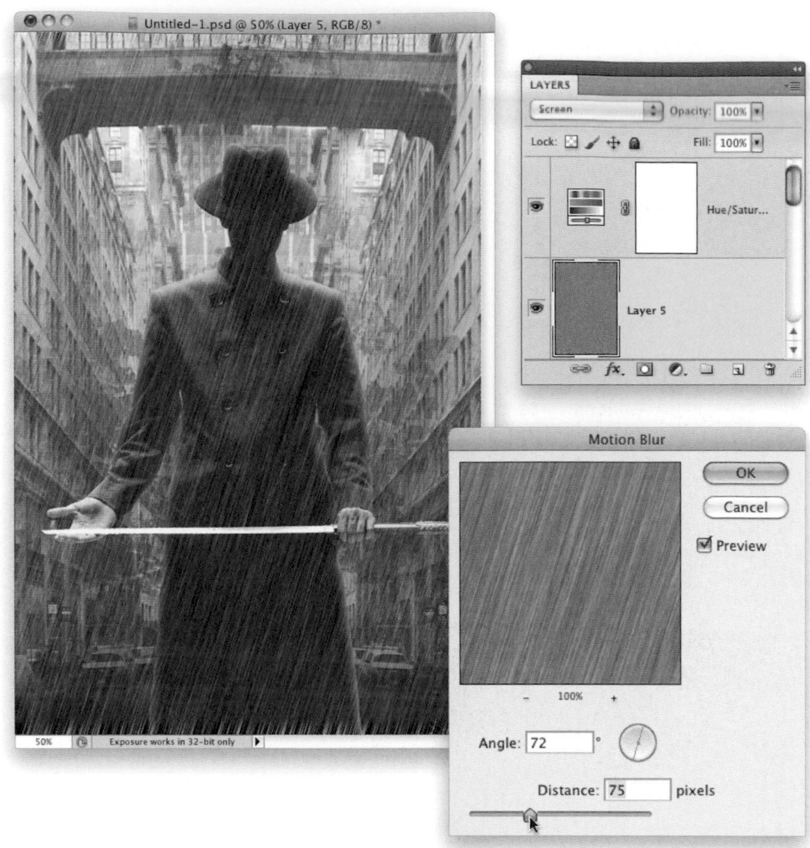

STEP 24:
I think it's a bit too much, so to lessen the effect, first drop the layer's Opacity down to around 80%. Then, press Command-L (PC: Ctrl-L) to open the Levels dialog, and use the settings I have here to greatly boost the contrast of the rain, reducing the effect on the darker areas, because the layer is in Screen mode.

STEP 25:

Next, I want to add a sort of blood splat effect on the image to, again, make it more dramatic. Remember the splat brush we created in Chapter 1? Select the Brush tool **(B)** and locate the brush, or go and create it if you haven't yet. Once you have it, create a new blank layer at the top of the layer stack, and then click on the Foreground color swatch at the bottom of the Toolbox to open the Color Picker. Choose a nice dark red color, click OK, and click once on the blank layer to paint one instance of the splat. Since it's on its own layer, you can use Free Transform to scale and position the splat anywhere you want. Here, I placed it behind where I'm going to add the title as a finishing touch.

You'll see in the final image that I added a tagline at the top (across the bottom of the walkway) and the title near the bottom (just below the sword) in Trajan Pro. I stacked the words in the title, then made the first and last letters of "Dark Assassin" a little larger, like we learned back in Chapter 2, and added a white line between the lines of text, like we did in the watch ad in Chapter 4. Then, just to make it look real, I added a movie copy block at the bottom.

Continued

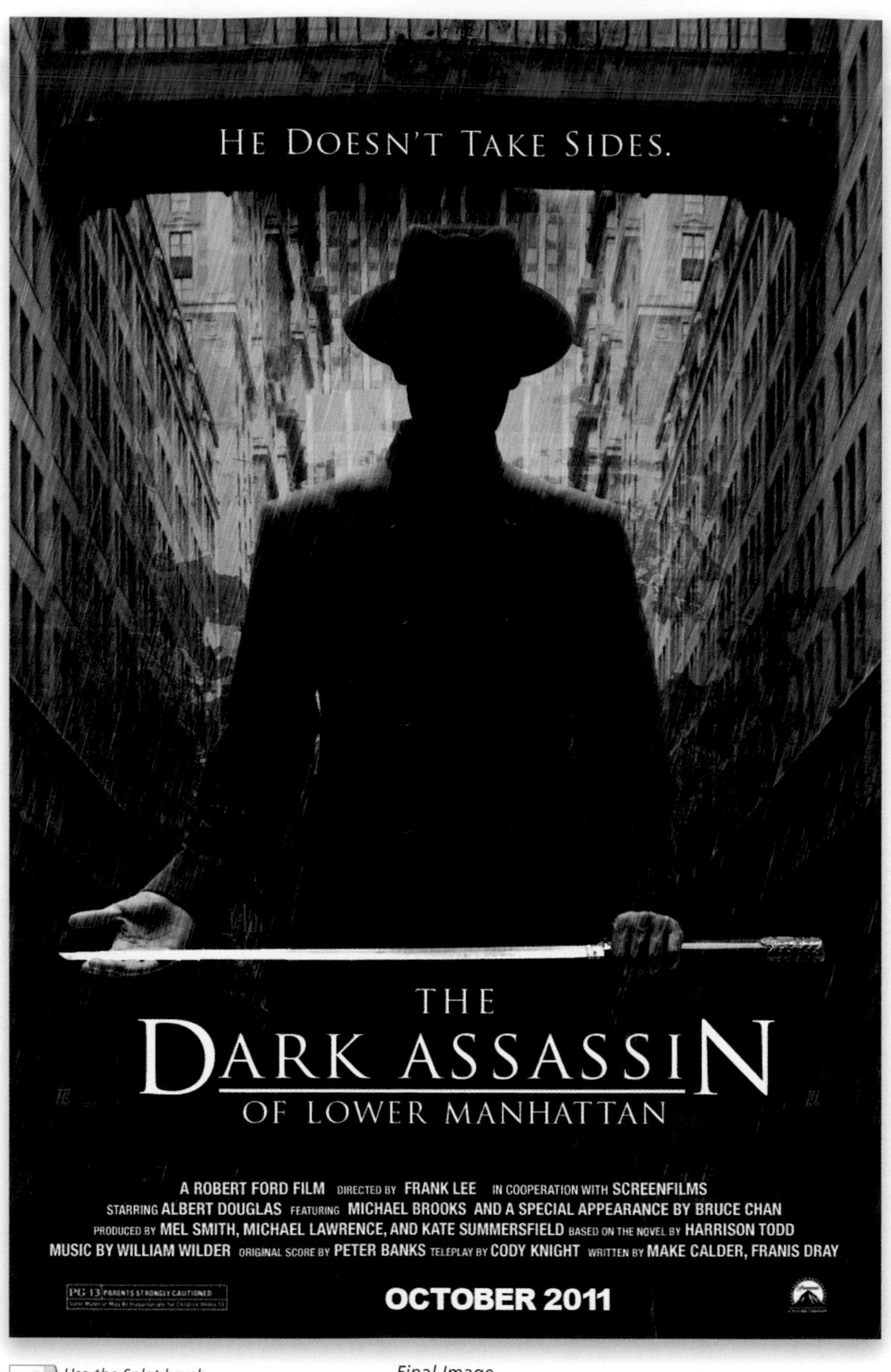

Use the Splat brush created in Chapter 1.

Final Image

A Dream Within a Dream

3D design effects

What if there were 3D capabilities in Photoshop that every designer could use to bring a whole new world of possibilities to an environment they are already used to? That would be a dream within a dream. Well, a dream it is not—as of CS5, Photoshop's 3D features have evolved into a nearly full-featured 3D application right inside of Photoshop. Because of this, the 3D features are only available in the Extended version of Photoshop. The Standard version does not support any 3D features. If you do not have CS5 Extended, please read through the following pages anyway to get an idea of just what's possible using 3D as a design tool. It may help you decide whether or not to consider the upgrade. (*Hint:* I realize upgrades can be costly, but if you're a budding designer, you would be doing yourself a favor by getting an edge on others with what is new and growing. From what I can see, 3D is only going to get better!) I've also created a video to show you how to use the 3D tools, since it is much easier to understand by seeing them in action than by reading a description of how they work. You can find it on the book's download page mentioned in the "12 Things..." at the front of the book.

3D Text Effects

One of the greatest leaps forward in Photoshop for designers is the ability to create and manipulate 3D objects, including 3D text. Here, we'll explore how you can create dramatic effects with 3D text and lights using the Repoussé feature. With some experimentation, this feature can take you on a creative path to all new possibilities.

STEP ONE:

Here, we're going to do two things: first, we'll set up the background image in 3D, and then we'll define a texture material from the background image to later apply to some text. So, open the background image shown here and make a duplicate of the Background layer by pressing **Command-J (PC: Ctrl-J)**. Then, go under the 3D menu and choose **New 3D Postcard From Layer**. This will put the 2D flat image in a 3D space.

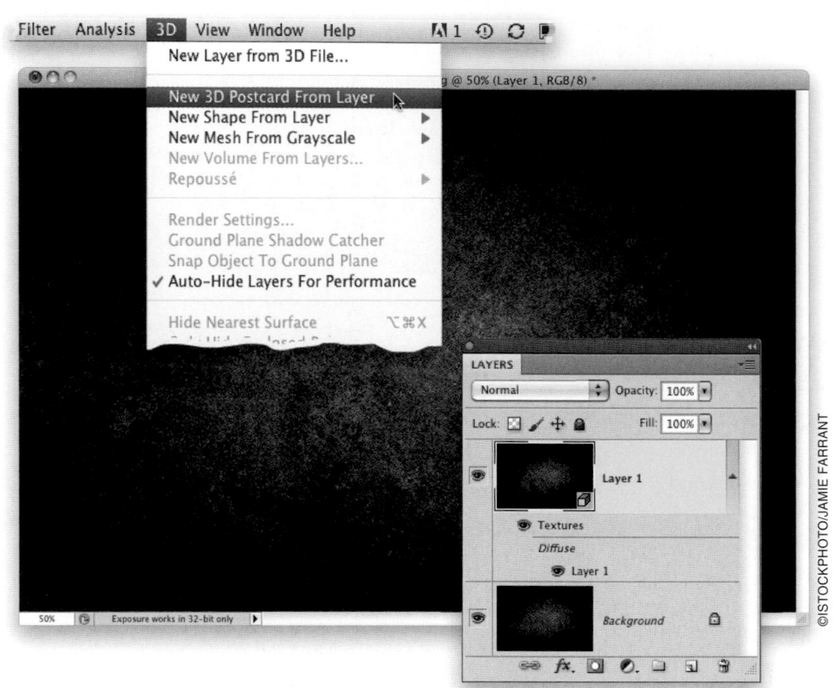

©ISTOCKPHOTO/JAMIE FARRANT

STEP TWO:

Go under the Window menu and choose **3D** to open the 3D panel. At the top of the panel, click on the Filter By: Materials icon (the third icon from the left) to open the Materials options, and then click on the material thumbnail to open the Material Picker. Click on the right-facing arrow in the upper-right corner and choose **New Material**. Give the new material a name and click OK.

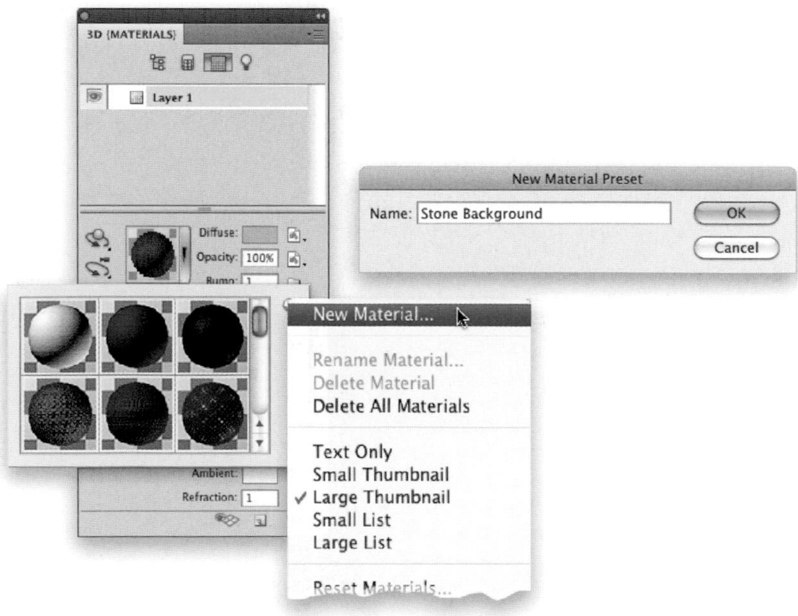

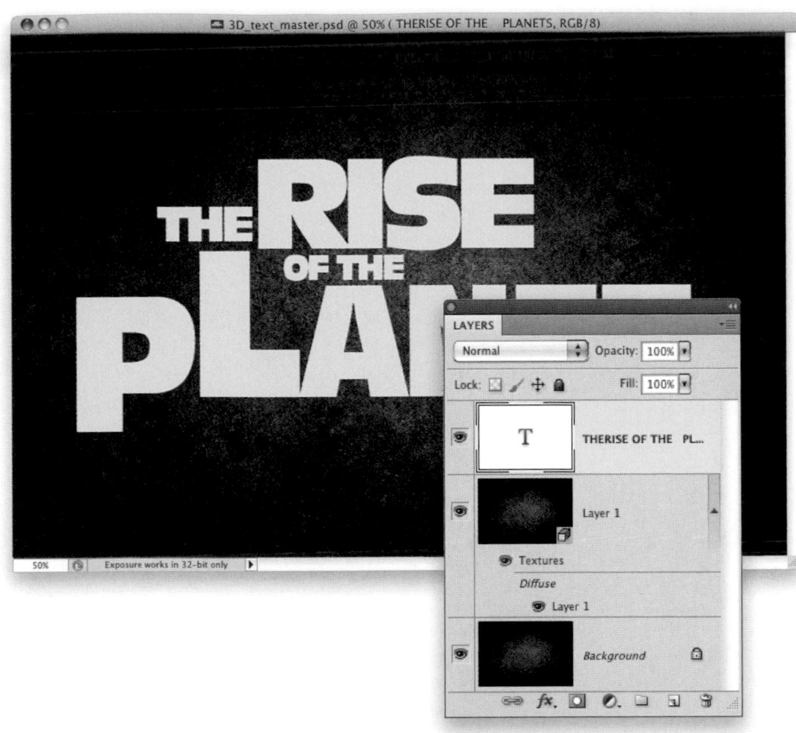

STEP THREE:

Now, it's time to add the text. You can use the Move tool **(V)** to click-and-drag the text layer I created here (using the font Incised901BT Compact; you can find it on the book's download site) onto your texture background to follow along with, or you can go ahead and grab the Horizontal Type tool **(T)** from the Toolbox and set your own text. Either way, make sure that once the text is set, its layer appears above the 3D postcard layer in the Layers panel.

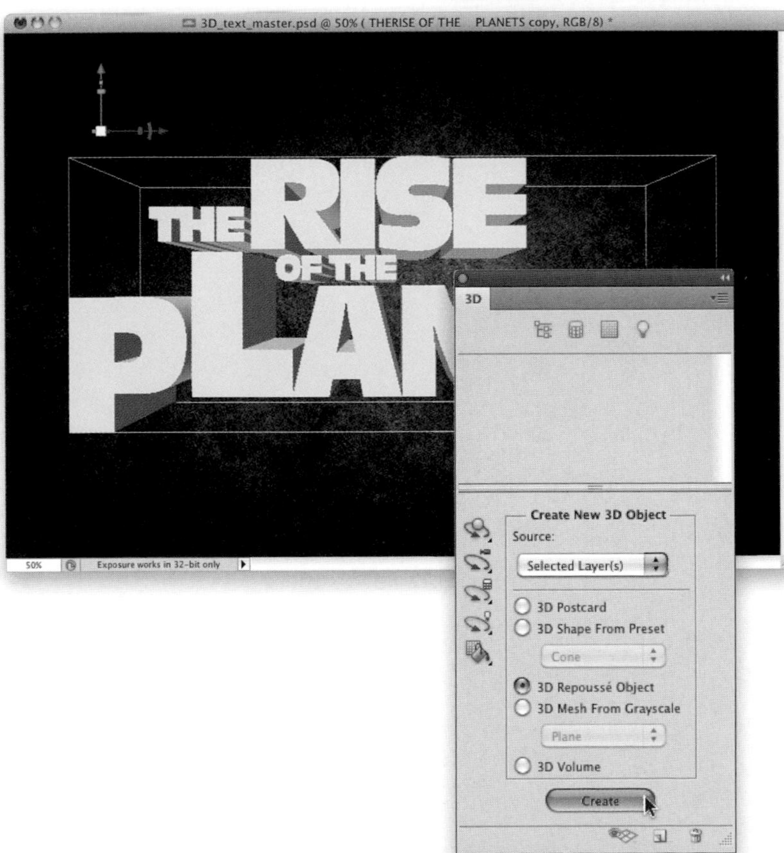

STEP FOUR:

With the text layer active, go to the 3D panel, make sure the Source pop-up menu is set to **Selected Layer(s)**, click on the 3D Repoussé Object radio button, and then click the Create button. This will apply a 3D effect to the text and will open the Repoussé dialog. (*Note:* The text will rasterize when converting to 3D, so you won't be able to go back and edit it. So, you might want to duplicate the text layer before you apply Repoussé, so that you can go back and change it if you need to. But, just be sure to click on the Eye icon to the left of the original text layer to turn it off.)

Continued

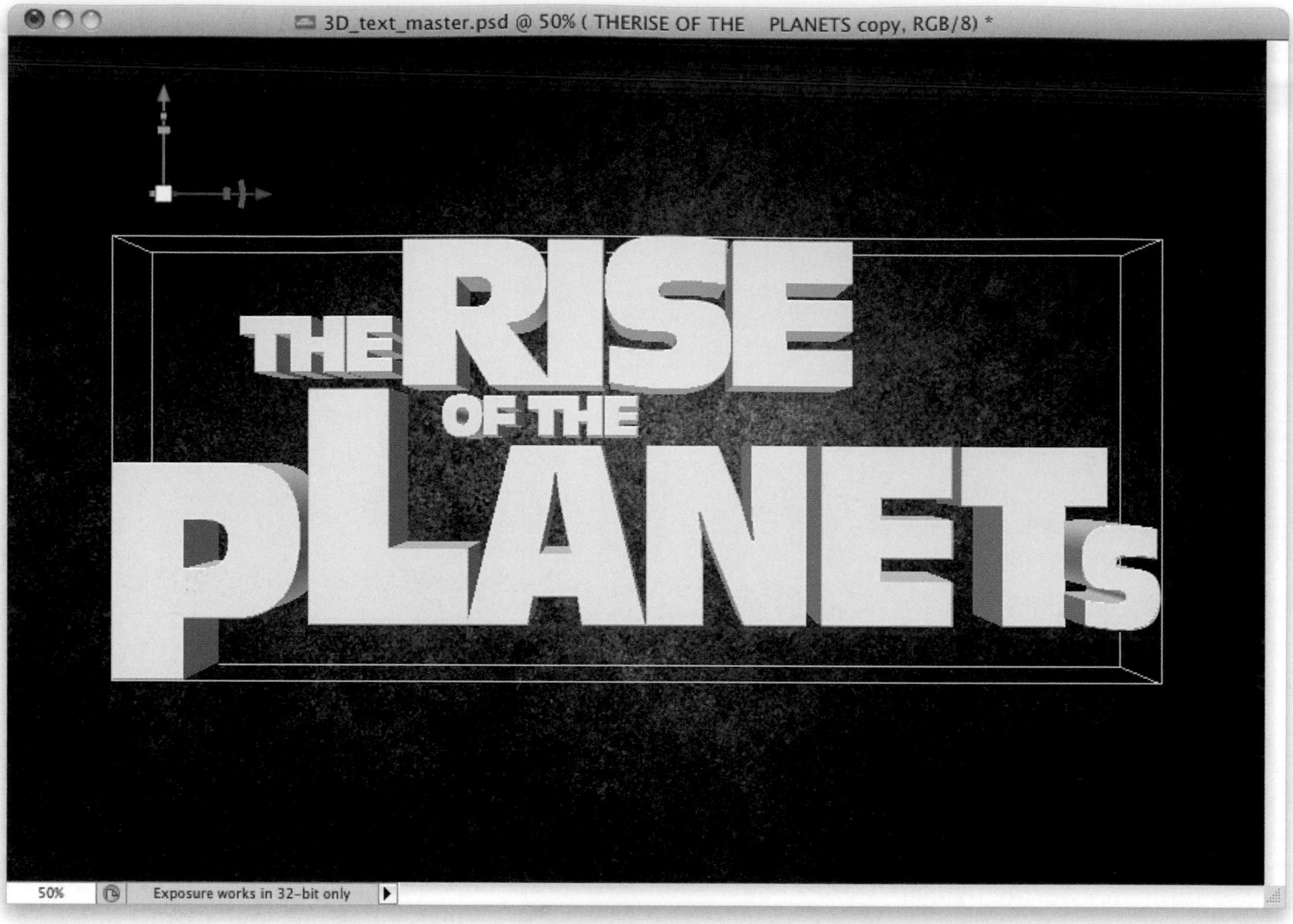

STEP FIVE:

In the Repoussé dialog, go into the Extrude section and set the Depth to 0.3. Then, go over to the Bevel section and set the Height and Width to 0.5. Don't click OK just yet.

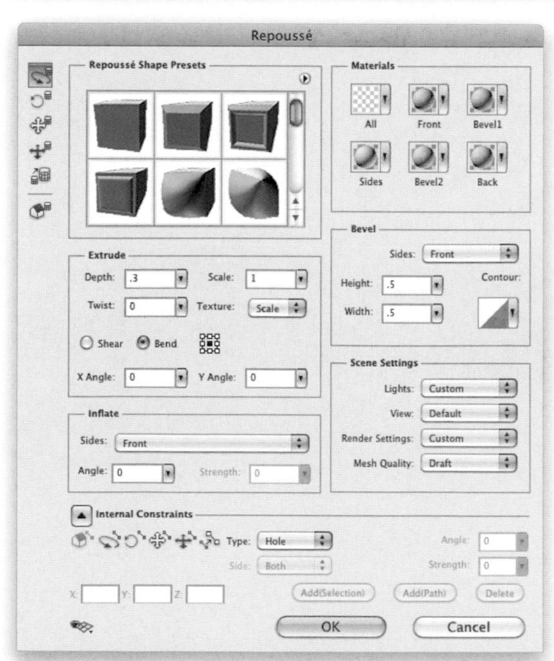

STEP SIX:

Go up into the Materials section, click on the All thumbnail, and then locate the new material we defined a moment ago. Like when defining new brushes, it will be located at the bottom of the Material Picker. Click on it, and Photoshop will cover all the sides of the 3D text object in that material.

Continued

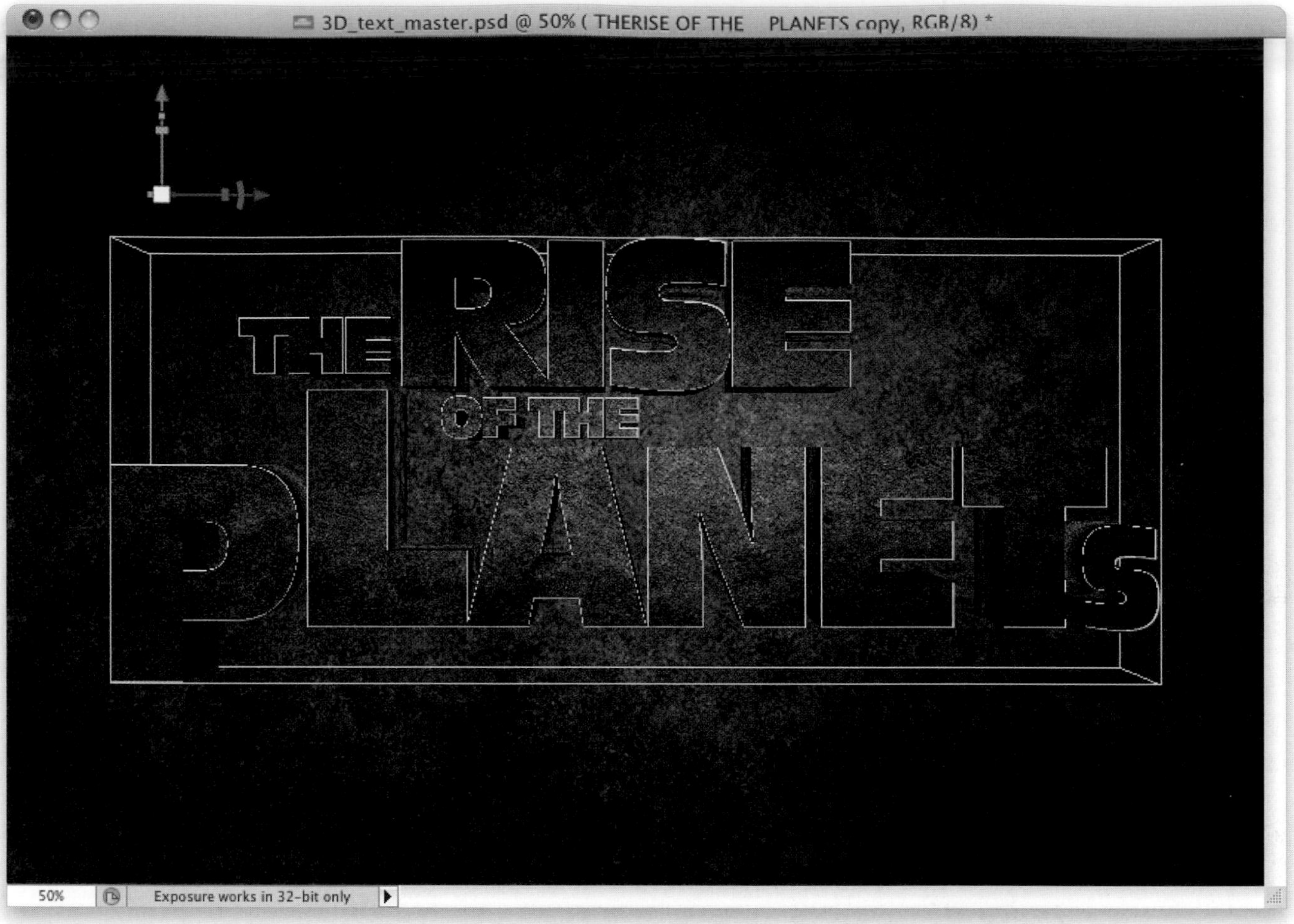

STEP SEVEN:

To help define the letters a little more, let's change the color of the bevel. Notice that, in the Materials section, there are thumbnails for Bevel 1 and Bevel 2. Bevel 1 is the front bevel we have on this object, so click on its thumbnail and, from the default set of materials, choose the Stone Marble texture. This will help define the front edges of the letters. (*Note:* Before clicking OK in the Repoussé dialog, click on the Return to Initial Mesh Position icon [the icon at the bottom of the toolbar on the left], so that you can easily get back to this position by clicking the same icon in the Mesh options of the 3D panel later.) Click OK.

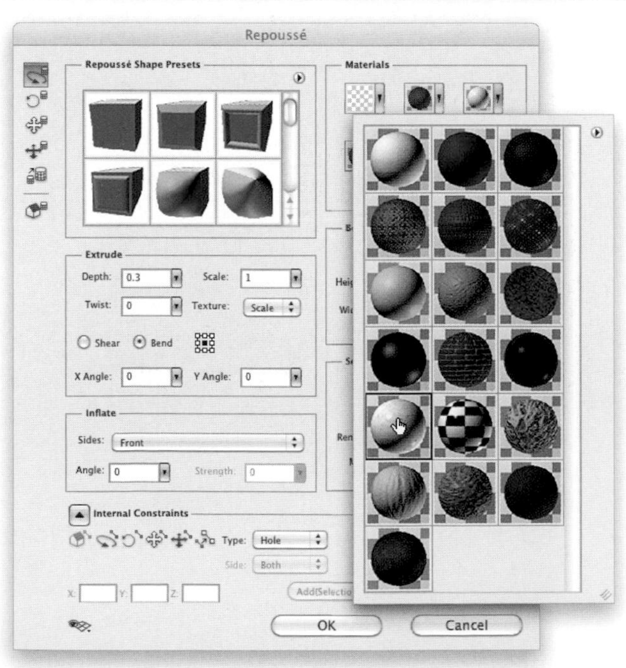

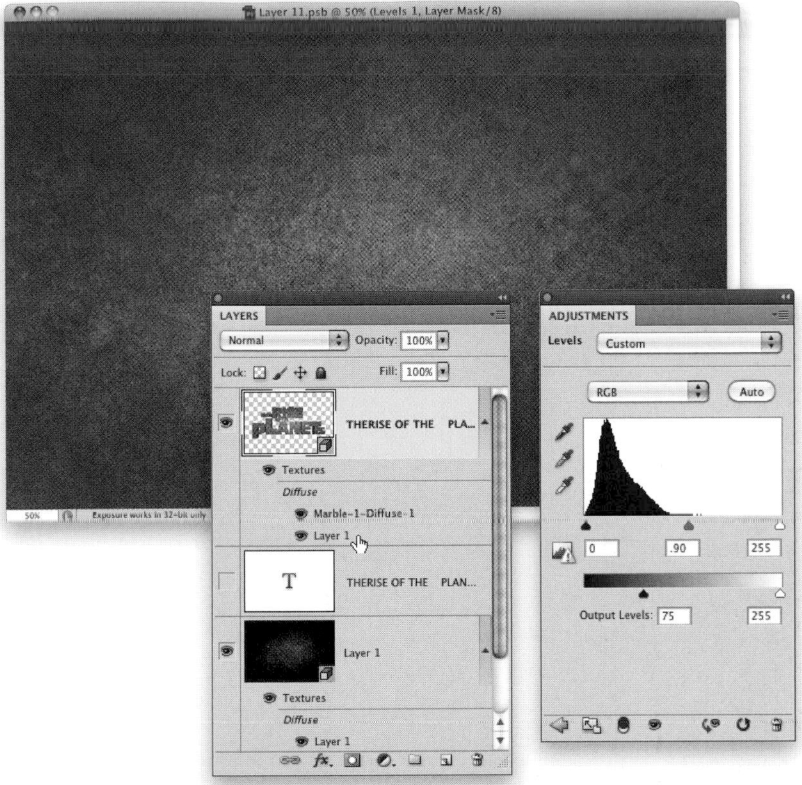

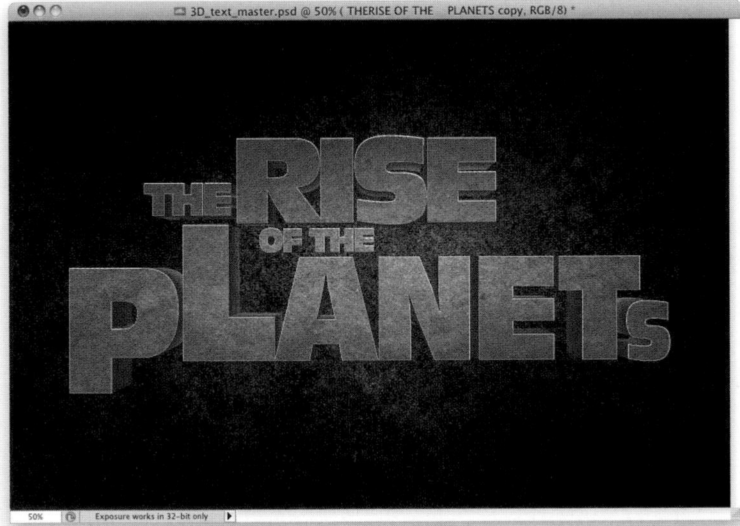

STEP EIGHT:

Now, with the text cover being the same texture as the background image, it tends to blend things a bit more than we'd like. So, we need to lighten up the text. In the Layers panel, double-click on the texture file sublayer (Layer 1) attached to the 3D text layer. This will open the texture file in a separate image window. Click on the Create New Adjustment Layer icon at the bottom of the Layers panel, choose **Levels**, and lighten the texture using the settings shown here. Save the changes and then close the file when you're done. This will update the texture on all the sides of the 3D text object.

Continued

STEP NINE:

In order for the 3D text and the background texture to interact, we need to combine them into a single 3D layer. This means we need to merge them, but not in the usual sense that you merge layers. Merging two 3D layers into one will allow you to modify the overall 3D object as a whole, but will also let you modify each shape individually. You can only merge two 3D layers at a time, though. So, if you selected and then tried to merge three or more layers, the merge feature would be unavailable. In this case, we only have two 3D layers, so Command-click (PC: Ctrl-click) on the 3D background layer (Layer 1), so both it and the 3D text layer are selected, and then go under the 3D menu and choose **Merge 3D Layers**.

STEP 10:

Now, when you merge two 3D layers, the objects have a tendency to shift their position. In this case, the text seems to have disappeared. In actuality, though, it shifted behind the background texture. So, go to the 3D panel and click on the Filter By: Meshes icon (the second icon from the left) at the top to open the Mesh options. Near the top of the panel, you'll see the two 3D objects that are contained in this one 3D layer. Click on the text object, then, in the toolbar along the left side of the panel, click-and-hold on the 3D Mesh Rotate tool to open its pop-up menu (the tools here allow you to modify the individual 3D object within the layer, whereas, the main tools in the toolbar [the top two] will manipulate the entire 3D layer). Since we need to bring the text forward in space, grab the 3D Mesh Slide tool.

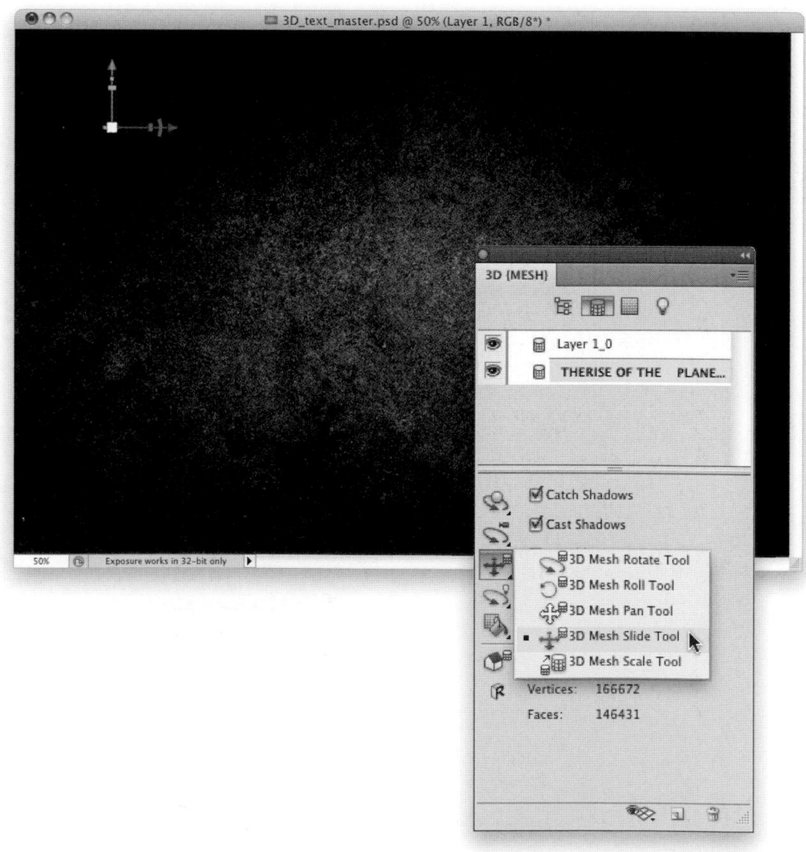

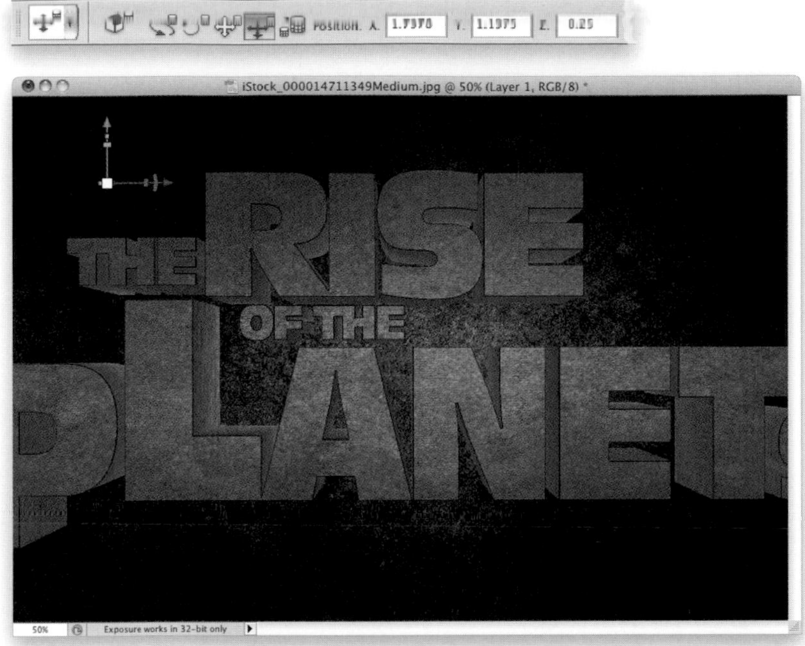

STEP 11:
You could now manually slide the text forward by clicking on it and dragging down. However, this feature is content-sensitive, meaning that it will automatically select an object as you hover over it. With the text being behind the background texture, this will not work. So, in the Options Bar, enter –0.25 in the Z field and press Return (PC: Enter). This will bring the text forward, coming through the texture, but not all the way.

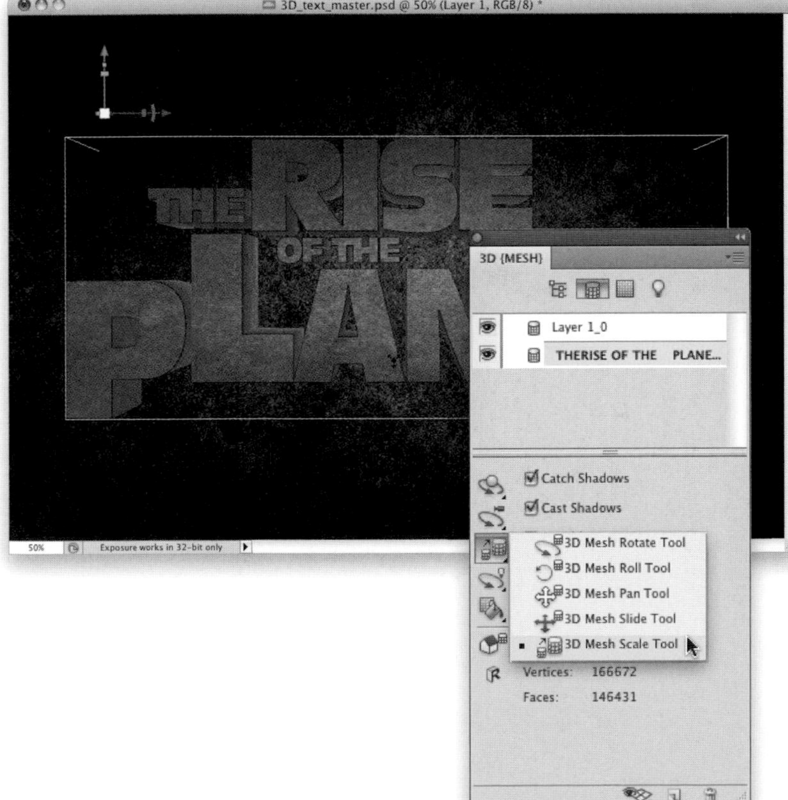

STEP 12:
We'll need to resize the text a bit now, so go back to the 3D Mesh tool pop-up menu and, this time, choose the 3D Mesh Scale tool. Then, just click-and-drag downward to resize the text.

Continued

STEP 13:
With the elements in place, we now need to light the scene. At the top of the 3D panel, click on the Filter By: Lights icon (the first icon on the right) to access the Lights settings. Right now, our scene has no lights at all. You can choose from four different types of lights, though, and I encourage you to play with all of them to get a better sense of what they are and how they work. In this case, double-click on Point Lights near the top, then click on the Create New Light icon at the bottom of the panel and choose **New Point Light**.

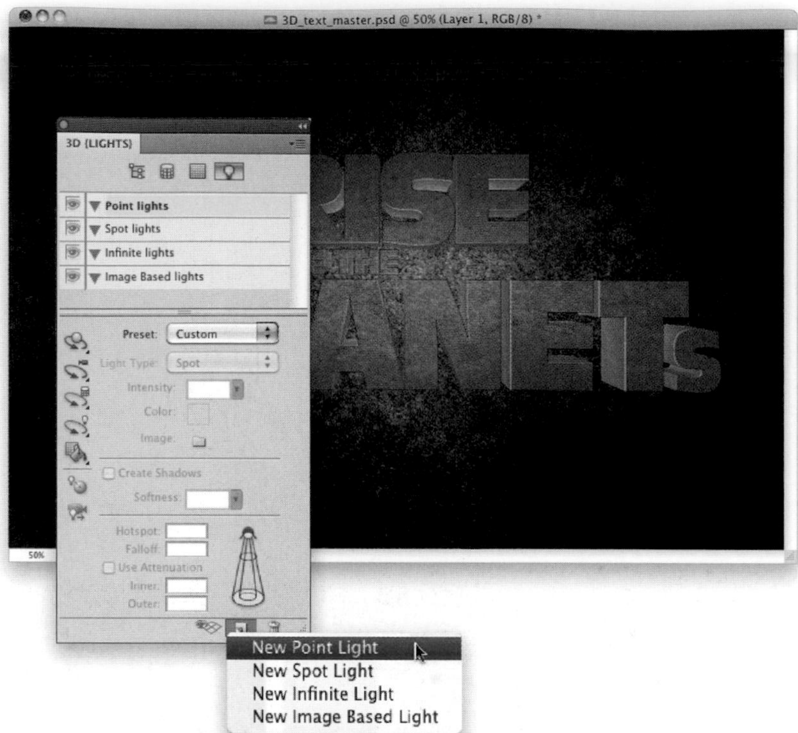

STEP 14:
Next, click on the Toggle Misc 3D Extras icon at the bottom of the panel, and chose **3D Light** to reveal the wire frame for the light.

TIP: Snap the Light to the Camera
When you create a new 3D light, there are times when you can't seem to get the light exactly where you want it, even with the wire frame on. If you use the 3D Camera tools in the 3D panel (the second icon from the top in the toolbar) to position the camera where you want the light to be, then click on the Filter By: Lights icon to view the Lights options, you can choose a light (by clicking on it in the list at the top of the panel), and then click on the Move to Current View icon (at the bottom of the toolbar). This will snap the selected light to the current camera position, and then you can move it with the camera, or choose a 3D Light tool and use it to tweak the light's position.

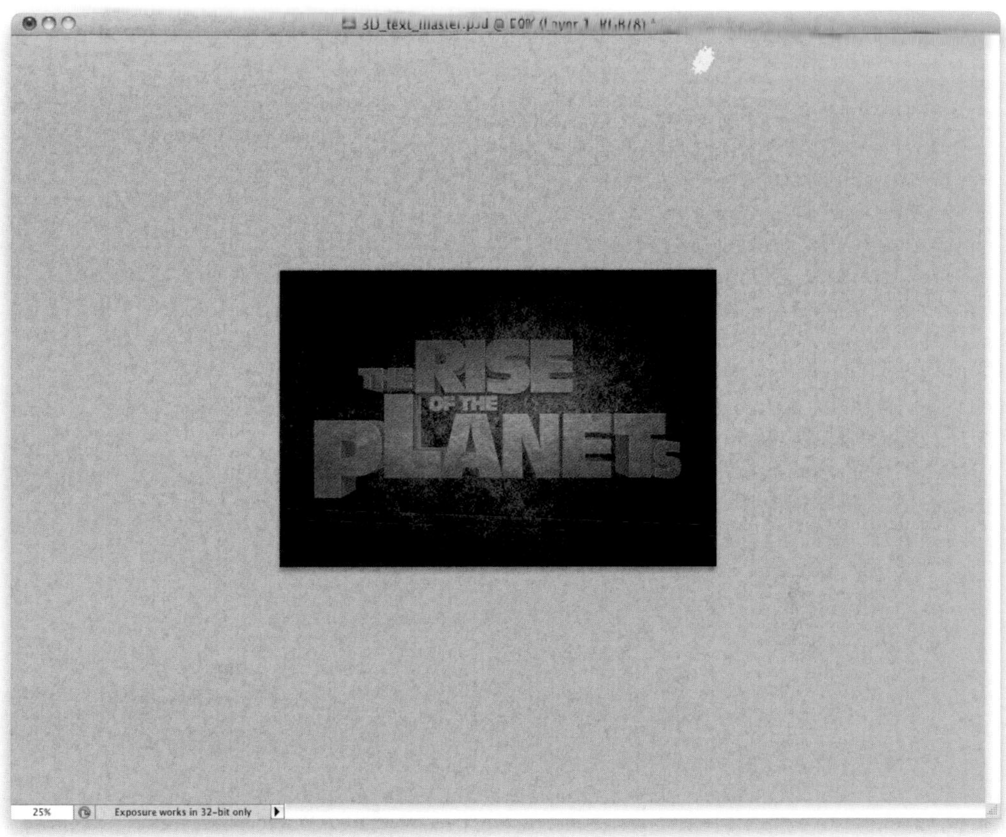

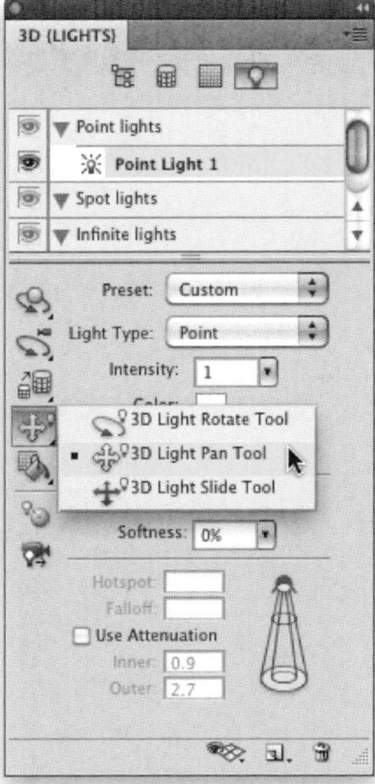

STEP 15:

Click-and-hold on the 3D Light Rotate tool (located just below the 3D Mesh tools) on the left side of the panel to open the pop-up menu. You'll use these tools to reposition the light. Chose the 3D Light Slide tool, and click-and-drag down to slide it forward a bit. Then, grab the 3D Light Pan tool, and reposition the light so that it's almost directly above the text and to the right just a bit. To see the drop shadow and the full effect of the lighting, we'll need to render. So, click on the Filter By: Whole Scene icon (the first icon on the left at the top of the 3D panel), make sure Scene is selected in the list near the top, then from the Quality pop-up menu, choose **Ray Traced Draft**. If you don't want it to render every time you change something, switch it back to Interactive (Painting).

Continued

STEP 16:

Now, with the light in place, click on the Filter By: Materials icon at the top of the 3D panel again, and this time choose the background item (Layer 1) in the list at the top. At the bottom of the panel, click on the Ambient color swatch and change this color to a somewhat darker gray. This will make the spotlight effect more prominent by lowering the apparent ambient light on the subject. (I rendered again here, so you could see the difference.)

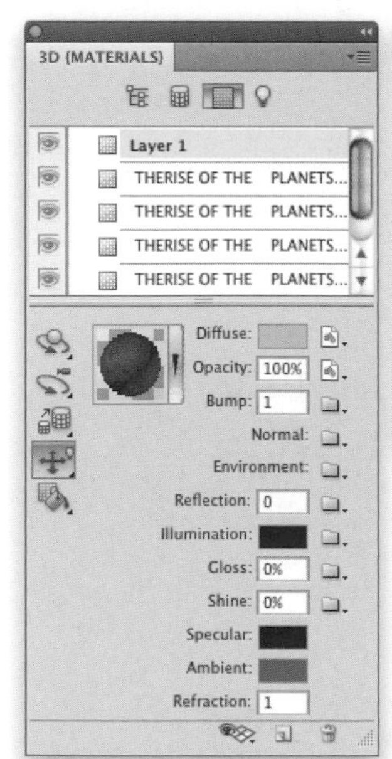

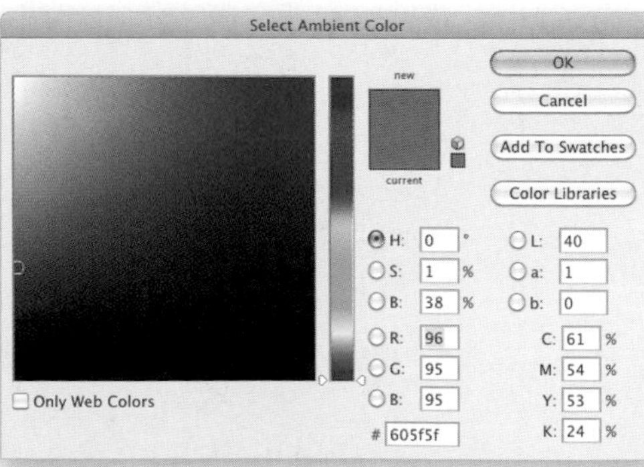

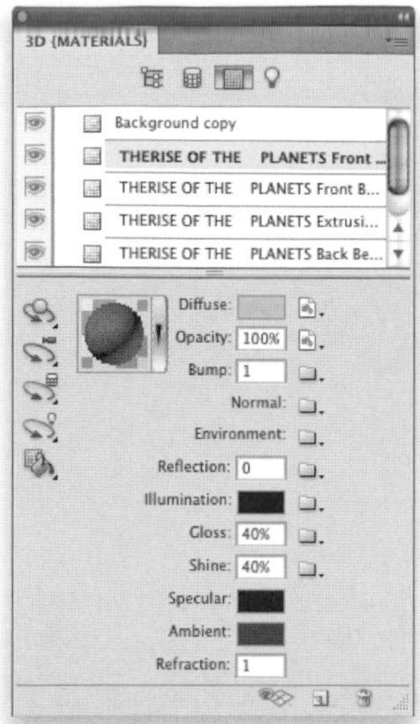

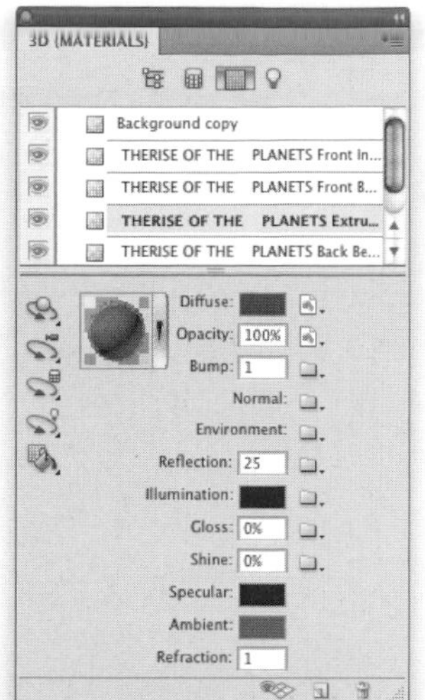

STEP 17:

Next, click on the text object's Front Inflation Material, click on the Ambient color swatch, and again, change it to a darker gray. Also, change the Gloss and Shine to 40%. Then, click on the text object's Extrusion Material and, as we have done before, change the Ambient color to a darker gray, and change the Diffuse color to an even darker gray. Then, increase the Reflection to 25.

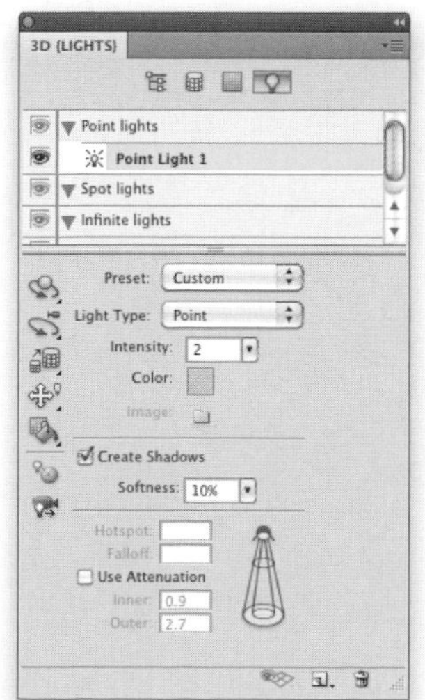

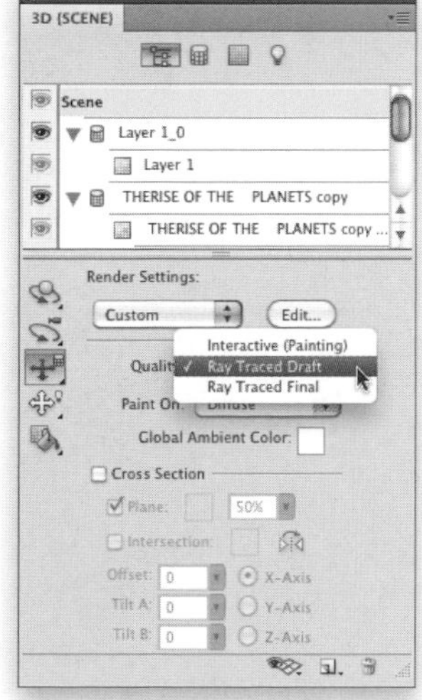

STEP 18:

Now, go back into the Filter By: Lights options and increase the Intensity to 2 (small changes in this setting have a big result, so be careful). Then, set the Softness to 10%. Again, sensitive settings, so start small! Finally, it's time to render again. You can see full results of this last render in the Final Image, where I also added a particle effect by turning the image we used on the decaying building in Chapter 6 into a black-and-white version, dragging it on top of the 3D layer, and changing the layer's blend mode to **Screen** to drop out the black background.

So, there you have it. Just a way of utilizing 3D in Photoshop to give atmosphere to text that was unheard of before. Be sure to experiment with these steps, as there are numerous possibilities. I also provided another example, showing the text from another angle, giving you even more options.

Continued

Final Image

Even though the finished image was viewed straight on, we can still rotate the view for a different look altogether. Note: *If you rotate using the 3D Object tools, then the lights will not move, making the lighting on the object change. To change your view of the object while keeping the lights in place, use the 3D Camera tools to change the angle of view.*

3D Postcard Effects

3D postcards (2D images placed in 3D space that have shadows and reflections from other objects) are a lot more powerful than you might think. With a little experimentation and some outside-the-box thinking, you can use these features to create interesting effects. In this project, we'll take a generic paint splash and use 3D postcards to create an interesting 3D environment. This effect will also work in CS4 Extended, as 3D postcards were first introduced in that version.

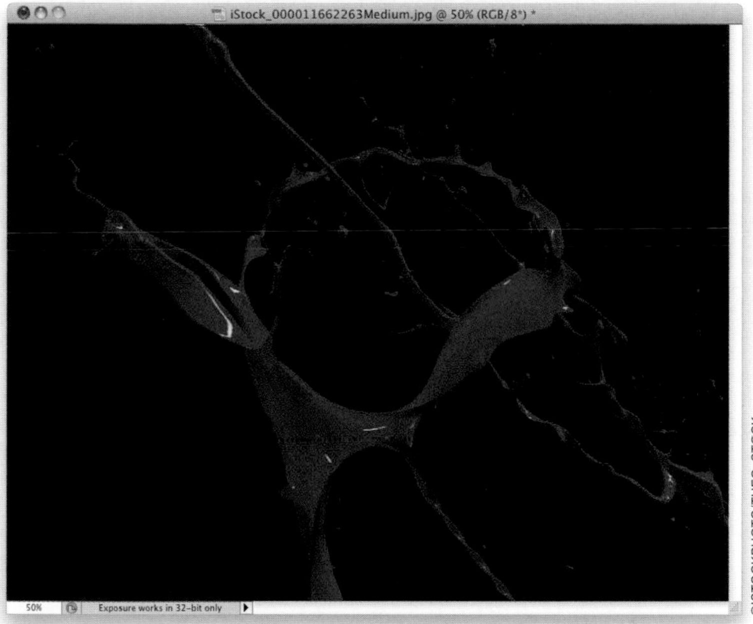

©ISTOCKPHOTO/THEO_STCCK

STEP ONE:

To begin, we need a nice abstract splash image. I went to iStockphoto's website and searched "paint splash," and it returned quite a few images. I think this one has a lot of interesting things happening and can be used in multiple ways. But, first, we'll need to extract it.

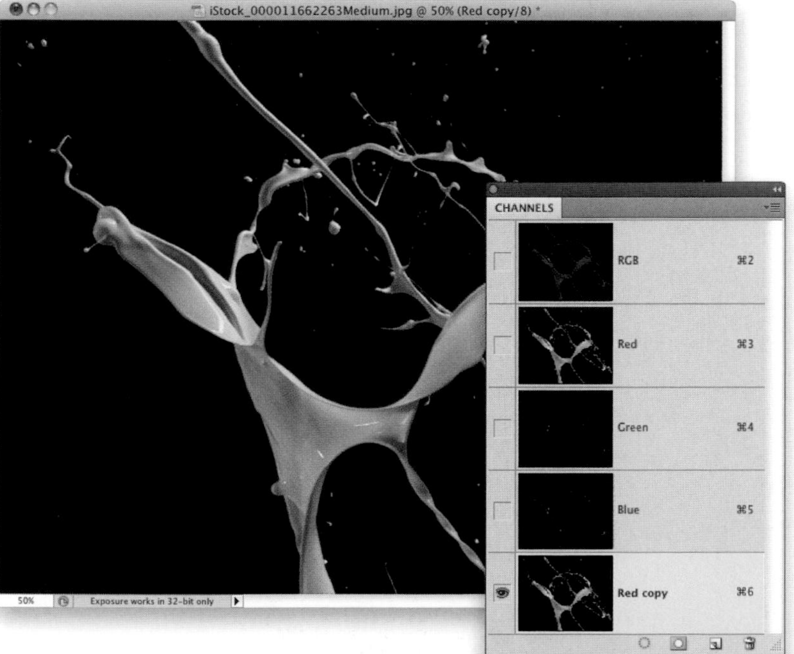

STEP TWO:

Since the splash was shot on a black background, we can use a simple channels trick to select it. Open the Channels panel (Window>**Channels**), click on the Red channel, and drag it onto the Create New Channel icon at the bottom of the panel to make a copy.

Continued

STEP THREE:

With the Red copy active, press **Shift-Delete (PC: Shift-Backspace)**, choose **White** from the Fill dialog's Use pop-up menu, and change the blend Mode to **Overlay**. Click OK. This will force a lot of the gray area to white. However, go ahead and apply this same fill a second time to get any last little gray areas, making the whole splash shape white.

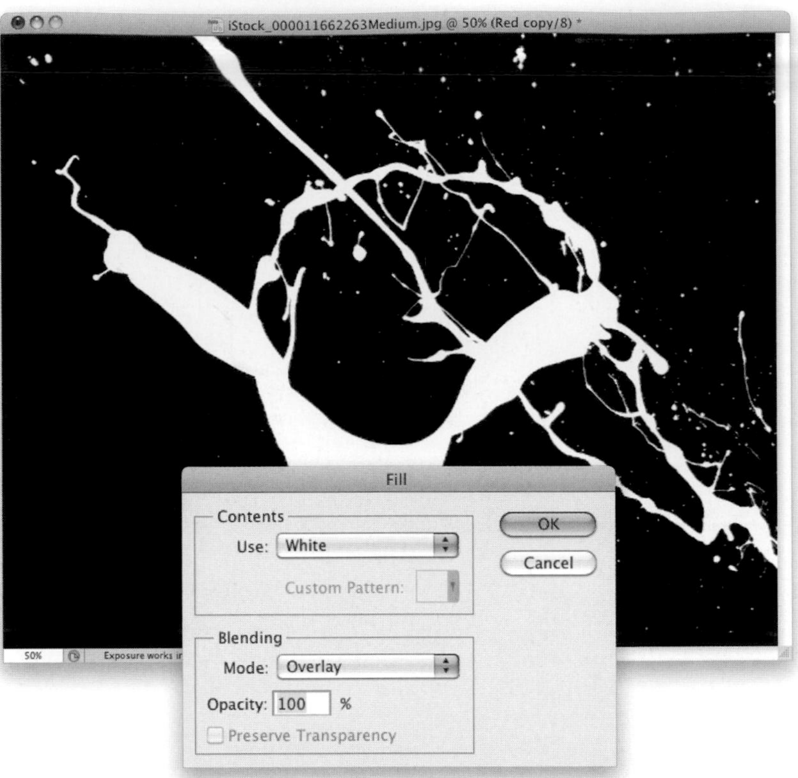

STEP FOUR:

The black area may have lightened a tiny bit, so for good measure press Shift-Delete again, and this time set the Use pop-up menu to **Black** and change the blend Mode to **Soft Light**. Click OK.

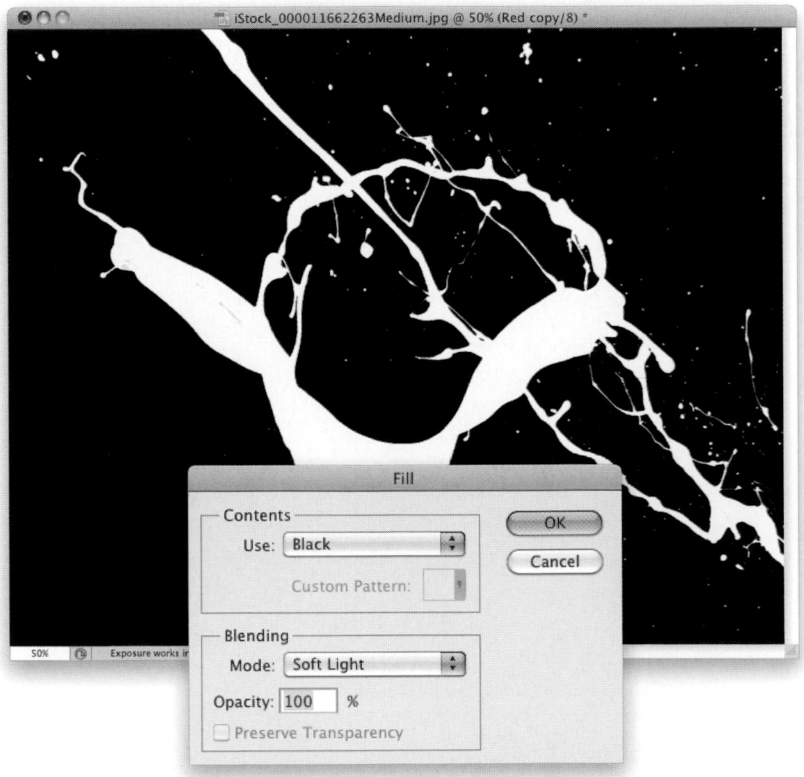

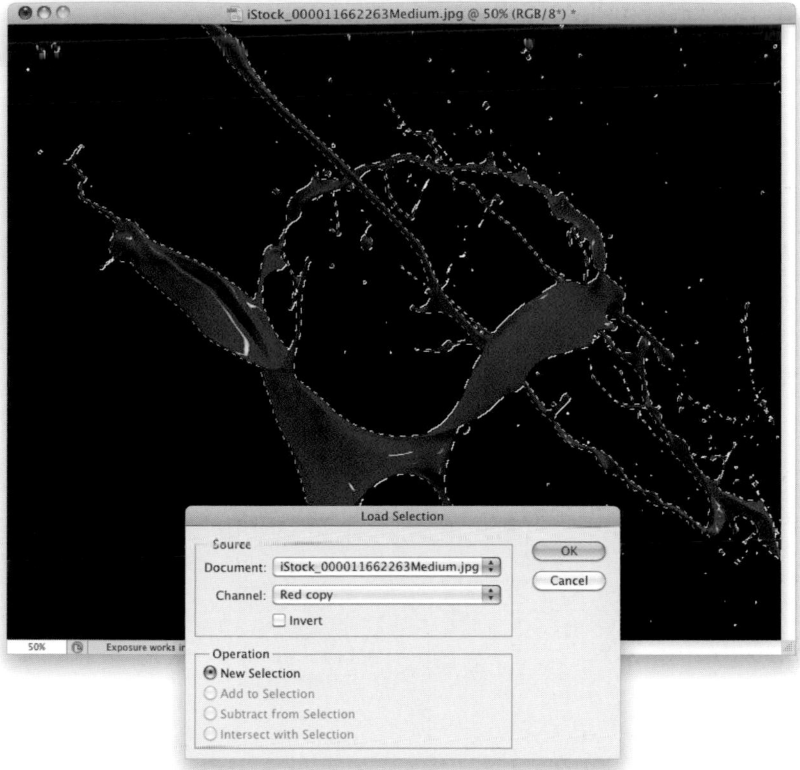

STEP FIVE:

Once the channel is made, click back on the RGB channel. Then, from the Select menu, choose **Load Selection**. Choose **Red copy** from the Channel pop-up menu and click OK.

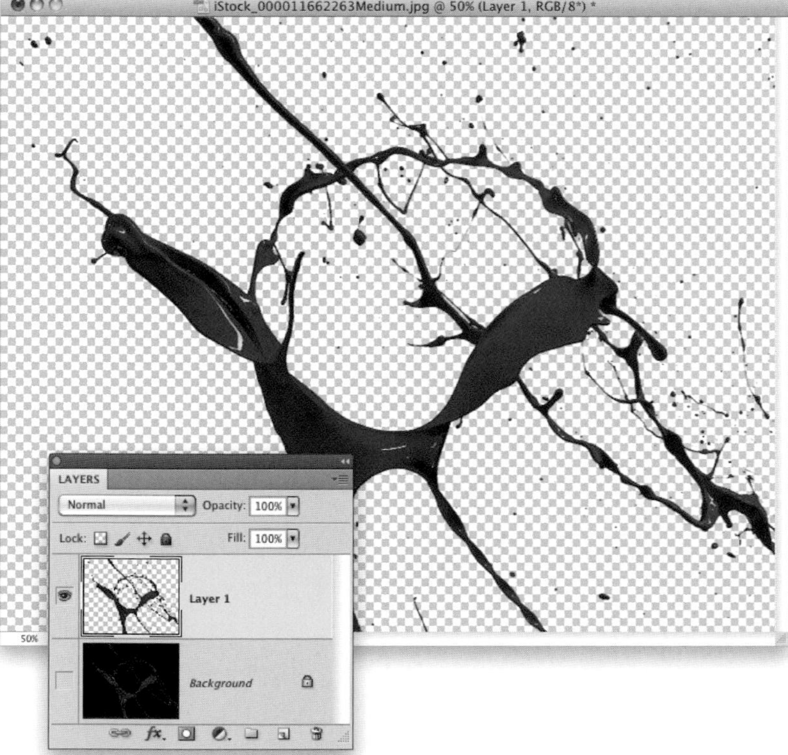

STEP SIX:

Press **Command-J (PC: Ctrl-J)** to copy the selected area to a new layer and now the splash is nicely extracted. Click on the Eye icon to the left of the Background layer to hide it.

Continued

STEP SEVEN:

To polish up the edges, go to the bottom of the Layer menu, under Matting, and choose **Defringe**. Set the Width to 2 pixels and click OK. This will clean up any anti-aliasing noise picked up from the background.

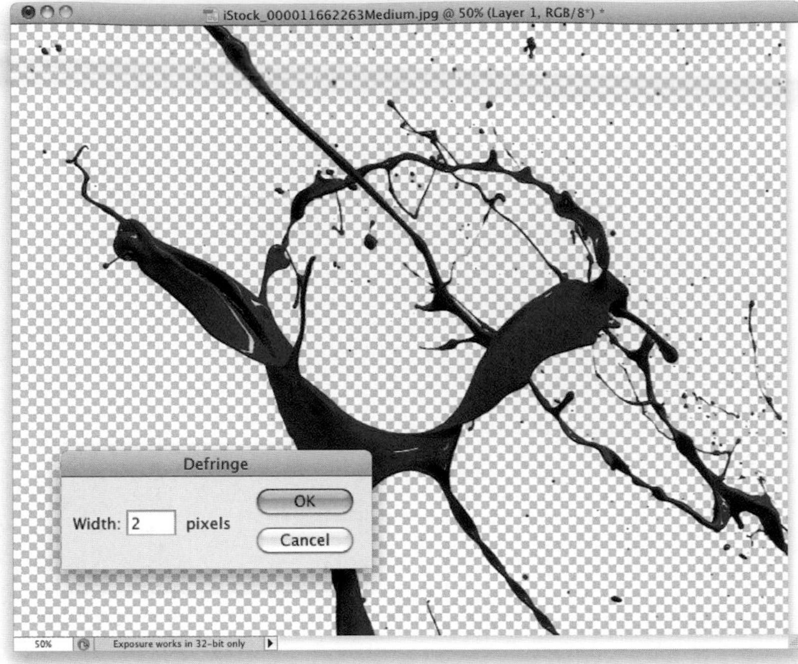

STEP EIGHT:

Now, the splash is a nice bright red, but that's not what we need. So, let's change the color by clicking on the Create New Adjustment Layer icon at the bottom of the Layers panel and choosing **Hue/Saturation**. In the Adjustments panel, turn on the Colorize checkbox, and set the Hue to 25, the Saturation to 60, and the Lightness to 20. This will make the paint splash orange.

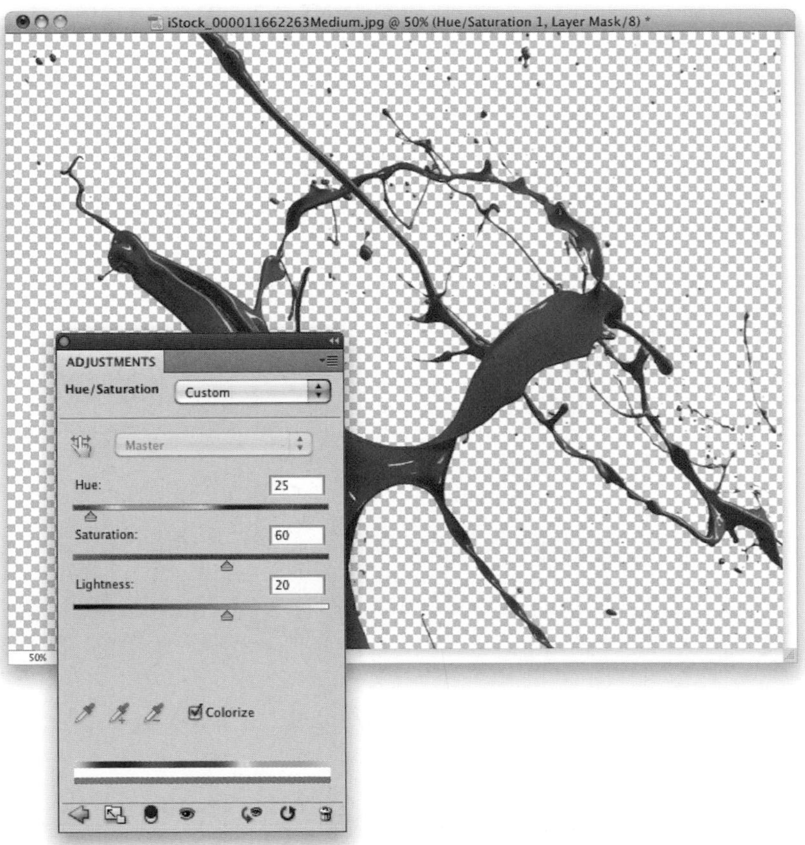

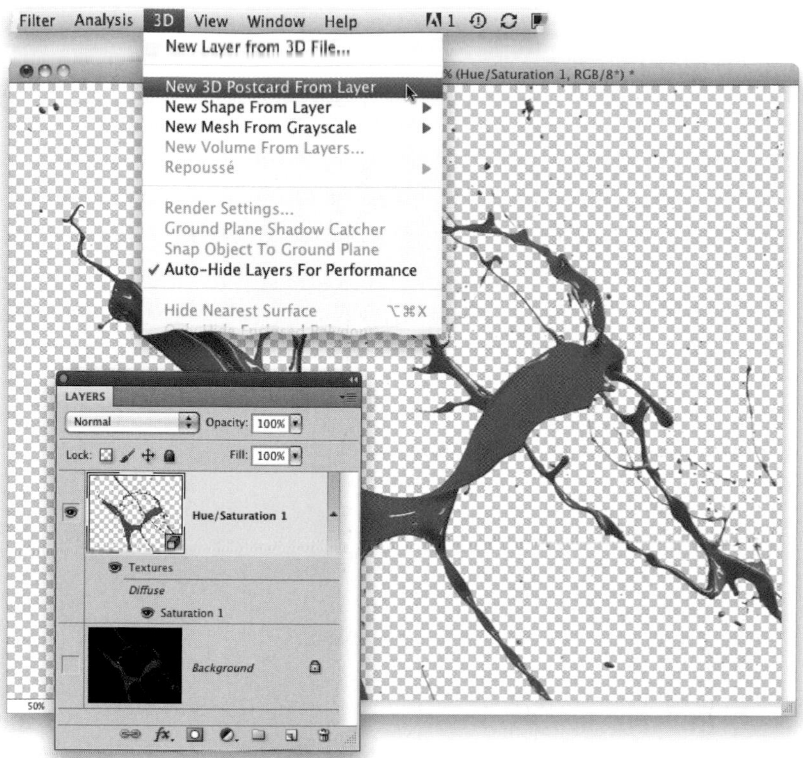

STEP NINE:

Command-click (PC: Ctrl-click) on the splash layer to select both it and the adjustment layer, then go under the 3D menu and choose **New 3D Postcard From Layer**. This will nest both layers inside a 3D layer, but will not flatten the image, making it possible to modify the color if needed later. Now, the postcard puts the image into a 3D space, but it's still a flat 2D image, hence the name "postcard." Though, with this effect, it will almost look 3D.

©ISTOCKPHOTO/BILL NOLL

STEP 10:

Open the background image, which we'll add the paint splash to. You can use the same method we used to change the color of the paint splash to change the background color, if you want. I changed it to blue using the settings you see here, and then I chose **Flatten Image** from the Layers panel's flyout menu.

Continued

STEP 11:

Now, using the Move tool **(V)**, drag-and-drop the 3D paint splash layer onto the background image. Remember to press-and-hold the Shift key as you drag, so it aligns to the center.

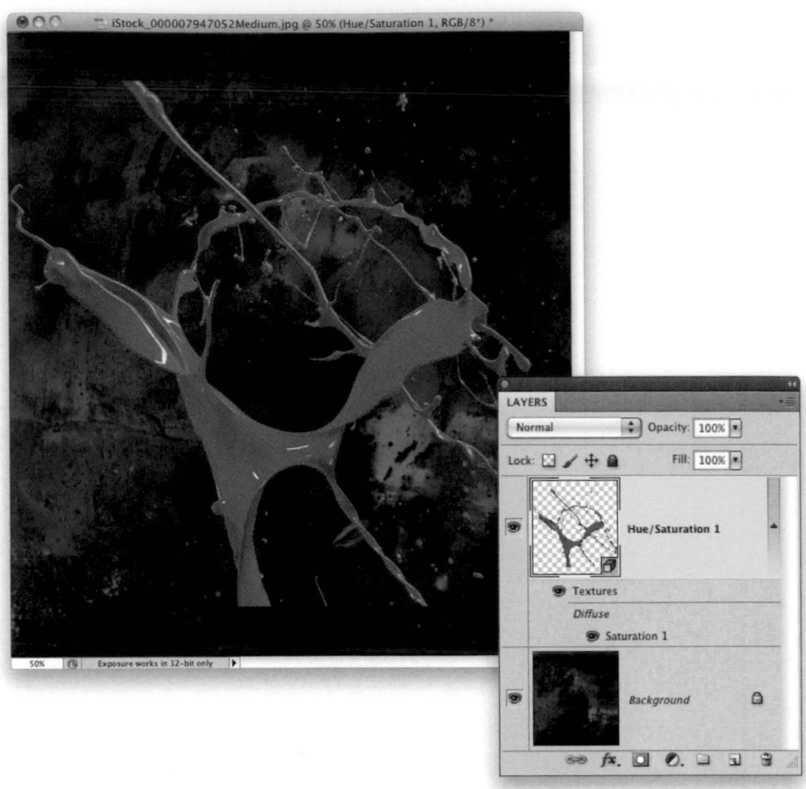

STEP 12:

Get the Horizontal Type tool **(T)** from the Toolbox and click on the canvas to set a text layer. You can use whatever type you like, but here I used Eurostile Bold Extended for the letters "GFX," then filled the text with 50% gray (I also turned off the splash layer while setting the text). (*Note:* The Shift-Delete trick will not work on a text layer for 50% gray. You'll need to select the text, then go to the Swatches panel [Window>**Swatches**] and choose the 50% gray swatch.)

STEP 13:

Once the text is set, go ahead and convert it into a 3D postcard, as well. Then, Command-click on the paint splash layer to select both 3D postcard layers and merge them into a single 3D layer by choosing **Merge 3D Layers** from the 3D menu.

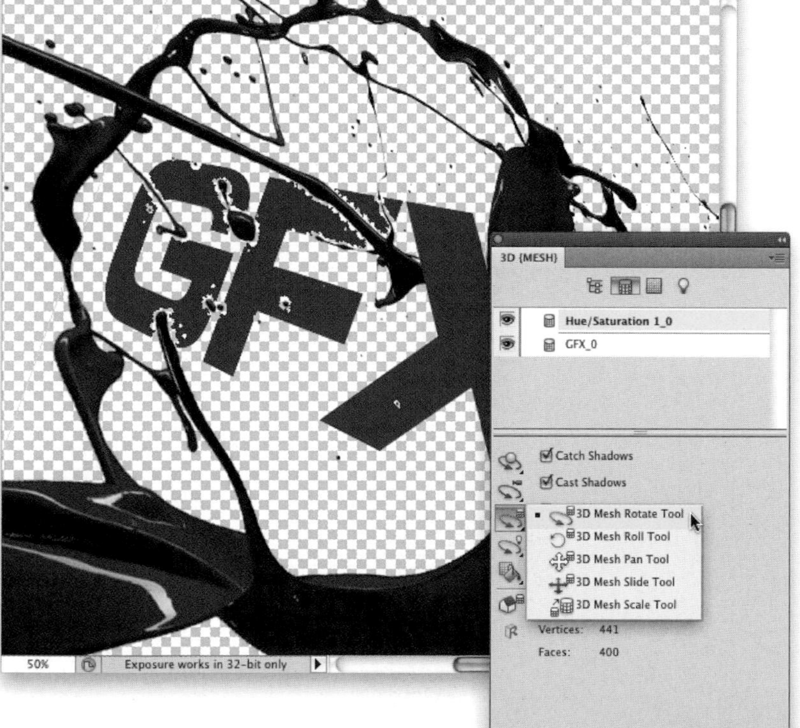

STEP 14:

Open the 3D panel (Window>**3D**) and click on the Filter By: Meshes icon (the second icon from the left at the top) to open the Mesh options. You can see the splash and text objects listed at the top of the panel. Simply, click on one and then click-and-hold on the 3D Mesh Rotate tool in the toolbar on the left side of the panel. The tools nested in this pop-up menu will allow you to modify each object separately in the same 3D layer. Use the 3D Mesh Rotate tool to rotate each postcard in the 3D space, and use the 3D Mesh Slide tool to bring the paint splash forward and hide its cut-off edges. The objects are content-sensitive, so the object will be selected when you hover over it, then click on it.

Continued

STEP 15:

Now for the lights. Click on the Filter By: Lights icon (the first one on the right) at the top of the 3D panel to access the Lights options. Then, double-click on Spot Lights (in the list near the top of the panel), go to the bottom of the panel, click on the Create New Light icon, and choose **New Spot Light**. Now, just working with the light is tough enough, so to make things easier, click on the Toggle Misc 3D Extras icon at the bottom of the panel and choose **3D Light**. This will show the cone-shaped wire frame of the light, making it easier to reposition.

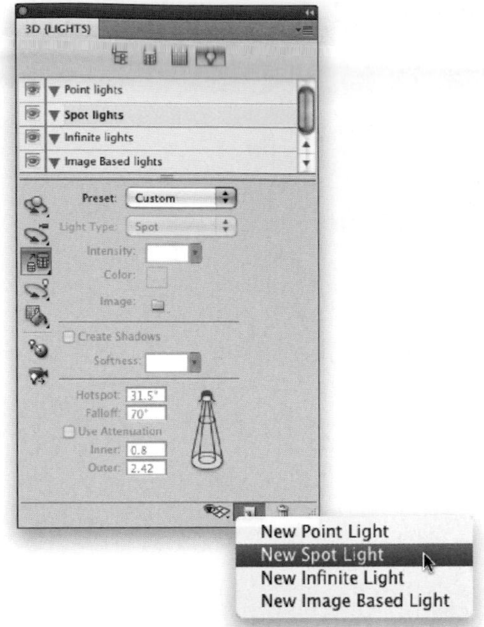

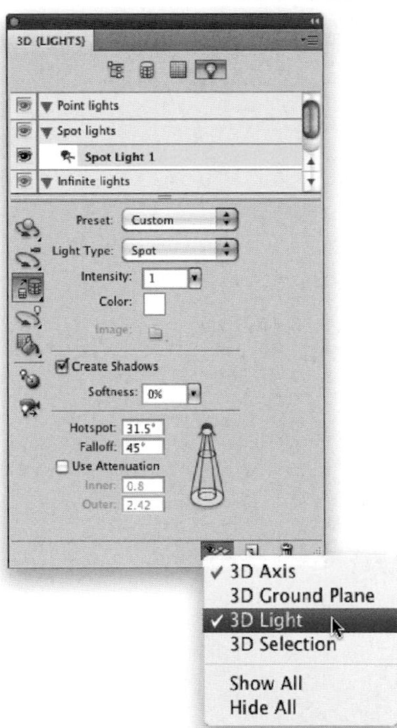

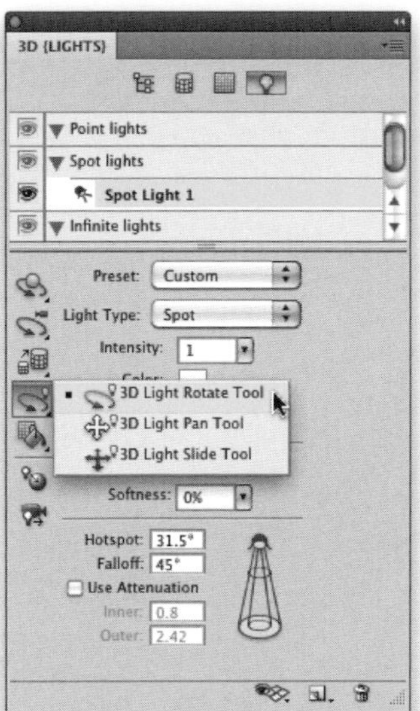

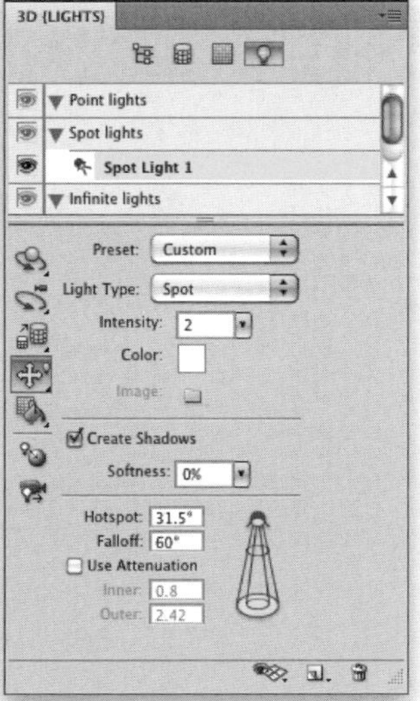

STEP 16:

Click on the 3D Light Rotate tool in the toolbar on the left to rotate the light, the 3D Light Slide tool to bring it forward, and the 3D Light Pan tool to reposition it on the upper-right corner of the image, pointing directly at the shape. Once the light is in place, in the middle of the 3D panel, increase the light's Intensity to 2. Also, go down to the Falloff field and increase it to 60°. This will widen the scope of the light just a bit. (*Note:* Don't forget, as I mentioned in the first project, if you're having trouble positioning the light, you can snap it to the camera.)

Continued

STEP 17:

Next, click on the Filter By: Materials icon (the third icon from the left) at the top of the 3D panel to access the Materials options. With the paint splash selected in the list near the top, go down and set the Reflection to 10, and the Gloss and Shine to 10%. Then, click on the Ambient color swatch and choose a neutral gray color. (*Note:* Just like in the last project, you won't see how all these changes are reflected until you render.)

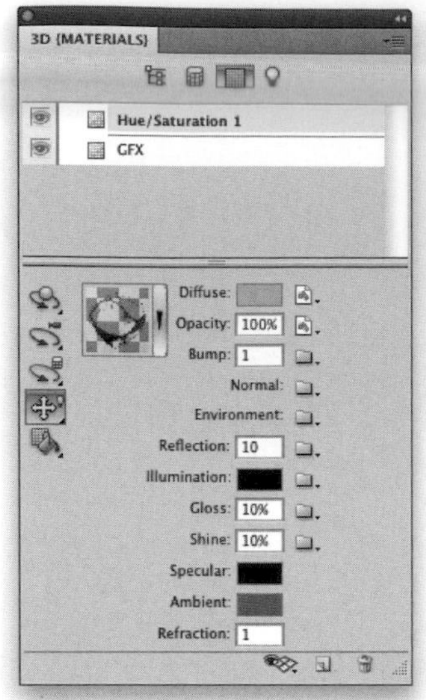

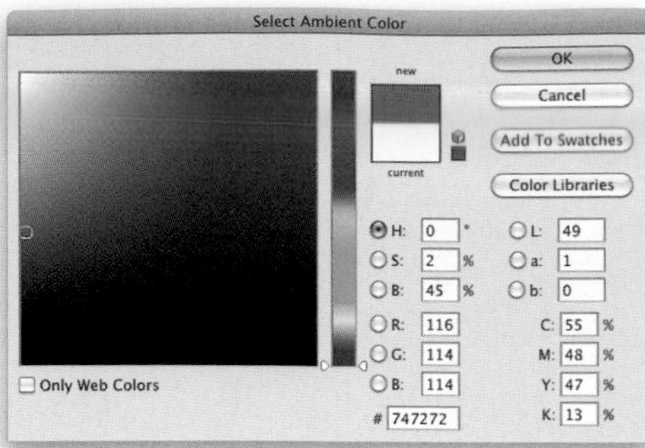

STEP 18:

Now, select the text object in the list near the top of the panel, set the Reflection to 50, and change the Ambient color to a neutral gray. By making the ambient darker, it makes the overall scene more dramatic.

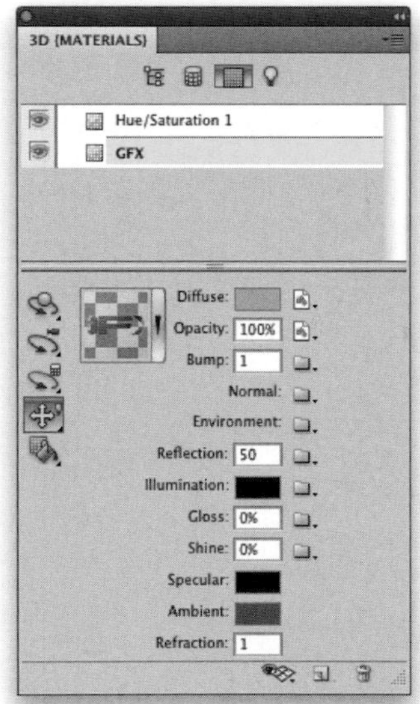

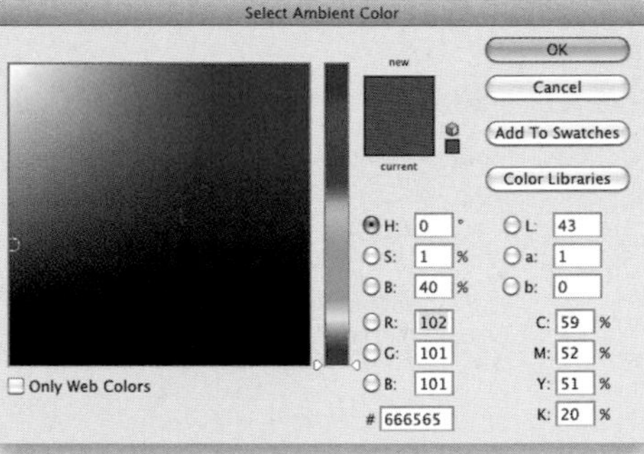

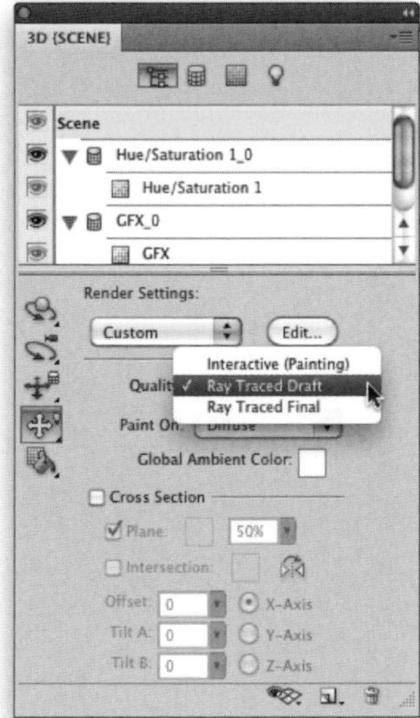

STEP 19:

At this point, it's time to do a quick render to see what we have so far. Click on the Filter By: Whole Scene icon (the first icon on the left) at the top of the panel for the Scene options. Make sure Scene is selected from the list at the top of the panel, then from the Quality pop-up menu, choose **Ray Traced Draft**. This will give you a quick render of the reflections and shadows, and will let you see if you need to make any changes to the positioning or angle of the 3D shapes. Use the tools we talked about earlier to make changes and then re-render. If you leave the Quality menu set to Ray Traced Draft, Photoshop will try to render after each change you make.

You can see in the alternate version how far some simple graphics in 3D can go. Just by changing up the colors and changing the angles a bit, you can get a completely different look altogether.

Continued

Final Image

For this alternate version, I merely went into the texture files and changed the color of the objects, then used the 3D Object Mesh tools in the 3D panel to change the angle of each 3D postcard. This just involves moving things around until you see something that grabs you. Have fun!

3D Logo Effects

We finally live in a world where you can create a fully realized 3D logo, complete with surface and light effects, wholly in Photoshop, without the aid of another 3D application. In this final project, we'll build a 3D logo from start to finish. Download the files relevant to this project and follow along to see just how powerful 3D in Photoshop is now.

STEP ONE:

I've discovered that when building a logo in Photoshop, it's best to use vector shapes—created in Photoshop, Adobe Illustrator, or another program—as they will give you the cleanest edges. Here, we have a logo I originally created in Illustrator, which you can download to follow along with (it shows up just like you see in the Paths panel here, as individual paths in the Start file). Notice in the Paths panel (Window>**Paths**) that I have the paths separated according to what part of the logo they are. Each one will be a 3D object of a different color.

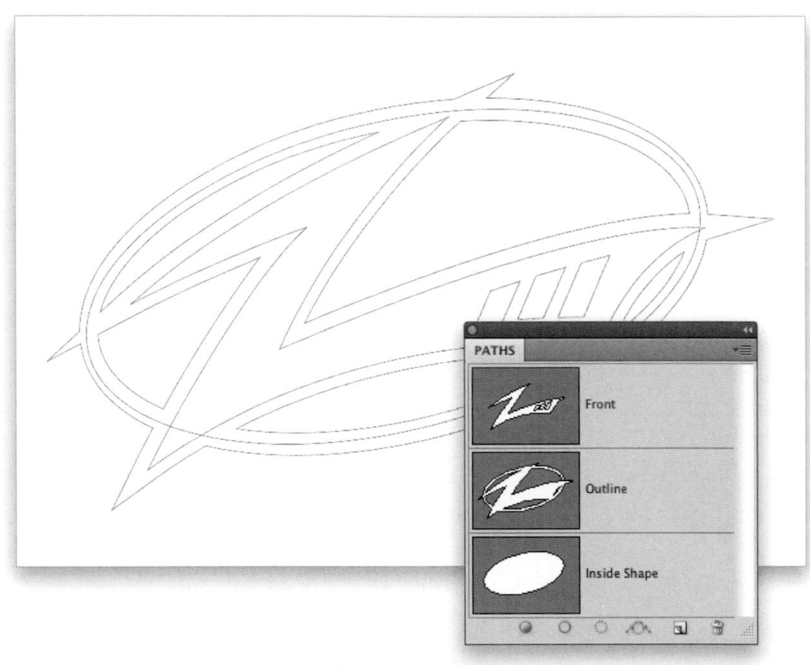

STEP TWO:

Next, you will notice in the Layers panel that I have three layers, each filled with a different color and named to match the names of each path layer. I also have a background gradient applied to the Background layer.

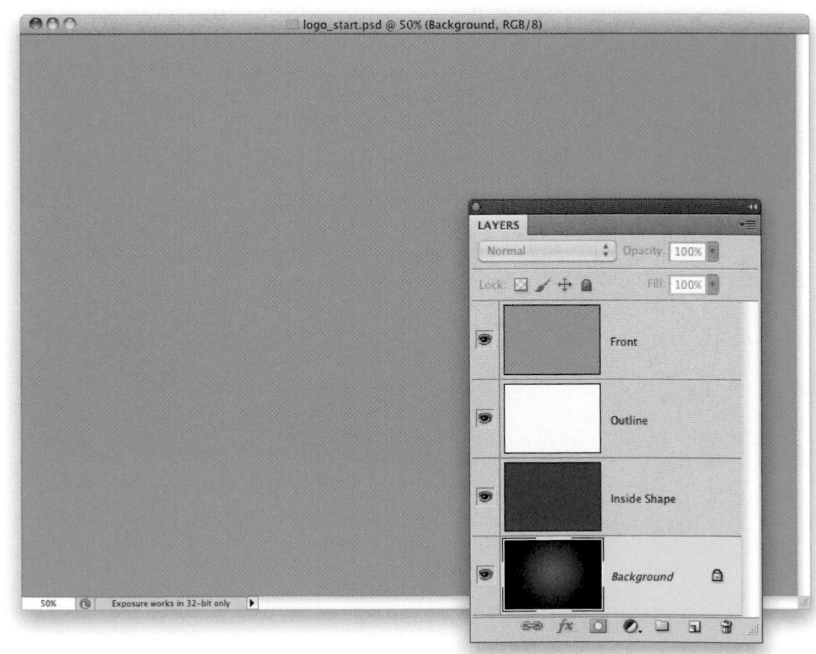

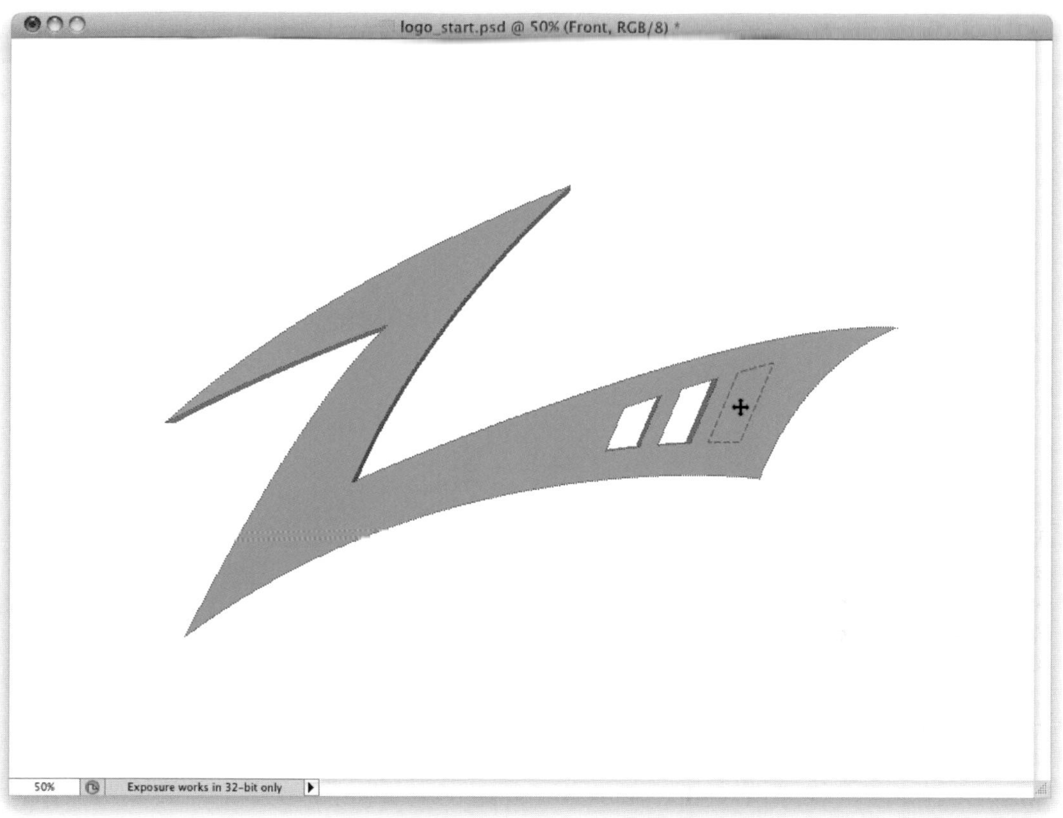

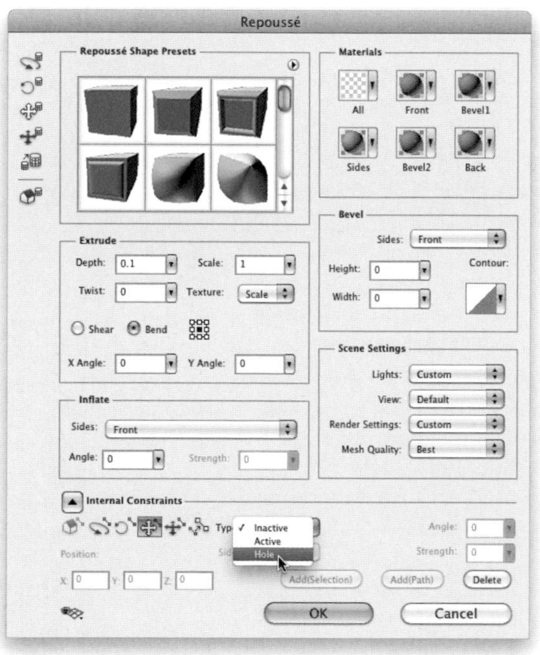

STEP THREE:

In the Layers panel, click on the Front layer and, in the Paths panel, click on the Front path to select it. Then, go under the 3D menu, under Repoussé, and choose **Selected Path**. When the Repoussé dialog opens, go to the Extrude section and set the Depth to 0.1. Next, go to the Scene Settings section, and change the Mesh Quality to **Best**. Go down to the Internal Constraints section and from the Type menu, choose **Hole**. This will knock out one of the three holes in the bottom right of the Z. Select the Pan the 3D Constraint tool (the fourth tool from the left at the top of the Internal Constraint section), hover it over where the next hole should be and, when the outline appears, click on it to select it. Then, change the Type menu to Hole again. Repeat this for the last hole, then click OK.

Continued

STEP FOUR:

Now, when the 3D object was created, it applied the green color fill to the front face, but not the extruded sides. So, go to the Layers panel and double-click on the Front Extrusion Material sublayer to open that texture file. You're going to fill the canvas with the same green fill as the front of the Z, so click on your Foreground color swatch, then click the Eyedropper on the green in the Z, and press **Option-Delete (PC: Alt-Backspace)**. Close the document and save the changes, and the 3D object will be updated automatically.

STEP FIVE:

Let's continue the process with the next element, which is the one labeled "Outline." Click on the Eye icon to the left of the Front layer to turn it off, so we only see the Outline layer and path. Click on the Outline layer in the Layers panel and the Outline path in the Paths panel, then go under the 3D menu, under Repoussé, and choose Selected Path again.

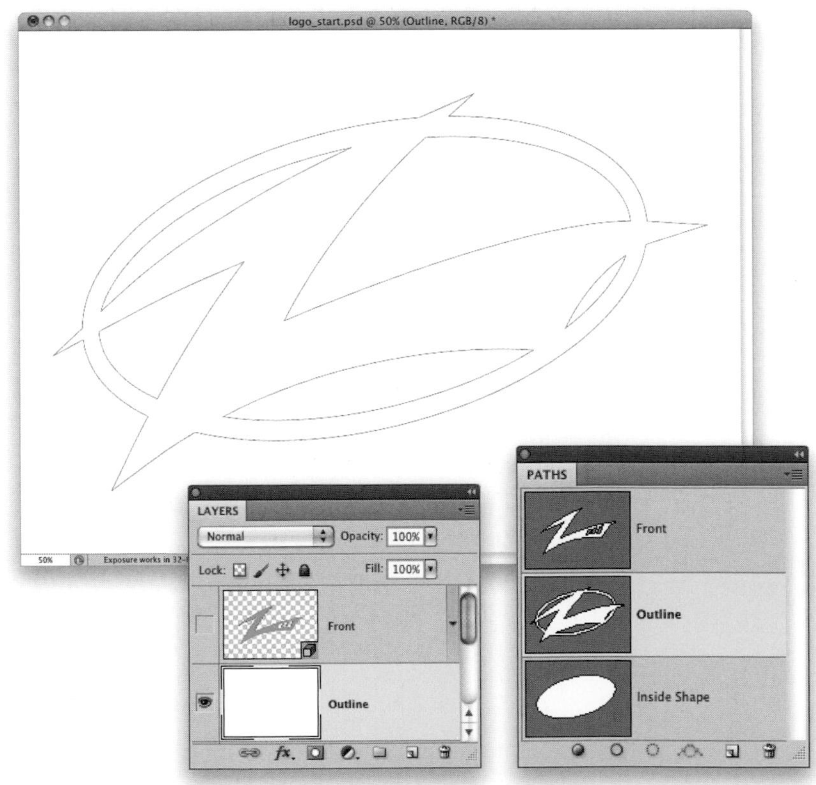

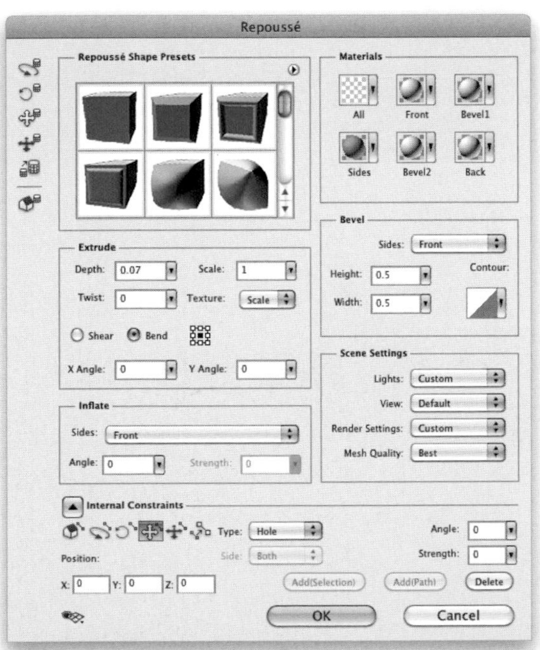

STEP SIX:

This time, in the Extrude section, set the Depth to 0.07. Then, go to the Bevel section and set the Height and Width to 0.5, and again change the Mesh Quality setting to Best in the Scene Settings section. Just like we did before, go to the Internal Constraint section and change the Type pop-up menu to Hole. Then, click on each of the other four areas that need to be knocked out, and change the pop-up menu to Hole. Click OK. Now, here the extrusion material has a default gray fill, which will be fine for the reflected effects we will add shortly. So, no need to go in and change it.

Continued

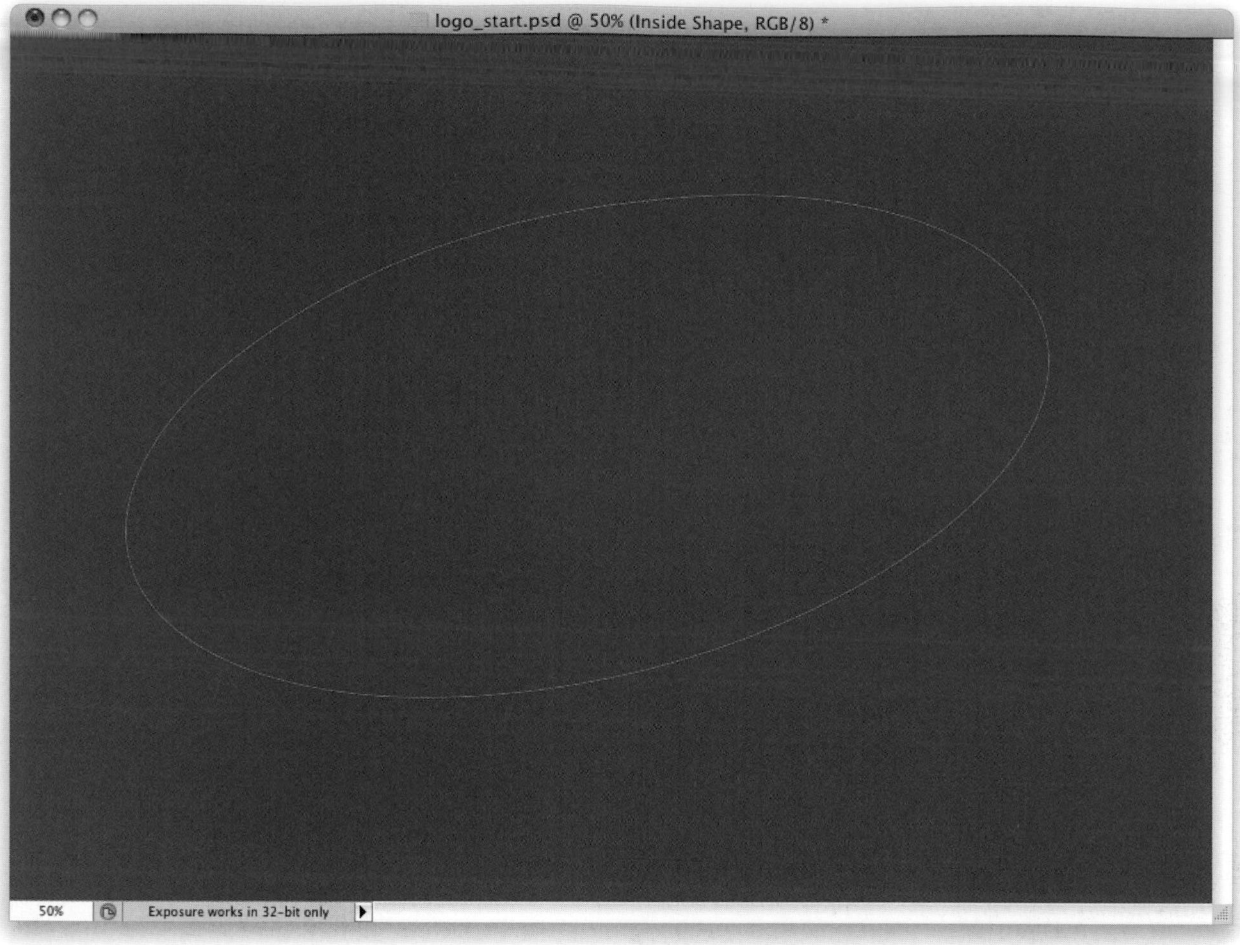

STEP SEVEN:

Now, repeat the process one last time for the final shape labeled "Inside Shape." Hide the Outline layer, so we only see the Inside Shape layer and path. This will be in the inner filling of the logo. Click on its layer and path and go into Repoussé.

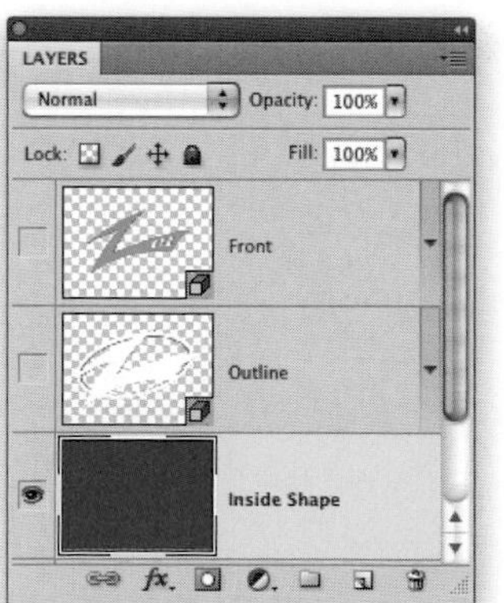

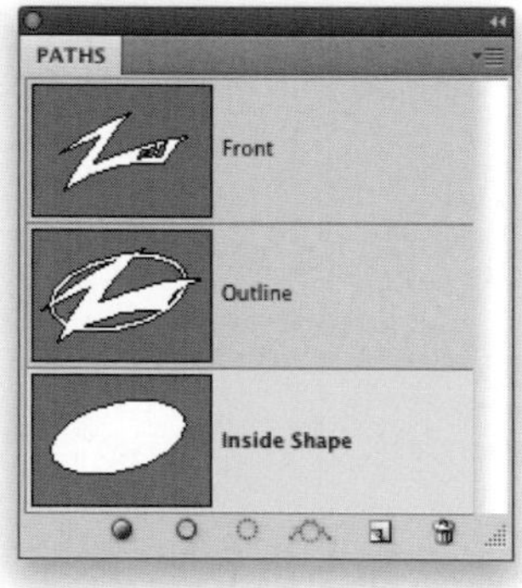

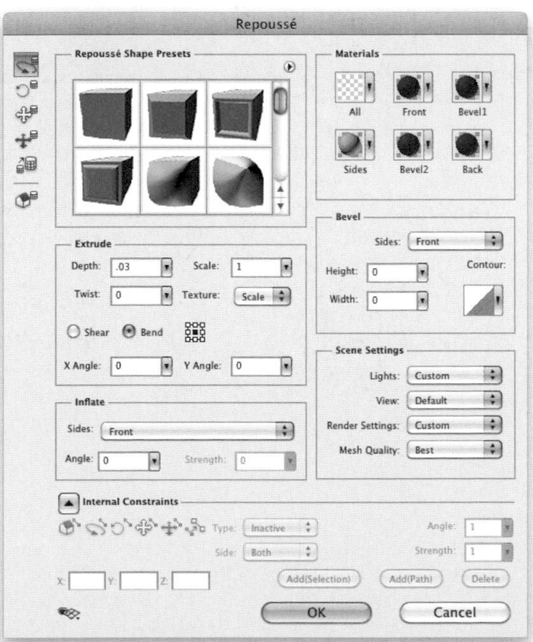

STEP EIGHT:

This object doesn't need a lot of thickness, so in the Repoussé dialog, change the Extrude Depth to 0.03. Then change the Mesh Quality to Best and click OK. Turn the top two layers back on by clicking where their Eye icons used to be.

Continued

STEP NINE:

Now, at this point, you should have three separate 3D layers, each one containing a different part of the logo. We need to merge them into one 3D layer so that these objects can interact with reflections, shadows, and light effects. First, go ahead and save the document, just to be safe (you should save regularly since 3D can take so long to create). Then, remember that you can only merge two 3D layers at a time, so Command-click (PC: Ctrl-click) on the top two to select them both. Then, go to the 3D menu and choose **Merge 3D Layers**.

Also, remember that objects will shift when merged. In this case, the Front shape is inside the Outline shape. To fix this, go to the Window menu and choose **3D** to open the 3D panel. Click on the Filter By: Meshes icon (the second icon from the left at the top) to see the Mesh settings. Make sure Front is selected in the list near the top, and then select the 3D Mesh Slide tool in the toolbar on the left side of the panel. In the Options Bar, you'll see the X, Y, and Z Positions. Enter –25 in the Y-axis field and then press Return (PC: Enter) to bring the green Front shape forward a little.

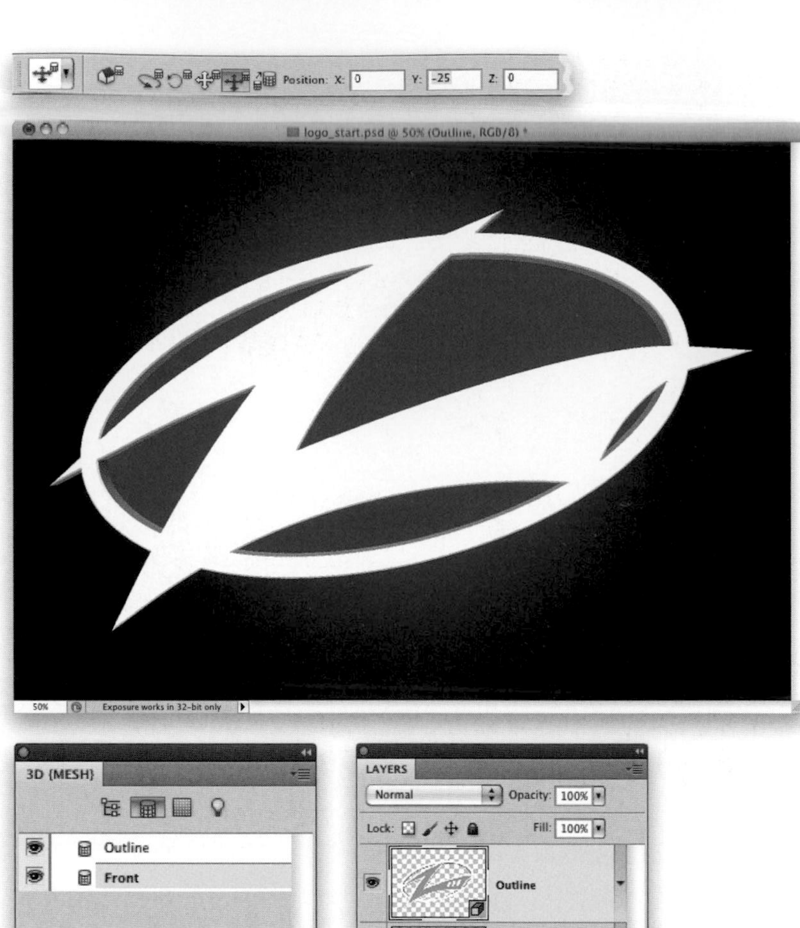

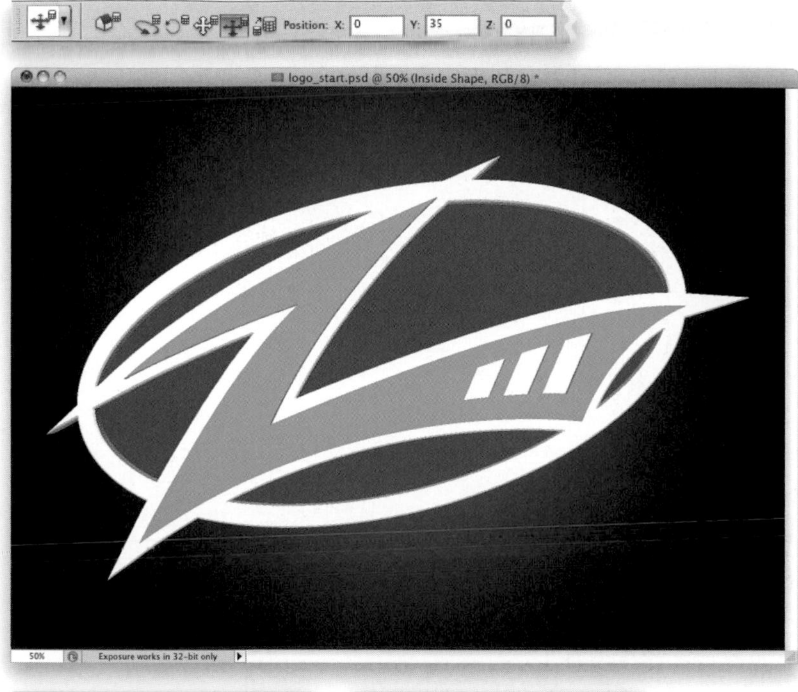

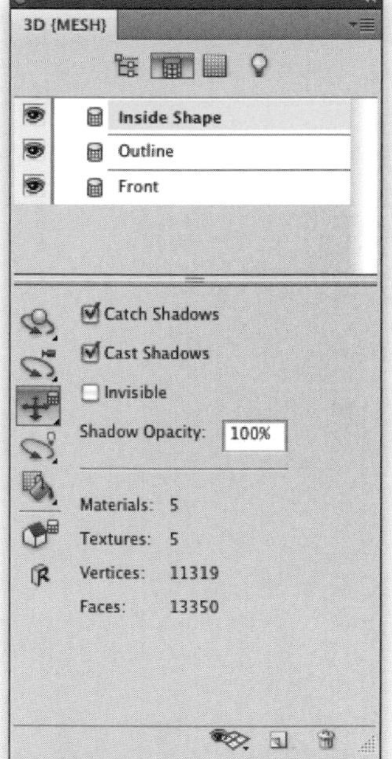

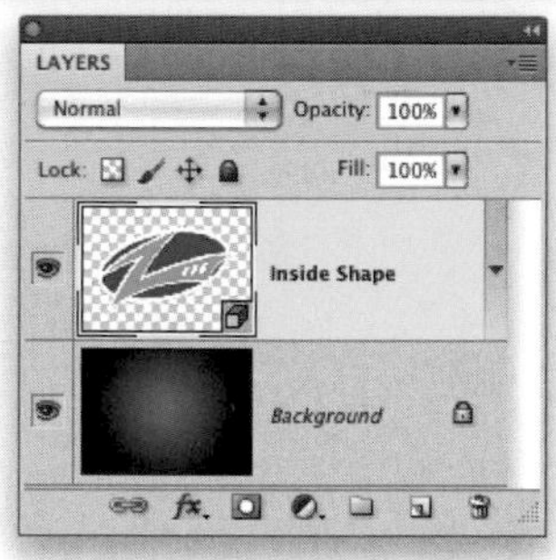

STEP 10:

Next, select the third shape's layer (Inside Shape) along with the new merged layer and merge them together the same way. In the Mesh options, make sure the Inside Shape layer is selected, and keeping the 3D Mesh Slide tool selected, change the Y-axis to 35 and press Return.

Continued

STEP 11:
To change the angle of the object, I prefer to change my angle of view, rather than change the object itself. This way, any lights you have on your object will stay in the same place in relation to the object. Near the bottom of the Toolbox, just below the 3D Object tools, there is a set of 3D Camera tools. You use them the same way as the 3D Object tools, but you'll discover that the movements are opposite. Meaning, if you click-and-drag left, the object seems to be rotating right. This is because you're moving the camera and not the object itself. Use them to get the object at an interesting angle, like you see here (I used the 3D Rotate Camera tool, the 3D Pan Camera tool, and the 3D Zoom Camera tool).

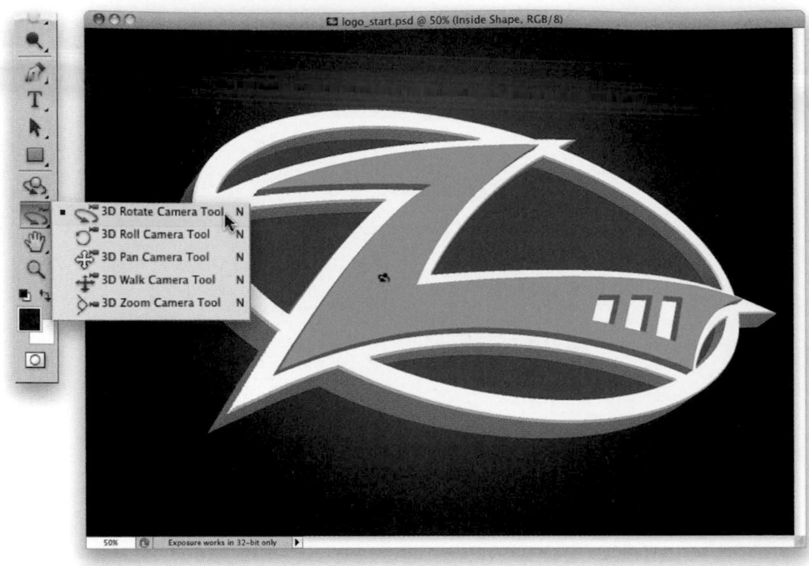

STEP 12:
Let's add an effect to the inside of the blue shape. In the Layers panel, double-click on the Inside Shape texture sublayer to open the file.

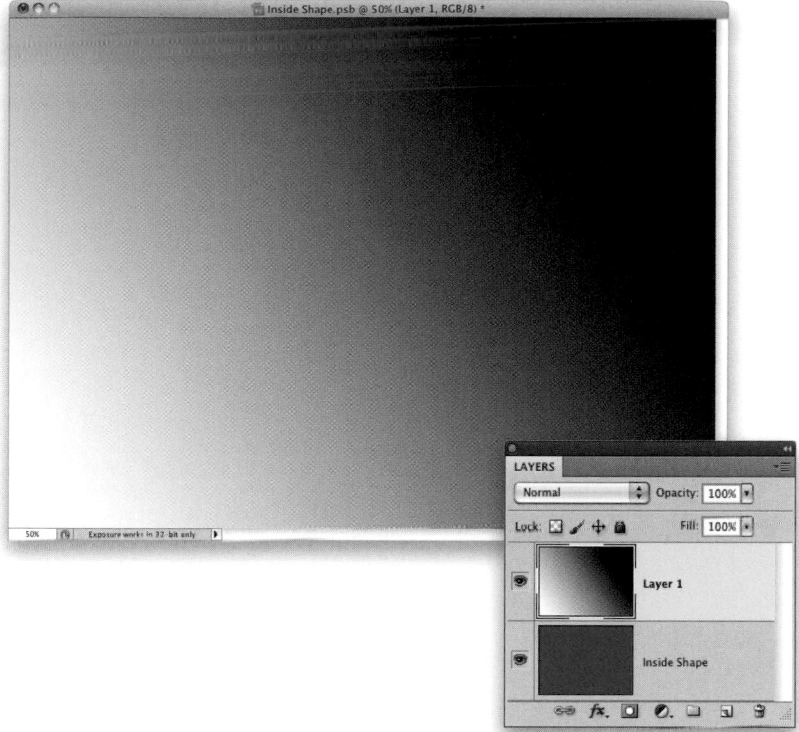

STEP 13:

Click on the Create a New Layer icon at the bottom of the Layers panel to create a new blank layer in this texture file, and then grab the Gradient tool **(G)** from the Toolbox. In the Options Bar, click on the down-facing arrow to the right of the gradient thumbnail to open the Gradient Picker, and choose the Foreground to Background gradient (the first one in the top row), then click on the Linear Gradient icon (the first icon to the right of the gradient thumbnail). Press **D** to set your Foreground and Background colors to their defaults of black and white, then click-and-drag out a gradient from the upper-right corner of the canvas to the lower-left corner.

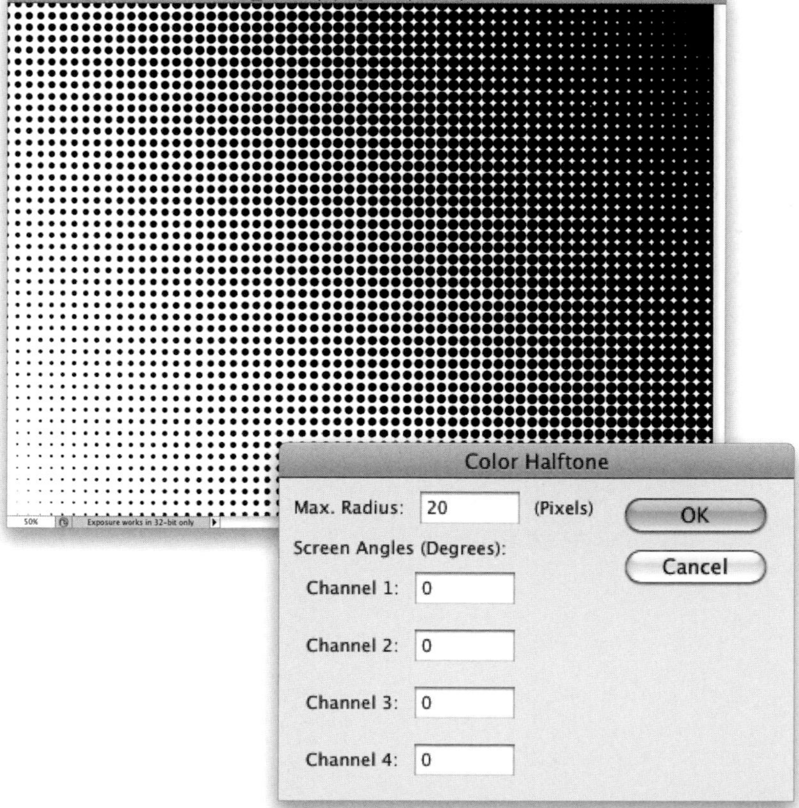

STEP 14:

Now, go under the Filter menu, under Pixelate, and choose **Color Halftone**. Set the Max Radius to 20 pixels and set all four channels to 0. Click OK.

Continued

STEP 15:
Next, drop the halftone layer's Opacity down to 25% and change the blend mode to **Soft Light**. Close the document and save the changes. You do not need to flatten, as these texture files support layers.

STEP 16:
In the 3D panel, click on the Filter By: Materials icon (the third icon from the left at the top) to access the Materials options. Select Inside Shape Front Inflation Material at the top of the list, and change the Reflection setting below to 25. Also, raise the Gloss and Shine to 100%, and click on the Specular color swatch and change it to black.

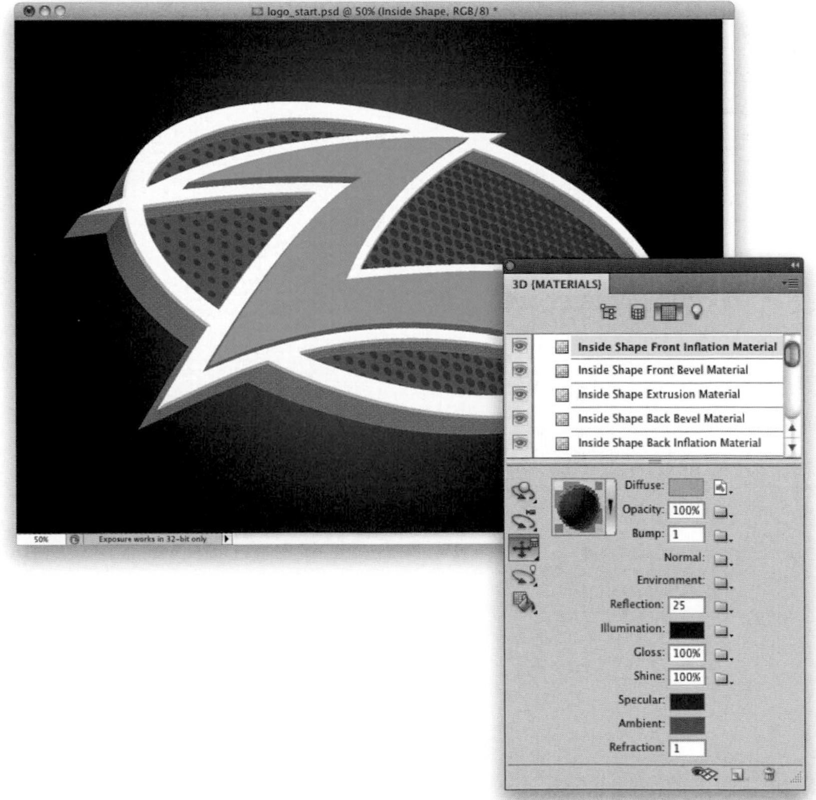

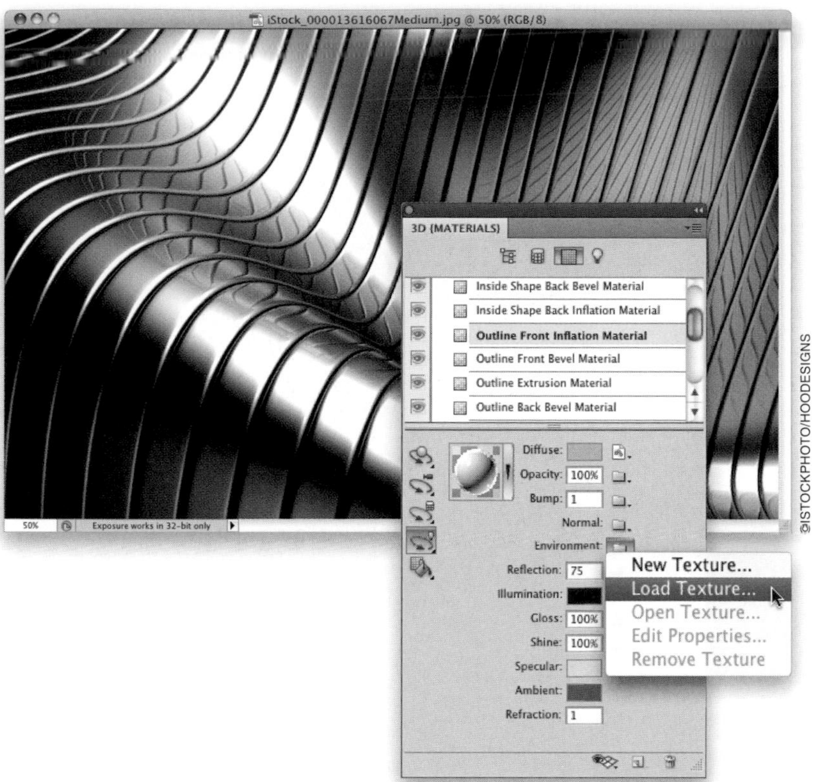

©ISTOCKPHOTO/HOODESIGNS

STEP 17:

Then, go back up top in the list and choose Outline Front Inflation Material. Go down and set the Reflection to 75, and then click on the folder icon next to the Environment setting and choose **Load Texture**. Locate the generic chrome texture file shown here, and load it as the environment. Change both the Gloss and Shine to 100%.

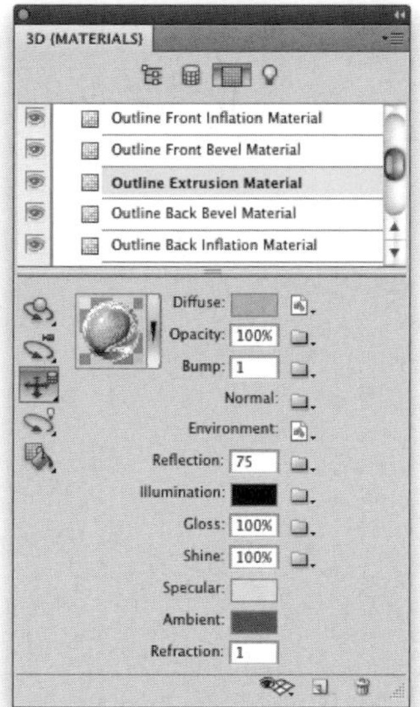

STEP 18:

Next, select Outline Extrusion Material in the list, and apply the same settings and Environment map to this mesh. You may get a warning telling you that you're already using that file. Just click OK. This merely means that all the meshes that use this exact file will be linked. So, if a change is made to one, it changes them all.

Continued

STEP 19:

You can now see the chrome effect reflecting in the sides. If you change the angle of view on the object, the reflection will change based on the angle, just like a real chrome object. Yet another reason why it's good to keep a library of textures and surfaces.

STEP 20:

Now, for the last shape: select Front Front Inflation Material in the list at the top. Then, add the same chrome texture to the Environment and set the Reflection to 5. Also, set the Gloss and Shine to 100% each.

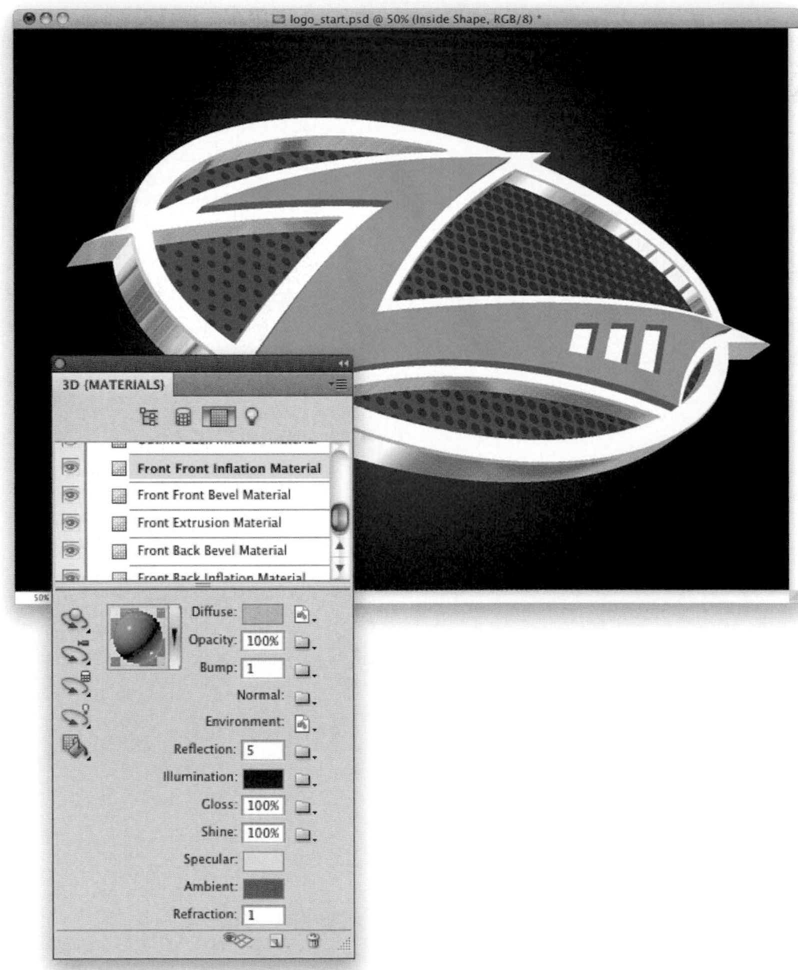

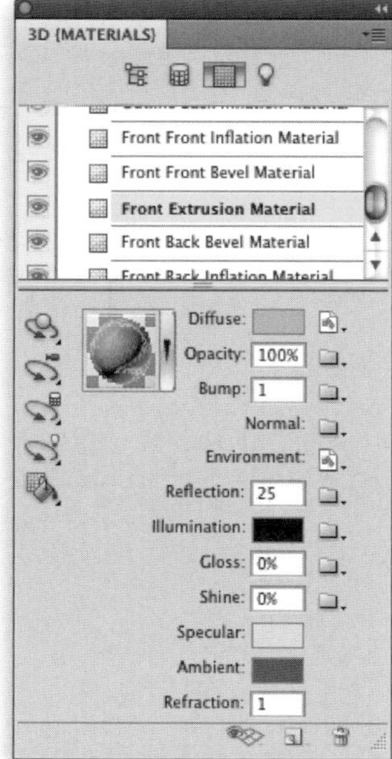

STEP 21:

Then, choose Front Extrusion Material, apply the chrome Environment once again, and set the Reflection to 25. Now is a good time to save again.

Continued

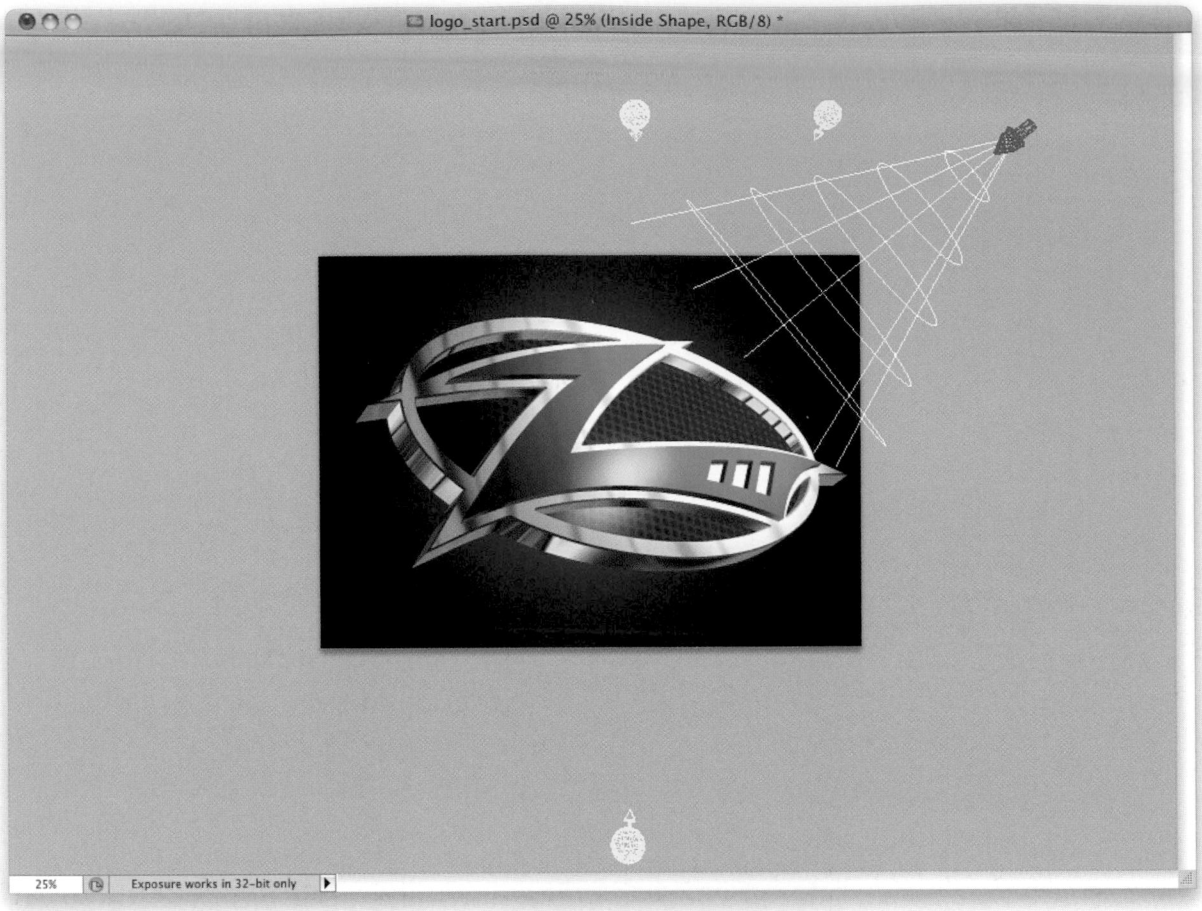

STEP 22:

In the 3D panel, click on the Filter By: Lights icon (the first icon on the right) to see the Lights settings. First, turn off all of the default Infinite Lights by clicking on the Eye icon to the left of their names in the list. Then, click on the Create a New Light icon at the bottom of the panel and choose **New Spot Light** from the pop-up menu. Grab a 3D Light tool (the fourth icon from the top on the left side), then click on the Toggle Misc 3D Extras icon, also at the bottom of the panel, and choose **3D Light** to show the spot light cone wire frame. Use the 3D Light tools to reposition the light in the upper-right corner, out beyond the document bounds, and aim it down directly on the logo, like you see here. Increase the Falloff setting to 60° to widen the scope of the light.

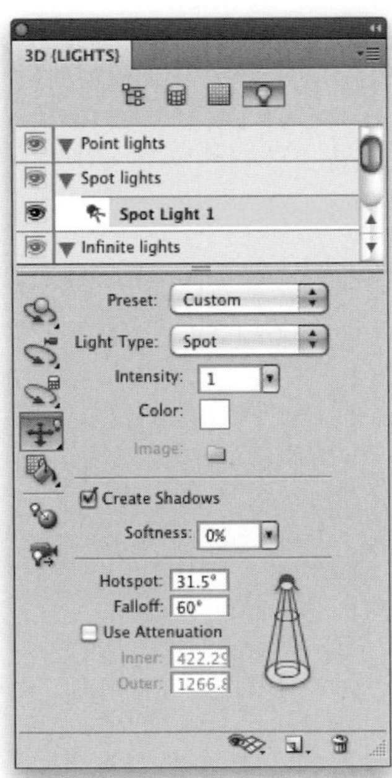

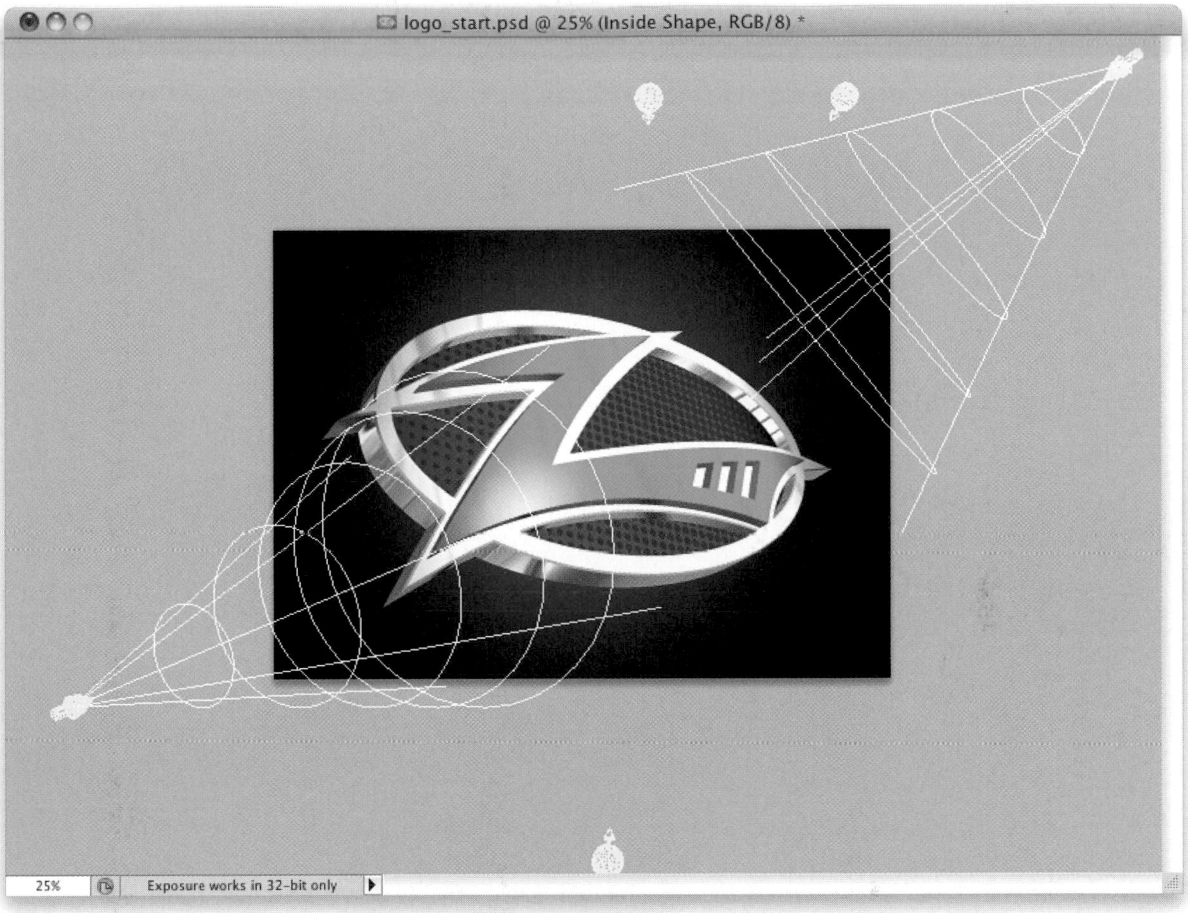

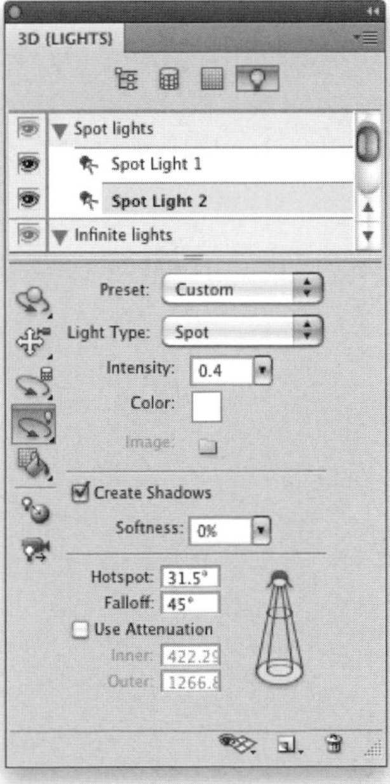

STEP 23:

Create a second spotlight and position it in the lower-left corner, shining on the logo, illuminating the bottom. Remember: Use the 3D Light Rotate tool to rotate it in place, use the 3D Light Pan tool to move the light from side to side, and use the 3D Light Slide tool to move the light backward or forward. It may be too bright, so go in the 3D panel and change the Intensity to 0.4. (*Note:* You can switch lights by clicking on the one you want to move in the list at the top of the panel, or if you hover your cursor over one, it's arrow will turn red, and when you click-and-drag, only that light will be affected.)

Continued

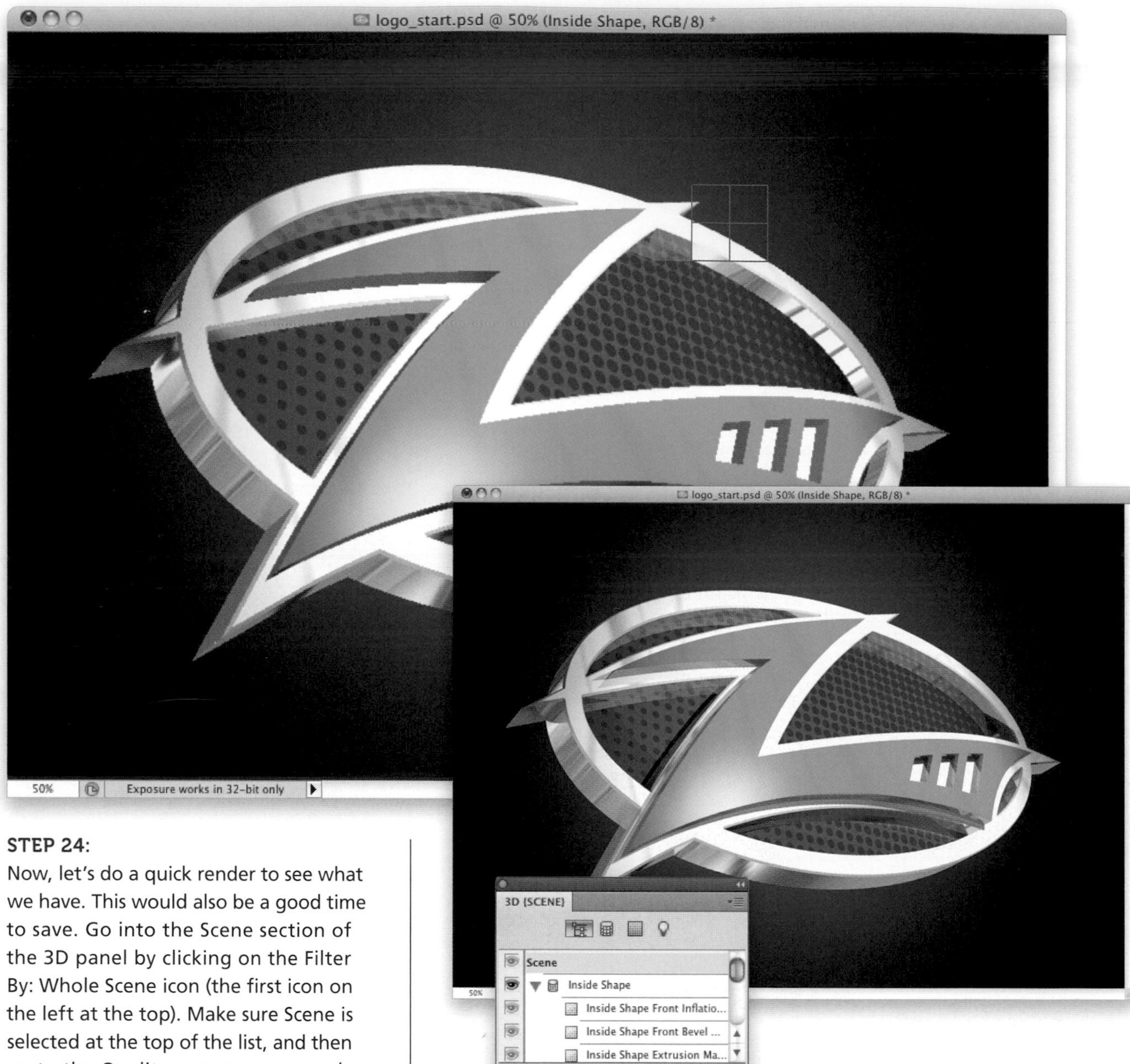

STEP 24:

Now, let's do a quick render to see what we have. This would also be a good time to save. Go into the Scene section of the 3D panel by clicking on the Filter By: Whole Scene icon (the first icon on the left at the top). Make sure Scene is selected at the top of the list, and then go to the Quality pop-up menu and choose **Ray Traced Draft**. After a few passes, you'll see the effect start to take shape. At this point, you can certainly go back and experiment with different settings and different angles, and even try different colors. The more familiar you are with what the features can do, the more that plays into your creative thought process. Let's add one final touch to this logo effect.

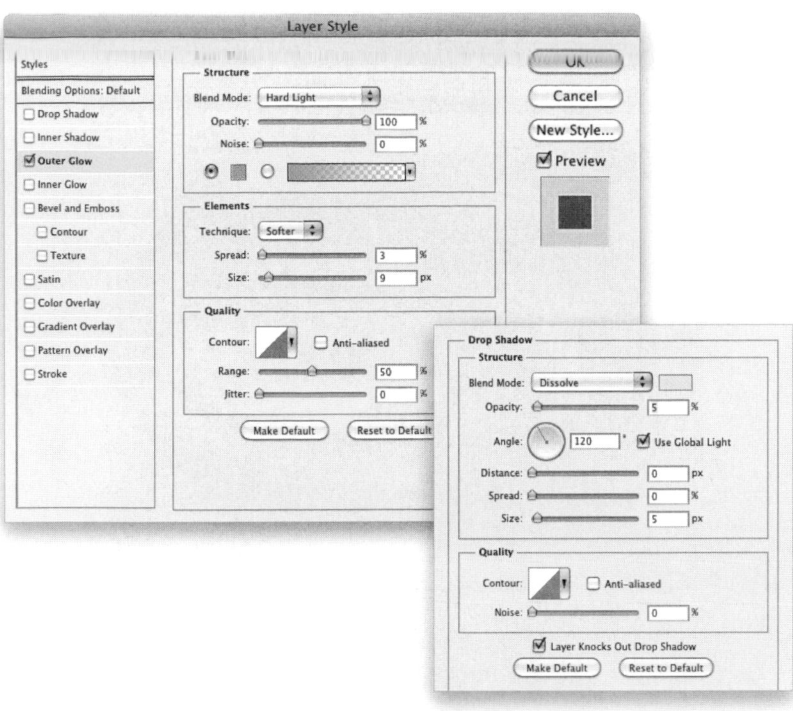

STEP 25:

Remember the lightning brush we defined back in Chapter 1? Get the Brush tool **(B)** and select that lightning brush from the Brush Picker (or go back and create it, if you haven't already). Then, create a new blank layer and click-and-drag it below the 3D logo layer in the Layers panel. Click on the Add a Layer Style icon and choose **Outer Glow** from the pop-up menu. Click on the color swatch and choose a lighter blue. Then, use the settings shown here. Click on Drop Shadow on the left to add a drop shadow to the brush, as well. Again, click on the color swatch and choose a lighter blue, then use the settings shown here, and click OK.

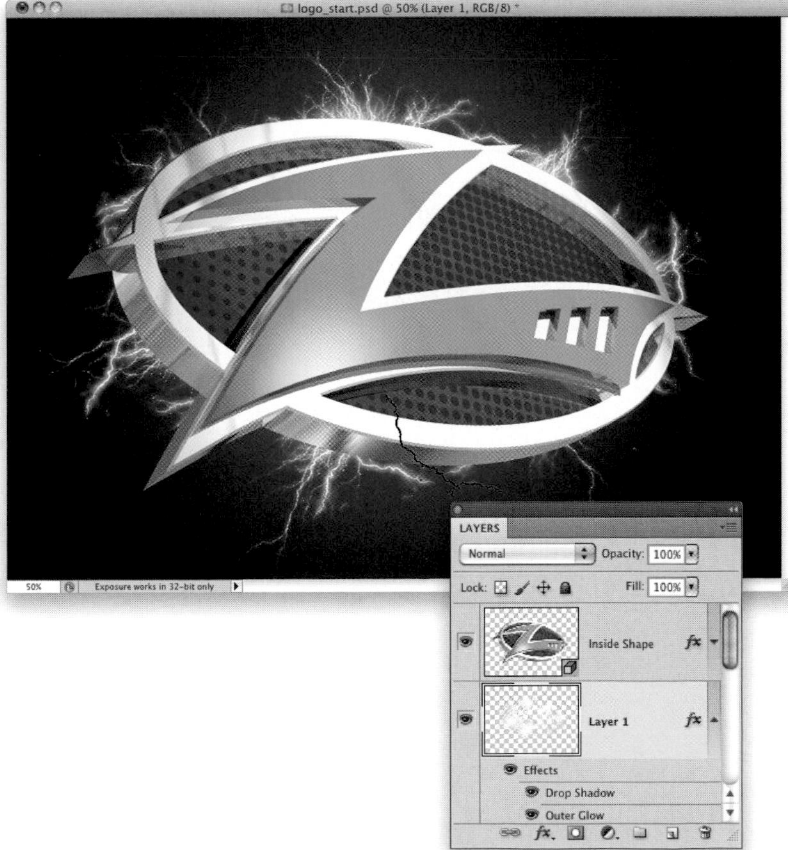

STEP 26:

Press **D**, then **X** to set your Foreground color to white. Use the **Left Bracket ([) key** to reduce the size of your brush, and paint some random lightning around the edge of the logo.

Continued

STEP 27:

Now, to enhance the glow, select the 3D layer in the Layers panel, and add an Outer Glow layer style to it. Click on the color swatch and set the color to white, then use the settings shown here to make it look like there's light behind the logo, thus enhancing the lightning effect.

In the Final Image, I thought the lightning would be casting a blue reflection on the edges of the logo. So, I created a blank layer above the 3D layer and, with my Foreground color set to the same blue I used in the Outer Glow on the lightning layer, I used a soft, round brush to paint a few spots around the edges. Then, to get rid of any spillover, I simply pressed **Command-Option-G (PC: Ctrl-Alt-G)** to clip the paint layer to the 3D layer. I also added a black-and-white grid image below the lightning layer, then warped it using Free Transform, changed the blend mode to **Screen**, lowered the layer's opacity, and masked out the edges of it.

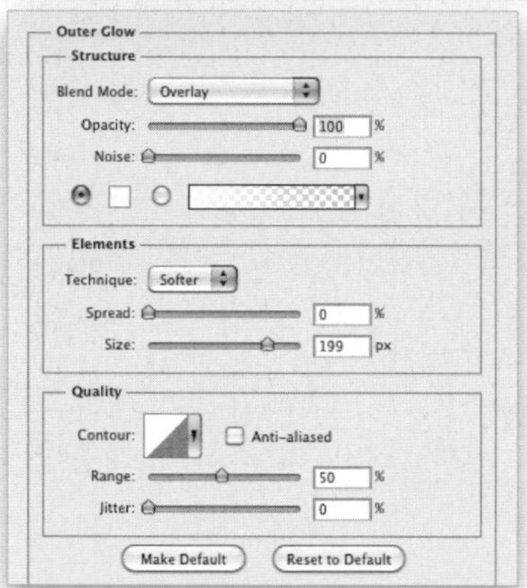

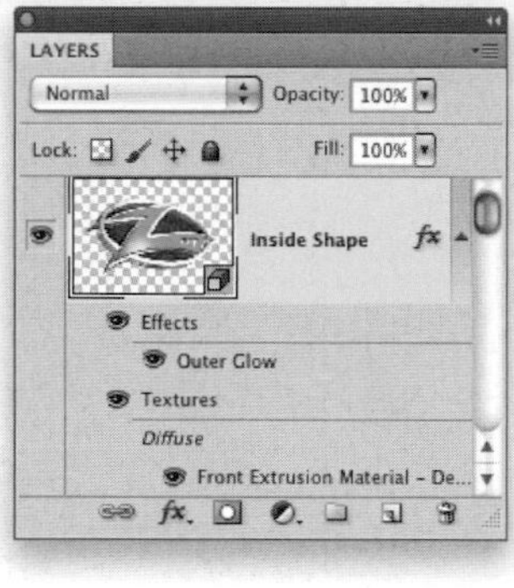

Use the Lightning brush created in Chapter 1.

Final Image

Where Can You Learn More?

Photoshop Videocasts & Tutorials: I am a co-host on the popular videocast *Photoshop User TV*, where we share tips and tutorials, and give away cool prizes, all in a frivolous and cheerful manner... most of the time! The show also features my fellow Photoshop Guys: Matt Kloskowski, RC Concepcion, Dave Cross, and, of course, Scott Kelby. You can check it out at **http://kelbytv.com**. I am also the Executive Producer of Planet Photoshop, a popular Photoshop tutorial site I update every week or so with fresh new video tutorials. You can see it all for free at **www.planetphotoshop.com**.

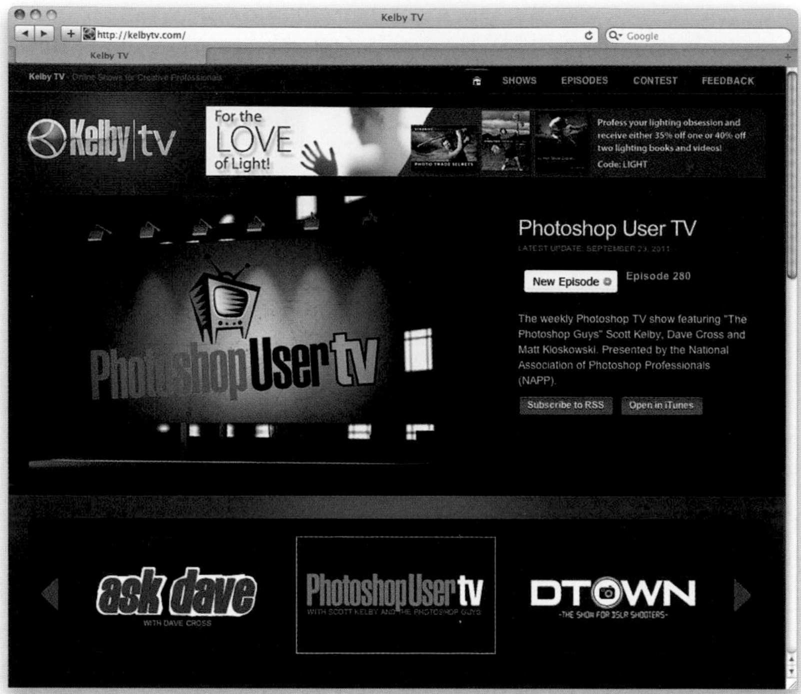

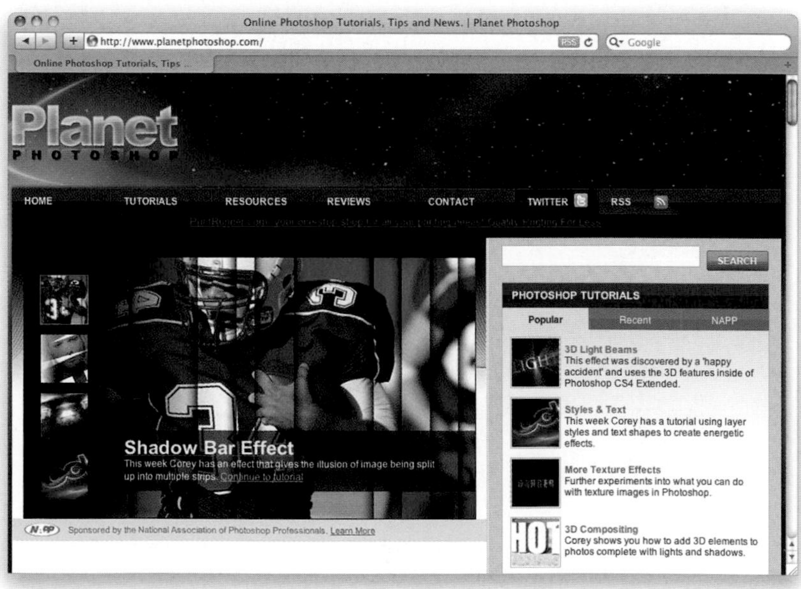

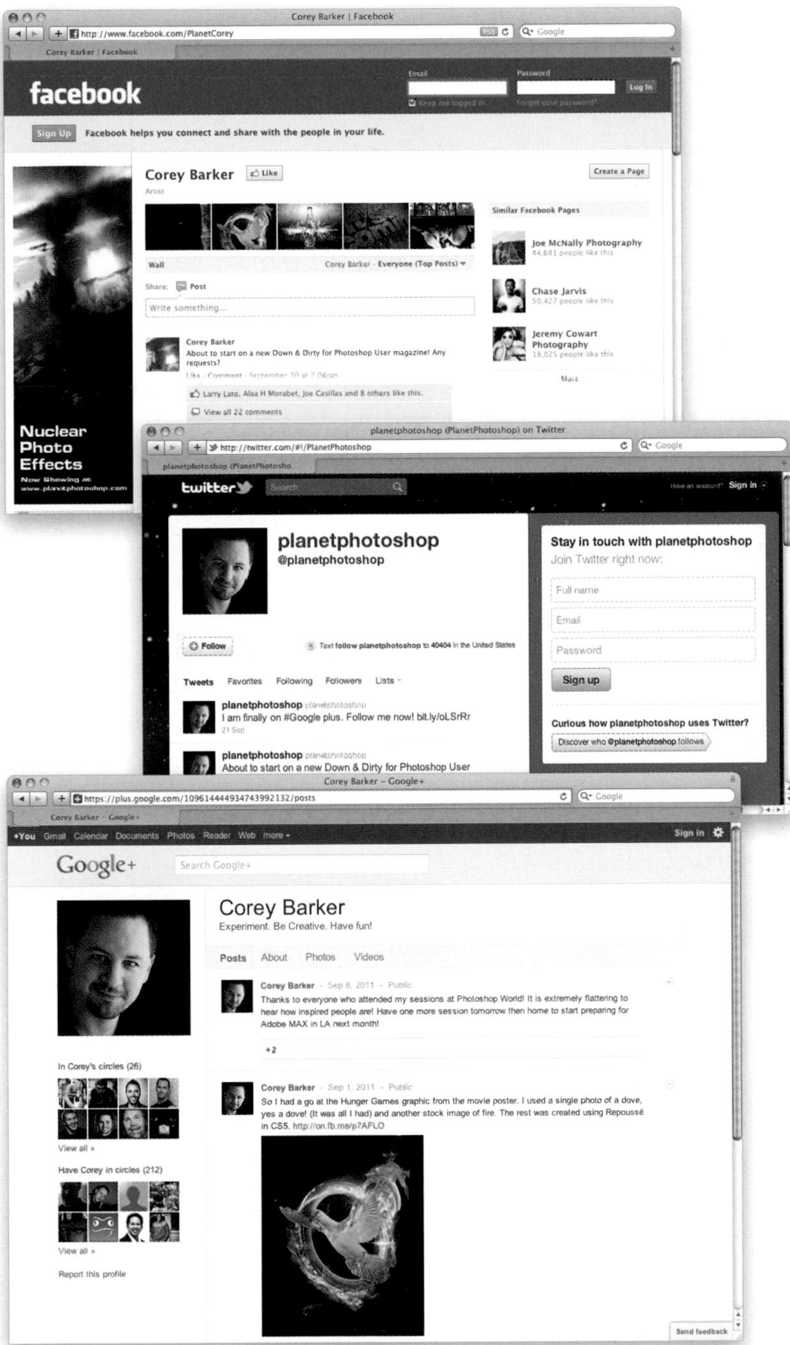

Social Media:

You can catch me all over the Web. I am regularly on Facebook, Twitter, and Google+, trying to stay in touch with everyone, find out what they are doing, and let them know what I am doing. If you like what you see in this book, message me and tell me why. You just might win something!

Facebook: www.facebook.com/PlanetCorey

Twitter: www.twitter.com/planetphotoshop

Google+: www.coreygplus.com

Continued

National Association of Photoshop Professionals:
I am a member of and instructor for the National Association of Photoshop Professionals (NAPP). I am a regular contributor for the official publication of NAPP, *Photoshop User* magazine, and provide video tutorials and support for the NAPP member website. We have exclusive NAPP member content, a lot like the material you see in this book, that is available to NAPP members all the time, not to mention other member perks, like a help desk, member portfolios, and discounts from industry retailers. You can find out more or join at **www.photoshopuser.com**.

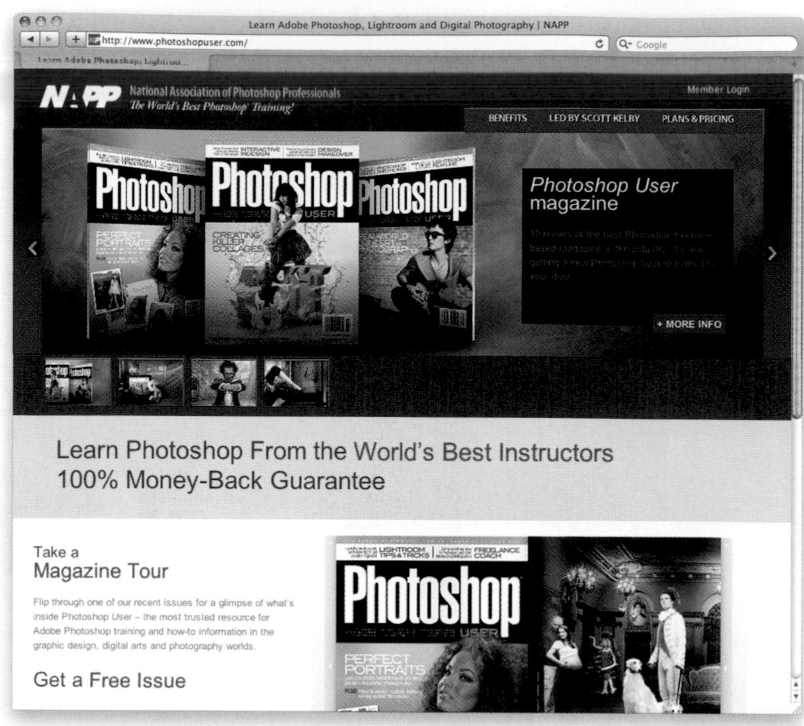

Photoshop Videos and Online Training:
I have also produced numerous DVD titles and online courses covering many subjects, like Photoshop design, effects, down & dirty tricks, and Photoshop 3D, as well as Illustrator. You can find out more, order DVDs, or try out an online training subscription at **http://Kelbytraining.com**.

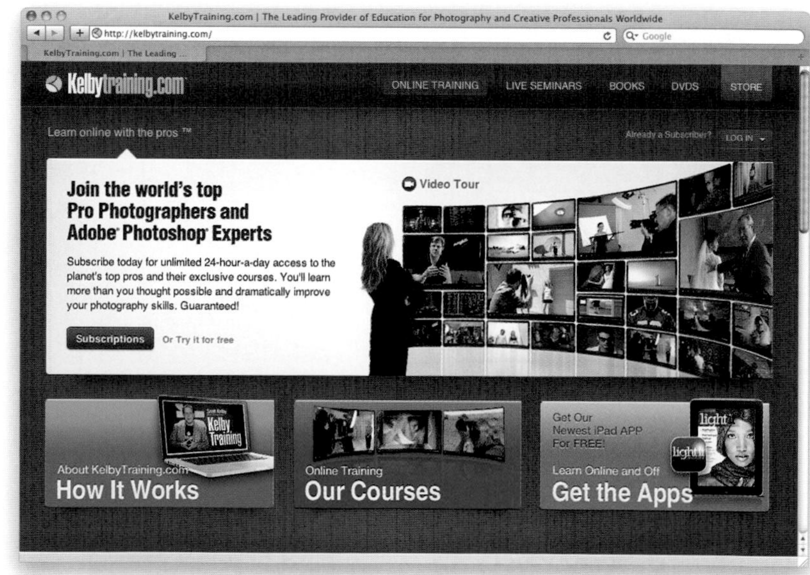

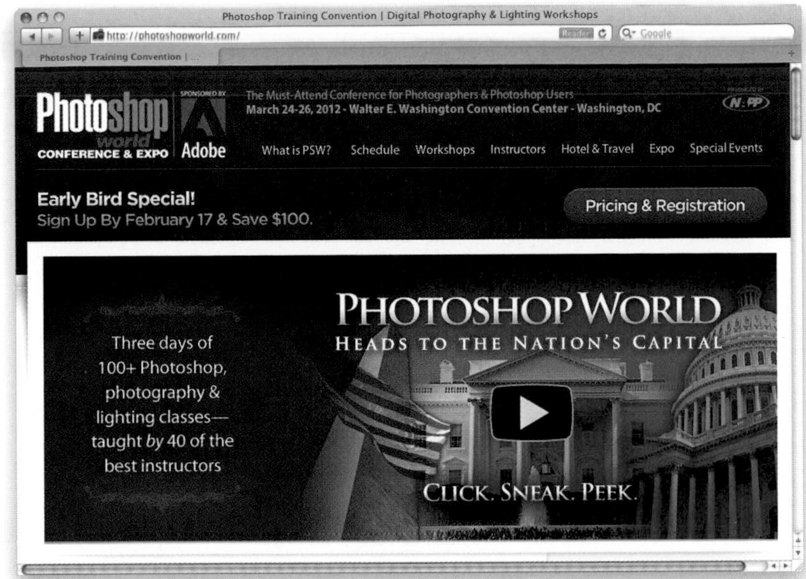

Photoshop World:
This has become what I have dubbed the Super Bowl of Photoshop events. I have been a fan of the Photoshop World Conference & Expo for years. It is truly a designer's and photographer's dream event. I get to teach alongside some of the biggest names in photography and Photoshop design for three days of geeking out! You've just got to love your Photoshop job, when there is a full conference dedicated to it. It is held twice a year, with new instructors and events happening every year. It is not to be missed! Find out about the next one, and read blog entries about the last one, at **http://photoshopworld.com**.

Index

C

E

F

I

K

L

M

N

O

P

Q

R

S

T

U

V

W

Z

Learn Online with the Pros
World Class Online Training for
Photographers & Photoshop Experts
At Kelbytraining.com you're always on-location and in-studio!
Become part of the action as we take you behind the
scenes of live photo shoots and show you exactly how
the pros do it, step-by-step, from start to finish.
COOL!
Join the world's top pro photographers
and Photoshop experts as they teach
you today's most advanced techniques.
UNLIMITED 24/7 ACCESS
$199 PER YEAR OR $24.95 A MONTH
100% Money Back Guarantee
Visit KelbyTraining.com for details.
Kelbytraining.com
EDUCATION FOR CREATIVES
Visit www.KelbyTraining.com to subscribe or for more info.
Adobe & Photoshop are registered trademarks of Adobe Systems Incorporated.